About the author

Mick Collins has had a diverse career since leaving school, working as a builder's labourer, infantryman, heavy goods truck driver, and living in a Buddhist Monastery. He has worked as an occupational therapist in an acute mental health setting and in a specialist psychological therapies team. He incorporated humanistic and transpersonal methods into his therapeutic practice. Mick also worked for ten years as a Lecturer in Occupational Therapy and Director of Admissions within the Faculty of Medicine and Health Sciences, University of East Anglia, Norwich, UK. He retired from academia in 2015 and trained as a Holistic Life Coach, and now works with individuals, groups and organisations to facilitate transpersonal awareness, growth and transformation.

Mick's personal transformative journey includes working through an experience known as spiritual emergency, which happened in 1986 after he had been living in a Buddhist Monastery. This deep encounter catalysed his sense of vocation to become a therapist, and eventually inspired his career as a writer, where he crafted academic publications on the subject of spirituality, including his doctoral thesis. His Ph.D. explored the relationship between individual recoveries from spiritual crisis, through new ways of doing, knowing and being, and how these may inform collective transformation. Mick is using his knowledge and experience to explore how humanity can face up to the impact of a burgeoning global crisis, which is also a spiritual crisis. He is interested in exploring new vistas of awareness and action that support the co-creation of an improved future.

His previous book *The Unselfish Spirit: Human Evolution in a Time of Global Crisis* won the 2014 Scientific and Medical Network Book Prize. He was 'author in profile' at the 2014 Hostry Festival, and was interviewed about his book at the 2015 International Hay Festival for Literature. He continues to speak at conferences and in 2016 he was interviewed about his work on Conscious TV. He lives in Norwich, Norfolk, UK with his wife Hannah. Mick's web address is: **www.epiczoetic.co.uk**

In The Visionary Spirit, *Mick Collins explores how the global crisis is also calling humanity to participate in a process of individual, collective and planetary healing and live in wholeness. A central theme that runs throughout the book is the wisdom from the imaginal realm, which he discusses in relation to a range of complex subjects, including science, myth, dreams, the ancestors, near-death experiences and indigenous wisdom to name just a few. Drawing on a large body of literature,* The Visionary Spirit *weaves together an exquisite thread of intelligent connections, showing us how our fragmented world can be transformed into a vision of wholeness, which is so desperately needed in the world today.* The Visionary Spirit *provides a meeting point between mystical and rational ways of knowing, where we are invited to re-imagine and co-create an improved future. Mick writes about the need for personal and planetary healing in this time of global crisis, where our hurts and vulnerabilities lead us to become 'wounded transformers', inspiring us to live authentic and whole lives. He says that it will be up to each of us to take full responsibility for 'undoing the restrictive knots that are tethering us to a one-dimensional destructive mindset, which continues to knock us out of balance with life as a whole'. It is without question that the global crisis is challenging us to find renewed ways of living in wholeness. This is a book that is full of hope, but it does not avoid the complexities of dealing with our personal and collective shadows, which are so evident in the world today. For this reason alone,* The Visionary Spirit *is like a beacon of light, guiding us to safety as we navigate the treacherous waves in our collective Night Sea Journey, leading us back to the Earth.* The Visionary Spirit *inspires us to draw on the wisdom and knowledge from the imaginal realm, and calls for us to put our dreams into action as we co-create the Transformocene Age.*

Katie Mottram, Co-founder and Director of the International
Spiritual Emergence Network, Founder of Emerging Proud campaign
Author of *Mend the Gap*

Mick offers thoughtful and exciting ways of shaking us out of our ignorance and denial. He convincingly argues that the imaginal is indeed a pathway to revelation. He shows that the enlivened soul can cope with the crushing order of scientism by enabling us all to reflect and open up our discourse and contemplation. What is critical for his exposition is the startling relevance of his propositions as laid down in his introduction for contemporary society, and especially for the coming generation. He is right to emphasise the one-dimensional view that ushers us onto destructive tram rails where the destination is so deeply wounding for so very many. He is right to claim that we all have within us the roots of sustainability with their focus on sharing, on compassion, and on reciprocity.

Tim O'Riordan, OBE, DL, FBA Emeritus Professor, School
of Environmental Sciences, University of East Anglia
Editor of *Addressing Tipping Points for a Precarious Future*

Mick Collins' The Visionary Spirit *is a transformational tour de force inviting readers to expand their ways of knowing beyond hyper-rationalist scientism and reconnect with the imaginal realm through dreams, visions and synchronicities. Our predominant paradigm has repressed other ways of knowing embodied in the mythic, sacred feminine and indigenous traditions. Mick gives readers the tools, not only through his exposition but also in reflections and exercises, to make a personal contribution to this redemptive quest by engaging in shadow work, recognising human moral evil in ecocide and accessing the daimon within in order to realise our individual and collective potential. His approach is one of re-imagination, deepening and resacralising our relationship to Nature. Importantly, he recognises the need to integrate the transpersonal with the transhuman in technologies of transformation that go beyond the robotic to a soul connection. It is clear that our overall human challenge is unprecedented and that our institutions are inadequate and unfit for purpose. As he inspiringly suggests, it is possible for us to exercise our visionary capacities to move from the Anthropocene to what he calls the Transformocene, but, as in all processes of birth and rebirth, the process will be intense on every level.*

David Lorimer, Programme Director, Scientific and Medical Network
Author of *Whole in One*

The Visionary Spirit *is a book much needed for our times. As climate change and ecological crisis quicken, so too does the denial of our perilous state, alive and well in Trump's USA today. Scientific facts are important – but facts alone do not enable the deep changes that are necessary for us to live in relationship with the earth. This is why this book is important. Collins writes: "This book focuses on how we can cultivate a deeper relationship between a manifest material reality, and the subtle world of the imaginal realm." Mick Collins writes with depth and breadth; he begins with a critique of the scientific worldview; he then weaves together a wide range of ideas describing how myth, the sacred feminine, relationship with ancestors and daimons, near death experiences, and more, can help us to transform our current ways of being in the world. In addition, he includes experiential exercises at the end of each chapter, with the hope that the reader can have a more embodied experience as they journey through this book. Brilliant!*

Mary-Jayne Rust, Art Therapist, Jungian Analyst, Ecopsychologist
Editor of *Vital Signs*

In The Visionary Spirit, *Mick Collins writes deeply about our neglected relationship to the dreaming realm. His book is a wonderful contribution to the activation of our total human potential for these troubled times.*

Dr Arnold Mindell, Founder of Process-Oriented Psychology
Author of *Conflict: Phases, Forums and Solutions*

The Visionary Spirit is a wonderful book to be read with care and to be read over and over again. It is masterfully crafted into a manual of wisdom that can guide us towards a positive future for mankind and the planet. Dr Mick Collins has built a case for us to wake up, as individuals and collectively, and draws from the works of others coupled with his own deeply spiritually transformative journey. He highlights how the rise of materialist science has progressed to the point of a disconnection and suppression of spiritual aspects of being human, culminating in a global crisis. A central theme of the book is the importance of addressing the greatly neglected realms of the mythical, dreams, near-death experiences, ancestors and the wisdom of indigenous peoples as a means to healing and becoming whole again. He emphasises the importance of reconnecting with our spiritual nature as well as attending to our shadow sides and remembering our ancestors, for when we return to wholeness the future is hopeful. This is one of the most important books that anyone, especially those who are passionate about life and the future of the planet, can read. It brings hope for a bright future amidst the current chaos that has been created in the world. It is a book I wholeheartedly recommend everyone read.

Dr Penny Sartori, Swansea University
Author of *The Wisdom of Near-Death Experiences*

The Visionary Spirit comes from a creative life force that flows through every human being and all that lives. We all have it. Mick Collins invites us to wander and wonder with him on a journey of deep encounter. In the modern world we have become caught up in the incessant noise of our whirring thoughts, seldom making room for the wisdom that is central to our experience of being human. I am reminded of the transformative experience of a Scottish engineer many years ago on an island off the coast of Canada. He just let himself become the bright light that appeared before him, and went on to share what he had learned with others. Sydney Banks famously said he had written more books than he had read. He realised that the personal mind and the universal mind are not separate. Similarly, in The Visionary Spirit, *Mick points to the universal wisdom that comes to us from the imaginal realm, through our dreams, synchronicities and other non-ordinary experiences. For example, the near-death experiences discussed in part three of the book reflect the kind of deep encounters people find difficult sharing with each other. However, such shared knowledge and wisdom could inspire a collective redemptive quest, which brings us to an emancipatory edge, where we are emboldened to tackle and transform the burgeoning global crisis before us. Back in the days when I was teaching neuro-psychiatry,* The Visionary Spirit *would have been a useful resource to show students how experiences of 'true mental health' are not the same as mental illnesses. Importantly, this book identifies the need for wholeness, which is based on wisdom and also the cultivation of a moral compass. Read and experience this book as the work of a fellow soul.*

Dr William Hughes, Fellow Royal College of Psychiatrists, MBPF
Analytical Psychologist, Training Analyst Guild of Analytical Psychology
Author of *Village Coaching*

The
Visionary
Spirit

Awakening to the Imaginal Realm in the Transformocene Age

Mick Collins Ph.D.

Permanent
Publications

Published by
Permanent Publications
Hyden House Ltd
The Sustainability Centre
East Meon
Hampshire GU32 1HR
United Kingdom
Tel: +44 (0)1730 823 311
Fax: 01730 823 322
Email: enquiries@permaculture.co.uk
Web: www.permanentpublications.co.uk

Distributed in the USA by
Chelsea Green Publishing Company, PO Box 428, White River Junction, VT 05001
www.chelseagreen.com

Front cover painting, 'The Imaginal Realm' by Mick Collins, 1991

Author's portrait by Guy Wilkinson www.guywilkinson.photography

'Re-imagining the Human: Re-imagining the World' Copyright Tim O'Riordan 2018

Typset by Rozie Apps

Index by Zoe Ross

Printed in the UK by Bell & Bain, Thornliebank, Glasgow

All paper from FSC certified mixed sources

The Forest Stewardship Council (FSC) is a non-profit
international organisation established to promote the
responsible management of the world's forests. Products
carrying the FSC label are independently certified to
assure consumers that they come from forests that are
managed to meet the social, economic and ecological
needs of present and future generations.

British Library Cataloguing-in-Publication Data
A catalogue record for this book is available from the British Library

ISBN 978 1 85623 315 6

Author's Note

The information in this book is educational in nature. The exercises at the end of each chapter are experiential, and should not be relied upon as means of self-healing. Professional advice or support should be sought from a qualified health practitioner for any medical or mental health matters. In addition, the illustrative stories conveyed throughout the book are real-life examples of people's experiences of change and transformation. These vignettes do not predict or offer any warranty or guarantee of the reader's experience. The author and publisher accept no responsibility or liability for the use or misuse of the information in this book.

The imagination is the vocabulary of the soul. It is where we craft a meaningful relationship to the Imaginal Realm, which enables us to create and narrate the myths of our existence. The imagination is our guide to interconnected living and wholeness.

Dedication

This book is dedicated to my granddaughter Martha who was born as I was working on the final pages of this book. It is my sincere hope that Martha and her generation have opportunities to create meaningful relationships to life as a whole, with one another, other species, and the natural world.

It was Einstein who said, if you want your children to be brilliant, read them fairy tales. And so, it is through our relationship to the imaginal realm that we show our children how to value and connect with the life of the soul. The children of today will only become Earth stewards of tomorrow if they know about the sacredness of the natural world. This book pays homage to the profound wisdom that comes to us from the imaginal realm, through our dreams, visions, synchronicities and angelic connections. These are the workings of the *Holy Spirit* in action, and this book is dedicated to the sacred forces, messengers and guides who illuminate our lives in numerous and numinous ways.

The human imagination has no boundaries

Contents

The relationship between the human imagination and the imaginal realm is co-creative, which finds expression in the world, through our tasks, relationships and quests to be whole. The sacrament of creative living values the seen and the unseen.

Acknowledgements

There are many people I would like to acknowledge for their friendship, support and love in helping to bring this book to completion. Firstly, sincere thanks go to Maddy and Tim Harland and the team at Permanent Publications for their vision and action in working for a more sustainable world. I am delighted to be working with such great publishers and such a good-hearted team. Special thanks go to Tim O'Riordan, Emeritus Professor, School of Environmental Science, University of East Anglia, who offered very helpful advice on content and structure after reading the penultimate draft of the book, and also for writing the preface. I would also like to express deep gratitude to Dr William Hughes for also reading the penultimate draft of the book and offering encouraging words. It is a blessing to have such wise and generous 'elders' as friends.

Many thanks to wise woman, Tchenka Jane Sunderland, for reading part of Chapter Three, and for our illuminating discussions on labyrinths and the sacred feminine. Also, I would like to thank Dr Alex Haxeltine for our many conversations on the global crisis over the years. Thanks also go to Doctors Max and Barbara Warminger for thoughtful discussions about the placebo, and Max's contribution at a time when he was recovering from a major life event. I would like to express my gratitude to all the people who have contributed their stories to the book. These wonderful accounts bring into focus the deep meaning that can accompany such non-ordinary and creative experiences in life. Sincere thanks to all the people who have endorsed my work and have helped the message in these pages find its way in the world. I would also like to thank the organisations that gave me permission to cite various works used in the text.

The evolution and development of my ideas have been greatly influenced by the work of Professor Carl Gustav Jung, and Doctors Arnold and Amy Mindell (co-founders of process-oriented psychology, or process work). Arny and Amy (along with other trainers and friends in the process work community) bring energy, illumination and awareness to many of the complex realities surfacing in these troubled times. The exercises throughout this book are inspired by my years as a student training in process-oriented psychology. In addition, the use of terms such as *consensus* and *non-consensus reality*, *growing edge*, and *channels* are used in accordance with the work of Arny Mindell.

Special thanks go to Bernie Sheehan, who worked as an editorial consultant on the early drafts of the manuscript. Bernie has the wonderful ability to 'purge and polish' a text of too much repetition or excess, and consequently my writing has improved over the years because of her editorial support. Bernie is always the first person to read my draft manuscripts and I refer to her as the 'canary in the mine shaft', due to her ability to keep the text as clear as possible. Bernie has enabled me to tell the story in the following chapters to the best of my ability. Big thanks go to Helen Wells for collaborating with me on ideas for the book cover. Her artistic and shamanic eyes are able to see the liminal in the material, which helped me to clarify the vision for the cover. Heartfelt thanks go to Richard Austin for agreeing to let me use his poetry at the start of the three main sections in the book. His work captures the struggles of existence and our redemptive urges. Many thanks go to Andi Sapey for photographing the front cover artwork, and also to Guy Wilkinson for taking the author portrait. Also, I would like to express my gratitude to Russ Thornton from Waiheke Island, New Zealand, who is an inspiration – not only as a gardener of the land – but also of the human soul.

I would like to acknowledge my wife Hannah, for her love, grace and support. I count my blessings for the day that we met, for the years we have spent together, and for the years to come. Hannah is an embodiment of the sacred feminine and it is no coincidence that her middle name is Sophia, which is reflected in her deep and wise connection to the life of the soul. I love you dearly. I would also like to send love and thanks to Rosie and Adam who have brought little Martha into this world; we are delighted and proud to be grandparents to this little angel. Also, I would like to say a huge thank you to all my family and friends for their love and good wishes. My heartfelt thanks and love go to my parents Gladys and Robert Collins for everything you did for me in this life. I am pleased we found a way through the difficult times. I would also like to send love to my birth mother, Ann. Due to circumstances beyond your control we were separated in 1956 and reunited in 2014. It was heartbreaking hearing about the traumatic way we parted. Thank you for all the love you sent me during the years we were apart.

This book honours the imaginal realm, which brings us wisdom and knowledge through dreams, visions and synchronicities. I have lost count of the times that unexpected and uncanny events have helped bring new connections to the diverse material represented in this book. It has been deeply challenging writing a book that covers such a wide range of subjects, but it has been my trust and faith in the workings of the imaginal realm which has enabled me to craft the pages that follow. Throughout my time writing this book, synchronous and inspirational ideas came without warning, as did impromptu meetings with remarkable people who shared their stories with me at just the right time. I have lost count of the number of times different books or articles came into my life when I was struggling to make connections in my research and writing. All these events confirmed to me that the spirit works in both mysterious and very specific ways. Writing this book has not only been an intellectual challenge; it has amplified aspects of my ongoing shadow work, which has resulted in deepening my connection and commitment to the process of individuation and wholeness.

Writing this book has also led to epiphanies and illuminations from the spirit world, where moments of grace have spurred me on. Such is the way when the soul is stirred, especially when it is seeking expression. I give deep thanks to the myriad manifestations from the imaginal realm, which is always seeking to find a way into our lives, in both ordinary and non-ordinary ways. Without discipline, our relationship to the imaginal realm can become a sideshow, but its real purpose is to help us be more loving and whole. It is my sincere hope that this book is a support to people in their sacred quests in these challenging times, and also for our species' collective odyssey.

Permissions

Every effort has been made to correctly attribute sources used in the book. I am very thankful to the following publishers for allowing me to use the material listed below. In the case of any errors or omissions the author and publisher will make any corrections in future editions if notified. Many of the myths and fairy tales shared in this book were communicated to the author in oral contexts. These stories have been written in the authors own style, and where possible a reference to the myth or fairy tale has been provided.

I am grateful to all the people who gave permission to share their stories in this book. Thank you.

Three Propositions for Deeper Living: Adapted and extended for this chapter. Used with kind permission from *The Scientific and Medical Network* by Mick Collins (2015). Global crisis or opportunity: We do therefore we evolve. *Network Review. Journal of the Scientific and Medical Network*, 116, p.17-20.

Introduction to Part One – The Imaginal Lineage: Poem 'Sun and Ice'. Used with kind permission from Chrysalis Poetry by Richard Austin (2014). *A Cold Fire*. Stroud: Chrysalis Poetry.

Chapter Three: Poem 'From the Place'. Used with kind permission from Tchenka Jane Sunderland by Tchenka Jane Sunderland (2004). *Walking the labyrinth*. Norwich: Jane Sunderland.

Chapter Four: Poem 'Psychiatric Shaman'. Used with kind permission from Changing World Publications by Mick Collins (2004). In *Alternative to war*, edited by Sara Halprin and Ursula Hohler. Eugene, OR: Changing World Publications.

Introduction to Part Two – The Redemptive Quest: Poem 'The Prisoner'. Used with kind permission from Chrysalis Poetry by Richard Austin (2014). *A Cold Fire*. Stroud: Chrysalis Poetry.

Introduction to Part Three – The Emancipatory Edge: Poem 'Philosopher'. Used with kind permission from Chrysalis Poetry by Richard Austin (2014). *A Cold Fire*. Stroud: Chrysalis Poetry.

Our 'worst' imaginings have led to the degrading legacy of the Anthropocene.
Conversely, our 'best' imaginings could reveal the wisdom of the Transformocene.
Cultivating lucidity in the nightmare of our own creation is the first step towards
deep transformation and 'living the dream'.

Re-imagining the Human: Re-imagining the World

An excellent narrative calls to the distracted to attract their attention. This is the purpose of Mick Collins in this powerful exposition. He talks of near death experiences, of serendipitous happenings, of spiritual insights, which change lives and outlooks, and always of the heartening sensitivities of the connected soul. This work complements his earlier expression of *the unselfish spirit* set in the context of the enveloping ecological transformation. He seeks an aftermath of the overwhelming human power of the Anthropocene in the Transformocene, the self-transcendence of the human realisation into an ecocentred holistic civilisation.

The strength of Mick's argument is that we can overcome three scourges of our contemporary age to reach the Transformocene. One is the power of rational and organised science and technology, which carry their own momentum and deftly shaped outlooks and experiences. Another is the systematic order of management structures built into legal, regulatory, and international arrangements, which lock in their participants into grotesque dances of obedience. The third is the rejection of imagination, of the freedom of thought, and the liberation of experience, which denies many from realising their inner spiritualties and the wonders of myth and the supernatural.

In Mick's creative hands and mind, these somewhat familiar critiques of our modern dilemmas are given fresh meaning and characterisations. He uses the platforms of philosophy, of religion, of anthropology and of spirituality to explore the outer limits of our scope for fullness. It is always at the boundary that exciting events happen. The boundary is where the familiar is loosened and the unfamiliar welcomed. The boundary is where the unimaginable becomes evident and explanatory. The boundary is where myth transfigures into fresh reality. He also makes marvellous use of thinkers and creative expressions to enlighten and illuminate his text. The stories from his own associations reached through his very special life in therapy and compassionate friendships bring into focus the electricity of the imaginary. And in the imaginary is the hope for the Transformocene.

In many respects Mick could be regarded as unconventional and dreamy. But there is a great strength and steely determination behind what he advocates. He should be read and heard. The world he fears is the world of the deaf and the bemused. There will be many who feel his text is well meaning but ultimately misguided and seemingly irrelevant. But please pause, dear reader. The globe is in trouble. The signs of danger and of disintegration are everywhere except where we are encouraged, and at times programmed, to look. Ill health stalks the land: famine malnutrition, toxic fumed air pollution, waterborne and vector transmitted disease, ill adaptation to weather events and coastal disruption never experienced before. All of these scourges are looming menacingly on a variety of unobserved horizons. Deeper still are the connections between terrorism, security, economic turbulence, military adventurism, and the driving out of sustainability across the land and seas.

Mick offers thoughtful and exciting ways of shaking us out of our ignorance and denial. He convincingly argues that the imaginal is indeed a pathway to revelation. He shows that the enlivened soul can cope with the crushing order of scientism by enabling us all to reflect and open up our discourse and contemplation. What is critical for his exposition is the startling relevance of his propositions as laid down in his introduction for contemporary society, and especially for the coming generation. He is right to emphasise the one-dimensional view that ushers us onto destructive tram rails where the destination is so deeply wounding for so very many. He is right to claim that we all have within us the roots of sustainability with their focus on sharing, on compassion, and on reciprocity. The birth of modern humanity took many generations to forge when the means for longer and happier lives were set in meanings of myth, of ancestries, of shamans, and of demons. The imaginal was the binding reality where intuition, story telling, recounting and reconciliation shaped behaviour and culture in creatively binding ways. This was the essence of prolonged living and of subtle but managed change. There is scope for its repetition but only if three outcomes coincide.

One is the awe and shock of realising the supreme power of the Anthropocene, where it indeed becomes possible that we can visualise an imaginal of almost universal dissipation and of despair. There is time to correct but only if there is leadership from the middle of society the world over to grasp the essentials of Collins' compelling analysis. This surely means that experiences in citizenship, in philanthropy, in cooperation and in reconnecting with the cosmos become central to learning. This process is beginning to take place in schools and community centres for no other reason than that social fragmentation is costly and dangerous. But it is surely much more to where Mick is taking his reader. It involves comprehensive experiences of the imaginal, it means mentoring and volunteering with the sick, the elderly, the depressed, and the inadequately trained. It means deepening the self-confidence of everyone so that everyone can be a mentor and a leader. It is not impossible to see this transformation in learning and social experience taking place in the coming decade as insidious change and ill preparedness engulfs as many as two in five youngsters.

A second is the emergence of a well-being culture, which slowly drives out the single-mindedness of much of modern economics. Again there are welcome straws in the wind; the talk of a universal social wage is but part of a wider notion of a social value and social return on caring which could become commonplace by the middle of the coming decade. Given this staging, there would be real opportunities for the kinds of imaginations which Mick extols.

A third is the progressive self and collective exploration of the deeper roots of sustainability, which could become the energising momentum of Transformocene. Here the basic tenets of Mick's propositions would bear fruit. For there has to be a supportive setting for his prescriptions. Right now the ground is somewhat barren but contains latent nutrition. Taking the steps from the expansive and imagined learning, to the trials and experiments of progressive community sustainability set in a socially caring economy, to the overall acceptance of holism, all of these taken together would surely bring us full circle, albeit in a thoroughly modern manner, to the living patterns and the connectivities to people and to nature that nurtured humanity for the many thousands of its evolving generations.

Tim O'Riordan, OBE, DL, FBA
Emeritus Professor, School of Environmental Sciences,
University of East Anglia

The intolerance of climate change deniers does not mask their uncertainty.
Their denial is no different to those who trivialise sacred knowledge and wisdom.
The 21st century 'culture of denial' is also our collective growing edge.

FOREWORD BY THE AUTHOR

A Climate for Deep Change

We live in interesting times

When I was completing the final draft of this manuscript, I read a story about a courageous nine-year-old girl from India, Ridhima Pandey, who filed a lawsuit against her government in 2017 for not doing enough to tackle climate change. She rightly points out that it is her generation who will have to tackle the burden of this generation's neglect.[1] This wonderful act by a very well informed young girl highlights the courage and creativity needed in our collective responses to the global crisis. If we are to improve our ways of living now, and for future generations, it will take imaginative and bold action. Ridhima Pandey is right to be concerned about the impact of climate change in her country. Researchers from the University of California have found that temperature increases in India are leading to worsening agricultural conditions, which is leading to a rise in suicides amongst farmers. The statistics are staggering. In 2015 12,600 Indian farmers took their own lives.[2] This is one example of the frontline problems connected to a warming climate and a burgeoning global crisis, which is not going to go away. A recent study at Washington University identified a 90% probability that global temperatures will continue to rise, which will result in worsening environmental impacts.[3] On this evidence alone, it is bewildering to learn that the US Department of Agriculture has officially told its staff to stop using the term *climate change*, directing them to use words such as 'weather extremes' instead.[4] It is interesting that this decision has occurred during Donald Trump's presidency, whose Chief Scientist at the US Department of Agriculture also dismisses the idea of human activity contributing to worsening climate change.[5] The denial of climate change is a serious threat to the well-being of humanity, other species and the planet. It is a supreme act of selfishness.

Ridhima Pandey's actions chimed with a conviction that underpinned my last book, which was published in 2014, *The Unselfish Spirit: Human Evolution in a Time of Global Crisis*. In the book I wrote about transformation through meaningful action, based on the idea that: "Change is not an option, it's a necessity". I explored how our modern attitudes and behaviours – towards each other, other species and the natural world – are outmoded, which is amplifying the planetary crisis. A central idea in *The Unselfish Spirit* is that the global crisis is also a spiritual crisis, which is becoming more pronounced as humanity continues to ignore the impacts of our collective assault on the natural world. We can no longer ignore the fact that the Earth is our *one and only* life-support system. To tackle worsening planetary conditions I put forward an occupational vision, underlining the interconnectedness of life, and how tapping into our *unoccupied* human potential could activate transformative actions, or *doing with depth* (archetypal occupations). Such actions enable us to participate in a living mystery, bringing us closer to a numinous and sacramental relationship with all life. In this way, we are opened up to a transpersonal consciousness, where our renewed attitudes and behaviours inspire us to co-create an improved and sustainable future. Each of us lives according to an occupational myth, which motivates us to *do* what we *do* in life. Imagine if we made a deeper connection to our *living myths* and harnessed them to a transformational vision, where our talents, skills and passions are used for the greater good. In such instances, imagination is the basis for holistic action.

There are no easy answers to the planetary problems before us, but I remain optimistic that a shift in collective consciousness is already underway; for example, there is a global resurgence and interest in a revitalised spirituality. I am convinced that radical change will not be initiated by our mainstream institutions for the simple reason that they are too invested in the outmoded ideologies that have led us to the current precipice. The administrative structures that are maintaining modern technocratic systems have wittingly or unwittingly been complicit in a form of mass indoctrination, where institutionalised *hyper-rationalism* has resulted in a stagnation of the collective imagination. We can see this in the collective inertia towards climate change and ecological degradation, which is *unimaginable* by our own supposedly *rational* standards. Building on the ideas that I shared in *The Unselfish Spirit*, this book explores the dynamic world of the imaginal realm, where we can be inspired by our encounters with non-ordinary realities and the irrational. Non-rational experiences may be unusual or even scary at times, but they can also be creative, enlivening and fun. One thing is for sure: anything is better than the mind-numbing predictability that permeates our modern consensus reality. Our politics and economics are shoring up a one-dimensional and technocratic habit, which is as much self-serving as it is self-annihilating. This critical observation is also a clarion call for humanity to engage a deeper and more creative relationship with the imaginal, which could inspire our rational efforts as we seek sustainable ways of living. Carrying on as normal is untenable and unsustainable.

We seem to be living in hope that our incredible scientific and technological nous will triumph as we lurch towards an uncertain future. However, our high-tech world is also revolutionising our lives in the fields of robotics and artificial intelligence, and we have no idea how these high-tech innovations will impact us. It is far from clear that these technologies are creating a world that we would dream of. Consequently, in the coming years there will be much discussion, debate and soul searching about the state of the world, the future of our species, and the consequences of investing in advanced technologies. Such discussions have been happening for many years. For example, in his 1999 book *The Age of Spiritual Machines*, Ray Kurzweil[6] speaks about understanding neuro-anatomical processes linked to spiritual experiences (which are much more developed these days), and how these could be enhanced in a brain that has been 're-created' computationally. My concern is we have become so steeped in a world of mechanistic science that our species' deep connection to a living mystery could soon be reduced to neural phenomena.

An example of how life may evolve in the 21st century is presented in Yuval Harari's book *Homo Deus*.[7] He writes about the best of our scientific lineage, which is propelling us into a brave new era, where health improvements and longevity are anticipated, via new technologies. He also points out that our rapidly evolving world of high-tech innovations could lead to *Big Data* becoming the new religion (*Dataism*). He writes critically (and sometimes justifiably) about the oppressive nature of our rule-bound religions, and he also warns that our cherished ideals of liberal humanism will probably collapse with the rise of information technologies (leading to techno-humanism). Much of what he says about information technologies is already apparent in the literature and media. However, I was more curious about his 'scientific-based' discussion, suggesting that the *soul*, *God* and even the *self* do not exist. Yet, in his book, Harari makes a few brief references to shamanism, Sufism and positive psychology, which he puts in the context of our unexplored human potential. It is difficult to know what to make of these inclusions in light of his efforts to show how modern science has 'allegedly' debunked the *soul*, *God* and the *self*. If so, what is the point of mentioning shamanism, which deals with *soul retrieval*, or Sufism, which is a mystical path of devotion to *God*, and even positive psychology, which is focused on *self-development* (inclusive of spirituality)? Harari mentions spirituality a few times in *Homo Deus*, but he does not seem to define the term adequately, which leaves the reader uncertain about what 'spirit' he is referring to?

Curiously, Harari has spent the last 15 years practising Vipassana meditation, which has its origins in Buddhism. Admittedly, in Buddhist teachings there is no *ultimate* self-supporting substantially existent 'I' (or soul), yet even Buddhist practitioners cede that there is a *relative* or conventional self, otherwise to 'whom' are the *Four Noble Truths* being addressed? Also, 'who' generates the karmic imprints (kleshas) that the Buddhists remind us to be aware of? Buddhists also teach that consciousness exists beyond our physical form, and that we can reincarnate into various realms of existence (depending on our karma), which reflects how we are bound to cyclic existence until we eventually awaken (enlightenment). Many of these issues are currently beyond the understanding of mainstream science, but as we shall see, people's encounters with near-death experiences provide us with compelling insights (and evidence) concerning a spiritual reality, which is beyond the material world. These deep spiritual encounters often have a life-changing impact on the ways people envision and engage their lives after returning to Earthly existence. They point to a non-material consciousness (or soul), which has profound implications for how humanity understands the sacredness of life. The idea that the Divine is just some sort of human fantasy is misleading and misguided.

In *Homo Deus*, Harari suggests that technology and data could potentially become the new God, but such a bold claim is complicated by a little *devil* in the detail. In the acknowledgement section of *Homo Deus*, Harari mentions that he could not have written his book without the support of his Vipassana meditation practice. This is essentially a *technology of transformation*, and there are many technologies of transformation, which are the legacy of our species' deep religious-spiritual heritage (prayer, vision quests, meditation, labyrinths and dream work etc.). I believe that the threshold between our *high*-tech innovations and our *technologies of transformation* is where our species will encounter the next *growing edge*, where a new spiritual renaissance will help us embrace a high-tech world more skilfully. I also believe that failure to embrace *technologies of transformation* at this critical time in our species' evolutionary trajectory will diminish our prospects for successful collective adaptation. *Homo Deus* points out the complexities of the new technological era before us, but the conclusion leads us into a *cul de sac*, where Harari fails to provide any alternative courses of action. In this book I explore how a sacred purpose lies at the heart of our evolutionary human journey, where technologies of transformation complement our high-tech innovations in creative ways. For example, it is through our deep, sacred and non-ordinary experiences where we meet the 'growing edge' of our species' evolutionary potential.

Honouring the sacred

The following life-transforming encounter happened to university professor Howard Storm[8] whilst he was on a trip to Paris with his wife. Storm experienced a perforated duodenum, which resulted in a near-death experience. Prior to this event he thought stories about *Hell* or *Heaven* were simply 'fairy tales', but his journey into the afterlife was about to turn this worldview upside down. In the initial stages of his near-death experience, Storm did not know what was happening to him, especially as he could see his wife sitting next to his physical body, which was lying motionless in a hospital bed. Then he heard friendly voices beckoning him, and he decided to follow these distant calls. Eventually he saw a group of pale figures that led him into a space, which became increasingly foggy and dark. He soon realised that he had been tricked, as these 'friendly' figures suddenly became more critical, nasty and vicious. Then, countless other figures joined the fracas, attacking him mercilessly. Storm was a committed atheist, but the sheer terror of this unrelenting assault made him cry out to Jesus, and he begged to be saved from the savagery that was now overwhelming him. Eventually a luminous and radiant 'being' emerged, surrounded by a light that was brighter than the sun. As the 'being of light' lifted him out of his misery, he was simultaneously relieved and healed, and he recounts how he cried uncontrollably as he was enveloped in an atmosphere of love. The being of light carried him into a presence, whose centre he described as 'the One'. He saw angels and colours unlike anything he had witnessed on Earth.

Howard Storm was encountering a Divine reality. Telepathic messages were communicated to him from the light, and he was taught about the importance of appreciating beauty and cultivating love. He learnt that near-death experiences are part of a *Great Transformation*, which is now beginning to unfold in the world. His descent into *Hell* and his ascent into *Heaven* taught him a profound lesson: that each of us is tasked with gaining self-understanding and bringing more love into the world. He was told that no religion has the monopoly on truth, and what matters most in life is how we are brought closer to the Divine (or God). I was touched to read how he was told that part of our *human pilgrimage* in this life is to wake up to the abuse we have inflicted *in* and *on* the world, including our attitude towards plants and animals. It is touching to read about a man who had spent years living as a committed atheist, and through a near-death experience was spiritually transformed and renewed. Storm was told that the Earth is *Holy*, and it is our responsibility to be reverential to all forms of life, where we are tasked with caring for the planet. In short, our human work in the world is to cultivate hope, love, patience and generosity etc. It is my firm belief that people's near-death experiences are contemporary spiritual teachings, which are communicated directly from a Divine source, and these revelations are akin to the most profound mystical teachings. Such encounters consistently reveal the sacrament of this Earthly existence. In this time of global crisis, such revelations are an important catalyst that could inspire a collective wake-up call, where we are inspired to transform our consciousness and live more soulfully and spiritually. It is a calling to live with more depth.

Carl Jung developed a more expansive approach to working with the depth of the psyche (soul),[9] and his research has provided us with a renewed (and dynamic) understanding of consciousness. It is a method that focuses on cultivating wholeness in life, where we are capable of encountering experiences of unity, similar to the mystics throughout the ages, who were opened up to a cosmos where all is in the 'One' and the 'One' is in all things. Jung's approach echoes the creative work of the alchemists, who deemed the imagination to be Heavenly, due to its illuminating and transforming qualities.[10] Such revelations point to the cultivation of a vibrant relationship, between the human imagination and the inspirations that come to us from the imaginal realm. In this way, our consciousness is awoken through dreams, visions, synchronicities and other non-ordinary encounters. It highlights the importance of Jung's soulful method of 'active imagination' and channelling it in our daily life and occupations, through what I call *imaginative action* as spiritual expression. The work of Arnold (Arny) Mindell is at the forefront of such imaginative and creative possibilities for living, where communities learn about the conflicts that kill, where conciliations can be considered, compassions nurtured and creative sparks celebrated. Wholeness takes commitment, which is cultivated through awareness, and emerges through working with our inner and outer worlds, where we learn about unity in diversity. It is through the depths of interconnectivity that our self-other knowing can incarnate love in action, which is one of the key messages from people's near-death experiences.

Deepening our relationship to life and wholeness is a step on from the modern culture of self-development programmes, which are often tethered to industries that promote individualism. It is true that self-development has become commercialised, but it is my view that these industries have sown positive seeds in collective consciousness, in that they have championed *awareness* and the importance of *holistic* living. I recently read an article that critiqued the modern culture of self-exploration, suggesting people should stop trying to *'find themselves'*, because personal growth is aligned to societal drives that are linked to consumption, acquisition and growth.[11] It is an understandable knee jerk reaction to a commercial industry. However, I take the opposite view, suggesting that our world is crying out for communities and cultures that are literate in holistic, sacred and deeper ways of living. And, I concur with the observation made by James Hillman[12] who identified a very clear distinction between 'soul making', from those activities that are allied to 'personality improvements'.

In the last paragraph of my book, *The Unselfish Spirit: Human Evolution in a Time of Global Crisis*, I wrote "the next frontier for human purpose is the emancipation of the human imagination, which acts in accord with the wisdom, compassion and intelligence of our full potential".[13] The main focus in this new book is concerned with the cultivation of a deeper relationship between a manifest material reality, and the subtle world of the imaginal realm, which is revealed in the work of German philosopher Frederick Wilhelm Schelling (1775-1854). He spoke about a *world soul*, where universal consciousness connects to self-consciousness.[14] This gives us some scope for understanding the important connection between the human imagination and the imaginal realm. It emphasises the inclusion of a spiritual reality, where as Schelling says: "Nature is visible spirit" and "Spirit is invisible nature".[9] This book honours diverse ways of knowing, which underlines the importance of both the manifest and the subtle worlds.

The collective task before us will be both demanding and enlightening as we seek a new vision for living, one that brings a renewed understanding of our personal, cultural, cosmological and sacred (numinous) connections, which are part of our mythic journey into wholeness.[15] It is through the *archetypal imagination*[16] that we can connect with the Divine, which also activates processes of healing and renewal, and deepens our relationship to the imaginal realm. We have to find the 'urge' in these 'urgent' times to live transformatively as planetary citizens. This is a vital part of our collective human evolution at this time, and I put it to you in the strongest possible terms: if we give up on our human potential, we give up on the world and ourselves.

Our reckless pursuit for wealth is now enshrined in the Earth's geological record. Yet, our real treasure remains hidden, locked away and ignored, lying deep and dormant in the vaults of our souls.

INTRODUCTION

From Anthropocene to Transformocene

Imaginal energies and planetary citizenship

I wrote this book with the intention of highlighting the importance of our relationship to a living mystery, the *imaginal realm*, which has served humanity for millennia through revelatory dreams, visionary experiences and synchronicities. We are blessed to have such a wonderful connection to a rich source of wisdom and intelligence, which comes to us when we live with depth. Compiling the research for this book and sharing stories of people's deep transformational processes has given me a great opportunity to do a stock-take of accumulated insights gleaned over the course of four decades. Throughout the book I show how 'non-ordinary realities' and 'supernatural' occurrences are part of a greater natural order, revealing how our species thrives when 'we' live with a better connection to a living mystery (and wholeness). When we are open to such numinous encounters they evoke and awaken a sense of awe within us, where we discover a deep intelligence that is active in the universe. In this way, a meaningful connection to the imaginal realm has an important function in relation to our personal and collective transformation in this time of global crisis. Throughout the book I show how our awakened human potential brings forth a renewed quality of participation in life, and how a revived connection to an awe-inspiring mystery rekindles and renews our relationship to life as a whole. Each of us is capable of connecting to an inspiring vision that ignites the imagination and energises transformative action. It is through such a reawakened sense of awe that we will be inspired to unlock the problems of the Anthropocene.

During the last 12,000 years humanity has flourished in an epoch known as the Holocene.[1] Yet, since the Second World War, increased globalisation has resulted in the 'great acceleration', with rapid increases in population growth, technological advances, and revolutions in communication systems.[2] A study published in the journal *Science* has revealed the extent and impact of human activity on the planet, from the amount of CO_2 and methane in the atmosphere, to the vast volume of plastics and concrete now present on the Earth, as well as the fallout from nuclear weapons testing.[1] A formal proposal has been made for a new geological epoch called the Anthropocene, which means that humanity has left its mark on the world to such an extent that it is now recorded in the Earth's geological record. The body of professionals tasked with determining this new epoch is the *International Commission on Stratigraphy*, and they are still evaluating the impacts of humanity's dominance on the planet. It is a record of catastrophic levels of ecological destruction. Evidence points to human activity being the cause of the sixth mass extinction, with vertebrate species dying at an alarming rate. Professor of Palaeobiology, Jan Zalasiewicz,[3] says that the parasitic nature of the human-created 'technosphere' is not functioning in partnership with the natural system of the Earth's *biosphere*. One thing is becoming abundantly clear: a more integrated, systemic and holistic approach to how we are living is needed to break the destructive march of mechanisation in the world today.[4] Despite the dire warnings mentioned above, we must not lose sight of that fact that our species is capable of great leaps in imaginative living, and impressive feats of adaptive functioning. Indeed, we are incredible survival specialists.

We cannot bypass the fact that as a species we need to make a radical shift in our ways of living to enable a more harmonious relationship with the world's ecosystems, of which we are a part, and on which we depend for our survival. We must face up to the impact of our cumulative behaviours on the Earth's biosphere, as we navigate the uncertainties of the Anthropocene.[5] The Anthropocene is undoubtedly the sharpest form of feedback about our species' need to adapt. It calls for us to reconsider our activities of daily living, and how we have degraded life, ecologically, economically, politically, technologically and most importantly – soulfully. It is a wake-up call requiring an epochal shift, underlining humanity's duty to become more caring and act as stewards for the Earth.[6] It means that we will have to rethink how our techno-culture operates; for example, Nicholas Carr[7] says all technologies are a reflection of human effort; therefore, we will need to make sure our future technologies work for the greater good of the planet as a whole. Indeed, Gaia Vince[8] reflects on the planetary conditions we have created and asks what type of Anthropocene does humanity want? This is a great question, because it forces us to think about (and feel) the consequences of our behaviours towards the natural world, and how as a species we can adapt and respond to the ecological changes ahead. The challenging times we are living in have been quite correctly described as a crisis of the imagination.[9] But if we take the trouble to re-imagine our relationship to life we can re-align soulfully and spiritually with the natural world.

In this book I contend that any viable response to the reality of the Anthropocene must include the activation of our imaginations to bring about a deep and creative response to change, which catalyses what I call the Transformocene. What do I mean by this term? Well, the Anthropocene potential is a geological marker resulting from accumulated layers of toxicity and debris in the Earth, which is simply a record of our unwillingness to reverse our destructive actions in the world. Conversely, the *Transformocene* is an attitudinal and behavioural shift that brings forth a new consciousness, which is committed to reviving and re-animating a sacred connection to the Earth. It calls for us to re-imagine and renew our relationship to nature and what it means to live as co-participants in a biotic community. To date, commercial and economic interests have increasingly dominated human 'progress', and our high-tech cultures of production and consumption have distorted what it means to live as responsible planetary citizens. However, the Transformocene is a dynamic response to planetary conditions, where humanity is called upon to take part in a process of individual, collective and planetary healing. Yet, in order to embrace such a transformational shift, we will need a new myth to galvanise this shared response to change.

Throughout human history myths have recounted the trials and tribulations that dramatically revisit successive generations. Wisdom and warnings are encoded in these highly symbolic renderings of the human condition, in which mortals confront forces they are often ill prepared to face. These mythic narratives resonate powerfully with humanity's struggles and achievements in life, which have existed since the earliest times and continue to echo in the vaults of collective consciousness. Yet today we seem to have lost sight of how these collective myths shape our worldviews and behaviours.[10] Since the Enlightenment the Western world has overly invested in a guiding myth based on reason and reductionism, which has sidelined alternative ways of knowing. Consequently, people in the modern world have become caught up in an ideology dominated by hyper-rationalism. But we are more than capable of re-awakening a meaningful and spiritual connection to life, via the imaginal realm, where our dreams and visions are instrumental in the process of awakening and transforming consciousness. Our species has a historical and instinctual connection to the imaginal realm, which can inform a renewed vision for our collective ways of knowing. Thankfully, we are living in a time where a new myth is trying to emerge.

William Irwin Thompson[11] speaks about the function of myths, how they bring the *known* and the *unknown* into a relationship of philosophy, science and art. Myths invite us to imagine, to dream and connect with life in meaningful ways. Rather than imposing a *worldview* on the collective, they encourage us to co-create a new *view of the world* through deep reflection and action. Indeed, mythic narratives bring us to liminal thresholds, where our imaginations are conduits that help us reconnect to a wider imaginal field, which Sufi scholar Henry Corbin[12] called the *mundus imaginalis*. This is not a fantasy world, but rather a subtle and sacred reality. How we create a meaningful relationship to our imaginative energies is set to become a burning question as we now seek ways of responding to the heat of global warming and its consequences. The imagination may well be our greatest asset, which helps us break out of modern one-dimensional ways of living, enabling us to engage our multi-dimensional potentials for transformation.

Philosopher Herbert Marcuse[13] pointed out over 50 years ago that the modern technocratic world has become increasingly invested in a one-dimensional mindset, which has altered the dynamic interface between rationality and irrationality. His counter-intuitive proposition for shifting this status quo is to honour the irrational, to bring us into an artistic relationship with life and offer us alternative courses of action. He noticed how the modern temperament has unquestioningly separated reason from imagination, and in doing so created repressive administrative structures in society, which continue to curtail our freedoms. He called for a dramatic reversal in the wholesale neglect of our human potential and its actualisation, insisting that it is our imaginations that can liberate us from the insidious binds of the world we have created and invested in. For Marcuse, the reclamation of the imagination was a political matter. Politics shapes our imaginative responses *in* and *to* the world, and it is for this reason that we should not underestimate the workings of the *Political Psyche*, as noted by Jungian analyst Andrew Samuels.[14] Engaging a meaningful and productive relationship to the psyche is a deeply political act, because it opens us up to the freedoms of the imaginal realm. For example, the psyche brings us into a dynamic connection with a living mystery, where the knowledge and wisdom found in the depths of the collective unconscious can serve our journey into wholeness. Such an undertaking means we will meet the irrational, but it is through a productive relationship between the rational and irrational that our vital life energies can be expressed creatively, as noted by Carl Jung.

Jung[15] understood the importance of the psyche as a source of eternal wisdom, which human beings have consulted throughout the ages. Today, in the modern world, humanity appears to have lost interest in understanding the symbolic meanings coded in myths, and consequently over the past 300 years knowledge has been dominated by one-dimensional science and technology, which has perpetuated a worn-out myth of gaining control and mastery over nature, rather than living in balance with the world. This one-dimensional myth was unmasked with the rise of a systems perspective (in science), where the web of life is understood through networks that interact within the context of a greater whole.[16] A systems view of life underlines the importance of holism. However, the force of reductionism remains ever-present in our scientific and technological methods (via scientism), and it is also evident in our economic and business activities.[4] If it is not transformed, the legacy of this one-dimensional trajectory will lead us further onto a path of alienation, where the Earth – our only life-support system – is treated objectively and ransacked for profit. Overuse of the planet's finite resources and destruction of ecosystems is not only symptomatic of a loss of wholeness; it is unquestionably an act of ecocide. Only a fool would deny that the planet is slipping into a deepening crisis year on year, with pressures of climate change, overpopulation, desertification of the land and acidification of the oceans, coupled to the problems of maintaining food security and supplies of fresh water. Yet, our economic and technocratic interests have tended to override our ecological responsibilities. This is the evolutionary edge before us, and we are tasked with galvanising our resolve to meet this transformational threshold imaginatively, co-creatively and cooperatively.

We need to have faith that we can transform the status quo. For example, *The Guardian* newspaper columnist Simon Jenkins[17] cites a YouGov poll in which 71% of Britons surveyed thought that the state of the world was getting worse. He writes about the dangers of pessimism, suggesting that we can afford a more optimistic worldview because of global improvements, such as reductions in poverty, starvation, child mortality, and increases in women's education, literacy and democracy. However, whilst such improvements are welcomed, it only reflects a human-centric view of progress. Exactly two weeks after the publication of this column, *The Guardian* reported a growing crisis in UK wildlife, with one tenth of wild species facing extinction, making the UK one of the worst nature-depleted countries on Earth.[18] This report underlines the fact that we must double our efforts to care for people, other species and the natural world equally. Humanity is facing a dilemma that will become more acute as global instability continues to increase. For example, social commentator Alvin Toffler[19] wrote about the bewildering pace of change in 1970, which he referred to as a *future shock*. That shock is now reverberating powerfully in the world. But we need to hold tight to the idea that shock and awe brings us into connection with the numinous, which is more than capable of sparking our transformative actions into life.

Toffler was alert to the inevitable collision between ecology and technology, and how our imaginations are capable of revolutionising our relationship to life. He proposed the construction of special sanctuaries in society, where our imaginations could be exercised. In a similar way, Theodore Roszak[20] speaks about the importance of being connected to a vision, which invites a quality of participation that is indivisible from the wider ecology. It is through our contact with the imaginal realm where we are opened up to new possibilities for living, which helps restore balance and wholeness. Roszak[20] reminds us of the importance of visions to our ethical actions, in the same way that soil is important to seed. That is, we need the right conditions in order to grow. Humanity is more than capable of moving beyond our current conceptions of life in order to bring forth new ways of living, rather than serving the status quo.[21]

The cosmos we call home

We are only now starting to wake up collectively to the importance of ecological security and sustainability, despite warnings since the 1970s from eco-activists about the state of the planet. Brian Swimme and Thomas Berry[22] suggest that we will have to actively engage in a shift in collective consciousness to alter the current course of our destructive behaviours. Of course, this is only possible if sufficient numbers of people and societies deem it important enough to act, but the problem is twofold. First, the very notion of altering our one-sided technological mindset and living more holistically is a radical proposition. Nevertheless, we know that humans are a transitional species[23] capable of great adaptation. Second, as Charles Eisenstein[24] points out, due to the scale of the global crisis, humanity does not know what to do. This is understandable, because we have never faced a collective problem of such magnitude. But we are a highly adaptive species and at some point we will be forced to engage our transformational potential. The choice is to live as deep and dynamic planetary citizens, or face the consequences.

The critical question is, will we embrace a shift towards wholeness and become empowered to make a difference in the world? Theodore Roszak[20] says that such a task involves finding out who we are as human beings, and most importantly, what we want to do in life. It will be up to each one of us to take full responsibility for *undoing* the restrictive knots that are tethering us to a one-dimensional mindset, which continues to knock us out of balance with life as a whole. Roszak goes on to emphasise the importance of exercising, expressing and expanding our creative possibilities for living, citing the work of Abraham Maslow, who championed the idea of actualising our full human potential. But will we do it?[25] It is here that integrating technologies of transformation into mainstream culture (via shamanism, dream work, vision quests, prayer etc.) could shift our current one-dimensional worldview (*high-tech vision*), from experiences of separateness and fragmentation to a unified vision of wholeness.

Technologies of transformation bring us into conscious relationship with life as an interconnected whole, and these methods bring us into stronger alignment with our sacred heritage, rather than say (for example) mindfulness techniques being taught to executives of a chemical weapons factory to help reduce their stress and aid performance.[26] This is a time where we are poised to move beyond a post-industrial culture, towards planetary citizenship[27] and co-evolve a new cosmological outlook that is fit for the 21st century. The Greek word *kosmos* refers to a sense of universal order, which Matthew Fox[28] says connects to *wholeness* (interestingly the Latin for 'universe' includes 'unus', which means 'one'). We need to hold onto the idea that a renewed cosmology of wholeness can be cultivated in the modern world. Interestingly, the seeds of change are already being sown in an international context.

The United Nations[29] has produced a sustainable development plan to transform our world by 2030. The report has the potential to act as a catalyst that kickstarts a renewed vision for improving human rights and dignities, as well as tackling issues such as climate change, poverty, and fostering greater harmony and cooperation in the world. Five broad goals are noted in the report where action needs to be taken: *people, planet, prosperity, peace and partnership*. Similarly, in the UK, the Welsh Government[30] drafted legislation that champions human potential and sustainability in the *Well-Being of Future Generations Bill*. The aim of the Bill is to create a more equal society, empowering communities to do the right thing through personal development, fulfilment of potential, and participation. However, in the United Nations' document, the section on people only makes a brief statement about cultivating human beings' aspirations to meet their *full potential* in life. I am curious why so little was written about a subject that is of such great importance. I hold to the belief that human potential (actualisation and transformation) is the driving force of the Transformocene and the co-creation of an improved and sustainable future.[25] I am also convinced that if a critical mass of people (from all walks of life) embrace a renewed vision for holistic living it will lead to tipping points for collective transformation.

When I speak about transformation I mean that we are willing to consciously 'die' to our old destructive habits, in order for deep change to emerge. The pathway before us in this time of global crisis is like a collective 'deathwalk', which Arny Mindell[31] describes as a process of acknowledging our vulnerabilities and the emotional impacts of living. It is where we meet our inner and outer adversaries, learn to let go of the past and open our hearts to life. The deathwalk is a process of emergence, which goes beyond rigid ideas of life and identity. It reflects the deep struggle of living an authentic life, between the forces at work within us, and the social roles or rules in the outer world.[32] This fluid approach to understanding consciousness and identity enables us to open up to the creative pulse of the imaginal realm, bringing forth a sacramental and transformational vision for living. Hence, the deathwalk is where we come alive to our transpersonal and occupational potentials, which intersect as we weave personal and collective paths of renewal, through our ways of knowing, being, doing and relating.

The wounds from which we learn, and heal

If we are to evolve as a species we will need to start to pull together collectively, and this means re-imagining our fractured relationship to nature. This journey into wholeness will also be a path of healing for us. Abraham Maslow acknowledged that when we are cut off from the transpersonal (wholeness) we become sick.[25] Awakening from our one-dimensional predicament will help us face up to our overinvestment in egocentrism,[33] and also our lack of awareness of a shared existence with others.[34] Therefore, a key part of becoming whole involves shifting the focus of human consciousness towards processes of Self-realisation, where we tend to our wounds,[24] including those we have inflicted on other species and the planet. It is imperative we understand how we have become *wounded* (in self-destructive ways), and how we are *wounding* (in eco-destructive ways) in a vicious cycle. We need more people to become what I call *wounded transformers*, who recognise the extent of the person-planet healing that is required at this time, who are also open to learning about the consequences of wounding.[35,36] From a mystical perspective, wounds are entry points for transformative living, where our deep reactions are brought into consciousness.[37] It means paying attention to the transformative potential that is trying to emerge in our lives, in our dreams and in our visions.

Reclaiming sacred ways of knowing opens humanity to wider parameters for living. The journey of psycho-spiritual transformation enacts a visionary process of renewal that garners insights, revelations and expanded awareness, which can then be integrated into everyday consciousness.[38] In this way, a sacramental vision underpins a path of collective healing and transformative action. In ancient Greek religion the word *Eusebia* described people's reverential approach towards the divine, their mother and father, the land and the ancestors.[39] It is a sacramental vision that is waiting to be revived and lived in the modern world. As a species, each and every one of us possesses imaginative and visionary energies that connect deeply to our transpersonal potential. Dying to our outmoded and redundant ways of living is where the deathwalk begins, where each step we take can be transformative, shifting our focus from destruction to global healing and renewal. Gary Reiss[40] tells us that the process of 'dying' whilst we are alive is a pathway to freedom. This powerful metaphor of *dying* consciously, creates opportunities to awaken our hearts, which not only means facing *who we are* and *what we have become*; it includes bringing more love into the world.

Peter Russell[33] speaks about an emergent evolutionary direction unfolding in our collective lives at this time, with opportunities for growing in awareness and affirmative action. Each year the stakes are rising for how we mitigate the worst effects of climate change and live sustainably. The collective silence on the subject of our global crisis is deafening and Mark Rice-Oxley[41] fears that even our hoped for high-tech solutions will probably not be enough to stave off the crisis. In fact, he believes sustainability will be dependent upon a radical transformation of civilisation, particularly in our ways of living. The most urgent action we need to take in the 21st century is to *renew our visionary energies* for deep change, as much as it is about investing in *renewable energies*. It is a time to dream big and act for the greater good. As David Whyte[42] says, the interface between the soul of people and the soul of the world cannot be ignored in the 21st century. It is up to each of us to revive a holistic relationship to life and co-create a re-enchanted connection to the natural world.[43]

This book has been written to stimulate and inspire the transformational potential we are all capable of actualising, individually and collectively. The 12 chapters in this book are divided into three sections, each exploring diverse and interconnected themes, which highlight the importance of the imaginal realm to the current shift in collective consciousness. This book was conceptualised as a way of activating the emergence of the Transformocene Age.

Three Propositions for Deeper Living is a call for renewal and wholeness in this time of global decay. Modern appetites and lifestyles are unsustainable, and they portray a self-centred and superficial understanding of existence. Yet humanity is about to be confronted with an increasingly complex future, which will require a radical departure from the hyper-rational and egocentric modes of consciousness that have created the crisis we are now facing. To reclaim a vision of wholeness, we will need to radically revise our ways of living, so that they are in balance with nature. It is here that a connection to the imaginal realm could inspire deep change. In addition, the much-maligned countercultural vision of hippie radicalism in the 1960s and its offshoot, the New Age, could inspire and initiate changes in collective consciousness today. This is one example for how the Transformocene could be seeded and actualised.

Part One: *The Imaginal Lineage*

Chapter One explores the role of science in society, which has become the dominant way of knowing in the modern world since the Enlightenment. Science has led to impressive breakthroughs and phenomenal gains that have improved human existence. However, an overinvestment in objective science and hyper-rationalism has contributed to a growing chasm in the relationship between humanity and the natural world. The global crisis is revealing that holistic and alternative ways of knowing are needed, such as those found in spiritual traditions with a deeper connection to the imaginal realm. Yet, the reality of a dogma called 'scientism' challenges the wisdom found in myths and mysticism, which are merely viewed as superstitious and irrational. I discuss how scientism is an impediment to holism.

Chapter Two considers how early Greek philosophers were alert to the wisdom found in myths and the meaning conveyed through their irrational narratives. An ancient Greek philosopher credited with appreciating the merits of both the rational and mystical worlds is Parmenides. He received inspiration from a goddess, and was connected to a spiritual tradition, where incubation and dreams were used in processes of healing. Such traditions highlight our mythic heritage as a counterbalance to today's hyper-rationalism. That a goddess inspired Parmenides underlines the important role of the sacred feminine in our imaginal quest towards alternative ways of knowing and wholeness.

Chapter Three proposes that the sacred feminine is vital to our ways of knowing in terms of our spiritual and mythic connection to life's mysteries. In this time of global crisis we are being confronted with the need to heal our wounds, including the damage we have inflicted on one another, as well as the natural world. It is here that soul work serves wholeness, and renews our connection to the *anima mundi* (soul of the world). The sacred feminine brings humanity into a deeper relationship with nature, opening us up to the imaginal realm and a process of creative unfolding. It encourages a deeper connection to intuition and dreams, which can revitalise humanity's relationship to life as a mystery, which brings us closer to the indigenous pulse that beats in the heart of humanity and nature.

Chapter Four honours our indigenous ways of knowing, anchored through a meaningful connection to the imaginal realm, as found in the Aboriginal dreamtime and shamanism. Indigenous wisdom reflects a relational worldview, based on an understanding that humanity lives in an intimate relationship with the natural world and the wider cosmos. Myths also have an important function within indigenous cultures, conveying traditional and ancestral knowledge, which is communicated across successive generations. Indigenous wisdom could inspire us to rekindle our relationship to planet Earth (our life-support system), through the cultivation of a renewed vision of wholeness. However, a key barrier to wholeness is the shadow that divides us, which needs to be addressed as a vital part of planetary healing.

Part Two: *The Redemptive Quest*

Chapter Five examines the impact of a neglected shadow on our personal and collective lives, due to the one-dimensional and hyper-rational attitudes that drive the modern world. Carl Jung conceptualised the idea of the shadow and his work has remained on the margins of mainstream culture. Yet, without a clear understanding of the unconscious processes that are operating in our hyper-rational modern world, we run the risk of using reason to explain all our behaviours, which is dangerous. Shadow work means that we must face the irrational, and in doing so, we enter into a transformational relationship with hitherto unconscious processes. As Jung said, 80% of the shadow is pure gold, and it is where we strike the rich seam of wisdom for living. However, a neglected shadow is where the seeds of evil are propagated.

Chapter Six clarifies that the shadow is not inherently evil; rather it is when the shadow is not examined that our unconscious projections can be strengthened and enacted. The collective shadow is a danger to any society, where *scapegoats* are targeted to take the blame for collective ills. Evil is a human construct, which is marked out by certain attitudes, values, and behaviours that are intended to do serious harm to others. Humanity has many mythic representations of the tensions between good-evil, which are often associated with titanic struggles in terms of spiritual awakening. Part of our collective wake-up call today is to reflect on the evil of ecocide connected to modern lifestyles and the destruction of the planet. Humanity has tackled questions of good-evil for millennia, which brings into focus the wisdom of the ancestors.

Chapter Seven celebrates the role of the ancestors, who since the beginning of time have left a legacy from which successive generations have profited. As Jung pointed out, the trajectory of human evolution has resulted in each successive generation contributing to knowledge that is part of the collective unconscious. In this way, the ancestral lineage acts as a numinous connection within our collective human heritage, where figures from the past are active in the imaginal realm, and can manifest in our dreams and visions etc. The myth of the ancestors brings into focus their achievements and the opportunities they squandered, or what they failed to do. Learning from the ancestors provides us with opportunities to learn from the past and invest in wholeness. The ancestors are like spirit guides, which also bring us into connection with the daimon.

Chapter Eight considers the role and function of the ancient Greek spiritual entity called the daimon, which awakens us at a soul level, stirring us to express our human potential in life. It is engaged through a deep sense of vocation, as found in the lives of people like Socrates and Jung. Working creatively with the daimon requires courage and wise discrimination in the ways that our true character is developed and expressed. *Eudaimonia* is about living with depth, subsuming all that we do into a transformational life, which becomes a blessing. It requires a deep understanding of the shadow, lest we fall into the trap of corrupting our daimonic potential. The daimon underlines the spiritual importance of living to our full potential before we die.

Part Three: *The Emancipatory Edge*

Chapter Nine evaluates the importance of what we are doing with our lives in the modern world, especially when compared against the revelations from near-death experiences and people's encounters with a life review. In the life review people 'feel' the consequences of their actions and how their behaviours reverberated in the lives of others. People may also be told that they still have life lessons to learn, and when these people are resuscitated they often make significant changes in their ways of living, for example, becoming more loving and compassionate. The life review puts human existence under the microscope, and such critical reflections may be vitally important to us as a species, especially with the rise of robotic technologies. We have much work to do to reclaim the soul from an increasingly one-dimensional technocracy.

Chapter Ten explores the important links between the imaginal realm, a soulful connection to life, and the expression of our human potential through doing. The work of Carl Jung has enabled us to develop a deep relationship to an archetypal reality, where we do inner work with the imaginal realm via active imagination. This creates a deep connection to expressing our human potential in daily life, where our outer work is connected to archetypal occupations (doing with depth), which is expressed through our imaginative actions. The interface between our *inner work* and *outer work* forges a dynamic and productive relationship between the imaginal realm and our imaginative energies. It is where we discover indigenous wisdom and the 'song' of the universe, which lives through everything. Such a connection brings an alignment between our actions and our subtle energies.

Chapter Eleven honours the relationship between the subtle energies (e.g. chakras) and our mythic and mystical physiology, which play an important part in our spiritual awakening. The subtle energies are part of our soulful connection to life and they play an important role in how we can fulfil our spiritual potential. Such awakening is an important part of regenerating a sacred connection to self, others, other species, and nature as a whole. It provides a necessary interface between a soulful and authentic representation of our true character (daimonic fate), and how our spiritual potential is expressed in life (angelic destiny). This deep and mystical alignment with our vital energies is an example of how *inner work* and *outer work* are part of our mythic quest. It exemplifies the need to re-animate a sacred connection to life as a whole.

Chapter Twelve encourages a deeper exploration between scientific and spiritual ways of knowing to assist in our stewardship of the Earth and all life. Science and spirituality are different, yet these complementary ways of knowing could model new patterns of living, via leading-edge ecological innovations like permaculture. Far from being nebulous, spirituality deepens our ways of relating to life through our ways of doing and being. In the same way that science is a discipline that elucidates life, spirituality also involves discipline, but the insights gained come from our deep experiential encounters with the imaginal realm. The biography of a 97-year-old Benedictine monk reveals the transformative possibilities of spiritual practice in the face of extraordinary trials, illustrating the relevance of mysticism for how we can live lightly on the Earth.

Afterword focuses on the subtle power of spiritual awakening and how it can profoundly shift our states of consciousness and our ways of living, even in the face of great adversity. Making a soulful connection to life helps us rekindle a relationship with the imaginal realm, and emboldens us to live authentically and be true to the deepest calling and character within us. The chapter tells the story of an inspirational man on death row. Although he is locked up in a living tomb, his story goes to the heart of spiritual awakening, in that it reflects a deep re-alignment to the soul we are all capable of making. The chapter concludes with the telling of the myth of the *Warriors of the Rainbow*. This is an indigenous prophecy about a time of global decay and transformation, which is a rallying call for collective action in the world today.

Transformative imaginations

The aim of this book is to investigate our connection to the imaginal realm, and consider it akin to a journey of exploration, rather like a novice traveller in a myth or folk tale who leaves behind the certainties of everyday life, and embarks on an epic voyage to uncharted lands. Such odysseys usually involve having to face the awesome power of nature, such as stormy seas or the forbidding precipices and chasms in mountain ranges, and of course the fear and disorientation that can occur when entering dense ancient woodlands. It is no surprise that nature plays such a pivotal role in the myths and stories of human quests, particularly in transformative rites of passage. Invariably, most of these fairy tales also feature some sort of adversary who adds a dynamic twist to what is already a formidable wilderness challenge. What myths and fairy stories teach us is that nature is powerfully represented in our psyches, and these tales can act as symbols or metaphors for the healing and transformative journeys we are capable of taking. Indeed, our experiences of the unconscious, and our inner journeys, can contribute to ecological Self-discovery and healing.[44]

We need to be inspired to act, which of course can include the use of humour. I remember hearing a joke in the 1970s about the fictional character *Rip Van Winkle*, who managed to sleep through many monumental events, including the American Revolution, the marriage of his daughter and the birth of his grandson. The joke deviates from the original tale written by Washington Irving, but it serves as a perfect metaphor for our global predicament today. In the joke, a friend of Rip Van Winkle decides it is time for his buddy to wake up. He goes to Rip's house and bangs on the door, shouting: "Rip, wake up". There was no answer, so the visitor thumps on the door again, this time shouting a bit louder: "Rip, get up". Once again, there was no response, and in a fit of frustration his friend bangs the door with a rock and screams: "Rip, waaaaake uuuup". Then, as Rip eventually stirs from his deep slumber, he shouts out: "How long have I been asleep?" and his friend shouts out: "20 years!" There was a long pause, before Rip replied: "Ok, just another 10 minutes".

For me the above joke holds two important messages. The first is we need to go deep into the realm of dreams and the unknown wilderness of the unconscious, which brings resources that help us transform. And second, we need to be persistent in helping each other wake up and put our deep insights into action. This last point is critical, because underestimating our human potential may be one of the greatest threats to humanity.[34] Perhaps our collective journey into the unknown in this time of global and ecological crisis would be easier if we used story, metaphor and symbol to stimulate our imaginations and engage our underused human potential. Narratives, stories, myths and tales are embedded deep within the human psyche and they are instrumental for inspiring and incubating change. For example, myths often show the best and worst of our human condition, revealing the importance of a transformative imperative. Deep down we are wise enough to know that preserving something as precious as the Earth and the beauty of the natural world, including the diverse range of living species on the planet, is well worth the effort. It is through the human soul that humanity is opened to the imaginal realm, which in turn, helps us connect to the soul of the world. This is how the Transformocene Age is seeded.

Exercise: The sacrament of wholeness

- In many spiritual traditions eating food is a way of connecting to sacred awareness (Tibetan tantra, the Eucharist, etc.).

- If you are fortunate to have enough food daily, consider how this is a privilege and blessing, one that many people in the world do not have.

- Bring to mind a fruit or vegetable that you enjoy eating.

- Think about this item of food and its origins in the natural world.

- Consider the nourishment this item of food gives you (protein, minerals, carbohydrate, vitamins, etc.).

- Reflect on the vitality and energy this item of food gives you.

- Imagine the vitality or energy of this item of food inside you now.

- Feel its influence in your body at a cellular level, keeping you alive and healthy.

- Go beyond the cellular level and feel the essence of this item of food.

- Imagine that this item of food is a spiritual gift for your life and wholeness.

- Next time you eat this item of food try connecting to it as a sacred offering from Mother Nature to you.

Imaginal intelligence is awoken through dreams, visions and active imaginations.
It is a vibrant pulse that connects us to wholeness, and reverberates with
the beating heart of the cosmos.

THREE PROPOSITIONS FOR DEEPER LIVING

A Call to Renewal

Overview

The three propositions for deeper living is a call for humanity to recognise the unconventional wisdom that could foster a holistic connection to living. We have arrived at a critical point in our species' evolution, where human and planetary problems exist in a destructive relationship. I discuss how alternative ways of knowing could inspire creative adaptations in our ways of living, as follows. Proposition one, *valuing wholeness*, underlines the importance of motivating human behaviour to shift away from a culture of empty consumption towards the fulfilment of our human potential. Proposition two, *opening to the imaginal*, points to the natural connection between humanity's use of visionary energies and creative living. I discuss the value of a resurgent countercultural movement today, which is continuing a shift in collective consciousness that began in the 1940s and erupted in the 1960s New Age. Proposition three, *engaging with the 'non-ordinary'*, argues for a creative relationship to naturally occurring phenomena, such as dreams, visionary energies and synchronicities, which breaks the spell of hyper-rationalism. These three propositions for deeper living are ways that the Transformocene Age can be understood and actualised.

Proposition one: Valuing wholeness

Cultivating an appetite for change

The most pressing problem in our collective lives today is the issue of climate change, but this only seems to make the headlines after some major ecological disaster, or when another scientific study informs us about the desperate state of the Earth. It seems that we are caught in a collective mindset of persistent indifference and inaction with regard to the well-being of people, other species and the planet. The way forward is fraught with inner and outer complexities, but these are the trials we face, if we are interested in wholeness. The bottom line is that climate change and human change are intimately linked, although we have yet to fully appraise the improvements that could create a new symbiotic relationship, between people and planet. Currently the squandering of natural resources on planet Earth mirrors the squandering of our human potential. Waking up to the state of the planet is synonymous with a collective wake-up call for humanity.

The Intergovernmental Panel for Climate Change (IPCC) has repeatedly warned that humanity is in a perilous position and we will need to take serious action to avoid the global crisis becoming worse.[1] To illustrate the scale of the problem, in 2016 Nicholas Stern revised his 2006 report on climate change, stating that he had underestimated the risks. However, he said that he had cause for hope and optimism because the Paris climate agreements (held in December 2015, involving 196 countries) only took 11 months to ratify. This good news is tempered by the fact that we now only have a 20-year window to start making adequate adaptations.[2] The decision by Donald Trump to abandon the Paris Agreement has not affected the resolve of the remaining countries to do the right thing. But we should be under no illusions that the global crisis before us is monumental in terms of its potential impact, with a warming climate predicted to cause further damage to habitats and ecosystems worldwide. In July 2016 temperatures rose to 54°C in Kuwait, and in Siberia thawing ice led to anthrax escaping from the ground, where it had formerly been trapped in subterranean permafrost.[3] In turn we can expect an increase in climate refugees and species extinction, which is expected to accelerate in 2020.[4] These climate change impacts will undoubtedly be compounded by predictions of global population increases from around 9 billion by 2050 to a staggering 12 billion people by 2100. There are clearly powerful tensions between the growing numbers of people on the planet and the increasing demands for natural resources we put upon nature, year on year. We also have the continuing threat of economic instability.

It is evident that our planet cannot sustain the rate and pace of consumption championed by Western industrialised nations, now being imitated by new economic powerhouses like China and India. 'Hyper-consumerism' is firmly embedded in the modern world, with an average of 50,000 products on sale in a typical US supermarket.[5] On this evidence, the scale of production (supply) and consumption (demand) appears to show no signs of abating in a global culture of industrial, agricultural and fiscal growth. Interestingly, it is gradually dawning on the Western world that material consumption does not make us any happier.[6] A study into the lives of 'modest consumers' by Teresa Belton[7] explored people's experiences of satisfaction in life, and found that well-being was not driven by material acquisition. Belton calls for a new direction in human development, beyond the materialistic impulses that are so rife in the world today. Her excellent book, *Happier People, Healthier Planet* explores human flourishing and how our ways of living can include a better relationship with the natural world. There is no doubting we are a successful species, which is reflected in our ability to adapt and continually thrive.[8] Humanity is more than capable of adapting to the global crisis, but whilst the supermarket shelves are brimming with goods and we can buy cheap flights to anywhere in the world, we are seduced by the idea that there is no problem and climate change has been overstated. However, any serious reader of the state of the world today will know the global crisis is presenting us with a reality check. We have reached the limits of sustainability in terms of our current ways of living. We will be challenged to craft adaptive responses to the threats before us. It will require all of us to use our imagination, intelligence, ingenuity and initiative like never before.

There are no simple answers to the global crisis; however, we can all play our part in adapting our behaviours. For example, Caroline Lucas[9] has suggested that tackling the problem of global warming is as much about psychology as it is about climate science. In other words, we could galvanise our collective motivation for change through reflection and action. We can begin such a process of behaviour change today by simply reflecting on our personal *appetites*, including those that drive our ambitions and desires. We only have to consider how certain foods, such as meat, take a disproportionate amount of land to produce (compared to vegetables), yet feeds relatively few people and contributes excessively to greenhouse gases.[10] The ethics of food production and consumption is one area where we can all make immediate changes in our lifestyle behaviours. Every year around a third of global food production is wasted or lost, while at the same time experts are calling for a 70% global increase in food production by 2050 to meet the demands of a growing world population.[10] Our consumer-based appetites also extend to the latest technologies, cars and household luxuries etc. The question is how can we begin to shift from consumer-based ways of living to behaviours that benefit the greater good?

One appetite that we could begin to cultivate concerns our *wholeness*, that is, adopting lifestyles and life choices that reconnect us to one another, other species and the planet. Our dissociation from nature is the consequence of our collective neglect of a deeper and more holistic relationship to life.[11] Indeed, whilst the industrialised world has invested in technological advances, it could be argued that neglecting our collective human potential (psycho-spiritual growth) has diminished our abilities to craft (*techne*) new ways of living that are more in harmony with the ecosystems to which we belong. Our Western industrialised approach has exploited the natural world, with disregard to the bigger picture, often with catastrophic consequences. In turning against nature (our life-support system), we have lost a vital connection to the life of the soul, the *anima mundi*, which is the soul of the world.[12] In short, we have failed to notice that beneath the burgeoning global crisis is a spiritual crisis. It is here that we somehow need to formulate a new myth and relationship to life, which is both sacred and whole.[13] It is time for a *New Renaissance* to emerge.[14]

In terms of collective behaviour change, there is a growing body of literature that underlines humanity's wholeness and how we live in an interconnected cosmos, as discussed by Ervin Laszlo.[15,16] Laszlo makes a persuasive argument for radical transformation, underpinned by a shift in consciousness. He proposes that our actions in the world are more connected than we may care to admit; indeed, what each of us does in the world will have ethical consequences for ourselves, others (including other species) and nature. This interconnectedness means we are all occupationally entangled, in that our actions and behaviours ripple subtly through the lives of others, both personally and globally. Understanding that we live in an interconnected world can help counter the rampant materialism and individualism that is increasingly unsustainable.

Doing deep and doing different

Humanity has never been challenged to adapt and change on such a scale before. Either we pull together collectively to work towards an improved future for all or we fall apart and fragment into groups of self-interest. If we are interested in pulling together we will need to find new ways of reflecting, acting and interacting. The global crisis is an unprecedented opportunity to develop a renewed relationship to life in all that we do. Doing and innovation have been important factors in our evolutionary journey, especially in the way they have mediated collective behaviour change. Just look at how successfully our ancestors adapted, survived, and thrived as they met environmental challenges (including a previous Ice Age). Human innovation and evolutionary actions have accompanied our species' developmental milestones, from early toolmakers to the technological advances that are continually shaping what we do today. However, *doing* in the modern world has been much maligned and misunderstood. We can see this in statements that profess: *we are not human doings – we are human beings.* Indeed, we are human beings, but without a complementary understanding of the depth and dynamism of doing, the engagement and expression of our full human potential is severely compromised.[17]

Our species' evolutionary trajectory continues to reveal the importance of being purposefully occupied, where the form and function of our actions have an archetypal root. For example, if we observe a clay pot from the ancient world, it is very similar to what we make and use today. In this way, doing is ancient and connects us to a shared human heritage, since these archetypal representations are graspable in terms of how they manifest in our daily experiences and work.[18] Moreover, cross-cultural patterns of doing reveal a shared human understanding of the importance of activity, for example cooking, art, craftwork or gardening etc. It is here that Carl Jung's concept of the archetypes could help us recalibrate a meaningful connection between the depths of our awareness and our actions. Jung also alludes to the important interface between occupations and archetypes, describing them as systems that are *ready for action.*[19] This point illustrates why *doing with depth* adds an important dynamic when working with our adaptive potential and collective transformation. The global crisis is challenging us to live deeply and live in wholeness.

Jung noted that symbolic representations of the archetypes arise from the unconscious, which brings us into contact with the sacred by virtue of the numinous power that accompanies them. Therefore, when we connect with the archetype of doing, through engaging in wholesome activities like gardening etc., not only can we encounter the numinous (mystery), but also such experiences have the potential to make whatever we do sacramental.[17] Doing has the capacity to bring about deep encounters in our everyday lives. Indeed, Jung acknowledged that because we know so little about the *demands* of the unconscious, he would often leave it to his hands to express what he could not articulate in words.[18] It is through our actions (doing) that we can deepen our reflections and awareness (being). In this way, archetypal actions (doing with depth) align with an ancient human lineage to create meaning, catalysing a creative spark in our ongoing evolutionary journey. A deeper mystical connection to doing could stimulate our interconnectedness to life as a whole.

Our modern ways of living and working are eroding our quality of life, which is not conducive for engaging the depth of living mentioned above. For example, research is beginning to identify how increases in workload demands and pressures on staff, driven by performance targets and financial efficiencies, impact on workers' lives.[20] The modern world is in the grip of a fiscal obsession that is anti-life and anti-wholeness. Jungian analyst Erich Neumann[21] noticed this trend developing in the mid-20th century and his diagnosis was that our consciousness is bankrupt. The evolution of consciousness is invested in wholeness, as opposed to the money-driven values in the modern world. Compare this with an alternative alignment between archetype and action in the characteristics of a Bodhisattva. Stemming from the Buddhist practice of Bodhicitta, or *awakened heart-mind*, the Bodhisattva takes vows to live compassionately, cooperatively, and creatively. Such altruistic behaviours can be witnessed in the actions of people from all walks of life, and a culture of adaptation could adopt such a transformational mindset. Bodhicitta is an expression of our innate 'basic goodness'.[22]

Essentially, the Bodhisattva is an *archetypal expression of compassionate awareness and action*, which is directed in the service of caring for all species, nature and the world.[23] Its opposite is the Buddhist mythic entity called the *hungry ghost*, which has a small mouth and a vast stomach, and no matter how much food this entity consumes, it is never satisfied.[24] *The hungry ghost* is an apt metaphor for the empty consumerism and insatiable appetites of our modern self-centred consciousness. Indeed, according to Arny Mindell,[25] Carl Jung would have viewed the *hungry ghost* as 'complex', which means that autonomous feelings (at an unconscious level) are activated and acted out behaviourally. We can see our collective complexes at work in our culture of consumption, where we have created vacuous industries that feed our narcissistic tendencies, resulting in *The Triumph of Emptiness*.[26] Just look at the advertising industry if you need a reminder of how superficial and seductive modern materialism has become. We *are* the *hungry ghosts*. However, imagine what sort of society we would create if we invested in the flourishing of our human potential? Professor of Jungian analysis Veronica Goodchild[27] points out that many of us are spiritually malnourished and hungry for deeper ways of knowing, aligned to a living mystery. She cites the importance of the imaginal realm, which we encounter through our visions, dreams, synchronicities and angelic connections etc. The imaginal realm nourishes us at a soul level, bringing us alive and inspiring us to live in wholeness.

Proposition two: Opening to the imaginal

Revisioning life

Our ancestors have demonstrated that evolution is never prescribed. Indeed, our evolutionary heritage is about facing challenges, cooperating, innovating and adapting.[17] In this time of global decay, we need to be firm in our collective resolve to engage and express our evolutionary potential for wholeness and sustainability for future generations, not just concern ourselves with today's fiscal bottom line. It is through a renewed alignment with our transformative potential that we can encourage a healing relationship to all facets of our daily lives, including self, other and the planet. If we can transform our worldviews and behaviours for the greater good and support the idea that *we are all in this together*, we may be able to harness the best of our human heritage, that is, to transform our lives through cooperation. Jungian analyst Marie Louise Von Franz[18] makes an important point, that before the emergence of ego-consciousness, our ancestors functioned in groups and were connected to archetypal behaviour patterns, such as collective rituals etc. Our ancestors evolved through cooperation and it is well within our grasp to realise that whatever we do in an interconnected world ripples throughout it. This realisation could possibly inspire greater cooperation and balance. It is in our daily lives and actions that each one of us can bring about the birth of a new era of shared responsibility and sustainability. Elsewhere I have suggested that human beings are more than capable of co-creating an improved future through our collective efforts, and such a proposition is aligned with our evolutionary potential: *we do, therefore we evolve*.[17] This shift in consciousness requires us to work together, to understand one another, and reach beyond our differences.

Arny Mindell and his colleagues have pioneered methods for collective transformation. Mindell, originally a physicist and Jungian analyst, developed theoretical concepts that facilitate greater collective awareness of diversity between people and cultures. His approach takes a *world work* perspective,[28] where people interact in large groups, guided by principles of deep democracy.[29] This approach means that within any group the dominant cultural viewpoints are acknowledged, but space is created for diverse perspectives, such as the voice of minority groups, the disenfranchised and dispossessed. In such a sensitive system even nature has a voice,[30,31] which can be expressed through participants, or indeed, if nature itself intervenes through the wind, thunder or the appearance of an animal. Mindell's work encourages us to understand and respect diversity in life (including other species), where our relationships, dreams and imaginations can be used to gain a greater understanding of the world from multiple perspectives. Mindell's *process work* with people uses a detailed blend of applied science, which follows subtle communication signals (through dreams, bodily responses, relationships and world). However, the method is also an art, which pays great attention to our everyday problems and experiences, while being watchful of the interconnected movements, images, words and feelings allied to our unfolding processes. Wholeness from this perspective values the consciousness linked to everyday consensus reality, but it makes room for information from the non-local field (transpersonal) to which we are all connected.[32] In this way, *process work* is a powerful method that integrates dreaming into our daily lives, which is a threshold to the imaginal realm.

A wonderful example of Mindell's holistic approach to working is captured in his interaction with a man in his eighties, who had been in a semicomatose state for six months. The hospital staff asked Mindell if he could possibly help the man, who was often agitated, groaning and shouting words that were incoherent. Mindell gently took the man's hand and created a pattern of lightly squeezing the hand in sync with the man's breathing, while also attending to any sounds the man was making. In his book *Coma*, Mindell provides a transcript of the process that unfolded, which resulted in the man becoming more able to articulate words coherently. The man was still in an altered state, but he was now able to enter into a dialogue with Mindell, which was focused on an internal vision he was having about a ship. Mindell followed the unfolding process and asked the man about the ship, to which the man replied it was going on vacation, but he was not able to go because he needed to get back to work. Mindell suggested that the man could take a closer look at the ship, and the man spoke excitedly about seeing angels at the helm. Mindell asked the man if he wanted to join the ship and take a holiday, and he received positive feedback, especially about not wanting to go back to work. The old man drifted to sleep in a peaceful state. Mindell left the man for a while, and when he returned 30 minutes later, the old man had passed away.[33]

This is such a touching story about the science and art of working with everyday reality and the imaginal realm, underpinned by a deeply compassionate attitude to life and wholeness. It shows how we can approach holistic living in all that we do. It reflects a deeper form of archetypal action, directed in the service of collective awakening, forging new appetites for wholeness and encouraging one another to serve the greater good (Bodhisattva archetype). To survive and thrive in the coming decades we will need to develop a greater sense of *altruism* based on cultivating our transformative potential and acting in accord with shared values, such as cooperation and kindness. Indeed, the *sanity of compassion* is one of the cornerstones for our personal and collective well-being[34] and Joan Halifax[35] says "visionary compassion" enables us to live closer to our hearts, which can embolden us to tackle the global crisis. Eco-compassion means a radical re-working for how we live in the world. It means that our institutions play a vital role in the cultivation of how we can care for one another and ourselves including other species and nature. To bring forth a new planetary culture, one that brings us into closer relationship with the Earth, we will have to develop new ways of living.[36] For example, the imaginal realm brings us into relationship with the symbolic world of dreaming, enabling us to connect with visionary, shamanic and synchronistic energies,[37] where we connect with the living breath of spirit and sacred inspiration. It is the opposite of our mechanistic lives in the modern world. The Western idea that the natural world can be treated like a machine is outdated. Transformative living is a call to open our hearts and minds to the deep intelligence that flourishes in the natural world.

Paul Kingsnorth[38] tells us about the intelligent networks that operate in nature via studies of plant interactions, where two-way communication exchanges occur. For example, a plant emits electrical impulses and pheromones that signal it is under attack by predatory insects. These distress signals act as an alert to other insects, which are then mobilised to drive away the invading insects and in doing so they protect the plants. It is a complex natural system of information exchange, also found in fungi, whose roots connect with countless other plants in a sort of interspecies communication network. Kingsnorth offers a view of the natural world as a living sentient entity. This is in contrast to humanity's relationship to nature over the past 300 years, which has been nothing short of eco-apartheid. Professor Susan Greenfield[39] quotes Prince Charles' 2000 Reith lecture, where he spoke about the consequences of treating life as if it were some grand laboratory, and our risk of breaking a sacred connection to life.

We have been mesmerised by our species' technological development, and we have overlooked how technology abounds in the natural world, for example in the way birds create nests and beavers build dams. A recent study has shown how beavers are capable of engineering and restoring habitats. Two breeding beavers were introduced into a 30-acre site in Scotland, which had been drained for pasture use and had resulted in the degradation of the land. Research showed how the beavers had transformed the area into a thriving wetland over a ten-year period. They built dams stretching for 200 metres, as well as creating 500 metres of canals and a series of ponds. The study contributes to existing evidence, showing the technologies employed by beavers slow downstream water flows, which reduces the risk of flooding.[40] We have lost sight of the fact that technology is not a uniquely human construct, but rather it is a creative force in the natural world. In fact, early Greek philosophers saw technology as metaphysical, meaning that technological progress was always in alignment with a cosmological order.[41] This revelation highlights why our technological engagement in the world needs to be accompanied by technologies of transformation, such as meditation, dream work and shamanism etc. The absence of technologies of transformation in our institutions underlines why our technological advancement is creating increasing levels of dissociation from nature and wholeness, as evidenced by the Anthropocene and the escalating levels of global crisis in the world. This important point underlines the need to rekindle a sacred bond with nature. This will be a real test of our imaginations and intentions to live more holistically.

Evolution to wholeness

The global crisis demands that we make major adaptations in our ways of living. The call for transformation today may sound like the hippie ideal espoused four decades ago, when counter cultural radicals were urging us to be more peaceful, loving and get back to the land. In the heady days of 1968, cultural historian Theodore Roszak[42] studied these movements that were challenging the status quo. He noticed how people were trying to break free from the imposition of a technocratic society, one that restricted their liberties and bound them to ways of living that were unfulfilling. The hippies saw through the false promises and illusory dreams peddled by a political and economic system that was literally all-consuming. William Irwin Thompson[43] provides a pithy critique of post-industrial Western economics, suggesting that capitalism is based on a subtle form of terror, encouraging people to amass as many financial assets as possible. The hippies wanted to live in freedom, not fear.

The very real tensions between post-industrial economics and the attempt to manifest a new planetary culture were not resolved by hippie radicalism. The revolutionary zeal that erupted in the late 1960s pointed to new horizons where consciousness could be transformed, but the sincere quest for freedom and wholeness that broke through the mainstream consensus at that time has now been subsumed into a culture of leisure and consumerism,[44] for example in the New Age economy of well-being. Professor Robert Winston[45] has noted that in its current form the New Age very much embodies a capitalist worldview, but it would be wrong to write it off just because it has to survive in the dominant economy. I believe that New Age spirituality still has importance, because it reflects an ongoing commitment to the ideal of holism, and at its core, promotes the shift in attitudes, behaviours, and consciousness that are much needed in our social and institutional infrastructures today. It is in the New Age literature that we still find a rallying call for a connection to the imaginal, through spirituality, synchronicities and dreaming, which are often linked to ecology and wholeness. But an even greater shift in consciousness is needed at a collective level to bring forth our transformational potential. Indeed, William Irwin Thompson[36] is correct in my opinion when he describes the current conception of the New Age as the last gasp of all 'Old Ages'. The New Age may be a clumsy precursor for a more radical eco-spirituality waiting to emerge in collective consciousness.[46]

The hippie revolution in the 1960s envisioned a New Age, which sought to revive a holistic vision for humanity after the devastation of two world wars, the Korean and Vietnam conflicts, and the threat of nuclear annihilation during the Cold War. The hippies and New Agers did not have all the answers, but they were asking decent questions about the state of modern consciousness. The hippies were interested in love, mystical awareness and peace,[47] which was subsumed into a broad New Age philosophy of healing, cultivating human potential and consciousness-raising activities, and valuing wholeness in relation to people, other species and nature.[48] Irrespective of the failings of the hippies and the New Age, their intentions were (in the main) good, and they uncovered important aspects of human potential that still remain on the periphery of mainstream culture. Interestingly, the roots of modern consciousness expansion were revived in 1943 when the powerful effects of LSD (hallucinogenic) became known after Swiss chemist Albert Hoffman accidentally ingested some. Consciousness expansion has continued ever since, revealing that alternative worldviews are possible.[49] We could say that the freethinking hippie ideal in the late 1960s was a sane and spirited response to the cumulative and destructive forces that were being unleashed throughout the 20th century. Yet, these innovative pioneers have now become identified as scapegoats in what can only be described as an attack on liberalism.

In an audacious attempt to colonise the collective imagination, it has been reported that US President Donald Trump's former special advisor, Steve Bannon, has made a film (*Generation Zero*) where he blames the hippies and the 1960s counterculture for causing the 2008 financial collapse.[50] This unconventional reading of history may raise a smile, but it hides a worrying agenda. Bannon, a former executive at Goldman Sachs, would probably prefer to scapegoat the hippies, rather than examine the political manoeuvring in the 1980s by the Republican and Conservative governments of Ronald Reagan and Margaret Thatcher. They created a new economic culture that championed financial deregulation,[51] which unleashed a frenzy of activity in global financial markets. Bannon's attack on the hippies can only be interpreted as a right wing smokescreen that is attempting to demonise liberal thinking. It reminds me of the shady propaganda that was used with devastating effect at various low points throughout the 20th century. One can only assume that scapegoating the hippies for the 2008 financial collapse is an attempt to obscure the reality of neoliberal-political deregulation (beloved of Reagan and Thatcher). Yet, since the 1980s the reality of neoliberalism has been responsible for 'boom and bust' economics, coupled to political drivers for increased privatisation and austerity, which has resulted in greater inequality.[52] It appears as though a neoliberal agenda is bankrolling our modern one-dimensional technocratic world, and we are all the poorer for it, ecologically, politically, psychologically, socially and spiritually.

However, I firmly believe that there is always wisdom in the symptom, and it could well be that the legacy of the hippies is a fulcrum for how humanity moves forward in freedom, not chains.

Proposition three: Engaging with the 'non-ordinary'

A path of renewal

The positive side of the hippie revolution over the past 40 years includes the mainstream acceptance of veganism, vegetarianism, yoga and mindfulness as well as the evolution of conscious living, wholeness, and interconnectivity. All of these build a solid platform for inculcating deeper transformation in collective consciousness. Hippie innovation has also made a valuable contribution to new science through the Fundamental Fysiks Group formed in the mid 1970s.[53] This small band of hippie physicists enthusiastically explored John Bell's theory, which postulates that when two quantum particles come into contact they somehow remain connected, even when separated at great distance. The spinning paired particles respond instantaneously to each other. This means that the particles are responding faster than the speed of light. Bell's theory reveals the existence of a subtle field, where sub-atomic particles are entangled and act non-locally. The Fundamental Fysiks Group wondered whether quantum non-locality and entanglement could help to explain phenomena such as telepathy and extrasensory perception. They set out to explore possible connections between Eastern philosophy and Western science, with notable publications in the 1970s such as Fritjof Capra's *Tao of Physics*[54] and Gary Zukov's, *Dancing Wu Li Masters*.[55]

Eminent mainstream physicists denounced the work of the Fundamental Fysiks Group as mysticism and moonshine, balking at any suggestion that consciousness was connected at a quantum level. Yet, these young hippie physicists noted how the idea of nuclear fission was also derided as moonshine before the Manhattan Project produced a nuclear bomb. However, it may well turn out that the Fundamental Fysiks Group were onto something. Today, we are moving much closer to understanding the interconnected and holistic nature of reality via systems thinking.[56] But we are still far away from opening to the knowledge and wisdom in the imaginal realm. In the early/mid 1970s Theodore Roszak observed how a wholesale adherence to technocratic living in the Western world had played its part in the loss of a sacramental vision, and that a gradual and corrosive separation from nature has made human experience poorer. Roszak was convinced that it had resulted in a fragmentation of humanity's imaginative energies that are, he argued, a vital source for transforming human consciousness.[57] Such experiences may result in encountering non-ordinary realities.

As a cultural historian, Theodore Roszak could see the evolutionary significance of new social movements and trajectories unfolding in contrast (and opposition) to prevailing mainstream ideologies. He viewed positively the flowering of the Human Potential movement, popularised by Abraham Maslow and others, particularly the transformative possibilities of transpersonal psychology, which he saw as a natural reaction to the persistent and pervasive underdevelopment of people's human potential in the industrial world.[58] The development of our collective psycho-spiritual potential cannot be prescribed; it has to be an organic process, which is awoken through a meaningful connection to the sacred. As a species we will undoubtedly draw upon the best of the psycho-spiritual traditions that have served us to date, but we also need to keep an open mind for the types of developments that sprung into life with the advent of the New Age. However, such innovative ideas are not always well received. For example, in his book, *Omens of Millennium*, Harold Bloom[59] writes about mystical ways of knowing (gnosis), which are not bound by dogmatic creeds, but which are connected to a divine spark within. He comments on the modern surge of interest in dreams, near-death experiences, angels and the New Age as adulterated and commercialised representations of their Gnostic origins.

Bloom is right to say that our modern interest in such phenomena should be tempered by what has been written previously on these subjects. However, we also need to remind ourselves that the imaginal realm is dynamic and works in mysterious ways, which can bypass agreed orthodoxies. For example a recently published book on *The Transformative Power of Near-Death Experiences*[60] by Dr Penny Sartori and Kelly Walsh is full of the most incredible stories. People share their experiences of encountering divine and unconditional love, as well as meeting angels and having a life review, which alerted them to the impact of their actions on others during their lifetime. One person encountered unpleasant shadowy figures, and another was given a glimpse of hell. They all experienced the interconnectedness of life, and one person was even able to see the life-energies surrounding plants on their return to an Earthly existence. Many had to face the impact of traumas, or great loss, and one person was sectioned in a psychiatric hospital for sharing their near-death experience with a doctor. Yet, a common bond that unites all the contributors in the book is that they are living transformational lives, based on love, not fear. An example of this is all contributors' royalties are being donated to a children's charity, whose motto is: Love, Care and Share. This is just one example of a resurgent and revitalised New Age at the leading edge of transforming collective consciousness, where the contributors are not seeking any commercial gain.

Spiritual awakening can happen in the most unexpected ways, and such occurrences are catalysts for living a transformative life. Harold Bloom[59] helpfully informs us that sacred ways of knowing thrive in relation to the imagination and creativity. Therefore, if spiritual ways of knowing are connected to creativity and imagination, then a genuine process of revelation, as outlined in the NDEs above, is undoubtedly an initiation into sacramental ways of living. For example, on their return to Earthly life, all the contributors in Penny Sartori and Kelly Walsh's book understood the pointlessness of living in fear, and now devote their life energies into paths of love and service. Jung understood that when the psyche is touched by the numinous, we are left in no doubt about the sanctity of life, which is always seeking to be born anew in consciousness. In this way, creativity and the imagination are a pivotal part of our alignment to wholeness. Is this not the essence of the creative imagination, especially when it has been opened through a connection with the imaginal realm?

Yet Bloom appears to take a dim view of Jung, whose psychology he refers to as a cult, emphasising that Jung viewed the unconscious as divine. In defence of Jung, it is only fair to point out that he discovered a meaningful connection between archetypal images and symbols arising from the unconscious and how these can activate the numinous (the Holy). For example, the archetype of the Self is where we connect with a transpersonal reality; yet this does not deify the unconscious; it simply reveals how numinous encounters can be experienced in the psyche, which brings a divine spark to our sacred ways of knowing (gnosis). Jung considered encounters with the numinous as an important contribution to our unfolding human potential and individuation (wholeness). Jung pioneered his innovative approach to healing through deep immersion in the world of the psyche (experiencing and encountering dreams, etc.), which was matched by an equally impressive intellect and scholastic temperament. Jung broke the mould for how a contemporary spiritual quest could be undertaken, which has probably assisted in the soul retrieval of countless people worldwide. Jung (in my view) cannot be understood by way of erudite explanation, but through immersion, encounter and experience. Jung should be credited for revitalising a relationship to the imaginal realm and the wisdom that resides in the collective unconscious and in our dreams.

Bloom goes on to tell us that in most religious traditions, dreams are considered as having a sacred function, yet he does not acknowledge Jung's unique psycho-spiritual contribution, which was realised through arduous inner work. Jung saw how dreams and archetypes are portals to the divine spark of the numinous. In this way, Jung's work is alerting us to the possibility of a genuine stirring and awakening in the human soul and a reconnection to sacred ways of knowing. Jung incorporated subjectivity into his method, which does not sit well in the detached world of modern academic and scientific experimentation, explanation, or erudite elucidation. Yet, if knowing (gnosis) is connected to creativity and the imagination as Bloom says it is, then it has to involve inner work. Such exploration takes courage, resolve, creativity and imagination to meet the unconscious forces at work in the psyche, which can inspire us to make radical changes in the outer world. In this respect, I consider Jung's work to be a way of guiding a renewed connection to sacred ways of knowing and wholeness. If humanity's connection to the imaginal realm can be found in traditions such as Gnosticism, Kabbalah and Alchemy, then Jung's work has to be acknowledged as a way of helping people find a way back to the imaginal. Incidentally, it is no coincidence that Jung's work is gaining more recognition today – at a time when humanity needs it most. Collectively we are being confronted with the need to do deep inner and outer work, which activates and actualises our transformative potential.

Bloom's assessment of the Millennium is important for understanding gnosticism in the context of modern people's interest in dream work, near-death experience and angels etc., but his caricature of the New Age is too critical (in my opinion). It is a mindset similar to that found in scientism, which has become a self-appointed debunker of 'cultural superstitions'. These attitudes expose the prejudice that exists behind the facade of such mainstream worldviews. We have yet to acknowledge (collectively) that when we enter the world of the psyche and reconnect with our imaginative and visionary energies, we can stimulate a path of transformative action. Theodore Roszak[57] envisioned that if we were to heal ourselves and live sustainably on the planet, we would need to make an evolutionary transition towards self-renewal to rediscover a greater purpose and meaning in life. Roszak's visionary acumen saw the divided state of modern humans and how our destiny and the plight of the planet are inextricably linked. Indeed, for Roszak the planet, like people, also has rights.[61] His research resulted in a major contribution to eco-psychology and he spoke about the consequences of a destructive division that has been forged by humanity in its objective treatment of the natural world.[62] Roszak was not anti-scientific, but he recognised the limitations and imbalances it has caused, which has also been noted by biologist Rupert Sheldrake.[63]

Visionary, Barbara Marx Hubbard,[64] has advocated for a transitionary shift in human capacities and consciousness, which brings forth a global experience of rebirth. It is here that Veronica Goodchild[27] points to Jung's method of individuation as an initiation into deeper ways of knowing (gnosis), inclusive of symbolic death and rebirth, which has parallels with shamanistic and alchemical traditions. She also reminds us that the mystical is as important as the scientific, and that human beings are as much visionary as we are rational. One of the key tasks in the Transformocene is to find meeting points between the mystical and the scientific. For example, Anthony William[65] discovered his healing vocation at the tender age of four years whilst he was sitting at the dinner table. He heard a voice, which called itself, Spirit of the Most High, who told the young boy to inform his family that his grandmother had lung cancer. He did not know what the words meant, but medical tests confirmed the accuracy of his grandmother's diagnosis. It is important that we remain open to non-ordinary experiences, because spiritual visitations can enrich human life. In another example, we learn that each night a muse dictated the epic poem, *Paradise Lost*, to John Milton.[66] However, the worldview of scientism does not like such stories, because they are believed to be 'superstitious'. Yet it is through such spirited holism that humanity is enriched, which is also a vital source of inspiration that will activate the Transformocene.

Exercise: Hungry ghost

- Reflect on the times when you have been greedy or covetous in life.

- Describe what happens to you when you become really greedy or covetous (e.g. being manipulative, deceitful, or secretive, etc.).

- Now, get to know this *hungry ghost* as a figure:
    - What does this figure look like?
    - What sort of things does this figure say?
    - What are the dominant emotions in this figure's experience?
    - How does this figure move?
    - How does this figure relate to others?
    - What is the worldview of this figure?

- Become this figure, play with it, and experience how it is so focused on getting what it wants.

- Go to the essence of the *hungry ghost* figure – find out what it is really hungry for.

- Create a poem or prayer that helps you to learn from the experience of the *hungry ghost*.

- What has this encounter with the *hungry ghost* taught you about your psycho-spiritual development?

PART ONE: THE IMAGINAL LINEAGE

Sun and Ice[1]

Ice breaking, did you know of the life below?

As winter sets upon midsummer
will its heart be any less the sun?

It is the will of our mystery
that we become everything,
not a tear missed
pain denied
joy lost.

Indeed the thin ice beyond reason.

Here the rhymes of childhood cease
voyages through unbelievable wisdom.

It is not for us to deny this
but to plunge onward and beyond
to views from the other side
of now!

If 'fire' is a symbol that represents the burning issue of climate change,
then the mythical phoenix is the perfect metaphor for the Transformocene Age.
It portrays a deep sense of renewal, a spirit that is reborn, rising from the ashes.

INTRODUCTION TO PART ONE

The Imaginal Lineage

Metaphors for collective transformation

The threat of the Anthropocene, reflects how our species' maladaptive behaviours are marking us out as a force for degradation of the planet. The question is, what will it take for us to adapt our ways of living, so that they are not only co-creative and sustainable, but also honour the sacrament of life as a whole? This question will intensify once humanity wakes up to the scale of the ecological problems we have created on Earth. We still have an opportunity to shift our ways of living to avoid worsening ecological conditions; however, if we fail to adapt, then the resulting calamity will make life increasingly pressurised and difficult. Professors of Environmental Science Tim O'Riordan and Tim Lenton[2] have published a book on *tipping points*, revealing the 'critical thresholds' for change that are likely to manifest regionally and globally. Tipping points present us with the unpredictable reality of complex systems, which can fluctuate for better or worse. Their book underlines the precarious state of the world at this time, emphasising how the cultivation of a sustainable future is dependent on understanding the interdependent variables that are interacting in life as a whole.

We are now embarking on a collective human trajectory that requires a *meta-vision* to help us understand the unpredictableness and interconnectedness of living on the planet at this time of burgeoning crisis. Tim O'Riordan, Tim Lenton and Ian Christie[3] point out that we are in a transitional phase of global change, which could be beneficial in a transformative way, but this outcome depends on how we respond collectively to the challenges before us. The authors remind us that the planetary crisis is not only about risk management, which is important, but also about harnessing new opportunities to direct our collective potential in restorative ways. In this way, they view tipping points as a useful metaphor for stimulating our awareness and imagination, as well as transcending our usual patterns of reasoning. We learn that the word metaphor comes from the Greek *meta-pherin*, meaning a shift or movement, and Giles Foden[4] notes its value for helping us explore new realities, opportunities and ideas. For example, information can be communicated linguistically and symbolically to enhance the transfer of ideas. This resonates with the ideas expressed by James Hillman[5] who believes that metaphor is the most expedient way to facilitate interactions between everyday consciousness and the unconscious. He points out that the language of the psyche is more closely connected to images and symbols.

Engaging metaphor as part of a shift in our collective consciousness requires ideas that convey a sense of wholeness, which 'speaks' to our human potential for adaptation,[6] enabling us to explore different ways of living. It is here that our connection to the imaginal realm is recognised as a powerful variable for initiating a deeper connection to life and living. The use of metaphor is particularly helpful when discussing the transformative potential of the imaginal realm, which is an experiential encounter that is not served well by factual or descriptive analysis. The use of metaphor to convey the power of the imaginal realm is well illustrated in the mytho-poetic worlds of visionaries, such as Coleridge, Blake and Keats,[7] who portray the 'creative edge' that exists between the human imagination and the imaginal realm. The metaphor of *the edge* is a good way of representing the interface between our everyday conventional ways of knowing (e.g. science) and the imaginal realm. There is no doubt that humanity is facing a 'collective growing edge', where we are being challenged to consider our outmoded attitudes and behaviours. In this way, scientific data about ecological tipping points can warn us about the state of the planet.[8] However, tipping points are also relevant to human attitudes, awareness and actions, especially when the human imagination is stirred. Therefore, scientific knowledge could be complemented by alternative ways of knowing, such as revelations from the subtle world of the *mundus imaginalis* or imaginal realm.[9] The inclusion of the imaginal realm in our collective odyssey needs to be understood as an 'outlier' perspective, and as Matthew Taylor[10] says, alternative worldviews are often overlooked in favour of established ways of thinking, especially when conceptualising and engaging change. However, outlier perspectives bring into sharp focus the '*edges*' between consensus reality and non-consensus reality.[11]

Re-imagining and deepening consensus reality

Part one of this book teases out the relationship between consensus and non-consensus worldviews. For example, if we consider mythic representations of transformation, the serpent that sheds its skin is an ancient and powerful symbol of change. Yet, a typical attitude that accompanies today's scientific-dominated consensus opinion might be: "What has a snake got to do with solving the problems of the Anthropocene?" It is a good question. Let us remind ourselves that the hyper-rational worldview so evident in the modern world is only one way of understanding life. Such a mindset does not accommodate the deeply symbolic and mythic connections for living that were commonplace among our ancestors. For example, we find in Ohio a 2,000-year-old serpent mound that stretches for half a kilometre across the land in a giant undulating sculptural wave, which protrudes from an embankment. The incredible effort that went into the construction of this serpentine symbol in the Earth conveys a clear message to the people from that cultural lineage: that this is a place of power, and it was designed to evoke the divine spirit and a sense of awe.[12] This vast Earth serpent also holds an egg in its mouth. The serpent and egg are ancient archetypal symbols of change and transformation. Awe-inspiring symbols bring us into relationship with the imaginal realm and have a vital role to play in our adaptive and transformative response to the degradation of the Earth, as represented by the Anthropocene. We need a renewed experience of 'awe' to galvanise our deepest intentions and efforts to co-create an improved and sustainable future.

Professors Tim O'Riordan and Tim Lenton[13] observe that humanity has yet to grasp the nettle in terms of waking up to the scientific evidence that could inspire adaptive action. They point out that the collective default position in our response to global events (such as climate change) is usually based on a momentary feeling of 'shock' or 'awe', not the steady and sustained cultivation of our adaptive potential and resilience. However, if we acknowledge that humanity still has the capacity to respond to awe-inspiring events, like the Ohio serpent was designed to evoke, then it re-situates the imaginal realm as an important variable in awakening our adaptive potential. If we can acknowledge the adaptive function of the symbolic world (as Jung did), then we are already primed to draw on our species' imaginal lineage and transformative heritage. This is an important connection, now that we stand at the threshold of the Anthropocene Age. Helpfully, another mythical symbol that comes to mind as I type these words is the phoenix, a bird that is burnt to a cinder and then rises from the ashes reborn. Again, it is a fitting image from an ancient heritage, which metaphorically illustrates how we may shift from the maladaptive behaviours that create the Anthropocene, and rise anew from the ashes into the Transformocene Age.

It was Joseph Campbell[14] who pointed out that myths are metaphors, and it is through our inner and outer experiences that we encounter a deep mystery in life. We are facing an epoch defining moment, and the mythic path we take at this time will have profound consequences for future generations (and us). Our mythic response to the current multi-levelled global crisis brings an opportunity to create blended ways of knowing, inclusive of science and spirituality. Such possibilities re-connect us to the fertile grounds of the imaginal realm, which can inspire a process of collective renewal. Mythic symbols and metaphors enable us to live more deeply, because they connect us to a greater sense of mystery and wonder in life, which brings us closer to the eternal.[15] Recent research into the impact of awe-inspiring experiences – from visiting giant trees in California, to whitewater rafting – identified that after the event, participants experienced greater levels of compassion and generosity, as well as increased ethical decision making, compared to the control group. Even people who experienced brief episodes of awe reported feeling more attuned to a shared sense of humanity.[16] If we are in any doubt that something is missing in our collective psyche, it becomes more evident when we learn that in the UK antidepressant use doubled in ten years from 2006, culminating in 64.7 million pills being dispensed in 2016.[17] The World Health Organisation champions the realisation of our human potential as one indicator for well-being. But it is curious that in the modern world we have neglected our connection to the imaginal realm, which plays an important part in helping us fulfil our psycho-spiritual potential.

What is truth and how shall we know it? The reductionist's razor dissects the part, but how does the holist proceed? Where are the scales vast enough to measure the immeasurable?

CHAPTER ONE

Scientism and Wholeness

Overview

In this chapter I explore the impact of a limiting worldview called 'scientism', which has resulted in the evolution of hyper-rational, objective and reductionist approaches to understanding life. This overinvestment in the dogma of scientism has resulted in a fractured relationship between humanity and the natural world. In this chapter I challenge the dogmatic assertions of scientism, which pass judgement on people's 'non-ordinary' experiences, believing them to be mere superstition. However, I point out that many leading-edge scientists have had non-ordinary experiences, contributing to breakthroughs in their thinking, which points to a creative and productive alliance between rational and irrational processes. At this time of global crisis, humanity needs all the creative resources at its disposal to support a process of collective adaptation, which could be informed by the wisdom found in myths and mysticism. Spiritual traditions reveal how a deeper connection to the imaginal realm can inspire alternative ways of knowing that are holistic. I discuss how the worldview of scientism is an impediment to holism and the activation of the Transformocene Age.

The soul of science

The pace of life today is becoming faster decade on decade, with information ceaselessly flowing into our communication devices from multiple sources, leaving us transfixed, or numb and overwhelmed. Technology has the potential to mobilise scientific and engineering knowledge to solve the ever-growing list of problems we are facing today, such as overpopulation, the impacts of climate change, securing energy, and managing scarcity of resources, such as fresh water and food production. Yet, for all the virtues of our technological prowess, we have failed to harness our imaginative and visionary resources to live soul-centred lives that serve the greater good. Social media technologies, for example, could assist in mass communication, inspiring us to engage our human potential and mobilise change and soulful transformation. We have the technology to encourage and mobilise a global vision of wholeness. William

Irwin Thompson[1] has spoken about the emergence of a revitalised sense of creativity, which integrates spiritual contemplation, art and science, linked to our imaginary and intuitive capacities. It will be up to each of us to make the commitment to tend to our souls, to harvest the fruits of our imaginative depths and nourish our creativities as we attend to the challenges before us. In short, we not only need to be the change, we have to also do it.

However, before we embark upon our collective transformative quest we need to be clear about what sorts of knowledge will engage our imaginative and visionary energies. There is no doubt that science has been good for humanity. We only need to consider the gains in medical science and how such knowledge has contributed to life expectancy to appreciate the good that it can do.[2] But science also speculates about subjects it is unable to answer, for example, it asserts that human beings do not have a soul, and that our existence is devoid of meaning, simply because we are the products of blind evolutionary processes, where life unfolds without any specific purpose or goal.[3] These are robust assertions, but there are limits to what science can prove or disprove. I have every respect for good science, but just because its methods cannot prove the existence of the soul, it has no real authority to denounce it. Essentially, science deals with *explanations*, whereas phenomena like the soul are based on *experience*, which connects us to the imaginal realm, such as found in indigenous knowledge. Cultivating a holistic relationship to the imaginal realm (via our imaginative and visionary energies) could complement scientific knowledge. Yet the one-dimensional and hyper-rational consciousness that is dominating the world at this time is created through division and separation.[4] We need an understanding of the forces of reductionism before we can evolve a more holistic perspective for living. However, science is also beset with ideological tensions.

Professor of biological sciences, Austin Hughes,[5] is troubled by a growing attitude within modern science, which assumes that its methods are the most expedient means for evolving knowledge. He notes that scientists who hold such views are overreaching their competencies in the mistaken belief that a higher degree in science gives them the right to speak out on any subject. He calls this "The Folly of Scientism", which overstates the power of science, and in some cases renders it no better than the superstitions it considers it is superior to. Science has an important role to play within the modern world, but it must expect to be challenged when it exceeds the boundaries of its methodological competencies. Other scientists have seen the charge of 'scientism' as an attack on science itself (which, in my view, it is not). Professor of psychology Steven Pinker[6] points out that the hallmark of a scientific movement is one that is capable of challenging false assumptions. Indeed, one can only applaud a science that questions the methods and knowledge arising from its own inquiries. For example, in 2015 the prestigious journal *Science* reported the findings of research that replicated 100 psychological studies previously published in top ranked psychological journals. Less than half of these studies were able to replicate the results of the original research. Psychological scientists have since reflected on the meaning of these findings, such as reviewing methodologies used and cohort sample sizes etc., so that they can learn and improve the quality of future research.[7]

Simply put, science is an important method for knowledge acquisition, but not exclusively so. Steven Pinker[6] advocates for a scientism that is based on understanding life from the perspective of physical laws and the 'machinery of life' which, he contends, has shown that cultural and religious beliefs about the origins of life lack any factual basis, including superstitions such as divine providence and karma. It would appear that scientism flourishes when scientists believe the physical laws they have discovered are perceived as the absolute truth. There are advocates of scientism who hope to eradicate superstitions, such as mystical beliefs, and are probably irritated by those scientists who have expressed mystical leanings, such as those discussed by Ken Wilber.[8] A recent example reveals how a scientist describes the process of doing research as both emotional and rational, saying the experience is like touching "a deep level of the psyche", which has a spiritual or mystical quality.[9] It is hard to ignore the experiential nature of scientists' deeper and subjective encounters with a mystical and interconnected reality. For example, neurosurgeon Eben Alexander contracted a rare form of bacterial meningitis and he was in a coma for seven days. During this time he passed through a life-changing near-death experience, which he describes as a form of death-rebirth. The encounter was so profound it opened him up from being a material scientist to a spiritual initiate.[10] It seems to underline an important point, that spiritual awakening happens through direct experience, not confirmation through scientific fact. However, whilst scientism appears to have adopted a role of debunking superstitions,[6] its reductionist outlook is on a collision course with eminent neuroscientists who appear to be moving towards a holistic perspective in the field of consciousness studies.

Dialogues between neuroscientist Christof Koch and the Dalai Lama have found that much of modern neuroscience research coheres with ancient Buddhist philosophy, where "consciousness is everywhere". Koch clearly takes an open-minded approach to scientific inquiry. He has collaborated with consciousness researcher Giulio Tonini and his *Integrated Information Theory* (IIT), which led to a test that measures the amount of consciousness (phi) in a human brain (using a magnetic pulse that reverberates in the skull from side to side, via neurons). The duration of the reverberations denotes the level of consciousness present, from the waking state, to sleep and even under anaesthetic. This cutting edge scientific research is opening up new possibilities that will extend to measuring the level of consciousness in animals, plant life and cells. It is also suggested that it will provide opportunities to test artificial intelligence, and whether machines can be conscious (this important issue is discussed in Chapter Nine). The exciting possibilities of this research is that it chimes with ancient philosophical understandings of consciousness, for example, early Greek, Buddhist and Pagan ideas of 'panpsychism' have upheld for thousands of years that "consciousness is everywhere".[11] It seems that progressive science is itself breaking free from the dogma of scientism and its superstitions.

Beyond reductionism

It is important to acknowledge that a gradual paradigm shift has been taking place in science, countering the material reductionism that has been the scientific default position since the 17th century. For example, the emergence of *systems thinking* is an ecological approach that is well placed to make a valuable contribution to resolving the global crisis.[12] Systems science functions in inclusive and interconnected ways, taking into account social and ecological factors, as well as political, philosophical and spiritual influences. It locates the human enterprise as working in cooperation with nature, not through control. In this way, a systems approach requires scientists to embrace an understanding of complexity, as well as lived experiences.[12] The scope of the systems perspective advocated by Capra and Luisi[12] is considerable and it certainly offers a viable way forward for humanity to begin responding to the challenges of the Anthropocene. For example the authors advocate for the inclusion and integration of qualitative and subjective states of consciousness (otherwise known as the *hard problem*). But systems theory still has more work to do in relation to integrating the *deep solutions* that can arise through our relationship to the imaginal realm, where dreams, visions and synchronous connections can deepen our relationship to an *omnijective consciousness*.

Nonetheless, the systems approach is capable of accommodating such a depth perspective,[13] which could help tackle a paradox that is at the heart of our brilliant high-tech modern culture. Put simply, in the modern world we are routinely ignoring a seam of wisdom that connects to the collective unconscious. Carl Jung[14] pointed out how humanity's lost connection to deep introspection and wisdom is born of the soul, and finds intelligent expression in our dreams and visions. We have a classic example of this in the case of chemist Friedrich Kekulé who was working on the problem of the structure of benzene. Kekulé dreamt of a snake eating its own tail, which led him to determine that the chemical structure of benzene was circular. This image is an ancient mystical symbol called the ouroboros, which represents the mythic and cyclic nature of renewal. But we also discover in alchemy, the precursor to modern chemistry, the ouroboros is connected to the spirit Mercury.[15] It is interesting that a chemist received an alchemical symbol to unlock a scientific problem. Such an observation would not have been lost on Jung. The question is, why has a deeper understanding of mystical traditions generally been lost in modern scientific discourse? For example, we celebrate Sir Isaac Newton as a scientist of the highest order, but not the fact that he was also a practising alchemist and mystic. Indeed, his alchemical knowledge was a foundation for his ground-breaking discoveries in physics.[16]

It is evident that a systems approach to life has the potential to shift us away from material reductionism, but for the whole to be truly taken into account it will involve a radical reconnection to the imaginal realm, which harnesses transformative possibilities. Evolving a sustainable relationship to life (as a whole) requires that we become whole, which changes our relationship to how we are living. For example, we can no longer view the Earth's resources as infinite commodities to be plundered and squandered for maximum profit, neither can we turn a blind eye to the ways we tacitly support the status quo through our consumer-based lifestyles. I shall not reiterate here the countless examples where humanity has become a global pariah, suffice to say, the consequences of our economic and industrial assault on the Earth (as evidenced in the Anthropocene) may force us to rekindle our relationship to one another, other species, and the natural world. It is evident that our modern attitudes to the Earth are divorced from our ancestral ways of knowing, which evolved through an intimate and sacramental relationship to the environment, not in opposition to it. Therefore, we need to recognise this trans-generational legacy, acknowledging that we rely upon the Earth for our well-being and survival, where our role in the world has to include the maintenance of healthy, bio-diverse ecosystems. If our ways of living continue to fracture our connection to the natural world, it will only lead to increasing levels of dissociation, desolation and destruction. Transformation begins with each of us recognising our individual and collective responsibilities to the whole.

Where does this global healing begin? If we do not pick up the challenge of adapting creatively and radically to the global complexities before us, we simply pass the problem on to the next generation, making the problems even more challenging to deal with. Perhaps a reasonable question to ask at the outset of our quest into the unknown is to find out where each of us is inspired to begin our transformative journey, via alternative ways of knowing, being and doing. As stated above, we live in a scientific and technological culture, which is the dominant way of knowing in the modern world with regard to how we understand facts about life. The current president of the Royal Society, Venki Ramakrishnan,[17] points out that our success as a species in the 21st century will be based on scientific innovation and knowledge. To this I would add the need to develop more expansive (transpersonal) ways of knowing, which would bring more depth to how science is understood and practised. William Irwin Thompson[18] says that it is impossible to conceive of a planetary culture without a new science. It points to a necessary shift in the scientific culture.

There is a need for more investment in holistic science, which combines the best of our scientific methods with the wisdom from ancient and indigenous cultures, in order to rekindle a closer relationship with the natural world. Our scientists need to be more than technicians[19] so that our tools and technologies enable us to create a more intimate connection to cosmic consciousness.[20] Such a worldview could catalyse a techne (craft) that brings forth an evolutionary shift in our ways of living, but such a vision needs to be allied to an emergent story or myth, enlivened through technologies of transformation (dream work, vision quests and meditation etc.). However, Stephen Buhner[21] and others have noted that our modern Western culture creates real pressure to abandon any metaphysical understanding of our place in the cosmos. It seems as though we are in a double bind, due to the mainstream agenda that prevails against myth, mysticism, visions and dreams, which paradoxically are the deep resources and assets we need to flourish as a species.

I hold the view that the human imagination and its revelations from the imaginal realm are the key for inspiring this shift to a new myth of wholeness. Myths can be woven into a common story, which helps to bind communities.[3] For example, in indigenous communities worldwide, myths are guiding stories that have helped generations to reflect on their relationship with sacred forces, as well as providing continuity for deep ways of knowing (via the ancestors). The deprecation of myth in the modern world has resulted in human consciousness becoming more and more alienated from a sacramental relationship to nature.[22] Interestingly, the loss of mythic meaning in the modern world has coincided with the ascent of rational scientism, and yet the root meaning for the Latin word science is knowledge, *scientia*, which had its origins in philosophy, and is concerned with the love and pursuit of wisdom. We seem to have lost sight of the deep wisdom connected to myths. The ancient Greeks did not have a specific word for science, but it would have been encompassed within a philosophical culture that sought to understand life (*bios*) and the craft of living (*techne*). What sort of explanatory knowledge and mythic narrative do we need to survive and thrive in the world today?

Science is not static, it evolves, and whilst its evolutionary development has been allied to materialism and reductionism, there is an emerging interest in holism. This holistic perspective is systemic, based on a web of intricate relationships that connect diverse and dynamic life systems, which intersect in a matrix of planetary ecologies[23] and wholeness, representing a world of living intelligence.[24] The emergence of a holistic vision in science is critical at this time to counter the over-reliance on reductionism and objectivity, which has resulted in an impoverished relationship to nature.[25] Indeed, our rampant materialist outlook has played a significant role in our separation from the natural world,[24] which begs the question, how did a one-sided materialism become the guiding vision of science? We can trace a lineage of key scientific luminaries who inspired the Royal Society (formed in 1662), where words such as "masculine philosophy" were used to describe its aims for establishing a certain type of knowledge.[26] Among the men of science who contributed to the Enlightenment during the 1700s was Francis Bacon (1561-1626), who advocated for a science that gains power over nature.[25] From the very beginning, science has viewed the natural world as something to be conquered and exploited, rather than revered and related to. For example, a key tenet in scientific reductionism is found in William of Ockham's famous razor (Ockham's razor). This is a process of thought used in scientific problem solving, which cuts away any extraneous variables to assist the most plausible reductionist explanation to emerge. Ockham was a theologian-philosopher who thought that there was no need for God and science (two ways of contemplating life), if science can clearly explain the phenomenal world.[27] However, Herbert Marcuse[28] likens Ockham's razor to a mechanism for slicing away other potential explanations, which means other opportunities, possibilities and ways of understanding life are sacrificed for the convenience of reductionism.

Ockham's razor is a way of thinking: it is not a law, nor is it an abiding truth; it is a tool that serves a particular approach to scientific inquiry (reductionism). Let's imagine what science could have looked like if Ockham had been interested in art, and developed the idea of *Ockham's paintbrush*. Such musings conjure the idea of a rich palette of life's colours, representing a holistic world of interrelationships. It contrasts with the *modus operandi* of the reductionist who metaphorically cuts open the phenomena being investigated, and in doing so, destroys the very thing they are seeking to understand.[29] This metaphor helps us understand how science has contributed to the ways we have critically separated and objectified life, which is the enduring legacy of René Descartes' dualistic philosophy.

Descartes' dream – Cartesian nightmare

Whilst there is a need for more investment in a holistic philosophy in the world today, it is important to recognise how humanity has benefited from logical thought and rationalism since the time of the early Greek philosophers. However, the evolution of scientific rationalism eventually led to a split from the dogma of religious influences.[30] Philosopher, René Descartes, provided the eventual *coup de grace* for the eventual divorce of science from religion, and in doing so he catapulted the rational mindset into a new orbit. However, it may come as a surprise to many people that Descartes' reductive philosophy was actually inspired by an irrational encounter. Professor of Physics Arthur Zajonc[31] informs us of the wonderful irony that it was a series of dream encounters that led to the emergence of Descartes' scientific method. Prior to his revelatory dreams, Descartes was in serious dialogue with many contemporary European intellectuals about the interface between spirituality and science. Then, aged 23, during a period of intense meditation and solitude, Descartes had a spiritual premonition (*le génie*) on 10th November 1619. He somehow knew that he would have a significant dream that night, which he asserted was divine guidance and had nothing to do with the human mind.[32] Descartes described the dream as the most important event in his life. Realising its significance, he made a spiritual pilgrimage five years later, walking from Venice to the shrine of the *Virgin of Loreto* (Italy) to honour the revelation that had been given to him.

Descartes' dream-revelation unfolded throughout the night in three parts. In the first part of the dream sequence, Descartes was out walking and he was struggling against a raging wind, which had already spun him around three times. In the midst of his struggles against the storm he saw the gates of a college (a seat of knowledge and learning) and he headed towards a church located in the college grounds, where he sought refuge, to say a prayer. But on his way Descartes realised he had failed to greet an acquaintance standing nearby, and as he turned to acknowledge the person he was once again caught off balance by the wind, which was blowing violently in the direction of the church (a sacred enclosure). He then met another person in the grounds of the college who told him someone had something they wanted to give him. Descartes speculated that the object must be a melon (an exotic fruit from distant lands). Interestingly, whilst his dream was unfolding, Descartes noticed that all the other characters in the dream were able to stand upright, whereas he alone was unbalanced by the power of the storm. It was at this point that he woke up in a state of pain and was filled with terror, because he feared that an evil spirit was attempting to influence him. He recited a prayer, asking for divine protection and then spent two hours ruminating on various actions he had committed during his life, and it was in this mood of melancholic introspection that he contemplated the nature of good-evil. Eventually, Descartes fell back to sleep, but he was awoken once again by a loud sound similar to a crash of thunder, which terrified him. Lying awake, he saw a host of *fiery sparks* shimmering before him in the room, and although such occurrences had happened to him before, this time he engaged with the experience (inspired by philosophical reasoning). He managed to gain control of the situation by working with his visual experiences, by repeatedly opening and closing his eyes and reflecting on the nature of his perceptions. His systematic response to his visual experiences had the effect of settling him down and once again he fell back to sleep.

In the final episode of this epic night-time encounter, Descartes dreamt about two books, a dictionary and an anthology of poems called *Corpus Poetarum*. He opened the book of poems and alighted upon a verse, *Quod vitae sectabor iter?* Meaning, *which path in life will I follow?* It revealed a question arising in a deep dream state concerning his free will and life direction. A man unknown to Descartes appeared and handed him another poem and he saw the words *est et non* (yes or no), then quick as a flash the stranger and the books vanished. Descartes then spent time reflecting on his dream revelations and he was convinced that the *Spirit of Truth* had come to him that night. Henceforth he decided to pursue a *science of reason*, one that would be pleasing to God. He further concluded that the books in his dream were also meaningful symbolic representations. For example, he thought that the dictionary connected to science (knowledge), and the *Corpus Poetarum* (poetry) reflected a union of wisdom and philosophy. Descartes viewed his dream-revelation as divine enthusiasm (a spirit within) and a connection to imaginative forces that flicker like sparks from a fire. Descartes also believed that such inspiration could be found in all human beings.[32,33]

There are many interesting elements in Descartes' dream (church, college, storms, good-evil etc.), some of which reveal a numinous quality. Descartes favoured a divine interpretation for his dreams, in which he was inspired by the *Spirit of Truth* which led him to develop a form of reductionism, based on a reasoned, scientific approach to investigating the material world.[32] However, there were also ominous resonances in the dream he did not reflect upon, such as his *imbalance* when a surging wind pushed him towards a church, where he was hoping to find refuge. It is interesting that he awakens shortly after this part of the dream sequence, and engages in a sort of *life review* of his past actions, where he reflects on good-evil. The next part of his night-time experience finds him being awoken by thunder, which is another powerful symbol associated with divine awakening in many mythic and religious traditions.[34]

As we reflect upon this extraordinary night-time sequence of dream encounters, we may well ask, was Descartes being awoken to some important divine revelation as a prophecy, or as a warning?

Descartes' dream work led him to create a radical dualistic philosophy, separating mind and matter, and his analysis led him to prioritise reason above all else, which he hoped would please God. Jungian analyst Anthony Stevens[35] discusses the nature of the melon in Descartes' dream, which in its natural environment is shaded by leaves and grows on the ground (an important symbolic connection to the Earth). The melon could represent the fruits of the material world, or it could connect to a quality of being grounded, which is in stark contrast to Descartes' overly rational and cerebral approach to life, best summed up in his famous quotation, *Cogito ergo sum* (I think therefore I am). Descartes' dream confronted him with dualities, such as sacred-profane, good-evil, and balance-imbalance, etc. These same polarities are all strong undercurrents that have been split off in our one-sided and hyper-rational modern world today. Science has a responsibility to reflect on these issues, as it embraces a more holistic vision that fosters a sense of wholeness.

Descartes' rational ego interpreted the dream sequences as favourable and divine, which led him to champion a particular course of philosophical action in his life. Yet, there are aspects of the dream which point to caution, for example, the powerful wind that pushes him in the direction of the church (a place of sacred refuge and reflection). Descartes was a very religious person, therefore the imbalance he experienced on his way to the church may well have reflected an inner conflict, between his faith and the scientific method he was pursuing. As we know, science eventually broke away from religious dogma and ideological constraints in its pursuit of knowledge. We are told that modern science is not bound to any dogma at all,[3] which I believe is misleading. Science has spawned a particular attitude called *scientism*, which judges reality by its own methodological yardstick, which of course is highly dogmatic. This objective worldview is dominated by hyper-rationalism, and it is fixated on facts and explanations. There is very little room for subjective or relational perspectives, and how these contribute to our understanding of life as an interconnected whole. We can see this in science today, where evidence from qualitative and subjective research is ranked much lower than quantitative and objective data from randomised controlled trials.

The dogma of scientism undermines the importance of wisdom found in traditions that access alternative ways of knowing, such as the spiritual traditions of indigenous people. Despite the benefits of material science, it has also contributed to humanity becoming more disconnected from nature, unleashing a technological assault upon the Earth. Rampant reductionism has contributed to a calamitous division between humanity and the natural world.[35] Essentially the global crisis we face today is the consequence of separating the material world from the spiritual world through hyper-rationalism, which continues to dominate modern ways of knowing. The unpalatable consequence is that an over-reliance on reason and reductionism has played a major role in our collective dissociation. It has rendered the human condition at odds with nature, with potentially fatal consequences.

Material scientism and rational imperialism

I have total respect for good science and open-minded scientists, but I have grown weary with the dogmatic assertions of some influential scientists, whose scientism is no better than ideological imperialism. Such narrow-mindedness has eroded any meaningful relationship with the rich heritage of humanity's wisdom and mythical traditions. For example, scientism singles out stories from the ancient world as mere superstition, which is blatant ignorance. A clear illustration of this is the sophistication found in Australian Aboriginal astronomy, which guided indigenous people's relationship to the land, and yet was completely overlooked by the Colonial British due to their prejudice.[36] This mindset continues today in the work of biologist Richard Dawkins who has written a book about science called *The Magic of Reality*.[37] In it Dawkins explores ancient stories and myths in a literal-minded way. He then draws comparisons between these mythic narratives and scientific knowledge in an attempt to put ancient and indigenous knowledge in its place, hoping to reveal that material science alone is what's really true.

One can only assume that Dawkins revels in opposing what he presumably views as soft mythical superstitions, before providing his readers with insights gained from hard scientific truths. Of course, to be fair to Dawkins, he is only doing what he has been trained to do as a biologist, which is to find a material explanation for a phenomenon under investigation, based on a methodology that can be replicated. Dawkins excels in the use of Ockham's razor to discard any extraneous information that he considers superfluous to *true knowledge*. This is how the irrationality of scientism works. For Dawkins science is helpful because it explains, but the *supernatural* is viewed as the enemy.[37] This is how the modern mindset of scientism has cut us off from the wisdom of the imaginal realm, where such prejudice divides and creates polarities. Yet, this is different from the gifted imagination of scientist Albert Einstein who understood that fairy stories could make the minds of children brilliant.

Theodore Roszak[22] was aware of the 'shadow' within scientism, which is now rooted in our collective consciousness. Because scientism is myopic, it discounts mythical and mystical knowledge, and consequently it has a biased approach to understanding our relationship to life and reality. It is a worldview that rejects out of hand metaphysics of any kind.[38] However, such one-sided scientism has failed to grasp that its methods cannot be applied to all areas of life.[39] To compare mythology and hard science, as Dawkins does, reveals the pitfalls of hyper-rationality, which can lead to an unbalanced view of life. For example, Dawkins is hoping to prove a point (on his own epistemological terms), but it is a point that cannot be proven, as mythology and science are two different ways of understanding life. When advocates of scientism approach complex problems from a mindset similar to Dawkins, they reveal a one-dimensional materialist philosophy at work. It is one that appears to have a sense of entitlement to cross boundaries of knowledge with an assumption of competence, which in reality only demonstrates a reductionist worldview steeped in prejudice.[39] It is a continuation of cultural imperialism, which has undermined indigenous ways of knowing for centuries. Dawkins'[37] attempts at deconstructing myths lack cross-cultural awareness or competencies about what these stories mean in terms of indigenous or ancient heritages.

I would like to share a creation myth about rainbows from native Australian culture called the *Rainbow Serpent*, as told by Bailey, McLeish and Spearman.[40] It must be remembered that there are often different versions of creation myths,[41] but the key point is that these stories help people connect to their cultural roots. Native Australian people lived on the continent many thousands of years before Western explorers 'discovered' the land in the 17th century. The Rainbow Serpent begins with an argument between a spirit snake-god and his son, which results in a fight, and the son injuring the father. The wounded snake-god then enters a *spirit river* and falls to Earth in agony, whereupon he slithers across the land and as a consequence his huge body creates ravines, which become filled with the water that flows from the *celestial spirit river*, bringing fertility and life to the Earth. In addition, the multiple colours from the snake's body are gradually represented in the world, such as blue for the sky, yellow for the sun and green for the plants. The rainbow serpent becomes the bringer of life, including plants, animals and humans. The story concludes with the healed rainbow serpent lying coiled up on the Earth. One day, huge tracts of storm clouds were forming as the sun shone, when suddenly the giant serpent leapt high into the sky, back to the spirit world. The only evidence of the snake was the trace of rainbow skin that had been shed from its body. The creation myth of the Rainbow Serpent represents a world that is alive, fertile and vibrant, promoting an attitude of reverence for all life. It is a myth that evokes a sense of awe.

The significance of this wonderful creation myth is that it cannot be separated from the lived experience of the people whose culture it represents. Dawkins and his ilk make no effort to understand the profound connection of indigenous myths to a spiritual reality, such as those described in the work of Charles Laughlin.[42] Laughlin speaks about the prevalence and variance of dreaming and altered states of consciousness in 90% of cultures worldwide, which gives us some indication of the importance of alternative ways of knowing in the human species. Indeed, the material scientism of Richard Dawkins *et al* uses the sharp edge of the razor to cut into perceived superstitions in an attempt to convince others that their beliefs are unproven, and in doing so, he attempts to colonise people's imaginations. There is a deep-seated prejudice at work here, one that has undermined indigenous cultures, like those of Indiginous Australians, for hundreds of years, as told by activist Stan Grant.[43]

In its cultural context, the myth of the Rainbow Serpent helps Indigenous Australian people to align with nature in a way that is interconnected and alive. Surely, this is the sort of knowledge that is crying out to be embraced in our parched and polluted world? Indigenous Australian elders kept alive the cultural stories of the *dreamtime* to the present day[44] through successive generations. Not only do these stories reveal meaningful connections to the ancestral spirits, they also keep alive a sacred understanding of life. They reflect traditional ways of belonging and living in harmony with the cosmos. These ancient cultures possess a deep knowledge about the lore of the land,[45] which enables them to survive and thrive in extreme conditions. Indeed, the dreamtime permeates all aspects of the Indiginous Australian way of life, civil and sacred.[44]

In his witting or unwitting attempt to trivialise myths, Dawkins also discusses earthquakes, and how science can explain the causes and devastating power of a *tsunami*, which for example, wreaked havoc and destruction on coastal communities across Asia in 2004. Yet, he omits to mention the story of an indigenous tribe who drew upon ancestral knowledge to recognise the warning signs of an earthquake in the sea, which alerted them that a tsunami was on the way. The tribe noticed changes in the way that the wind was blowing and the behaviour patterns of birds, and they heeded the warning signs, allowing the whole tribe to survive by taking evasive action.[46] Now, an open-minded scientist, interested in exploring knowledge from different perspectives, would find ancient tribal *ways of knowing* a fascinating phenomenon to study. But Richard Dawkins appears to be more interested in the promotion of a certain type of geological explanation gathered rationally. We have to conclude then, that this type of one-sided scientism is more concerned with generating facts to understand how the world works, which is fine. But, when it is used to undermine other forms of knowledge as superstitious and irrational, I am left wondering why scientism is so anxious to be seen as right. Yet the indigenous knowledge of a tribe enabled them to survive an environmental disaster, because of their *deep experiential relationship* to nature. These ancient cultures have access to wisdom and knowledge, which help them to connect with life in creative, inspiring and symbolic ways. It is an understatement to say that we could learn a lot from these people and their traditions.

A wonderful book by Jules Perry[47] chronicles how people from diverse communities and across cultures live cooperatively with nature. Perry cites examples of knowledge connected to ways of living that are passed on traditionally, and cultivated over generations, in which deep relationships are forged with the land and to other species. In one example, Perry describes how a Māori community, working with a researcher, actually predicted the imminent arrival of an extreme weather pattern called *El Niño*. However, we are informed that this indigenous method of predicting weather pattern changes has yet to be '*validated*' by the scientific community. Why are we so slow to credit the ancient wisdom of indigenous cultures when they appear to have knowledge that is outside of our scientific understanding? The problem is that scientism abhors metaphysics, myth or mysticism. In other words, from a material scientific point of view, a rainbow is the result of refracted light, which can be reproduced via experimental conditions, such as when white light is passed through a prism to reveal a spectrum of colour that was previously unseen by the naked eye. Material science may think it has had the last word, but the mysterious function of the rainbow is revealed in other surprising contexts.

The rainbow body

We need to ask some serious questions about the type of science that serves society as a whole. Do we want a holistic science that is open-minded, free to enquire and evolve, or are we content to put up with a scientism that propagates a materialist and reductionist ideology,[48] which limits our worldview and feeds a dogmatic understanding of life. What is at stake today is how we cultivate a myth for living in the modern world, one that supports our efforts to live in balance with nature as a whole. Theodore Roszak[22] reminds us that science cannot measure and know all the various ways that human beings experience life. For example, the spiritual practices of Tibetan Buddhist monks reveal knowledge that might have important implications for understanding human functioning and development.

Physician Herbert Benson[49] researched the effects of meditation practice on Tibetan Buddhist monks. Initially, Benson and his team had read accounts of Tibetan monks who were able to generate intense body heat as a by-product of advanced meditation practices, with anecdotal reports of monks melting the snow beneath them. These monks had developed a level of mastery in their meditation practices, called *inner fire*, or *gTum-mo*. Benson sought permission from the Dalai Lama to study these monks, who meditated throughout the night at a temperature just a few degrees above freezing. He and his team witnessed the monks dipping 3 x 6 feet sheets into icy water, which they then wrapped around their almost naked bodies. Within a few minutes the sheets were steaming and within 45 minutes they were completely dry. Benson says the monks continued to repeat the feat with ice-cold sheets two more times. He reported that the monks showed significant physiological changes in bodily functioning with regard to heat production. To put the experiments into context, most human beings would not fare well in these conditions; some would even die.

The meditation practices of Tibetan Buddhist monks are based on centuries of well-developed knowledge, which is primarily focused on spiritual awakening and the cultivation of an enlightened consciousness. Practitioners become highly proficient in working with subtle energies that flow through the body via channels (nadis) and chakras. While mainstream science has no conceptual or theoretical understanding for the existence of these subtle energies and chakras, it means practitioners of scientism are free to ignore these results and label them superstitious or irrational. Yet the research findings of Benson and his team point to latent spiritual and energetic potentials that could be developed in human beings. They reveal how a group of Tibetan Buddhist monks are producing replicable results that defy the normal parameters of biological functioning in extreme conditions, which means Benson was engaging in an area of legitimate scientific research.

Another example from Tibetan Buddhism is the phenomenon of the rainbow body. It is well known in Tibetan Buddhism that highly realised meditation masters actually cause a rainbow to manifest when they die, which surrounds the body of the deceased. A YouTube film, *Rainbow Appears During Parinivarna of Tibetan Master*, shows a rainbow manifesting in front of a temple complex in Namdroling Monastery, in Mysore, India following the death of His Holiness, Penor Rinpoche, the former spiritual head of the Nyingma school of Tibetan Buddhism. It is easy for material scientists to dismiss phenomena like the rainbow body as impossible, but such attitudes seriously undermine a spiritual tradition that has an intricate and highly developed cosmology of body, mind and universe, where eminent meditation masters have witnessed and written about the rainbow body phenomenon.[50,51]

On a similar theme, Jungian analyst Jerome Bernstein[52] recounts a time when he participated in an indoor Navajo healing ceremony, which lasted for eight days. Part of the ritual included making a painting out of coloured sand, which depicts a mythic representation of where the *Holy People* learnt their songs (in the direction of the North), a holy place illuminated by rainbows. The sand painting includes a rainbow, which receives medicine from the *Holy People*. Bernstein describes how the sand from the painting was applied to the patient's body as part of the healing process. At the close of the ceremony, all the participants then filed outside for the concluding ritual. It was at this point, just as Bernstein had stepped outside, that he saw in front of him, in the middle of a clear and cloudless sky, a rainbow with one end of the arc in a north facing direction. Bernstein recounts how none of the Navajo participants at the ceremony commented about it, but when he mentioned the rainbow they said it was a clear indication that the *Holy People* had attended the ceremony. It is a worldview that runs counter to the dogma of scientism, where such events are not meant to happen.[53] The worldview of scientism appears so entrenched in many of its practitioners, who cling tightly to their hyper-rational beliefs, which have contributed to humanity's ongoing alienation from the natural world. It is hardly surprising that humanity has eroded a sacramental understanding for life as a whole.

Physicist Michio Kaku[54] is correct when he says that science exemplifies our species' incredible creativity and productivity in terms of discoveries that will continue to improve the human condition, such as nanotechnology etc. But he also notes that science has a destructive capacity, for example through technologies developed and used in wars etc. Kaku[54] interviewed over 300 of the world's leading scientists, who are all engaged in research that will shape our lives in the 21st century. Yet, as impressive as the book is, Kaku does not appear to provide an overarching myth or collective narrative that is guiding such a bewildering array of discoveries and what these mean for an emerging worldview. Kaku does ask the question about where technology is leading humanity, and he suggests that a planetary civilisation is emerging, but what sort of planetary citizenship this is remains unclear. However, Kaku does give us a hint of the scale of scientific discoveries and the need for wisdom. He imagines that the destiny of science by the end of the 21st century will include harnessing powers that were formerly occupied by the gods, which will enable us to shape reality and gain a level of mastery over nature. It is a statement that made me pause and reflect. I am in no doubt that human beings are capable of connecting with the divine, as revealed through the lives of mystics from all spiritual traditions. But when I hear a scientist say we will occupy powers that used to belong to the gods, it is the word power that causes me most concern. We are most certainly a highly creative species, even co-creative, but we are not *the Creators* of life. It is on this single point alone that I contend we need to include technologies of transformation (mindfulness, prayer, dream work, shamanism etc.) as complementary ways of tackling the potentially inflatory attitudes and practices that drive our hyper-rational and high-tech world.

We are living in a time of almost techno-hypnosis and seem to be losing the ability to question attitudes, such as the pursuit of god-like powers. If this is a myth that is underpinning scientific progress we are in trouble. Interestingly, *The Guardian* columnist Simon Jenkins[55] warns scientists not to play with the idea of being gods, to which the President of the Royal Society, Venki Ramakrishnan,[56] responded in a letter that scientists have no desire to be seen as gods. However, the statement by Kaku reveals an underlying attitude that is associating scientific discoveries with powers that used to belong to the gods, which carries all the potential for a one-sided ego inflation that could get out of control. It is an attitude that in the ancient world would have been represented mythically as a warning of the dangers to come. William Irwin Thompson[57] warns that science only allows us to think big when we keep our experiences out of the equation. It is no wonder that we are witnessing such worrying levels of dissociation in our high-tech world, due to such objectification of life. A letter in *The Guardian* newspaper in May 2017 suggested that the ethical, moral, political and social basis for science would be well-served if graduating scientists had to take the equivalent of the *Hippocratic Oath*, stating their intentions to use knowledge responsibly.[58]

I believe science, on balance, has the potential to be a force for good. But the lack of a guiding myth in science today is a worry. When modern worldviews are contrasted against humanity's ancient and indigenous heritage, where balance and a harmonious sense of belonging to the cosmos are ingrained into all facets of lived experience, we begin to understand the scale of our modern one-dimensional ways of living (this issue will be discussed in Chapter Three). Yet, for all our overinvestment in reason, there still persists an uncanny relationship to mysterious forces that work in our lives, such as the revelatory dreams that inspire our imaginations to produce extraordinary shifts in our evolutionary trajectory. There is no doubt that these uncanny forces can unlock potentials hitherto unknown to us. The dawning realisation is that the prevailing attitudes of scientism impede the development of a more holistic relationship with nature. This is in contrast with indigenous cultures, where myth has played an important function within those communities, revealing a respectful and universal connection with life. Of course, what works for one culture would not translate to a diverse planetary civilisation of billions. But the point I am trying to make is that the global crisis is made worse when it is coupled to a one-dimensional scientism that drives ideas of technological progress in the modern world. I argue that our over-investment in an objective view of life has left us woefully underprepared to embrace a holistic perspective, where as planetary citizens we can co-exist with others, other species and nature as whole.

In the next chapter I will discuss the implications of dismissing the so-called 'superstitions'. There is more to life than explanations and facts, which are generated by objective and dispassionate methodologies. Such one-dimensional and methodological servitude, according to Roszak,[22] could easily become the preoccupation of mediocrity. We are missing a soulful connection to life, because the hyper-rationalism in our technocratic world is eroding the language of mystery from human life.[59] We need an honest appraisal about what types of knowledge best serve humanity, including how we can prepare ourselves to become planetary citizens and co-create a better world, which includes the recognition and actualisation of our human potential. Indeed, there is a real paradox in the notion that creative and intuitive scientists are more similar to shamans than technicians.[18] But such a realisation is not the welcome in the world of mainstream scientism. Richard Dawkins[37] is right to suggest that science needs to improve its methods to explore phenomena that cannot be explained. He calls for a revolution in science, which would be unrecognisable to previous generations of scientists. However, it is evident that the scientism advocated by Dawkins is all about objective methods. There is no call for scientists to develop their human capacities and explore their transpersonal potential. Yet there are alternative and complementary ways of knowing, which seem to be beyond the reach and understanding of modern scientism at this time.

One of the questions I explore in this book is how we can re-imagine our human potential in relation to an overarching collective purpose, one that realises the importance of us all working for the greater good, where we are able to respond to the fluctuating ecological conditions that will define the 21st century. Is it even possible that we can *dream up* a shared vision that helps us re-imagine our way into an unpredictable future? I hold the view that such a guiding myth is one of the most important shared objectives facing humanity today. We need a renewed vision for life that encourages holism. We need to break free from the shackles of scientism, which attempts to debunk the soul and propagate dispiriting ideas, such as the notion that personal meaning is no more than a mere delusion.[3] In my book, *The Unselfish Spirit*, I address the issue of *meaning* and I make a clear distinction between speculations concerning the *meaning of life*, as distinct from the cultivation of *meaning in life*, which emerges through our ways of living. There is a huge difference between these two ways of approaching *life* and *meaning*. It goes without saying that the objectification of life, coupled to hyper-rationalism, distorts our understanding of reality, as warned by Carl Jung.[60] Indeed, Jung believed that modern notions of *meaningless* were symptomatic of illness, and a barrier to wholeness.[61]

I concur with the view expressed by William Irwin Thompson[18] who proposes that science needs to be delivered from scientism, so that wisdom and compassion can be cultivated to help restore a sense of balance (remember Descartes' dream?). Jean Hardy[62] reminds us that as a species we have gained in many ways from scientific knowledge. But, as she wisely points out, science cannot represent all there is to know about reality, which means if we adhere to its methods unthinkingly, it is capable of restricting what we know. She cites the words of Giambattista Vico (1668-1744), who warned against the idea of scientific rationality as a means to discover the 'truth', because it only gives us a particular view of reality, which is based on a system of rules. Therefore, we need to ask, what has been left out of our hyper-rational worldview? We should feel emboldened to ask what it would take for scientism to honour ancient and indigenous wisdom, where the imaginal realm and the world of dreaming are revered, which could bring humanity into a more intimate relationship with wholeness? It is a worldview where science and spirituality are honoured for their respective and complementary ways of knowing.[63] A key task at this time in human evolution is to re-engage the relationship between the human imagination and the imaginal realm as a way of connecting self, other, world and cosmos. We are in desperate need of a philosophy of life that represents a genuine *love of wisdom*, where reason and our imaginative and visionary energies honour the depth of our relationship to wholeness. I am speaking about living soulfully. In this way, a renewed sense of holism is the heart and soul of the Transformocene.

Exercise: Blended ways of knowing

- Bring to mind an issue in your life where you are stuck, or are finding it hard to gain a solution to a problem (at work, or in a social situation etc.).

- What is your rational appraisal of the situation?

- How does this rational appraisal inspire or motivate you?

- Now add another dimension to this rational way of knowing, and imagine an 'as if' scenario developing, where you take time to day dream:
  - Remember a time when the natural world inspired you in some way. It could have been a majestic tree, the elements, the wilderness, an animal or a plant etc.
  - Recollecting this experience (seeing, feeling, hearing, etc.), how does it connect you soulfully to the natural world?
  - How does this connection to the natural world bring a sense of well-being or wholeness to your lived experience in this moment?

- What insights can you take from the reflections made above?

- How does nature support your inner well-being?

- How do you reappraise the problem at the start of this exercise from the position of your innate wholeness?

The love of wisdom is intimately bound to the love of knowledge, which connects to the alchemy of transformation. The injunction to 'know thyself' is an initiation into death and rebirth. This is the mystery of renewal.

CHAPTER TWO

The Mythic Journey

Overview

The discussion in this chapter is centred on an alternative vision to the one-dimensional and hyper-rational reality that has modern consciousness in its grip. I explore how wisdom in Ancient Greece was bound to myth and meaning, as found in the philosophy of Parmenides, who is credited with integrating rational and mystical worldviews. It is believed that Parmenides was connected to the spiritual traditions of Apollo and Asklepios, where incubatory practices and dreams were used for healing. The mystical tradition of Parmenides was overlooked in favour of a more rational lineage, which contributed to the gradual marginalisation of *irrationality* in Western philosophy. I illustrate this point further by drawing on the example of how modern scientific medicine abandoned its connection to the Asklepian tradition in favour of Hippocrates (cause and effect), yet in Ancient Greece these traditions were complementary. I point out that the placebo response provides us with the clearest evidence that rational and irrational forces can work together, based on imaginative resources. I argue that we need a philosophy of wholeness, which is aligned with the imaginal realm to inspire our efforts in the Transformocene.

Reclaiming the depths

As discussed in the previous chapter, we live in a time where reason and rationality are the dominant *ways of knowing* in the modern world, which have contributed to our collective dissociation from nature. But the state of the planet and our impoverished relationship to the natural world suggests that the perspective of *deep ecology* could help us awaken to the interconnectedness in nature, and help us deal with the unfolding ecological crisis.[1] We need to explore the problems connected to our ecological illiteracy and begin to find *deep solutions*, which means connecting to deeper experience of living as a way of harnessing our adaptive potential.[2] Theodore Roszak's[3] eco-psychological perspective references the importance of Jung's ideas of the collective unconscious, which according to Roszak harbours our species' *ecological intelligence*, having played an important (and wise) role in our ongoing survival. Our collective navigation in a time of global crisis will require all the adaptive resources we can muster to re-imagine changes in behaviour that will help co-create an improved future. I have argued elsewhere that the global crisis is a spiritual crisis, and the potential rise in the numbers of people experiencing spiritual emergencies is part of the transformational imperative of this time.[2] This is why adopting a systems perspective (mentioned in Chapter One) is an important first step that offers a deeper understanding of the bifurcations and tipping points that are occurring in collective consciousness at this time. Such systemic and transformational shifts in the modern world need to be seen as initiations into holistic consciousness, but we will have to go deeper. In this regard, Jung's *deep phenomenology*[4] is a well-developed experiential method for encountering the depth of the unconscious,[5] which finds support in the work of transpersonal philosopher Michael Washburn.[6] He writes about the possibilities of activating unconscious processes that can eclipse our egos, which (if managed wisely) can serve a greater process of transformation in human development.[7] In short, this view recognises that humanity is more than capable of participating in radical processes of change, including transformations in consciousness as part of a deeper ecology for living.[2]

It is evident that in the modern world there is scant recognition of the value of a deeper process of living as part of our evolutionary potential and our development as a species. Jung[8] pointed out many decades ago that humanity has failed to understand how our lack of connection to the depths of the psyche, (which is part of nature), has contributed to a soul sickness that makes us rootless and gives rise to meaninglessness. This collective disconnection to the deeper experiences of the psyche is long-standing. It is an issue that has been discussed by Peter Kingsley[9] who explored the early origins of Western philosophy and the evolution of an intellectual tradition based on rational thinking, which gradually overlooked the importance of mystical initiation. As stated in Chapter One, the achievements of Western philosophy and science, based on logic and reason, have resulted in some phenomenal breakthroughs, and therefore it is only correct we should celebrate our ability to reason and discern. However, I agree with Matthew Fox[10] who says that our modern philosophical quest has been *un-spirited*. In this regard, the deep experiential value of Jung's work is an important contribution to Western philosophy (in that it takes mysticism seriously), which chimes with philosophical ideas from Ancient Greece, before the focus on rationalism and materialism became more developed.[11] We need to ask ourselves, has Western philosophy and science helped us understand life as a whole? To begin answering such a question we have to reflect upon what has been left out of our modern philosophical and scientific worldviews.

We know that scientism is interested in debunking superstitions and providing us with explanations and facts. Yet William Irwin Thompson[12] wisely points out the structures and stories that surround science are also mythic, which unconsciously guides its activities. It underscores the subtle distinction between the science of facts (explanations) and the stories (myths) that shape our ways of interpreting and understanding the world we live in. Thompson reflects on one of the key problems in the emergence of a planetary culture, where our technologies are now being governed by systems of scientific management, yet the *uncanny* nature of life and the mystery of consciousness are not so neatly formulated.[13] If we are interested in cultivating a holistic worldview, we are confronted with the task of understanding and integrating the *rational* and the *irrational*. We might think such an idea is heresy in an age of hyper-rationality, but if we consider Eastern philosophy as a counterpoint to our discussion, we find practices in Zen Buddhism, where the irrational is used as a more reliable method for spiritual awakening (wholeness). For example, a key technology of transformation in the Zen tradition is the Koan, a riddle that makes no rational sense, but when combined with structured meditation practice, can assist in awakening consciousness (enlightenment). A typical Zen Koan is: "What's the sound of one hand clapping?" Zen masters use a combination of rational and irrational methods to help adepts awaken to wholeness.

Similarly, Peter Kingsley[9] notes that pre-Socratic philosophy (love of wisdom) was concerned with becoming a whole human being. He offers a perspective about the original purpose of philosophy, which at its heart seems very different from the dry academic disciplines of today. He rightly questions the one-sided rationalism that has gradually eroded the importance of mysticism and the language of the soul: for example, when we encounter the views of popular academics espousing a one-dimensional worldview, announcing that the soul has no existence.[4] Wisdom must include the intellect, but it is also soulful, which encourages us to embrace good heartedness, justice, service and love.[15] Kingsley mounts a challenge to modern academic philosophy, based on the fragments of work left by pre-Socratic philosopher, Parmenides, who lived around the start of the 5th century BC, in Elea, *Magna Graecia* (now Italy). Parmenides' philosophical position, according to Kingsley, was a blend of reason and spirituality. He touched on matters such as the nature of truth and the world beyond the five senses. Indeed, the writings of Parmenides reveal that he was orientated towards the *mystery of life*.[16]

Kingsley's analysis of Parmenides has been challenged as being too polemical, and the criticism levelled at his work accuses him of breaking away from pre-Socratic scholasticism, because he gives primacy to mysticism and suggests that ancient spiritual perspectives could be relevant for people in the modern world.[17] Whether Kingsley has over-stepped the boundaries of academic philosophy is an interesting point, particularly if the mystical ideas of ancient philosophers like Parmenides do appear to have relevance for the modern world. Whilst we do not have much written evidence of Parmenides' work, we do know that he lived in a time of strong beliefs in the Olympian Gods and he may have even participated in rites such as Eleusinian mysteries. Although we have no written records of the Eleusinian mysteries, a monument of this rite shows the *mystes* kissing a giant snake, which represents the power of the Earth, or *chthonic mana*.[8]

It points to a deep mythic and symbolic connection to the Earth. It is little wonder that people with an interest in the experiential aspects of philosophy like Peter Kingsley (who are undoubtedly in a minority position) are challenging the one-dimensional reasoning that seems to have a stranglehold on our imaginations and institutional thinking today. Far from being irrelevant, a mythic and symbolic connection to our lived experiences is a gateway to the imaginal realm, where we are inspired to live a soulful connection to life.[18] It is how we also experience a sense of mystery and renewal.

To make sense of Peter Kingsley's work it is important to consider the ideas he puts forward in comparison to someone like Carl Jung, who was deft at weaving the rational with the irrational, and has given us an intellectual and experiential understanding for how to work with the complexities of the living unconscious (mystery). Kingsley's thesis proposes that one of the key founders of the Western philosophical tradition, Parmenides, was also a priest of Apollo. He draws on archaeological evidence from three separate carvings made 2000 years ago, which bore inscriptions that were linked to the god of incubation and healing, Apollo (also known as Iatros). A few years later in a nearby excavation, another ancient marble inscription was found close to a statue of Asklepios (with a snake carved on his robe), which bore an inscription identifying Parmenides as a healer.[9] Both Apollo and his son Asklepios were the gods of healing, whose interventions occurred during a process of incubation (sleep), and in the mystery of darkness. Their healing method was essentially an induction into the imaginal realm through dreams. Kingsley's research suggests that philosophy in the ancient world was connected to visionary energies, where the imagination was used as a means of entering into a sacramental relationship with divine forces. In this tradition, mysticism and healing had equal merit to rationality in terms of ancient ways of knowing. Kingsley is suggesting that we may well have discarded an important part of our sacred heritage, namely our deep connection to the imaginal realm.

Kingsley proposes that we need *both* the rational and the irrational to go beyond *duality* if we are to create new possibilities for living. Such a proposition offers us a renewed relationship to philosophy, which is also spiritual, experiential, imaginative and tinged with myth and mystery. The missing philosophy of Parmenides, as told by Kingsley, re-aligns us to a mytho-poetic reality that gives equal value to mystical experience and rational thinking. Kingsley tells the story of Apollo and the creation of his shrine at the great temple of Delphi, where a divine oracle advised and counselled the ancient Greeks. Priestesses served the oracle at Delphi, where a huge sacred snake called Python was connected to the goddess Gaia.[19] Kingsley informs us that in the Apollonian myth the Olympian god fights Python, who possesses the gift of prophecy and whose hissing sound, or *syrigmos*, has magical properties. Apollo eventually won the fight and in doing so he was able to harness the snake's prophetic powers, which he did by burying the giant serpent under the floor in the centre of his shrine at Delphi. It was here that the snake became an ally to Apollo the healer, who visited supplicants as they slept in the temple in the darkness of night (incubation). Apollo's presence was always accompanied by a hissing sound, which is why the snakes associated with the healing god are considered sacred.

According to Kingsley's interpretation of ancient Greek sources describe the experience of incubation as an induction into altered states of consciousness. Kingsley compares this to awakening the subtle energies associated with Kundalini, which are activated when practising tantric yoga, where people experience vibrations and hissing sounds in the process of spiritual awakening. Interestingly, in Hindu tantra, the awakening of the Kundalini energy happens through the divine feminine energy, *Shakti*, which is located close to the tail of the spine and is symbolised as a serpent power, and where the Goddess is represented as a snake. Once awakened, the Kundalini energy flows upwards through the central energetic channel (*Sushumna*), where the feminine Shakti meets the masculine Shiva at the chakra located on the crown of the head in mystical union.[13] It is a process of awakening our latent sacred energies, where two channels (*Ida* and *Pingala*) cross the central channel (*Sushumna*) at each chakra (energy centre), from the base of the spine to the crown of the head.[20] Interestingly, the pattern of the Hindu chakra system and central energy channels are configured similarly to the serpentine symbol of the Greek messenger of the gods, Hermes (or Mercury in the Roman pantheon), whose symbolic staff is called the Caduceus. The imagery is so similar and striking that it has to be more than coincidence.

Parmenides: priest, philosopher, poet, prophet

Although Parmenides was the philosopher credited with cultivating reason (the rational), evidence from the ancient world suggests that he was also a priest-healer in the cult of Apollo, which adds a mythical twist to his mystical philosophy (the irrational). Thomas Rickert[21] quotes a poem written by Parmenides, *On Being* (*Peri Pheseōs*), about the journey of an initiate descending to the underworld (*katabasis*), who experiences altered states of consciousness and divine revelations from an unknown goddess. Kingsley speculates that the identity of the goddess is Persephone, a representation of the divine feminine, who interestingly is strongly associated with the Eleusinian mysteries, and is also intimately linked to Apollo. The name Persephone derives from *Sophe*, which translates as *wise* and shares its origins with Sophia the Greek goddess of wisdom.[22] The philosophy of Parmenides resonates for the times we are living in, because he was concerned with preparing people to be liberated from the mundane pre-occupations of everyday life, which interestingly requires the complementary functions of *sacred inspiration* and *reason* to work together and bring about an awakening in consciousness. Such a philosophy sounds ideal for countering the one-dimensional technocracy that is squeezing the life out of people and planet today.

The priest-healers of Apollo, or Iatromantis, were mystics who were not only adept at stillness and entering deep states of consciousness, they also used poetry, incantations, oracles, incubation and dreams to inform their learning and healing abilities.[9] Essentially, it was a mystical tradition, where Parmenides spoke about the need to 'die' before one's physical death, which is allied to the sort of symbolic death that accompanies transformations in consciousness. It is similar to shamanic initiations of death and renewal, as well as mystical awakenings found in other spiritual traditions. Indeed, the practice of dream incubation happened in many other countries around the same time it was flourishing in Ancient Greece.[23] It also points to fertile possibilities for cross-cultural exchange in terms of trade, as well as sharing philosophical ideas and also sacred teachings and practices. The philosophy of Parmenides reminds us of the importance of cultivating a relationship to the imaginal realm. Kingsley tells us that in this tradition the divine world is *ever-present*, shimmering through the appearances of everyday life. In this way the Iatromantis would have enabled people in Ancient Greece to connect with a sense of wholeness and healing.

Whilst we will never know the complete truth of Parmenides' philosophical-healing vocation, we need to keep an open mind about Peter Kingsley's work for the following reasons: Western philosophy and science has developed a habit of marginalising ways of knowing that do not concur with a rational consensus. For example, in the field of medicine the figure of Hippocrates (born on Kos, 460 BC) is considered the founder of Western natural medicine, based on his interest in exploring the rational cause and effect of illness, as illustrated in the body of work produced by his followers, the *Hippocratic Corpus*. Yet it is more than curious that our medical traditions today do not celebrate more robustly the news that Hippocrates was an Asklepiad, or healer in the Asklepian tradition. It is wonderful to reflect on one version of the Hippocratic Oath, which starts with swearing an allegiance to Apollo, Asklepios, Hygeia and Panacea, as well as all the gods and goddesses, which puts Hippocratic medicine in line with the sacred and spiritual dimension. I have previously written about the medical tradition of Asklepios[24] and how this god of healing is associated with *religious medicine* in rituals that took place in temples and sanctuaries known as *Asklepieia*.

Whenever you see a medical symbol of a staff with a single snake wrapped around it, you are looking at the ancient symbol of Asklepios, whose non-venomous snakes were part of the healing process (renewal and rejuvenation). Supplicants spent time in the temple (*temenos*) preparing themselves to participate in the climax of the healing ritual, which involved the ritual act of *enkoimesis*, or sleeping overnight in the inner sanctuary (*abaton*), where they would receive a healing dream, or message. Samples of the cures recorded in the Asklepian temple at Epiduras in Greece survive to this day, carved in the temple stone (*stelai*). We need to be clear that this was not a small cult; it was a major healing tradition that lasted for centuries[24] and its prominence is put in perspective when we learn that there were around 300 Asklepian sanctuaries in the ancient Greek empire.[23] This was the dominant healing paradigm in early 6th and 5th century BC Greece. There is also a record of Hippocrates having a vision of Asklepios, where he sees serpents following the great healer, which are making whistling/hissing sounds as Asklepios walks towards him, followed by his attendants who are carrying medicines. Asklepios then reaches out and offers his hand to Hippocrates.[24] The visionary gesture of an outstretched hand provides a graphic image of the link between Asklepian (religious) and Hippocratic (natural) healing. Incidentally, dreams were used in both traditions. We have clear evidence of a vibrant holistic healing tradition of which Hippocrates was a part (Plato referred to Hippocrates as the Asklepiad of Kos), but this important healing lineage is all but absent in the modern world. However, despite our best efforts to create a completely rational understanding of life, the imaginal realm has an uncanny way of appearing when we least expect it. In this regard the placebo poses intriguing questions for us.

Placebo dreaming

In Asklepian temples, priest-healers would encourage supplicants to prepare for healing by making inexpensive offerings to Asklepios, such as honey cakes. People would bathe and unburden themselves of negative attitudes. These preparations were done in an atmosphere of building expectation and enthusiasm. The Greek meaning for enthusiasm (*en theos*) is the god within, and it was on this basis that Asklepian healing activated supplicants' endogenous (inner) resources.[24] Essentially, the imagination played a significant role in the process of Asklepian healing, which has powerful resonances with placebo medicine that continue to confound scientists to this day. The origin of the word placebo, 'I shall please',[24] is from the Bible (Hebrew Psalm 116). However, the full Latin translation, *placebo domino in regione vivorum*, is a declaration that people's actions and ways of living reflect a spiritual aspiration: 'I shall please the lord in the land of the living'. In addition, the Anglo Saxon origins of the word 'heal' connect to the word *whole*, and it is here that placebo healing works through the imagination and expectation. I consider the placebo response to be a way of bringing the worlds of healing and wholeness together. However, whilst I am excited by modern research into the placebo, I worry that the rigid methodological parameters for studying this fascinating phenomenon may also restrict our understanding of it.

Ted Kaptchuk and John Kelley[25] inform us that the usual routes for administering placebos, such as saline injections and sugar pills, are found to be helpful in cancer treatment by reducing the experience of pain, nausea and fatigue. However, the authors infer that placebos cannot shrink tumours. Yet, much earlier in his career whilst living in Asia, Kaptchuk had witnessed his Chinese godmother recover from thyroid cancer after she visited a Buddhist priest and folk medicine practitioner, whose shamanic method divined a treatment for her, and she was advised to drink a special brew of plum tea for four weeks. Kaptchuk's godmother drank the plum teas daily, and she cried and prayed devoutly to the gods, which against the odds produced a cure. The tumour totally disappeared in the four-week period.[26] Clearly, tumours are capable of shrinking, but these occurrences do not seem to happen in research conditions. It is understandable that researchers are only looking at their data sets, and not wanting to speculate and raise expectations about possible cures for cancer, which cannot be substantiated. But, the question has to be asked, what is going on when tumours shrink against the odds?

An interesting case study reported by Dr Klopfer in 1957 indicates placebos may well be able to shrink tumours. Dr Klopfer was part of a research trial into a new cancer drug, and a patient in the hospital (Mr Wright) asked to be included in the study. Yet Mr Wright's cancer was deemed too advanced to be considered for inclusion in the research trial. But this did not deter Mr Wright, whose persistence and enthusiasm eventually changed Dr Klopfer's mind. Mr Wright's condition improved dramatically when he was given the drug, all his tumours shrank, and he left the hospital shortly afterwards. However, early reports in the press about the efficacy of the new wonder drug were disappointing and when Mr Wright heard this news his tumours returned. Once again he was admitted to hospital and Dr Klopfer became very curious about the dramatic twists and turns in his patient's health, so much so that he decided to help his patient in a rather unorthodox way. He lied to his patient, telling him that a newer version of the same drug was being trialled, and he asked Mr Wright if he would like to join the study. Immediately, Mr Wright became very enthusiastic about receiving the latest version of the wonder drug. At the point when his doctor administered the saline solution (water) Mr Wright was in a heightened state of anticipation, and once again the tumours shrank.[27] The placebo response is quite a mystery: its healing potency appears to be activated by imagination, emotion and a touch of drama.

All good dramas have twists and turns, and the benefits of the placebo response are no exception. For example, the placebo has a twin, who is called the nocebo, and it works in direct opposition to the healing power of the placebo, in that it has a harmful impact. It means that something intangible, like a word or a particular tone of voice, can act as a trigger for healing (placebo), or the opposite (nocebo). Such an account happened to a patient with a very serious heart condition. On the day in question, during the cardiologist's ward round (accompanied by the medical team), the doctor used the word 'gallop' to describe the poor functional state of the patient's heart. Against all expectations the patient recovered. It was only at a follow-up appointment that the patient told the cardiologist what a relief it had been to hear that his heart was as strong as a 'horse'. The patient had associated the word gallop with equine vigour.[24] It shows the importance of being *mindful of the imaginal* when engaging in healing conversations. I sometimes worry about the impact of medical researchers' intended and unintended messages when speaking about their research. For example, when researchers suggest that on balance, placebos can help with pain, but they can't shrink tumours, it potentially marginalises and excludes case material (like Mr Wright), which may well be pointing to deeper potentials for healing that lie outside the limiting controls of a randomised control study. I fully understand the need for caution, but I also think we could be more expansive in our approach to understanding the imaginative possibilities connected to the world of placebo responses.

Modern medical research generates objective evidence, where the findings are only relevant when they are statistically significant. It is a responsible way of managing procedural interventions, which does not give false hope to people. However, the imaginal does not bow to the rational. It means that when a well-intended message, drawn from objective research, tells people that the placebo cannot shrink a tumour, it may well be promoting an unintended nocebo message in collective consciousness. Reductionist science needs to be mindful of how its methods might be limiting the imagination. In this regard, the placebo and nocebo responses may well be as elusive as the world of quantum physics. For example, quantum experiments reveal that when photons (particles of light) are fired at a barrier with one slit open, a particle passes through it. But, when a barrier with two slits open, the particle that is fired collapses into a wave. It is a conundrum, and physicists have had to conclude that at the most subtle level, there is indeterminacy. Most importantly, the observer who sets up the experiment is recognised as having an influence on the outcome of the experiment. Similarly, I am suggesting that the imaginal realm and the human imagination are not reductive phenomena; they are more aligned with the paradoxical world of quantum possibilities, which means we need to tread carefully about what we think the placebo is and isn't. For example, a report in *New Scientist*[28] mentioned how a study into nausea, using verbal suggestions, was intended to reduce the experience in one group and promote it in another, but the interventions ended up having the opposite effect on each group. This is the paradox of working with the placebo, which should fireup our imaginations for the wise and intelligent resources that are available to us.

The mystery of healing

One of my favourite placebo stories comes from Joe Dispenza.[29] He recounts a time when he was 23 years old, and was involved in a terrible accident that left him with six broken vertebrae. He was taking part in a triathlon competition, and whilst cycling on a difficult part of the course an SUV vehicle travelling at 55mph knocked him off his bike and dragged him along the road. The accident damaged his spine and the shattered fragments of bone threatened to sever his spinal cord, which could have rendered him paralysed from the chest down. Dispenza was offered surgery to insert metal rods to help reconstruct his broken bones. However, as a chiropractor, he knew that this procedure would likely result in a lifetime of chronic pain. A second medic also said the surgery option was the only viable intervention available to him. Yet Dispenza believed in his body's ability to heal itself, and so he refused conventional medical treatment and discharged himself from hospital, and went to stay with friends. He spent weeks lying face down, and worked on focusing his energies to support the body's natural resources to heal.

Each day, for two hours, twice a day, Dispenza did inner work and focused his intentions on imagining a process of healing in his spine. It took him six weeks to break through the frequently occurring negative and intrusive thoughts that constantly interrupted his visualisations. However, his persistence paid off, and gradually he was able to train himself to enter into an effortless presence in terms of focusing his mind and body. Worrying thoughts no longer distracted him, as he entered into a more peaceful and silent space, living in the present. As he steadied his healing vision he noticed more joyful feelings, which in turn inspired him and brought greater conviction to what he was doing. He then started to extend his vision by imagining enjoyable social events with friends in the future. It dawned on him that fate and destiny are ours to create through our thoughts and feelings. He started to feel blessed. After nine weeks and a few days, he stood up and walked. This is such an inspiring story, and it points to deep (unconscious) intelligence at work in body, mind and spirit, which is activated by the imagination. Our work is to have the courage to acknowledge this incredible resource, and then, like Joe Dispenza, bring its potential for wholeness to the fore. In such examples, the mystery of healing is like an alchemical process, where transformation happens. Such events cannot be explained by the facts associated with rational science. In fact, it opens up a wider view of reality, where the power and potential of placebos bring an imaginative connection to the mystery of the imaginal realm.

In my practice as a therapist and coach I have witnessed the healing power of the imagination when working with people's physical and psychological symptoms. For example, I have used a method developed by Arny Mindell, where people are invited to use their imaginations and personify their difficulties as a *symptom maker* (e.g. turning the symptom into a character). I have seen first hand how radical processes of healing happen (some immediate, and some over a period of time) when the symptom maker is embodied and enacted, which leads to unexpected (and sometimes unconventional) wisdom and insights. Mindell teaches people to follow the moment-by-moment multi-channelled signals linked to the unfolding process. Following the information flow between consensus reality and the signals from the dreaming requires the discipline of a scientist, coupled to the mind of a shaman or mystic.

There have always been threads of mysticism woven into the psyche of the Western world, for example in the alchemical and romantic traditions. But,religious intolerance led to the persecution of mainly women psychics and healers, who were often burnt alive in what can only be described as an obsessive and irrational hunt for witches. Later, religious power waned due to the steady rise of scientific progress (following the Western Enlightenment in the 17th century and later on during the Industrial Revolution). However, the purge of mysticism and the imaginal realm continued in more subtle ways through the dogmatic worldview of scientism, where sustained accusations of superstition have attempted to inhibit explorations of alternative ways of knowing. In the modern world, mainstream scientific thinking continues to exert a powerful influence on modern consciousness, as exemplified in the story of Carl Jung, a well-respected psychiatrist and scholar. He published ground-breaking work detailing his deep and dynamic approach to working with the psyche. However, it was Jung's own personal explorations, recorded in his *Red Book*, that laid the foundations for his innovative ideas and theoretical developments. In essence, Jung's published scientific works were being fed by his personal healing encounters with the unconscious, where he undertook active and imaginative journeys into the depths of his own psyche. In this way, Jung's work was an important breakthrough, which offered a radical approach to understanding a transpersonal connection to life. Yet he was marginalised by mainstream science, despite the efficacy of his healing method for countless people who were retrieving their souls in an increasingly mechanistic world.

Jung married the mystical, mythical and dreaming levels of the collective unconsciousness and formulated these into a rational and scientific understanding of human development and wholeness. It is for this reason that Jung is an important figure in the modern world, and a good example of someone who was able to enter the dark and irrational world (the unconscious) to find the pearls of wisdom that can nourish our journeys into wholeness. Jung occupied a role in the collective that had been lying dormant in the Western psyche for many years, namely the role of the Iatromantis, the priestly-healer in the natural sense of the word. Jung was a prophet of our times, a psychiatrist of the soul who gave voice to the deeper layers of meaning and healing in the psyche. The fairy story of cobbler and the elves illustrates the insights that are incubated and brought forth in our unconscious processes. In the story, the cobbler was struggling in his business, but after he went to sleep one night a group of elves set to work making shoes and upon awakening the cobbler discovered the well-crafted footwear left by these industrious spirits.[30] Such is the way that the wisdom of the unconscious works when the rational mind is not in a dominant role.

Jung was a modern shaman who ventured to the depths of his soul and returned with a method of working that enabled humanity to engage with the symbols, signs and symptoms from the unconscious that had been long neglected, overridden, lost, or obscured in the modern world of reason, but which had always been calling to us in our dreams and visions. Jung died in 1961, and his *Red Book* was published 50 years after his death in 2009. It is only now that we can fully appreciate the extent of his inner work. Jung pioneered an experiential method, which offered Western philosophy and science the chance to reclaim the mystical and spiritual. He recognised the recurrence of archetypal symbols that arise from the depths of the collective unconscious, which we encounter in dreams, fairy tales and myths. And he enabled us to understand that these dreamlike occurrences not only come from the unconscious, they also evoke it.[31] Many years ago when I was a psychotherapy student I recall hearing the Grimm's folk tale called *The Spirit in the Bottle* (see Arny Mindell's *Dreambody*). It is a very poignant story dealing with the raw energy and potentials unleashed when working with the unconscious and the spirit world. The story serves as a wonderful illustration of how we can approach the complexities of the symbolic world of the psyche, and how such journeys can profit us in terms of healing and wholeness. Here's how I tell the story.

The bottled-up spirit

The story begins with the son of a woodcutter, who was attending school and had aspirations to become a medical doctor, but with hardly any money to support his studies, he is forced to abandon his education and return home to help his father in the woods in order to build up his funds. One day, after toiling long and hard in the forest, the young man stops for a break and decides to take a leisurely stroll through the dense canopy of trees, whereupon he comes face to face with a huge old oak tree. Whilst marvelling at the majestic tree, he hears a cry coming from its base, "Help, get me out of here – get me out". As the young man moves closer, the voice gets louder, "Let me out – let me out". He located the spot where the voice was coming from and started to clear the undergrowth, whereupon he came across a tightly sealed glass bottle wedged in the roots of the mighty oak. The young man was perplexed: how could a voice come from within the bottle? Then, out of curiosity, he opened the bottle, and with great force a spirit flew out and grew in stature, quickly becoming half the size of the oak tree. The spirit then announced that he was Mercury, the messenger of the gods. Mercury was furious at having been cooped up in a tiny bottle for such a long time, and said to the young man that whoever releases Mercury must die. The young man, who was very bright and quick-witted, said to Mercury, "How can I be sure that you are the voice I heard coming from the bottle? Look at the size of you, compared to this small vessel." Mercury was incredulous at this unexpected challenge to his identity, and in a fit of anger re-entered the bottle to prove his authenticity. Then, quick as a flash, the young man replaced the top and sealed the bottle once again. Mercury realised he had been duped and took a different approach to negotiating his release by offering a reward to the young man if he let him out of the bottle. After agreeing terms with the aspiring young doctor, Mercury was once again released from the bottle and he gave the young man a piece of cloth with instructions on how to use it. "If you place one end of the cloth onto a wound it will heal, and if you place the other end of the cloth onto metal it will turn into silver." The young man tested the cloth on his axe, and sure enough it turned into silver, which he sold for a lot of money, enabling him to resume his studies. Not only was he able to take care of his elderly father, but also the cloth helped him to become a prolific healer.

It is interesting that the human-spirit encounter takes place at the root of an ancient oak tree. Jung[32] compared the process of individuation to the acorn that grows into an oak, while Michael Meade[33] also speaks about the mighty

European oaks (which were considered sacred trees) as a perfect symbol for the sacred journey of transformation and the seeding of our human potential. In the story, the forest is a metaphor for the unconscious, where it is easy to get lost and disorientated. Here, the spirit Mercury has been bottled up for a long time, symbolising our neglected relationship to the unconscious. This story is a powerful reminder that we need to be prepared when working with the unconscious. Indeed, it highlights the danger of letting the *genie out of the bottle* too soon and finding ourselves in a situation that is out of control. Essentially, the story is about cultivating a wise relationship to unconscious forces and the imaginal realm.

Carl Jung championed an imaginative approach to the psyche as a whole, and he encouraged his clients to start a dialogue between the ego and the unconscious. In the story, the young man had to think quickly in order to contain what was potentially a life-threatening force. It was only when Mercury was back in the bottle that an effective dialogue could be established, one that was not overwhelming to the young man's ego. Once a productive relationship was established with the spirit, the young man was then granted resources that supported his vocation in life. The beneficial two-way relationship led to an effective process of integration, and allowed Mercury to do his work: communicating, initiating and activating the young man's full potential. In the story, Mercury gives a cloth to the young man with a dual purpose: first, it can turn ordinary metal into silver, which illustrates the alchemical process at work – quicksilver (another name for Mercury) is always an active agent in the process of transformation of base metals into precious metals. It also symbolises the *Magnus Opus*, or the Great Work, which activates our unmet potential to produce an awakened process of consciousness transformation. Second, the healing cloth radically alters the young man's life path, allowing him to pursue his vocation and enter into a path of service to help others. The story reveals the dual process of doing both inner work and outer work if we are serious about transforming our life path, in order that we may grow. Working with the forces in the unconscious is often like a deathwalk (as noted by Arny Mindell), where our habitual and redundant patterns die, and we are reborn through the engagement of our human potential (Jung called this individuation, or becoming whole). The *Spirit in the Bottle* is all about managing transformative potential, where we are cautioned to work wisely when connecting with the imaginal realm, which cannot be mediated by ego-consciousness alone. It is why the transformational process is deemed alchemical, and all those who release Mercury must die (as in transform).

The symbolism in *The Spirit in the Bottle* provides helpful insights about how to engage more deeply with the psyche. In my career I have worked as a professional therapist, university lecturer and holistic coach, and whilst I have always taken an overarching rational approach in my relationship to working with people, doing my best to support their human potential, I can think of countless examples where I have entered into seemingly irrational processes, which have yielded unexpected insights, creative responses, and new avenues of exploration. I will be sharing some of these stories in this book. It is important to recognise that when working with the imaginal realm the process will invariably involve the irrational, yet I can safely say that I would not have witnessed such profound insights and transformations in the people I have worked with had we not explored the unconventional wisdom found in their dreams, visions and musings. The point I am making is, when we engage the imaginal realm, terms such as *rational* and *irrational* are not only meaningless, they are irrelevant. The imagination does not make such distinctions. Indeed, it could be said that the imaginal realm is our greatest ally, that is, if we learn to trust the deeper processes at work, we may discover innovative solutions to personal, collective and global problems. Trusting in the power of the unconscious helps us to connect with our lived potential as Albert Einstein remarked, reading fairy tales to children is one way to make them brilliant.[34] What he meant was, if we feed children's imaginations, then creativity is alive in them and they are alive to creativity. It is my belief that we never lose the ability to activate our imaginations and connections to the imaginal realm.

As a species we are capable of the most profound feats of endeavour, endurance and enterprise. But, of course the opposite is also true, and currently many of the worst human traits are coming to the fore, such as greed, waste and cruelty. Whether we like it or not, humanity is on a collective odyssey, where we have an opportunity to face and resolve the global crisis before us. The question is, will it be a voyage of shared awakening, or collective destruction? In the ancient world our ancestors had a closer relationship with the natural world, which they saw as animated and spirited. This is why myths and fairy stories have reverberated throughout time: they reflect our symbolic connection to forces in the natural world that resonate with deeper connections and awakenings in life, as do our dreams. In the vignette below a woman recovering from a life-threatening illness worked with me on a dream that indicated a deepening of her healing journey. It is interesting that she encountered a giant snake, which, as stated previously, is a collective symbol for prophecy, healing and transformation.

_____ The snake and the underworld _____

In the dream the woman, accompanied by her husband, was invited to a big glamorous party in a luxurious hotel in Sydney (Australia), which was also attended by some of her old friends. Two hotel staff appeared (male and female), who then took the woman and her husband to their room, but rather than going to the luxurious bedrooms where all the other guests were staying, the staff led them down a deep, dark tunnel, which was directly under the hotel, and where the rooms were still under construction. The tunnel leading to their half finished bedroom was sloped with a very steep downward gradient and low ceiling, which made it very difficult to walk. The tunnel was dark, damp, narrow and claustrophobic. In addition the ground was littered with loose rubble and stones, which made the footing very unstable and they slipped and stumbled.

Suddenly, without any warning, the woman saw a huge snake appear in the dream, sliding powerfully along the floor in front of them. She said the group froze and she whispered, "What do we do?" Then quick as a flash the snake reared up and sunk its fangs into her forearm, where it hung on and gripped tightly with its teeth. She tried to pull the snake off, but it would not let go. Then she remembered a technique, which she had learnt years ago, connected to a martial arts move that recommended pushing into a grip rather than pulling away from it. In the dream the technique worked and the snake let go and quickly disappeared. The group continued to walk towards the accommodation, and the dreamer noticed a variety of small exits leading off the main tunnel. Eventually the couple arrived at the turning that led to their bedroom. The woman said the tunnels were like a maze, and she asked the staff how she and her husband would be able to find their way back to their room after the party later in the evening. One of the members of staff pointed to a drip coming from the roof of the tunnel, which was leaking in the corner, and suggested that this could act as a signpost. They then entered their bedroom and were surprised to find that it was not even finished, and that it was a shared space with other beds, like a dormitory. It was very uncomfortable, cold, dark and damp.

I asked the woman about her associations with Sydney, and she spoke about having lived in the city for one year when she was 26 years old. She spoke about how the city symbolises an easy-going life, good times, sunshine, fun, and glamour. She described her time living there as carefree, and it was a time when she was confident, independent, and sociable. This was in contrast to the years following her illness, when she endured intensive medical treatment and has been on a path of recovery ever since. I then asked about her associations with the snake. She said that when she saw the snake in the dream she felt a sense of fear, panic, and horror because the serpent represented a very real threat and could seriously harm her in some way. She spoke about the moment in the dream when she froze and didn't know what to do. The conversation reminded her of actual snakes in Australia, which can be poisonous and often deadly. But she was proud of the way she had acted decisively and powerfully in the dream to get out of a difficult situation. She went on to say that once the snake had let go of her, she felt fine and was not overly concerned that she may have been poisoned. We spoke about how the snake is a symbol of healing in the Apollonian and Asklepian traditions of Ancient Greece, and how these healing cults have powerful mythic connections to the serpent's power, which represents the sacred. The serpent is seen as a symbol of transformation, where shedding of the skin represents renewal, rejuvenation and recovery. Jungian analyst Jean Shinoda Bolen[35] also points out that the snake is a symbol of feminine power and when it appears in dreams it is an opportunity to reclaim that power.

Whilst listening to the dream, I also had an instinctual feel that the drip, which was used to signpost the direction to her hotel room, may have been significant. I asked the woman about her associations with the constant dripping coming from the roof. I suggested that she actively entered into the quality of the dripping, and she allowed herself to go deeply into the experience. At first she thought the drip was merely a consequence of the construction work, and typical of what *one* might find in a dark, dank tunnel. However, as she went further into her direct experience of the drip, she found that she was becoming at one with each droplet, and she described it as like being in a hypnotic state. She said there was an ancient feel to the experience, as if it had always been there and always would be there. As she went further into the quality of the dripping experience she noticed that it was very centring, and she felt like it was acting as a guide, which connected her awareness to a cellular level, as if each drip was reverberating throughout every cell in her body. At the end of the session she looked at peace and said that it was a calming and meditative experience.

This woman had undergone extensive medical and scientific treatment to save her life, but the dream shows us that the process of healing and wholeness was continuing to happen. We could say that her healing process is a blend of rational influences (medical science) and irrational influences (dreams). Dreams can be our most faithful guides if we learn how to listen and interact with them. It never ceases to surprise me when I come across dreams that have an obvious archetypal connection. This happened when I read the excellent book by Jungian analyst, Veronica Goodchild,[36] who shares one of her own dreams about serpent initiation. Goodchild's snake dream is detailed and deep; however, I will share a précis of the dream to illustrate some of the parallels with the dream of my client above. Goodchild encounters two giant snakes blocking her exit at each end of a corridor, which forces her to enter a room that has a pool with snakes. She finds herself in the pool and one of the snakes enters her mouth, and moves down to her stomach. The initiatory experience brings a sacred connection to the serpent, and also a sense of aliveness at a cellular level. The snakes become her allies and in the dream she is told to know the meaning of the *unknown*, and that the time is right for *snake initiation*. As we shall see in the next chapter, this may well be a prophetic dream for the collective, as well as being personally meaningful for the dreamer.

Our Western culture has ignored an important dimension of wisdom, knowledge and healing available in dreams, which is lost to us if we only favour a rational approach to life and living. The anti-superstitious attitudes found in scientism have resulted in a narrow appreciation of consciousness. For example, Robert Moss[37] explains that whilst neuroscience is naturally focused on understanding neural networks in the brain, its reductive methods cannot account for the *mystery of dreaming* and our connection to the collective unconscious and the imaginal realm, which would be akin to taking a television set apart in the hope of finding out how programmes are made and transmitted. Indigenous wisdom reveals a sophisticated understanding of the role and function of dreams, where interconnections occur in a dynamic, alive and intelligent universe. Reductionism has no way of responding to life as a whole, and it is a holistic understanding that is important for the well-being of people and planet at this time.

Reconnecting with depth

Our dissociated and one-dimensional ways of living have caused a warming planet, rapid species extinction, as well as acidification of the oceans, desertification of the land, and erosion of fresh water aquifers worldwide, overpopulation, as well as health and economic inequalities. The stakes are high. Humanity's relationship to the natural world, including the psyche, needs to be radically revised if we are to break out of the claustrophobic and deadening impasses created by our consumer-based lifestyles, which Theodore Roszak[38] calls the *technocracy*. Roszak[38] believes humanity is capable of connecting to a *cosmic vocation*, one that encourages a proper relationship towards nature, which brings forth a radical shift in our understanding of life. If we recall the fairy tale, *The Spirit in the Bottle*, Mercury is a sacred messenger, a trickster-like figure who accompanies processes of transformational change in alchemy. The story of the *Genie* acts as a powerful metaphor for how we can re-imagine our vocational potential, through inner work and outer work. The story reveals how the young man is motivated to serve (healing), which means going deep within to discover our talents and gifts to help each other, other species, and the world. Yet, engaging our human potential takes effort, motivation, commitment and courage. My own experience has shown me that once we embrace a path of transformation, we will encounter opportunities and challenges, but we also discover that we are capable of wholeness and living more holistically. It is through our relationship to the imaginal realm that our actions are directed in the service of the greater good, expressing our sacred vocation.

Connecting to a sacred vocation requires us to explore our human potentials. There are already organisations across the world that honour this work: for example the Institute for Noetic Sciences, Findhorn Foundation, Schumacher College, Naropa University, Deep Democracy Institute, and the Californian Institute of Integral Studies, the Institute of Heart Math, as well as other groups of pioneering researchers, such as the Scientific and Medical Network. But, generally, our social institutions are woefully unprepared to address the question of living in wholeness. Our Western political manifestos, educational, health and social services, local governments and places of work are locked in a self-serving *technocracy*. The first step for any social institution interested in serving the greater good is to offer support for people to discover and express their psycho-social-spiritual potential, and help them connect with a vision that co-creates a better world for people, other species and nature as a whole. Essentially, a creative response to the planetary crisis is needed, one that involves the engagement of the imagination as an integral part of the transformative process.[39] Renewing our understanding of myth can nourish our sense of vocation and empower us to acknowledge our connection to the universe.[40] We can begin a process of transformation by doing something about injustices that are committed against people, animals and the natural world, as well as tackling inequality and poverty by living modestly and sharing resources. This is a tangible way of being connected to the creation of a more compassionate and loving world.

In my book, *The Unselfish Spirit,* I wrote about the embodied, vocational and imaginative energies that live through us, in our everyday actions, as an occupational myth. This is where our deepest potential for wholeness finds transformative expression, and embraces the challenge of joining with others to co-create an improved future. But, as Larry Dossey[41] says, humanity will need to develop a fuller understanding of consciousness to appreciate our connection to the unity, or *One Mind,* of which we are all a part. Furthermore, it will take real fortitude and resilience to work through some of the dualistic binds that underpin our current conception of life, such as the tensions between our personal egos and our capacity for Self-realisation (wholeness). A mythic imagination is required if we wish to relate effectively to the imaginal realm and engage in what William Irwin Thompson[42] refers to as immersion in a process of changed *perception* and *participation.* This reflects a world where our personal boundaries become permeable to the subtle realm. This is described very clearly in the work of Stephen Buhner[43] who notes how our species' deep connection to a *living reality* is alive and brimming with intelligence. For example, in the plant world, science is starting to identify the complex and intelligent networks that are highly sophisticated and which function in profoundly interconnected ways.[43] But science focuses on gathering factual knowledge and seeks to explain the phenomenal world, which is very different from the experiential knowledge gained by entering the imaginal realm. It is here that our *rational ways of knowing* could be complemented by the wisdom (*Sophia*) of intuitive ways of knowing. It is the realm of the sacred feminine, which inspires our efforts to initiate and activate the Transformocene Age.

Exercise: The tree of your life

- Imagine your psycho-spiritual growth represented as a tree.

- What sort of tree comes to mind?

- Imagine this tree planted deeply in your soul and connected to your subtle body.
    - Feel the roots deep and anchored within you (and in the Earth).
    - Feel the trunk, firm and flexible.
    - Feel the branches growing and spreading out.

- Meditate on the sap rising slowly and strongly in your tree.

- Feel the 'life force' in your tree flourishing.

- Notice how your tree helps you to connect with nature, inwardly and outwardly.

- Feel a sense of resilience connected to your tree as it grows steadily.

The serpent of 'her' knowing is chthonic wisdom. Her hollow, shedded skin lies on the Earth as a ghostly reminder of the transformation we ignore. This translucent symbol of metamorphosis haunts the modern imagination.

CHAPTER THREE

The Sacred Feminine

Overview

In this chapter I explore the connections to deeper ways of knowing, which are allied to the tradition of the sacred feminine, where we are brought into a more intimate relationship with a living mystery. The knowledge and wisdom linked to the sacred feminine was oppressed and marginalised by a patriarchal worldview that resulted in the hyper-rational mindset of today. In this time of global crisis, humanity is being confronted with the need to heal the wounds we have inflicted on one another, other species and the natural world. I discuss how cultivating a relationship to the Earth, as Gaia, brings us into connection with life as a sacred mystery. Such a shift is based on a soulful relationship to life, where we are open to the *anima mundi* (soul of the world), and learn from nature in similar ways to indigenous people. I discuss how the sacred feminine opens us up to the imaginal realm, through dreams, intuitions and synchronicities, and facilitates a process of creative living and unfolding. In a time of collective renewal, humanity can be revitalised through a deeper connection to life as a mystery, which guides the hearts, minds and souls of humanity to bring forth the Transformocene.

The light of wisdom in depth and darkness

As long ago as 1976, Ruth Nanada Ashen[1] was writing about the impact of our destructive behaviours in the world. She spoke about a new era of evolution that was unfolding, requiring the development of wisdom to enable our collective flourishing. If ever we needed a revitalised philosophy (one that is not overly dominated by a reason and explanation), it is now. Our ways of knowing must include feelings, intuition, and direct experience, to align us more soulfully with life as a whole. Such a shift requires a closer relationship with the sacred feminine, where our transformative journey into wholeness will involve encountering polarities, such as yin-yang; feminine-masculine; soul-spirit; and good-evil, etc. It is no surprise that there is an upsurge of interest in the wisdom of the sacred feminine at this time in history, particularly as it brings us into a deeper and more holistic relationship with nature. William Irwin Thompson[2] says that a new planetary culture requires a worldview that is based on a *knowing* relationship to the Earth, or *Gaia*.

More recently, Thompson[3] has elaborated on this point, saying that a *new enlightenment* is emerging, connected to female emancipation and embodied ways of knowing. Of course, this new enlightenment will undoubtedly highlight dark and shady recesses that have hitherto been ignored in a world fixated on illumination and hyper-rationalism. In discovering what we have lost, each of us, women and men, will undoubtedly experience grief and alienation, which is the shadow side of our modern culture's fixation on success and achievement, not to mention the tragedy of ignoring ecological destruction. We desperately need a counterbalance to the masculine and patriarchal structures that have dominated the world and led to destructive imbalances. Mary Harrell[4] says that we meet and engage the feminine through intuition, the imaginal, and the unconscious. Harrell speaks about the collective repression of feminine consciousness, which is now breaking through and bringing forth renewed connections to the imaginal realm. The following vignette is a touching story of a woman who was feeling grief for her personal loss in life and also for the state of the world.

_____ **The living flame** _____

I did some coaching sessions with a woman after a succession of lifeevents had left her feeling stuck. She was a retired health professional and it transpired that she had never fully planned for her retirement. During her retired years she had cared for her brother who had been very ill, and one day she had found him dead at home. It was a great loss as they were very close, and it brought home her feelings of isolation, particularly as her brother had been her last living relative. It transpired that she had many acquaintances in her life, but no longer anyone she could call a close friend. In addition she spoke about a lack of purpose in her life. When she arrived for her first coaching session with me we identified that she was experiencing a deep sense of loss, fear, anxiety, and anger, especially in relation to feeling invisible when around people. But it transpired that she was able to make lively connections with children, and very much enjoyed their company. She said she was often quite critical of people, and feels very angry about the state of the world and the plight of the planet.

We started our work in the cold winter months and explored how the woman's fear and anger were impacting on her everyday engagement in activities of daily living. In the first session we explored these emotions as well as the woman's desire for peace. As she spoke about these two sides of her experience, the wood-burner in my room suddenly made a series of five mini-explosions in fairly quick succession (this would be a rare occurrence if it happened only once). I had an intuition that the fire bursting back into life repeatedly was symbolic of the woman's life energy, and we explored the meaning of the spluttering wood-burner. She became choked-up and it brought tears to her eyes, and she said: "I want to be a Shaman". Many years ago she had taken a deep interest in Pacific Shamanism. The bellowing fire was a meaningful coincidence (synchronicity), which held possibilities inspiring a new connection to her life energies, which were trying to burst back into life.

Over the next few sessions the aim of the coaching work was to help the woman explore her *visionary energies* further, to find a way of *igniting* her motivation and find greater purpose in her life. However, it was apparent from the beginning that her negative self-criticism was persistent and 'annihilating'. We found out that her deepest wish was to cultivate self-love and renew her sense of identity. Over the weeks, the automatic barrage of negative and destructive thoughts continued relentlessly, but the coaching sessions appeared to provide some respite and temporary relief. It gave her some hope that her situation was amenable to change. Gradually she was able to develop a deeper sense of trust in her process and eventually we were able to access the inner saboteur (critic). It was an oppressive presence, like a heavy cloak (which she took off and hung up), yet the woman recognised that there were times when this could be helpful, for example, when she needed to be challenging or in difficult situations. She also started exploring the work of Carl Jung and found information about the shadow and Pacific Shamanism, which she found helpful. She said understanding the shadow, "is about learning and accepting that the 'ups and downs' are OK – they are not out to destroy me, but are knocking at my metaphorical 'door' to awaken me to the light and learning about the previously hidden and feared darkness".

The metaphorical journey into the woman's *visionary energies* continued, and in one of our sessions we did some work outside in nature, using a method developed by Arny Mindell[5] called the *vector walk* (the Latin for 'vector' is *vectus*, meaning 'carrier'). In the natural environment she had a strong connection to a tree, which was a meaningful symbol for her. Next to the tree were three dark containers full of composting material, and somehow she had a realisation that her growth (tree) needed to be nourished by the transformed garbage (compost). This enabled her to make a tangible connection to the critic-shadow work we were doing, and she began to appreciate how these difficulties were also part of her growth. The tree became an important symbol, especially in the way it can be flexible and able to withstand storms. She reasoned that whilst some branches will naturally fall off, the tree could respond by sending its roots deeper and deeper into the Earth, which then nourishes the new growth. This was a potent symbolic representation of her own transformation, for like the tree, she may have appeared broken at times, but as she recounted, "That does not matter, because the 'true' me is hidden in the depths of the Earth, out of sight but infinitely stronger!" Witnessing my client's connection to her tree, I was reminded of the shamanic *world-tree*, which symbolically represents different levels of reality: the underworld, the material world and the upper world. As we concluded the session we somehow veered into a discussion about the transformational nature of Greek myths and she said, "The myth that seems to sum up my life is Medusa." This seemed an appropriate myth, as Medusa is a much-maligned figure, and yet her origins are connected to a powerful goddess, with great powers of creation and destruction.

My client took a courageous and imaginative journey into understanding the destructive and creative forces of the dark goddess. Such honest encounters are crucial for evolving our consciousness in terms of who we are and what we do in life. We can see in the vignette that polarities of dark-light or destruction-creation are processes that need to be engaged with to open up the prism of awareness. Such deeper layers of reflection help us understand the visionary energies at work within us, and the spectrum of opportunities and alternative paths of action.

The case vignette above illustrates the power of the imaginal, and how our visionary energies connect with transformative processes. This is particularly evident in my client's casual reference to feeling identified with Medusa in one of our conversations. Medusa has links to North African shrines, which personified female mysteries, particularly death and renewal.[6] Although maligned by the ancient Greeks, Medusa is a powerful medium for transformation and healing.[7] The Hellenic representation of Medusa as a monstrous aspect of the feminine to be confronted and destroyed is a deeply political myth, revealing the threat posed by the wild and dark aspects of the Goddess to society dominated for centuries by patriarchal attitudes. The Gorgon masks (with unblinking gaze) worn by priestesses of Medusa signified the need to protect the mysteries of the sacred feminine[6] and Medusa's head of snakes represents her sacred wisdom.[8] The eventual beheading of Medusa by Perseus, who in the Hellenic myth was aided by Athena (the wise and rational personification of Greek feminine power) led to the demise of the shrines to Medusa, and it reflected a further shift towards patriarchal power and the continued undermining of the mysteries associated with the sacred feminine. When Perseus decapitated Medusa the blood that poured out of the left vein in her neck was poisonous and deadly, whereas the blood from the right vein was life-giving and healing. In an ironic twist, recognising her destructive and creative potential, the blood of Medusa was given to Asklepios, the god of healing[9] and his ancient symbol of medicine, a serpent coiled around a staff, is still used today (as discussed in the previous chapter).

Serpent rising

Anne Baring and Jules Cashford[10] chronicle the sacred feminine from the early representations of the goddess found in Upper Paleolithic carvings, made around 20,000 BC, through to modern shrines, such as those dedicated to the Virgin Mary. Interestingly, Baring and Cashford reveal that the serpent was a powerful symbol associated with the goddess from ancient times, either in literal snake form or as a spiral, and they cite representations of a snake goddess existing from Neolithic times 4500 BC, as well as the Minoan goddess at Knossos temple on Crete 1600 BC, who is depicted holding aloft a snake in each hand. The serpent is acknowledged as a totem of feminine power[8] and in the ancient world different incarnations of the great goddess presided over rites of initiation, healing, revelation or prophecy. She is found across all the great spiritual and mythical traditions, for example as Isis, Hera and Kali etc. We must not forget that the sacred feminine also works with the sacred masculine to awaken a consciousness of wholeness (as discussed in Chapter Two). In the Hindu system of tantric yoga the latent Kundalini Shakti energy (located near the base of the spine), symbolised as a coiled serpent, travels up the body (parallel with the spine) and unites with the sacred masculine energy or *Shiva* at the crown of the head.[11] Interestingly, Sufi scholar Henry Corbin[12] speaks about the *creative feminine*, and how mystical visions and revelations arrive through sacred contemplation, where the *eternal feminine* is a divine and creative force.

The sacred feminine and the serpent are familiar motifs in antiquity, where the snake is not only a companion,[13] it also represents the dynamic forces of life-death, regeneration-renewal and healing-restoration. Yet, a Judeo-Christian myth appears to run contrary to our emerging vision of the divine feminine, as told in the story of Adam and Eve. I will focus on the part of the myth that informs our discussion, where a serpent in the Garden of Eden suggests to Eve that she eats fruit from the tree of knowledge of good and evil, which results in the expulsion of Adam and Eve from paradise. This patriarchal myth claims that Eve was duped by the Devil (as a serpent) and thereby contributed to the downfall of humanity. Yet Kelly[14] reveals that grammatical differences informed the translation between the Hebrew Bible figure of Satan, as adversary, and the Greek *diabolis* (devil). Consequently, the myth of Adam, Eve and the serpent in the Garden of Eden appears to have been interpreted to fit in with the New Testament personification of the Devil. However, according to Kelly[14] there is no mention of the Devil in the Book of Genesis. In fact, the Old Testament reveals an interesting relationship between God (*Yahweh*) and Satan in the story of Job. Satan is sanctioned by God to test his faithful servant (Job), which illustrates how the *adversary* is working for God.[15] In addition, if we are led to believe the snake was bad, we should also ask why Moses carried a staff that could turn into a serpent and heal snakebites.[16] This healing-serpent connection has much in common with the tradition of Asklepios (discussed in Chapter Two).

Interestingly, Elaine Pagels[17] cites the early Christian Gnostic author who wrote the *Testimony of Truth*, which discussed the myth of Adam and Eve from the perspective of the snake, who is revealed as a divine teacher, and wanted to help the couple be more conscious of life. This is a viewpoint that chimes with the work of Anne Baring and Jules Cashford[10] who contextualise the myth of Adam and Eve as a story of humanity's initiation into consciousness. Baring and Cashford reflect on the actions of Eve, who instigates a divine awakening connected to curiosity, instinct, intuition and wisdom. Baring and Cashford's analysis coheres neatly with Pagels'[17] study, which points out that in the 2nd century AD, the story of Adam and Eve was commonly understood to illustrate themes of moral freedom, responsibility, and *self-mastery*, which are exercised through life choices made, actions taken, and how experiences of good-evil are managed. At its root the myth appears to be underlining the importance of human free will, and how we determine our fate and destiny as conscious beings. Joseph Campbell[18] points out that Eden is a metaphor for unity, inclusive of masculine-feminine and good-evil etc. From this perspective our *human journey* starts from a place of integration

(Eden), which means, if we are wise, we would place the sacrament of unity and wholeness at the centre of all that we do in our pilgrimage in our Earthly lives.

According to Pagels[17] it was St Augustine in the 4th century AD who doubted humanity's capacity for self-governance, equating Adam and Eve's behaviour with original sin. Essentially, he believed people could not be trusted to make wise choices (free will). This idea became part of Orthodox Church thinking and is a typical example of how paternalistic beliefs were propagated in our Western spiritual traditions. Like all myths, the story of Adam and Eve is not literal.[19] If we consider the myth in its symbolic form, perhaps Eve (as feminine consciousness) was awoken to the human capacity to exercise free will (hitherto dormant in the psyche). Eating the 'forbidden fruit' initiated a new experience of self-knowledge allowing Adam and Eve to see their naked bodies for the first time (embodied consciousness). In this telling of the story, the serpent initiates transformation.

In her Magnus Opus (Great Work), Jungian analyst Anne Baring[20] speaks about a dream that prompted her to resume her writing on the sacred feminine, which she had started some 20 years previously. She dreamt of taking a walk with her grandmother and friends, when she suddenly became aware that to her right was a resplendent and luminous winged serpent, which had a radiant red underbelly and a golden top half. Baring says in the dream she voiced her concerns in case the snake bit anyone, and they carefully avoided the beautiful creature as they walked on. But the serpent soon reappeared (again on the right side), only this time it moved towards Baring and eventually bit her at the base of the thumb on the right hand. A few days later she made a connection between the *right* side, which had popped up three times in the dream, and she took this as a sign that she should *write*. The book that she eventually wrote, *The Dream of the Cosmos*, bears testimony to the need for a reintegration of the sacred feminine in the world. In the dream the serpent is viewed as *awesome* and is treated with great respect, which leads Baring to make a meaningful connection to the imaginal realm. The dream was a call from the deep, asking her to bring forth her considerable knowledge and wisdom about the sacred feminine in the context of our troubled world today.

Anne Baring's interpretation of serpent energy is very different from the one taken by US preacher George Went Hensley. In 1909 Hensley was inspired to take the word of Jesus literally to *take up serpents*. In the middle of a sermon, Hensley produced a fully-grown rattlesnake and took hold of it, presumably to make a point that the snake (as the Devil) need not be feared. The practice of holding live rattlesnakes in church services caught on, yet tragically this literal interpretation of the words of Jesus has caused around 120 people to die of snakebites (including Hensley) between 1909 and 2005.[15] Of course, the preferred teaching method of Jesus was parables, which are stories and metaphors. If we recall, Jesus quite categorically implored people to be *wise as serpents*. Perhaps what he meant by *taking up serpents* was to become wiser, which could be a symbolic and archetypal representation of *wisdom*. For example, the symbolic meaning of the ancient Minoan snake goddess (Crete) who holds aloft a serpent in each hand is not known, yet it suggests the need for *wise handling* of powerful and regenerative forces, which would not be out of place in this discussion. A serpentine connection to the sacred feminine symbolically formulates a wise relationship with the imaginal realm in the psyche, as the following vignette reveals.

Serpent of transformation

Publisher and eco-activist Maddy Harland recounted an experience that she had a few years ago when she was in Thailand. She was part of an international group (formed in Findhorn), where she was helping to develop an Ecovillage Design Education course. These courses have now spread throughout the world under the auspices of Gaia Education. Maddy speaks about an experience on that trip that had a profound and lasting impact on her: "We were staying in an ashram North of Bangkok in the countryside, far away from city life. The ashram had designated spirit houses, and one day I ventured into one, but I had a strong feeling that I must leave the building." Maddy spoke about sensing an energy presence that was not welcoming, and she intuitively knew that it was because she had not been initiated into the medicine of the spirit houses; she had not been invited. She left immediately.

The accommodation in the ashram was typically a small hut on stilts accessed by a ladder, because poisonous snakes are prevalent in this land. However, a snake did make its way into her hut one night, via her dreams. She recalls falling asleep in complete darkness and dreamt a huge snake, which towered over her. The giant serpent reared up revealing its large deadly fangs. Maddy says: "I knew that it was omnipotent and that I was tiny and helpless beneath it. The snake wasn't there to bite me; it was there to devour me, to swallow me up." The dream chimes with the process of shamanic initiation, which involves death-rebirth. In this way, the serpent is a force for regeneration and renewal, representing an induction into the mysteries of the sacred feminine, as embodied experience. In the dream Maddy realised she had no choice in the matter, but her sense of everyday identity recognised the power of this ominous experience. She goes on to say: "I screamed out in mortal fear as the giant serpent lunged down to consume me (apparently my neighbour heard my distress!). I knew that all I could do was surrender as I faced my impending death." In the dream, Maddy understood the futility of resisting the power of this numinous encounter. She knew that she must surrender and meet her fate. The dream catalysed a deep reflection about whether she had led a good life, and made a contribution to the lives of others and the world (life review). She had a sense of the snake as an arbitrator of karma. There was nothing she could do. No means of recompense or alleviation. Just surrender.

She woke up in pitch darkness, sweating and surprised to find that she was still alive. The next day she mentioned the dream to one of the Thai hosts linked to her group. He said it was tremendously fortuitous to meet the Naga in a dream, but he did not tell her what the dream meant. Nor did he share with her the teachings of the Naga in Thailand. The dream had such a powerful impact on Maddy and it has remained an important thread between her 'being' and the imaginal realm ever since. Jung would have appreciated that this is an example of a Big Dream, which is connected to initiation and individuation. Once again, it is more than coincidental that a woman is inducted into the mysteries of the imaginal realm, via a serpent. But this vignette reveals a more nuanced relationship between symbolic death of the old self, and the connection to 21st century eco-activism in the service of Gaia. This is a beautiful representation of what such deep encounters are like when the knowledge of the sacred feminine is awoken so powerfully.

It is impossible to calculate the real cost of suppressing the sacred feminine in the modern world, but Helen Luke[21] writes about how the instincts and the irrational were *killed off* long ago by a dominant rational consciousness, and she believes this will eventually poison civilisation. Perhaps the serpent is the perfect symbol for a resurgent sacred feminine and our species, reconnection to depth, healing and wholeness. Anthropologist Jeremy Narby[22] has explored a universal connection to the sacred and the imaginal realm, noting the regularity with which cosmic serpents are found in the creation myths of ancient cultures, including the Americas, Australasia, North Africa, across the Mediterranean and Scandinavia. Snakes continually appear in myths, dreams and visions worldwide, representing a creative, life-affirming force, which brings a deeper connection to life, as well as imparting important knowledge. Jeremy Narby says that no worldview has a monopoly on what 'reality' is, and he makes a very pertinent observation about the levels of dissatisfaction in the lives of modern people. Carl Jung[23] acknowledged this sickness and lack of meaning, and was fond of emphasising that our way to wholeness and individuation is circular, which is similar to a labyrinthine journey (symbolic of serpentine wisdom) that takes us to the centre of our being. The labyrinth is a wonderful example of a deep technology of transformation, which provides us with the means to regenerate and renew our relationship to life as a whole.

Cycles of revelation

I have always taken the opportunity to explore labyrinths in the course of my spiritual journey over the past few decades. I have also used them in my professional role as therapist and educator, for example when running weekend workshops or as part of an annual lecture I run at my local university on a Masters in Clinical Education course (using a finger labyrinth). Essentially, I have used the labyrinth as a means to encourage people to dream and reflect on their psycho-spiritual development. The depth and power of walking a labyrinth is akin to entering a mandala, one that leads us in a circular way into the centre of our experience.[24] It is like entering a liminal space, where we encounter new thresholds or possibilities for our life directions. The reason why the labyrinth can be such a deep experience is because it is a *temenos*, or sacramental space, where we are opened up at a soul level in unexpected ways. For example, as part of a conference on spirituality I was co-organising when I worked at the university, we constructed a labyrinth on the lawn outside the venue. The labyrinth was one of a number of experiential workshops, which complemented the more traditional conference presentations, and it was a great success. I have an abiding memory of some of my faculty colleagues, who had not attended the conference but spent time at the end of the day walking the labyrinth, and how some had acknowledged the quality of reflection they had encountered when entering its pathway.

I live in Norwich, a small city in the East of England, and one day a few years ago whilst visiting our 800-year-old cathedral I noticed a newly laid labyrinth in the central lawn, which is framed by a beautiful quadrangle of cloisters. Naturally, I was drawn to enter the labyrinth's pathway and the contemplative atmosphere of the setting was conducive for a deeply reflective and rich experience. I later found out that the labyrinth had been designed and created by Tchenka, a local astrologer whom I had first heard about in the mid 1980s but only recently met. In 2014 I contacted Tchenka to find out if she would draw up an astrological chart for me. We met on two occasions over a two-year period. The first meeting coincided with the writing of my first book, and the next was when I was in the middle of writing this book. It was during the latter meeting in 2016 that I asked Tchenka if I could write a vignette about her connection to the labyrinth. This opportunity came when I casually mentioned that my new book contained lots of unintended references to snakes, which seemed to be popping up in almost every chapter. She turned to me and said: "Of course, the labyrinth is a coiled snake pattern." Naturally my instincts were aroused and I also found a reference to snake symbolism whilst reading Anne Bancroft's[25] work on the *origins of the sacred*, where spirals, zigzag lines and dots were all said to symbolise the serpent. Meeting Tchenka also revealed we had a shared interest in the sleepy town of Walsingham in north Norfolk, the national shrine of England, where in 1061 the Virgin Mary appeared to Lady Richeldis. In response to her prayers and petition to Mary, Richeldis had a vision of the original Holy House in Nazareth, and Mary instructed her to construct a replica of the house in Walsingham.[26] The building of the Holy House, around a thousand years ago, revealed a hidden well and the healing waters of Walsingham continue to flow to this day, attached to the Marian shrine.

Carl Jung[23] speaks about the role of the sacred feminine in relation to the Assumption of the Virgin Mary by *Pius XII* in 1950, which he equates with the Church recognising Sophia (wisdom). In one of my conversations with Tchenka, she spoke about the importance of the sacred feminine in this time of global crisis, and how *She* brings an awareness of '*bearing witness*'. Tchenka likens this to: "Holding a consciousness and experience for the pain that is going on in the world" (e.g. due to climate change, deteriorating environmental conditions, and increasing tensions and divisions between people). She illustrates the dynamic presence that accompanies the process of bearing witness through the vigil of

Mary Magdalene, who sat at the foot of the cross and witnessed the unfolding agony and passion of Jesus. Tchenka wondered if it was Mary Magdalene's devotion to witnessing Jesus on the cross which led her to be the first to witness the risen Christ. My conversation with Tchenka underlined my appreciation of living close to Walsingham, where the sacred feminine is honoured.

Walsingham is a deeply spiritual place, and the entire town is pregnant with healing energy. This is no surprise, as the north Norfolk coast has been home to many ancient peoples from the Beaker people to the Celts, Romans, and Saxons. The ancient spiritual credentials of the area are further strengthened by the discovery in 1998 of Seahenge, a circular shrine enclosure made of ancient upright oaks surrounding a central altar made from an upturned base of an oak tree. It was in relatively good condition, having been submerged in the sand and seawater of the north Norfolk coast for thousands of years. An exceptional tide unearthed the sacred enclosure, providing us with further evidence of our ancestors' spiritual connection to nature. I was fortunate to visit Seahenge before it was removed and preserved. North Norfolk has an ancient feel to it, and the village of Walsingham itself was previously the site of a Roman sanctuary, where figures of the goddess Minerva were found (the Roman equivalent of Athena, a powerful Greek goddess). In ancient Britain, temples dedicated to Minerva are linked to the Celtic goddess of healing, Sulis. For example, in the ancient Roman city of Bath, Minerva is known as *Sulis-Minerva*. Anne Bancroft[25] confirms that Minerva was strongly identified with Sulis in ancient Britain, and it is well known that the Romans would build temples on pre-existing religious sites, which is probably the case in Walsingham. As well as the Minerva connection, archaeological excavations at the Roman temple at Walsingham have also unearthed figures of the god Mercury, the equivalent of Hermes (the Greek messenger of the gods), whose symbol, the *Caduceus*, is two snakes entwined around a staff with two outstretched wings at the top of the rod. And so, the spiritual heritage of Walsingham has a positive mythical link to the serpent.

Walsingham is located in a geo-sacred hub of interesting connections to the ancient world. For example the great St Michael and St Margaret ley line (the serpent way), crossing from the West of England to the East,[27] connects two geographical areas with major sites celebrating the sacred feminine. Glastonbury sits on the ley line[28] and Walsingham is around 50 miles away from it.[26] Also, it is worth pointing out that the feminine was powerfully represented in the pre-Norfolk Celtic people (Iceni tribe) who honoured the warrior goddess Andraste. The Iceni were led by the fierce warrior queen, Boudica, who led a spectacular Celtic uprising against the Romans, sacking Colchester and London, before losing the fight against the battle hardened legions of Rome in open countryside, which favoured their highly organised fighting tactics. The East of England has ancient and powerful connections to the sacred, regal, and warrior dimensions of the feminine. Thus, the tranquil north Norfolk village of Walsingham seemed the perfect place to make a pilgrimage with Tchenka, to honour the sacred feminine, and the memory of all the sacred traditions of the land, as well as taking time to discuss the deep meaning of the labyrinth, and to drink the healing waters from the holy well. I was also keen to learn more about Tchenka's pilgrimage in this life.

A walk on the wild side

Since childhood the stars have fascinated Tchenka, and when she was 15 years old she purchased an old Victorian book on astrology. She carefully followed the directions, which enabled her to draw up her birth chart. The energetic pattern it portrayed mirrored her inner experience of her *Self* so accurately that she was immediately hooked and from that time onwards she has embarked on a life-long journey of learning. In 1984 Tchenka became a professional astrologer, but in the meantime she passed through two damaging relationships, which catalysed a process of self-empowerment in 1990, leading her into a deeper relationship with her spiritual development and a more intimate connection to the dark aspects of the divine feminine. Tchenka's astrological wisdom gave her the confidence to follow the promptings of her *deep instinctual Self* and she started to follow her own path. She entered a potent time of emergence and unfolding, and was guided by the synchronous discovery of a library book on the subject of the Cretan seven-circuit labyrinth, which is the oldest labyrinth pattern in the world. Tchenka devoured the contents of the book, which suggested that the Iron Age ridges around Glastonbury Tor, one of Britain's most ancient spiritual monuments, are the remains of a labyrinth whose pathways mark the ritual approach into the mystery of this sacred place.

Tchenka decided to try and walk the Glastonbury Tor labyrinth in gratitude for her connection to the divine goddess. In 1991 she made a pilgrimage to the West of England and arrived in Glastonbury at the time of the summer solstice that coincided with the full moon in the sign of Cancer, which created a powerful astrological connection to the Mother. Tchenka's deeper calling and spiritual path emerged during that 1991 Glastonbury labyrinth experience. She said that "It was real magic at work". From this time onwards she has immersed herself in the study of the history, geometry and construction of labyrinths.

In the summer of 1992, Tchenka saw an advert for the *Rainbow Circle Astrology Camp*, which rang a bell for her and she followed the call. Her participation at the Rainbow Circle camps over the years enabled her to make a deeper connection to the dark side of the divine feminine. It was a time where she flourished and started to develop workshops that explored 'Her' power, especially via the serpentine pathway of the labyrinth. It was also around this time that Tchenka felt she had emerged authentically and that her vocation had found fertile ground. She described what the labyrinth meant to her as a tool, but she felt the word tool did not do it justice, so I suggested the word *technology*, particularly as the ancient Greek word *techne* means craft. Tchenka agreed and said, "It is like a *technology of transformation*." For Tchenka the seven-circuit labyrinth is an ancient technology, where the patterns and pathways create the potential for opposites (like yin-yang energies) to be brought into connection, and where a void state is created in the centre. In this way, the pilgrim enters the labyrinth and transcends polarities by walking both clockwise and anti-clockwise, which leads to a centre, bringing a sense of the whole.

When I returned home after meeting Tchenka, I found a book about the labyrinth in my library by Lauren Artress[29] who also found the word 'tool' inadequate to describe the function of the labyrinth. She preferred the word 'transformation'. In fact, she states that the *archetypal experience* most *active* in walking the labyrinth is the process of *transformation*. For Tchenka, the labyrinth is a portal to nature's power, connected to growth, change and transformation: "When I walk the labyrinth my mantra is '*move me*', which reminds me to surrender to my destiny, to wait to see where it leads me." Tchenka spoke about how the labyrinth is the most potent technology and symbol of the divine feminine, because its snake-like coils are the actual serpentine pathways that lead us to a 'dead end'. It is where we have the opportunity to shed old skins, to die to old and redundant patterns that no longer serve us. It is an encounter, wherein we meet our potential for rebirth, which starts to emerge as we make our way out of the labyrinth, on the way to being reborn. Following her own labyrinthine mantra of 'move me, move me', Tchenka's path took her down unexpected turns. She was invited to construct a large-scale labyrinth in Norwich Cathedral, which in turn precipitated a seven-year period when she lived and volunteered at Schumacher College in Devon.

It was at Schumacher College that Tchenka constructed the first labyrinth to which she had free and constant personal access. She walked it every day, in sunlight, moonlight, sunshine and rain, and in this practice she came to understand how knowledge of the divine feminine is incubated, revealing the power of the feminine, and the sacred connection to snakes. She recalled the times when she used to walk the pathway of the Schumacher labyrinth and when she arrived at its centre, her arms would rise spontaneously above her head and the movement was accompanied by a hissing sound. She then experienced a simultaneous flow of energy coming from above and below, which was like an integration of the *masculine and feminine*. She realised the truth of the old alchemist saying, that "Nature is the teacher" and that it's no good only *thinking* about life, "the labyrinth path *must* be trodden; you have actually got to *do* it". In her publication, *Walking the Labyrinth*[30] Tchenka writes about the *moving spirit of nature*, which cannot be understood by thought or the mind, rather it is about encountering a mystery, which needs to be met through experience as a rite of passage. The following poem written by Tchenka sums up the labyrinth as both a pathway and a deep encounter with Mother Nature:

From the Place

From the place where
there is nowhere else to go,
I call you.

From that place where,
after all the twists and turns,
there is no way forward.

A Dead end.

The centre of the labyrinth.

Where to be
is to be simultaneously
at an end and at a beginning.

Come to me.

Explore my mystery.

It is evident in Tchenka's story that her path of initiation into the mysteries is powerfully accompanied by the incubatory practice of walking the labyrinth, whose pathways are designed to loosen our rational bearings.[11] It is akin to a process of symbolic death and renewal, which brings wisdom from the depths. Tchenka's story reminds us how the psyche flourishes when our overly rational minds are set aside and we trust ourselves to enter the unknown.

Our Mother who art in the Earth

Today most people who have grown up in the west will inevitably have been inducted into a set of values and assumptions that reflect the reductionist and materialist philosophy of the Enlightenment, when a succession of talented philosophers and scientists (Bacon, Descartes and Newton to name a few), oversaw the birth of a scientific method that resulted in an increasingly mechanistic way of understanding life. Since the Enlightenment the benefits of science have been incalculable, but the rigid separation of matter (nature) from mind has made a substantial contribution to the current global crises we are experiencing. It is hard to imagine what sort of world we would be living in today if an authentic representation of feminine spirituality had not been suppressed in favour of major religious beliefs and philosophical traditions dominated by patriarchal attitudes. Humanity has failed to cultivate a meaningful relationship to the sacred feminine and we are now paying the price. It could have brought a more rounded approach to our human development, rather than the modern one-dimensional *ascent* we have today. In short, the modern world has too much *yang* and not enough *yin* (as Jung pointed out). The feminine encourages us to *descend* and also to connect with the Earth. Sylvia Perera[31] says that the sacred feminine takes us into darkness where polar opposites, such as beauty-ugliness etc., exist side by side. It brings a more authentic and holistic representation of the sacred feminine into the collective. We need a greater connection to the sacred feminine within society, especially in systemic-holistic sciences, which encourages us to honour our relationship to life as a whole.

In the 1960s James Lovelock and Lynn Margulis conceptualised the Gaia hypothesis, which considered the planet as a single, living and whole organism.[32] Gaia of course is the ancient Greek goddess of the Earth. It is also a wonderful irony that Lovelock and Margulis's scientific theory of Gaia portrays the planet functioning as a unitary whole, which also represents the sacred feminine. William Irwin Thompson[2] considers Gaia theory as a way of opening to the imagination and encouraging processes of transformation, to create a new landscape of cultural ecology. In the early years Gaia theory was savagely attacked by certain quarters of the scientific community because it did not conform to the tried and tested methods of reductionist science. Gaia theory confounded reductionist views of science, because it was a paradigm shift reflecting a more complex and holistic view of planetary systems. Stephen Buhner[33] cites the radical philosopher Buckminster Fuller on the need for humanity to connect with and be guided by Gaia: to find out what *she* needs and what we can do to make a difference to life on Earth. Using the goddess Gaia to communicate a vision of wholeness from a scientific perspective could not be bettered; she is a divine representation of what it means to live on Mother Earth. She symbolises a sacrament of wholeness, in our sciences, philosophy and technology, in our economics, politics and ecological awareness, and in our bodies, minds and souls.

The sacred feminine opens us up to diverse ways of knowing that could complement the skills of logic and reason that have been well honed since the Enlightenment. Anne Bancroft[25] provides a glimpse of pre-patriarchal cultures' relationship to the Earth, which was considered womb-like and humanity's earliest experience of a deep spiritual connection. Bancroft tells us that the *Earth Mother* was subsumed into the *Great Goddess* with the rise of agricultural settlements, and they were viewed as indivisible. Archaeologist Maria Gimbutas[34] explains that in the ancient world the Goddess was central to religious life, and far from only being a symbol of fertility, she was intimately connected to the mysteries of life, particularly processes of death and regeneration. Around this time women often officiated as priestesses at sacred ceremonies in the temple.

It is evident that patriarchal structures have de-potentiated the goddess and feminine ways of knowing,[35] and Edward Whitmont[7] believes this has resulted in the repression of the psyche (soul). Today, Jungian analyst Carolyn Baker[36] explains that the patriarchy is firmly rooted in our *techno-corporate* world. She points out the need for a creative renewal, for example in the ways we can connect to our bodily wisdom, as well as our relationships and the ecosystems to which we belong. For this to happen, Baker argues that we will need to foster a fertile relationship to the dark goddess, which means honouring the wise feminine, personified in the figure of the Crone, and encountering processes of dissolution (death) and transformation (life) in the underworld of our experiences.[4] In order to revive a soulful relationship to life and rekindle a sacred connection to nature, the *Dark* is an essential counterpoint to the persistent glare of the *Enlightenment*, whose intense illumination casts a long shadow that we continue to ignore at our peril. Whitmont[7] suggests that a renewed and resurgent relationship to the feminine would make us more receptive to the depth of human experiences, including an appreciation of our wounds and pain, as well as our joys and beauty – and help us connect to life's deeper mysteries. Humanity would be more in tune with life's seasons and cycles, as well as processes of growth and decay. Carolyn Baker[36] outlines some creative ways that people can connect to the Dark Goddess through activities such as poetry, storytelling, dream work and art etc., which she suggests is where we are likely to encounter the realm of our imaginal energies.

Mary Harrell[4] recounts a story about her connection to the sacred feminine and the imaginal realm at a time of deep childhood distress. When she was thirteen, Mary's mother was pregnant and there were no complications. Then, one night, young Mary had a dream that her mother had died and the family were choosing a coffin at the local funeral director. Naturally in the morning Mary was distressed and was reassured by her mother. However, almost three months after Mary's dream, her mother passed away after complications in childbirth. The following day the family visited the funeral director and Mary knew which coffin would be chosen for her mother, so accurate was the dream in its detail. Mary Harrell writes beautifully about the grief and trauma in her life, as well as her journey of spiritual awakening to the sacred feminine, which connects to her process of individuation. Two years after her mother's passing Mary started to have visits from a female spirit who would communicate with her telepathically. Obviously, Mary was scared. During the apparitions she was unable to move her body, as if she were momentarily paralysed, but the spirit woman would materialise gradually, moving slowly, and kindly telling Mary that she wanted to give her a box. Over a period of 22 years the figure returned to visit Mary many times, but Mary never took the box. However, she believes that the gifts in the box materialised in the form of her healing and the deep soulful connection she made to life.

For me, a resurgence of the sacred feminine is about humanity honouring depth, intuition and an immersive experience into the sacrament of wholeness. It requires us to find a connection to our deepest natures, free from the internalised and externalised oppression of the patriarchy, which continues to oppress women and inhibit the emergence of positive male energies.[36] If we are truly interested in co-creating a more soulful and balanced representation of our human potential, we need to integrate our feminine and masculine energies. Carl Jung conceptualised the idea of the anima and animus as soulful qualities in women and men, and later Emma Jung[37] wrote two very accessible essays on the subject.

The anima is a feminine soul figure in men, and the animus is a masculine soul figure in women, and these contra-sexual forces are part of our awareness work that are integrated in the process of individuation, or becoming whole. Working with the soul at a personal level is a way to connect with the *anima mundi* (the soul of the world). When men (for example) work with the anima, not only does it create a shift in attitude towards the feminine (within and without), it can also awaken a renewed and reverent attitude towards nature. Such work is desperately needed in the world, after millennia of patriarchal oppression. However, we also need to take great care not to assign rigid gender stereotypes, attitudes, beliefs and values to the anima and animus. Nor must we be seduced by the idea that dark is bad and light is good when we are dealing with the flow of yin-yang in relation to our wholeness. Both are needed, and each contains the seed of the other. For example, visionary and mystic Julian of Norwich experienced God as both *Mother* and *Father*, which is a wonderful way of communicating the unity of the sacred.

John Lamb Lash[38] writes about the repression of the sacred feminine over the past two thousand years, which has atrophied our sense of vision, awe and humility. He explores the *mythos* of Sophia (wisdom) and says that the imagination (*epinoia*) is an endowment given to humanity by the goddess, which is vital for engaging human potential. The Gnostic vision considers the Earth to be the divine dwelling place of Sophia, who is also connected to Gaia, and they bring humanity into a sacred connection with the natural world. In this way, humanity can be brought into a living connection with the 'imaginal dimension', where the cultivation of *divine intelligence* (*nous*) leads to a sacred 'biopsychic' relationship with the Earth (*ecognosis*). We are inspired to love Gaia-Sophia and to care for her plants and animals etc. It is a way of *knowing* that is connected to the heart (*cardio gnosis*).[38]

Because any meaningful relationship to the sacred feminine has been marginalised in the modern world, we all have much work to do. For example, Susanne Schaup[39] encourages us to understand the sense of wholeness connected to Sophia, as 'One-in-All', which represents unity in diversity. She points out that the 'dark' has for too long been equated with evil. We learn that before the dark goddess *Lilith* was demonised, she presided over the animal kingdom, science and the crafts. Therefore, Schaup suggests that it is necessary to unite Sophia and Lilith to arrive at a more complete representation of the sacred feminine. It is also an important first step in healing the dualities that are running out of control in the modern world, such as: nature-spirit, body-soul, dark-light etc. Carolyn Baker[36] stresses the need to re-imagine our relationship to the *dark feminine*, both within ourselves and within our societies if we are to transform our consciousness, and to honour our *inner indigenousness*. The word indigenous (from the Latin *indigena*) means one who comes from the land,[39] but more interestingly the breakdown of the words *indu* (in-within) and *gene* (beget-give birth) reveal an intimate connection to the feminine, as in *birth* and *Earth*.[40]

Indeed, the psyche is where we make a deep connection to the feminine. It should also be remembered that the various groups that make up Western culture all emerged from indigenous tribes, such as the Norse, Celts and Gauls etc.,[41] whose genetic imprints we carry today. In this way, we all have access to an inner indigenousness. The question is, how can our indigenous heritage help us evolve a planetary consciousness? It is here that Jung's discovery of the collective unconscious reveals that we all have access to a deep mythic nature, which enables us to live more creatively,[42] especially in relation to engaging our transformative potential. Such a worldview brings opportunities for revitalising new connections and creative meanings for living. In this way, the emergence of the Transformocene Age is initiated through indigenous wisdom, which brings deep inspiration and heart-centred action.

Exercise: The labyrinth within

Use a search engine and find a seven-circuit labyrinth that you can print off onto A4 or bigger. Or, if you live near a labyrinth that has been constructed in the Earth, which you can walk on, then please feel free to use that instead.

If you are using the paper labyrinth you will be using your finger to enter the pathways. This is a different experience from walking the labyrinth, but it can be just as powerful, if done mindfully.

- Place your finger at the entrance to the labyrinth (or stand at the entrance if you are walking). Reflect on the direction of your life to date. Pose a question to yourself, one that connects to your deeper purpose in life.

- Then, when you are ready, open your heart to the experience, and mindfully move your finger (or walk) along the labyrinth pathway. Hold the question you have about your life purpose and make your way to the centre.

- When you reach the centre of the labyrinth, just pause. Enter into a meditative state and wait for the imaginal to connect with you, either through an image, word, message, feeling, sound, or the natural world. Do not analyse what came to you; just be with your experience. When you feel like you have made a meaningful connection with the imaginal, prepare yourself to return to the labyrinth's pathways.

- Again, run your finger (or walk) along the pathways in a meditative state. When you reach the exit, pause and reflect. Bring to mind the question you took into the labyrinth, and also the connection you made to the imaginal in the centre. Now, put these together and notice how they inspire you to live closer to your life purpose.

The imaginal realm permeates the indigenous soul, like a dream within a dream.
Here, the wisdom of the anima mundi – the soul of the world – is revealed.
The whispering mysteries of Mother Earth are enfolded in her creatures,
rivers, forests and mountains.

CHAPTER FOUR

Eco-Imaginal Energies

Overview

In this chapter I outline how the modern world has treated indigenous wisdom with contempt. The modern drift into a hyper-rational worldview has resulted in a lost connection to alternative ways of knowing and initiatory rites. These rites of passage bring a more animated relationship to life. I point out that it is through the cultivation of a wise relationship to the imaginal realm that we come into contact with a deep intelligence, which brings inspiration and guidance. It is through indigenous ways of knowing, as found in the Aboriginal dreamtime and shamanism that we learn the importance of a relational worldview, which highlights the importance of vision quests, enabling us to re-imagine and renew our relationship to self, nature and spirit. I discuss how indigenous knowledge brings us into a more intimate and mythic relationship with the natural world and the cosmos, where ancestral knowledge from a lineage of successive generations is honoured. The ways of indigenous wisdom could help humanity rekindle our relationship to the Earth and take care of our one and only life-support system. I contend that such knowledge is at the heart of the Transformocene, where we are inspired to connect to wholeness on our journey of personal and planetary healing.

Our eco-covenant with nature

James Hillman spoke about the dissolution of personal boundaries the older we get.[1] We already know from transpersonal psychology that we all belong to a greater cosmological whole, where a wider experience of consciousness reveals how we are interconnected with all life.[2] Such expansive and liminal experiences of belonging bring our everyday ego-consciousness into a deeper connection with the dreaming, the collective unconscious, and the imaginal realm, where nature is experienced as alive and intelligent. But how long can we go on abusing the life-giving resources that flow bountifully from nature? Unless we wake up and take action soon, we face an exponential growth in eco-destruction. One immediate antidote to our compromised relationship with nature is to take time to experience the shimmering beauty in the natural world, and to witness how the Earth is a living and numinous sacrament.[3] Then, in a spirit of honouring our wholeness, we can allow that sense of connectedness to inform our thoughts, feelings, and actions as we make a commitment to sustainable living. However, we also need to be prepared to heal the split within ourselves. Our modern one-dimensional egos have been cut off from the deeper layers of the psyche, which is the place where nature is alive within us, and where we are alive in nature. Jerome Bernstein[4] calls those who are experiencing a deeper need for unity and healing from our dissociated relationship with nature, 'borderland' people. It is evident that we have arrived at a *collective growing edge* at this time in world history, and we are the generation who are tasked with initiating a process of healing, where we also evolve a more sacramental relationship to nature. If not, we face the consequences of continuing on a collective path of indifference, or inertia.

I have written elsewhere about the evolutionary importance of transpersonal studies, which entered into Western culture in 1969 thanks to the work of Carl Jung, Abraham Maslow, Stanislav Grof and others. The field of transpersonal studies heralded a paradigm shift, which honoured a more expansive sense of self, and what it means to live in an interconnected cosmos. A transpersonal perspective champions the idea that without this experience of a universal Self, we are prone to alienation, depression and boredom.[2] Psychiatrist and psychoanalyst Stanislav Grof devoted his whole career to the study of psychedelic therapy, spiritual emergency and holotropic breath work, and he witnessed how material science influenced medical psychiatry, favouring a pathological explanation of expansive and holotropic states of consciousness.[5] Interestingly, there is now a growing interest in transpersonal studies in Western culture; for example, studies in spiritual emergency are gradually being taken more seriously in psychiatry.[2]

Recent studies in the use of psychedelic therapy are revealing beneficial impacts for people experiencing depression, and scientists are starting to question why. Professor David Nutt from Imperial College London is open to the possibilities that mystical experiences associated with psychedelic therapy may be significant. He is entertaining the idea that when we connect with life in a way that is 'more' than our everyday conceptions of self (inclusive of a wider cosmos), it suggests that we may well 'need' mystical experiences.[6] Transpersonal scholars have said all along that experiences of *universal connectedness* have been central to human experience from ancient times to the present, as found in shamanic and indigenous cultures. It is time we focused on what it means to activate our full human potential and health (salutogenesis), rather than the endless quest to find more elaborate labels that show us how sick we are (pathogenesis). We only have to look at the size of the Diagnostic Statistical Manuals, from edition one to five, to observe what I call *Syndrome Syndrome*, e.g. the obsessive practice of looking for mental illness everywhere, which itself is part of the sickness of the modern technocracy. I once had a poem published about the initiatory processes linked to shamanic crisis, awakening and the birth of indigenous healers and warriors.[7]

Psychiatric Shaman

Mental health, whose guess?
From the centre to the margins
a quivering extreme,
waiting to erupt.

The daimonic dance,
a wild, freaky paranoia warp,
twisting the path that cuts
containing its pulse, to oppress or die.

Mental wealth is richness in states
a stream, a main line to the deep,
this echo, reverberating throughout time.

Ancient blood, warrior's soul.

The poem was composed at a world work event (linked to *process-oriented psychology*), where people from around the planet gather to process global events and how these impact our lives. The poem is recognition that our altered and extreme states are also connected to ancient paths of healing.

Recognition that something needs to change in our understanding of what constitutes mental health was signposted by James Hillman and Michael Ventura[8] when they spoke about the world getting worse, despite the best efforts of psychotherapy during the past hundred years. It's not so much that psychotherapy is missing the mark; it's more to do with the collective malaise inflicting our technocratic world. The point they are making is psychotherapy is battling against the cultural malnourishment, which is gnawing away incessantly at the remnants of our *collective mental health*. In effect, we are doing nothing about the sick world of our own creation. We have overlooked a simple truth: that our pathologies are really signposts for transformation.[9] It is here that Jung was ahead of his time, in that he saw how our *collective consciousness* was not rooted in a deeper understanding of the *collective unconscious*, which is where we connect with the wisdom of the imaginal realm. It is for this reason that Arny Mindell's[10] emphasis on *City Shadows* seeks to understand the wisdom that is communicated through our altered and extreme states of consciousness in a collective global context.

It is beyond doubt that humanity will be rudely awoken by the growing crisis in the world, and it may well be that in the midst of distress, anguish, and chaos we discover new initiatory pathways in a way our indigenous brothers and sisters would understand. For example, the notion that crisis is part of a *transformative rite of passage*. We have arrived at a critical point in our ways of living. A transformational shift in our knowledge, attitudes and behaviours and in our relationship to one another, other species and the natural world is much needed today. Such an *eco-covenant* with nature would relocate humanity in relation to the *biotic community*, where all forms of life have equal rights. Such a commitment would forge a sacramental bond and awaken a greater sense of belonging, one that goes beyond self-interest and the sickness of exploiting natural resources. Naomi Klein,[11] in her book *This Changes Everything*, calls for a mass mobilisation of people, to rival the civil rights movement of the 1960s, demanding an end to the damaging impacts of our treatment of the world and one another. I would add that humanity would also need to renew its relationship to a transpersonal dimension of consciousness, to reconnect with the natural world and recover a sense of our place in the cosmos. I have written elsewhere about the value of a transpersonal perspective, which aligns our human consciousness to a greater sense of universal connectedness.[2] Such a transpersonal perspective enables us to forge a conscious alliance between the everyday functions of our ego and a greater Self-representation for living. In this way, we become more sensitive to others and life as a whole, and our personal boundaries open up to a greater transpersonal connection in life.

Professor Tim O' Riordan[12] has commented on the urgent co-habitation problems humanity faces as ecosystems fluctuate and in some cases diminish. Again from the perspective of survival, social cooperation and collective functioning, it is most important that we establish an eco-covenant with nature. It will allow us to cross a threshold, from our limiting experiences of ego-consciousness to new opportunities that cultivate a transpersonal relationship to life. Such a shift promotes a loosening of the overly individualistic boundaries championed in the modern world, which have restricted our psycho-spiritual growth and potential. Such an evolutionary transformation within human consciousness could revolutionise our relationship to nature, and recalibrate our understanding of what it means to be a planetary citizen located within the biotic community, not separated from it. Indeed, as Baird Callicott[13] says, we need to embody and communicate an alternative vision for an ecological worldview infused with spiritual potential to bring about radical change. This point of view chimes with the call made by Brian Swimme and Thomas Berry[14] for greater creativity in the process of transforming human consciousness, incentivising us to engage our collective spiritual potential. It is here that we can take inspiration from our indigenous sisters and brothers, who for millennia have revered the Earth and made offerings that maintain an active relationship to the spirit of the land. Of course, I am not so naive as to romanticise indigenous cultures, believing that they always live more harmoniously with fellow humans, other species and the planet. This is not always borne out in anthropological research.[15] However, we can learn much from indigenous cultures and practices that celebrate their harmonious relationship to nature, life and living.

The wisdom of the Kogi

The Kogi tribe who live in Columbia are descendants of the Tairona indigenous culture, who fled to the mountains to avoid the invading Carib forces, and later the Spanish conquistadors. The Kogi have maintained their indigenous culture and lifestyle by keeping the outside world from entering their lands. The Kogi regard themselves as the elder relatives of modern humans, who they view as younger siblings.[16] The Kogi have a well-developed cosmology, based on the emergence of a cosmic egg, which was created by *The Great Mother* and encompasses seven directions: North, South, East, West, Zenith, Nadir and Centre. There are also different levels represented in this cosmic schema, for example, the Kogi philosophy for living is based on the recognition and existence of dualities, such as female-male, light-dark, and good-evil, etc., but these opposites are viewed as complementary relationships rather than strict polarities. The Kogi have a highly developed spiritual culture, full of guardian spirits, mythic symbols and figures. This spiritual connection fosters an integral bond with nature, which connects them to ancestral lands that surround a sacred mountain.[17]

We have invaluable insights into the Kogi way of life after a filmmaker was invited into their lands at the request of the tribe. They expressed their concern about modern humans' attitudes and behaviours, which are having such a devastating impact on the Earth. The first film was released in 1990 and the Kogi used it as a platform to warn of impending disasters, and they advised modern people to change their way of life to avoid increased levels of ecological destruction. Their message was ignored, and in 2013 another film, *Aluna*, was made at the request of the Kogi after they realised that their warnings had not been heeded. In fact, the 23 years between the releases of the two films has shown how their concerns were correct, as profiteering corporations continue to abuse the land, causing deforestation, landslides and floods. The latest film shows how modern attitudes are very much at odds with an indigenous culture that has an intimate understanding of the land and how the Earth is sacred. Interestingly the word *Aluna* roughly translates as *universal consciousness* and it is this cosmic connectedness that informs how the Kogi live. The spiritual vocation of Kogi priests known as Mamas starts from a very early age, where they are kept in *darkness* until the age of nine years. During this time their Mothers and tribal elders care for the young children, as they are initiated and instructed in ways that are attuned to *Aluna*. It is where they learn to carry out important spiritual functions, through their connections to a cosmic consciousness.[18]

The film, *Aluna*, follows a group of Kogi led by *Mamas* as they trek hundreds of miles along the Columbian coastline, laying a sacred thread, carrying out rituals and praying at key spiritual places on the journey. On the trip a gentle narrative unfolds with the elder Mamas revealing their deep wisdom and understanding of the interconnectedness of the surrounding ecosystems. The film also provides a touching endorsement of Kogi ecology from an Oxford University academic, a specialist in ecosystem recovery, who confirmed the wisdom of the Kogi and their ancient ways, which reflect their deep understanding of the intricacies that contribute to the maintenance of flourishing ecosystems. What the Kogi show us is the importance of understanding the balance between ecosystem interactions, but also that humanity can impact positively on those ecosystems when we live in harmony with nature. What makes a difference in the Kogi way of life is a spiritual connection to the Earth, and how they live lightly on the

> planet. The Kogi show us how to live holistically with nature, revealing that the planet is alive and how the spirits and the ancestors need to be honoured. The enduring success of the Kogi, despite the attempted intrusions from the outside world, is their ability to connect with a universal consciousness that inspires a deep regard for *The Great Mother*.

The inspirational story of the Kogi shows us that when human consciousness connects to a universal consciousness, it provides us with a meaningful sense of our place in the cosmos (the whole). Our task is to use our imaginations to connect with the imaginal realm, or the dreamtime, where we too can participate in an evolutionary shift, one that moves away from the mindless actions that have led to eco-destruction, and helps us reconnect to a greater ecological consciousness.[19] Indeed, Charles Eisenstein[20] urges us to be bold and empowered as we seek to engage a new narrative, one where we can all become *miracle workers*. It is on this point that I turn to the power of the imaginal realm and the human imagination to highlight the spiritual gifts that can come to us as divine inspiration, especially when we tap into a transpersonal reality, which brings a visionary connection to the cosmos, as noted by Sufi scholar Henry Corbin.[21] He talks about the noetic (mystical way of knowing) and the creativity that can be experienced when we are in touch with the imaginal realm. It is this relationship with life as a dynamic and intelligent force which underlines the importance of an indigenous perspective that could inspire us and re-enchant our activities of daily living, as found in the cosmology of the Kogi. But to transform our consciousness we will have to shift our worldview, which means breaking free from the crippling ideologies that prize reason and rationality far more than mystery, and where history is valued more highly than myth.[22]

Creative urge, creative edge

According to William Irwin Thompson[23] we need a healthier appreciation and understanding of consciousness and how it can be harnessed to transform culture. He points out that in these complex times, the dynamic nature of the imagination could be a major factor inspiring transformation: where we wake up to the creative potential between the known and the unknown.[24] This could include the fertile ground between mainstream consensus reality and the unconscious processes at work in our psyches and cultures. It is a call to re-imagine what we are capable of becoming.

The modern world is on a collision course between polarities that are being played out in the collective, such as person-planet, good-evil and rational-irrational etc. Despite the warnings from scholars such as Theodore Roszak, humanity seems to find it hard to awaken from the sleep walk to destruction, where our *collective somnambulism* is the default position of our current consensus reality. Forty years ago Theodore Roszak[22] probed our collective conscience and asked whether we have the imaginative resources to evolve a higher sanity, which draws on our latent potentials to inspire a lived *quality of experience*, one that touches into the *mystery in life*. Indeed, the value of acknowledging mystical consciousness is that it is part of our nature (transpersonal). It is an inner resource that humanity can readily draw upon,[25] but only if we are motivated to do so. The question is how can we collectively tap into our vital imaginative energies to stimulate a renewed focus for living? For example, when our imaginary energies are activated, they grip us from the inside and arouse our instincts to such an extent that we cannot fail to be motivated by a creative force that is alive within us.

From such an inspired perspective, we are capable of touching into a passion for living that is dynamic, alive, activated, and tinged with the numinous. It is here that our creative instincts become potent, like the soul of a poet, who is awoken through the mystery of deep experience, and finds soulful expression in words that capture and evoke a quintessential moment in verse. When we are in touch with a creative pulse, we understand how sounds can quicken the heart of a musician, or how the body of a dancer flows with inner and outer movements, and how colour and form flirts with the senses of painters and sculptors. These are examples of liminal entry points, where our bodies, minds and souls are brought into connection with the imaginal realm, which open us to the mystery in life's wholeness, as: form and formlessness; flux and flow; function and freedom.

When we trust and cherish our imaginative energies we are open to 'eureka' moments of wonder, joy and discovery. The Greek word for eureka, *heúréka*, means *I have found it*,[26] but it's more like the imaginal has *found its way to us*. The process of working imaginatively and creatively allows our creative urges to lead the way to such moments, which are potent carriers of our human and numinous potential. Indeed, the *creative urge* often brings us to a *creative edge*, and dynamic opportunities for our emergent potential to unfold, like a living art form.[27] Each of us has the capacity to connect with the imaginal realm, allowing our imaginative responses to life, to open us up creatively to the process of self-exploration, embodiment and empowerment. As we welcome these epiphanies into our lives, we can start to *know* that we are connected to a bigger process of transformation in action. Creativity is essential if we are to evolve a consciousness fit for the 21st century, where our imaginative energies expand our purpose for living. The creative and transformative imperative is wonderfully illustrated in the following story of a client I worked with. It reveals how the imaginal is always finding ways to enter our lives.[28]

_____ **Return to the Mother** _____

I worked for six sessions with a deeply spiritual man who was seeking a renewed connection to his unfolding life process. Before the last session he experienced a series of panic attacks, which seemed to be pointing to a transformative urge within him. We met on a glorious sunny morning and went into the garden to do a vector walk. I said to my client that I consider the process of entering the subtleties associated with the imaginal realm to be like a living prayer, akin to meeting an angel of imagination. I pointed out that the work could be deep and inspirational, which supports us to shed old patterns of behaviour that are no longer serving our life path (deathwalk). I asked the man what he wanted to let go of, or give up. He pondered this question and somewhere deep down he knew that certain beliefs and attitudes were no longer serving him. I suggested that he started the process by scanning the garden in a dreamlike way until something stood out and caught his attention, or as Mindell says 'flirted' with him. After a short while he turned to me and said, "There is a large black plastic compost bin tucked away in the corner of the garden, under the tree." We walked slowly towards the composter and he said: "This bin is a contradiction for me, because on the one hand its purpose is useful and needed [recycling], but on the other hand it's a large plastic container, which also means it's part of the ecological problem we are all in."

We stood looking at the composter for a while and then took off the lid to feel the heat and smell the intense alchemical process at work, where transformation was already happening. The waste material was already breaking down, transforming into fertile soil, which would eventually nourish further growth in the garden. It seemed such a wonderfully potent symbol that captured the dynamic process of change my client was facing. I encouraged him to go further with his associations and he said the plastic container was like those aspects of the modern world which represent the falseness permeating our daily lives. We stood there looking at the compost bin and I said: "What do you want to give up?" Immediately, he said "fear" and went on to elaborate: "The...fear...that prevents action".

Standing before the black compost bin, my client started to experience images flash through his mind of patriarchal figures from his life. Interestingly, it was at this moment that I had a sensation as if I were being hung by the neck from a branch of a tree that was directly above our heads. The feeling was so strong that I wanted to see if it connected with my client's process, and so I tactfully mentioned the experience to him to find out if it had any resonances with his process. The feedback was immediate and positive: he spoke about giving up the outmoded opinions of elders, whose patriarchal beliefs and attitudes were paralysing. He called these outmoded beliefs the "opinions of the grey beards". Standing before the black compost bin he decided to let go of these limiting ideas and beliefs and metaphorically hung them on the spot. He said that the experience felt good and liberating. My client's decisive response also relieved me instantaneously from the strangling sensation that I had experienced moments beforehand.

As we entered the next part of the vector walk, I asked my client what it was that he was seeking to connect with in his life. He scanned the garden in a dreamlike way, and the strongest 'flirt' came when he looked through the bushes and made eye contact with his Czechoslovakian wolfhound, and her 'knowing eyes' as she gazed at him, whilst lying patiently on the ground. The eye contact with his beloved dog was very emotional and powerful, which stopped him in his tracks. He said that: "She represents the wilderness, mountains, freedom and being wild. But, when I try to move towards her it is like my feet are stuck." It took a few minutes for my client to acknowledge the depth of his connection before he was able to walk. Then, as he approached his large majestic companion, she sat up attentively, ready to connect. It was at this point that he saw the power of the wolf in her, a fierce predator and hunter. But he also recalled how the wolf brings harmony and balance to ecology, such as happened in Yellowstone National Park, after Aldo Leopold noticed that wolves were a key variable in that ecosystem.[13] As my client stood still before his trusty companion, he felt deeply energised and relaxed; his shoulders naturally rolled back, and as his chest rose up his spine became straighter. He went on to say: "I had a clear image of me standing high on a mountain top, looking out over mountain ranges that stretched far into the horizon." He said that he felt like a Spartan warrior, fearless and in the prime of his life. He also spoke about humans being top predators, and he became very conscious of humanity's responsibility for how we direct our power and energy in the right direction: "Otherwise our actions will be harmful to us and those around us. Our life energy is powerful and we need to use it wisely, or it will use us." As I watched my client's bodily energy and posture become more aligned, we focused on the crown of his head and his heart. He went on to say: "I could feel the energy surging through me, it was amazing, my spine felt like it was iron, I had a strong feeling that I must take my life calling and existence seriously, I must take hold of my life with both hands and own it."

The final part of the vector was about my client connecting to his life path, or calling. He was still feeling very connected to the radiant energy in his body and he was scanning his environment to see what part of the natural world would flirt with him next. As he stood in the garden he heard and felt a gust of warm air envelop him, swirling around his body, which made the hairs on his arms stand up. He felt the gentleness of the wind gather behind him, as if it was gently pushing him forward, and he then decided to follow the wind to see where it would lead him. It was as if the wind were prompting him to be free and to move freely. As he slowly and freely walked forward he eventually came to an old large apple tree, and interestingly the wind stopped blowing just as he arrived at it. The old tree had a lovely feel to it, and an unusual feature, in that two large branches had grown horizontally from the base of the trunk where they formed an oval shape, which was close to the ground. My client climbed into the centre of the oval branches and after standing there for a while he said that he was reminded of the words of the Prophet Muhammad: "The Garden [heaven] lies at the feet of your mother." The experience brought my client into a very deep connection to *Mother Nature – Mother Earth*. He felt like the experience was a confirmation of the importance of following his instincts and not the rules. This experience led to a tacit way of knowing, which was encouraging him to fully trust his life path. Along with this deep realisation, he felt the warm rays of the sunshine upon him, and whilst standing in the middle of the oval branches he said it was as if he "was in a womb".

My client's process revealed how his life was pregnant with new possibilities and opportunities. The result of the vector walk was that he felt a sense of peace and a dawning realisation that deep down we all know those times when we must act. And he went on to say that when we are aligned: "Creation reveals the way and guides us along the path."

The living dream

When the imaginal stirs within us, it often evokes an urge to connect with something more vibrant and vital and brings us closer to the edge of our unfolding destinies. Edges can be scary because they often represent the unknown, or a dramatic shift, but it is said that when the edges of two ecosystems meet there is often richness in biodiversity. In human terms, I would view such edge systems akin to the meeting between the *ego* and the *unconscious* (as originally formulated by Jung). The imaginal space between the ego and the unconscious is fertile ground for inspiring and gestating new patterns for creative living. For example, the ego helps us to be orientated in the world, enabling us to manage our social relations etc., whereas at the level of the collective unconscious we are connected to the dreaming and the imaginal realm. Working at the edge, between the ego and the unconscious, generates new perspectives for creative living. As a society we have not been educated in working with the collective unconscious, and it is understandable that we might feel trepidation when coming into contact with our limitations or edges, which are determined by personal and collective ideas about what life 'should' be. But, if we champion the idea about what life 'could' be, it means that we embrace the uncertainty, as summed up in the Chinese word for stress, which recognises that the experience can be framed as either a crisis, or an opportunity. Meeting edges provides us with opportunities to evolve imaginative responses to life. It means that we have to value the unconscious, which in turn brings us into a more productive relationship with the imaginal realm. We should not overlook the fact that inspiration often has its roots in the imaginal realm, through our dreams and visions etc., and in this way it has been an ally to humanity. But the idea of *living the dream* in the modern world is a far cry from the creative and spirited connection to the imaginal realm that runs deep in our human heritage.

The Western economic dream has become synonymous with the one-sided pursuit of financial and material success. The marketing triumph of the mid 20th century onwards has involved the mass hypnosis of successive generations into believing that they will find happiness and fulfilment by buying into a consumer vision of life. For example, we already know that the winter solstice pre-dates the celebration of Christmas. The festivities originally offered a potent opportunity for spiritual reflection at a time of seasonal transition. Yet the modern celebration of Christmas has morphed into a powerful festival of consumerism. Santa Claus is a central figure of the festivities, and of course he is an amalgam of the Norse God, All Father (Odin, who rides through the sky on a sleigh), and St Nicholas, who was a generous Christian holy man who gave gifts to help people. So, Santa Claus certainly has a powerful spiritual pedigree, but we can probably agree that in this day and age his temple is the shopping mall.

Richard Shweder[29] captures the spirit of modern cross-cultural consumerism when he writes about someone visiting a Tokyo department store during the season of Christmas, and being confronted by a figure of Santa Claus with outstretched arms, nailed to a cross. This depicts something very tragic and real about the confused state of our collective mythic lives. It suggests that the spirit of giving and generosity (symbolised in the figure of Santa Claus) has been *sacrificed* on the *altar of consumption*. But, as we know, there is no redemption in the shopping mall, and a crucified Santa graphically illustrates the commercial killing of the spirit. It is true that myths do morph, but we no longer appear to value the transformational nature of such stories, and how they can guide our actions in the world. Today, the most popular use of myths is in the fields of advertising and entertainment, rather than in the service of our psycho-spiritual-ecological growth.

The human potential movement, which came to prominence in the 1960s, proposed an alternative idea for *living the dream*. Yet Carl Jung deserves credit for equipping humanity with methods that enable a soulful reconnection to wholeness, through the collective unconscious. This important discovery revealed how the archetypes are the shared symbols of humanity. Not only that, but the imaginal connection to the collective unconscious takes us to a liminal threshold, where we experience a sense of *mystical participation* in life.[30] It is fitting that one of the last dreams Jung communicated before he died was of a huge round stone situated in a quadrangle, which was located upon high ground, and the words carved on the stone revealed that the circle is a symbol of *wholeness*.[31] The significance of Jung's dream is a living testimony of a man who dedicated his life to helping others reclaim their wholeness. He advocated a process of individuation, through cultivating a relationship between the personal ego and a transpersonal Self. He showed how big dreams are as close as one can get to the *Holy Spirit* (numinous) working within each of us, like a spiritual key that unlocks the mystery of the soul, which can inspire and sustain us on our journey to wholeness.

In a world of increasing hyper-rationality and one-dimensionality, Patrick Harpur[32] is correct when he says that dreaming may be the last refuge of initiation, where a deep connection to life is an induction to soulful living. In a world of mass conformity, dreams and dreaming are humanity's most lively connection to the wild.[33] Meeting the wilderness within can bring forth an unmediated experience of the psyche, revealing images and visions arising from the imaginal realm.[34] From this perspective, dreaming is a deep and wild form of participation, exposing us to a natural force that is calling us to adventure. Dreams provide us with sacramental knowledge that has stoked the fires of the human imagination for thousands of years. In my book, *The Unselfish Spirit*, I honour the place of dreaming and associated revelations that have led to scientific breakthroughs. When we are fully engaged with a problem or a subject in the waking state, we are likely to experience dreams or visions that are connected to our work.[35] For example, in chemistry, Dmitri Mendeleev was preoccupied with finding ways of organising the elements, and a solution, which we now call the periodic table, appeared to him in a dreamlike state. Another example is Nobel Prize winner Otto Loewi, who dreamt of experiments that showed how chemical information is transmitted via nerve cells. He is often acknowledged as the founder of neuroscience.[36] Nobel Prize-winning physicist Wolfgang Pauli called dreams a "secret laboratory".[37]

William Irwin Thompson[24] discusses the particular state of consciousness at work in such revelations, and the type of *scientific* mind that is open to receiving them, which he says is also poetic. We see these glimpses of reverie at work in other luminaries, for example the engineer Elias Howe could not work out where to position the needle hole in his new invention, the sewing machine, until he dreamt of an indigenous tribe who all had holes in the tips of their spears. Upon awakening he knew exactly where the hole should be placed in the needle. In the field of medical research Fredrick Banting discovered insulin after instructions for a procedure came to him in a dream. One of India's greatest mathematicians, Srinivasa Ramanujan, who advanced mathematical knowledge at Cambridge University, spoke about how a Hindu goddess would show him equations in his dreams, which he would write down upon awakening. The list goes on, from the discovery of musical instruments, to creative inspirations in the field of electronics, etc.[38,39]

One of my favourite dream discoveries is told by Patricia Garfield,[35] who writes about Professor of Anthropology Hermann V. Hilprecht when he worked at the University of Pennsylvania. He was researching the discovery of two ancient Babylonian rings, which dated back 3,000 years. The rings were in a museum in Turkey and he was in the United States working from drawings that had been sent to him. His scholarly publications about the rings concluded that they were separate items, but he was having difficulty classifying them. Then one night he had a dream of an ancient priest from Babylonian times, who told him how the rings had come to be made, saying that they were originally made from a hollow cylinder, which had an engraving across the surface of the tube. The priest told the professor that when the rings were cut they were to be used as earrings for a sacred statue. The priest then told him that if he placed the two rings together he would be able to read the inscription, and the priest even told him what the words would say. Hilprecht immediately travelled to the Middle East and was able to physically inspect the two rings together. Everything that the priest had revealed to him in the dream was correct, including the inscription. The priest had also told the learned academic about the existence of a third ring, but he said this would never be found. This was a wonderful dream that shows the wisdom in the imaginal realm.

Dream guides

Not only do we find incredible wisdom in dreams, but we enter a liminal world, where synchronous events seem to manifest as subtle connections between psyche and matter, also revealing interconnections between our inner and outer worlds, which Jung referred to as a "psychoid archetype".[40] A powerful example of a synchronicity that happened to Jung one night was when he dreamt of being shot in the head. The dream was so frightening that it woke him up. However, the following day he was told that one of his patients had committed suicide that night by a gunshot to the head.[41] Synchronicities, as meaningful coincidences, bring the imaginal realm into our direct experience. Another wonderful example of synchronicity is told by lecturer in psychoanalytic studies, Roderick Main,[42] who recounts a time during a conference presentation when professor of biology, Adolf Portmann, was about to share a story of a praying mantis. At that very moment, an actual praying mantis entered the room through a window, and flew above Portmann before landing in front of the projector, which resulted in the insect's shadow being projected onto the screen. These synchronistic connections are no different to the experiences of shamans, which can occur in all our lives. For example, I once woke up in a dreamy state and sat quietly in the living room. When my wife woke up, she came downstairs and the first word I said to her was "cake". Hannah then told me she had been dreaming of cakes. Reductionists might label this as *mere coincidence*. However, Jung would say that such synchronicities (as meaningful coincidences) happen because we live in world where we are more connected than we care to understand.

In October 2017 I had an interesting experience, which happened just before I was due to facilitate a discussion and experiential session on the subject of 'the daimon' to a group from the *Auriga Mysteries School*. I learnt that the group name has a symbolic connection to the spider and web (linked to the Auriga constellation). Just before I spoke I went to the toilet, and as I pulled the cord to turn on the light, a spider fell onto my neck and bit me. It was the first time I had been bitten by a spider in my lifetime. I managed to remove the spider from my body without harming it, and the bite only caused a mild reaction (stinging sensation and slight headache). By the end of the evening I was already considering the synchronous and symbolic meaning of being bitten by a spider just before talking to a group whose name has a symbolic connection to the spider and its web. From an indigenous perspective the spider in North American indigenous traditions is associated with Grandmother, who weaves the mysteries. The spider is also represented in myths across cultures, including Ancient Greece and Egypt, as well as in Celtic traditions etc. The spider symbolises awareness of how we weave our fate, including symbolic death and rebirth. It was interesting that my talk on the daimon also included reference to the *Amor Fati* – the love of your fate – and the cultivation of *true character* (inclusive of symbolic death and rebirth). As a holist, I often wonder what would happen if we encouraged one another to open up a bit more to such synchronicities and support each other's psycho-spiritual growth?

If we are receptive, synchronicities and dreams are capable of jolting us, and inspiring us to reflect on our lives and the directions we are taking. They provide us with revelations that do not necessarily follow the standard scripts from consensus reality for how life 'should' be lived; on the contrary, big dreams are like little miracles that inspire a path of discovery and self-awareness. They can be luminous, ominous, numinous, vivid and symbolic, leaving us with a lasting impression that we have crossed a threshold in consciousness, finding ourselves in sacred territory.[43] Dreams are where we can have a feeling, a sense of knowing, or a sign that somehow, something of great importance is being communicated to us.[44] Yet, how often do we reflect on the richness of the human soul in our technocratic world today? I suspect the answer is occasionally, perhaps in the consulting rooms of depth psychologists and coaches, or in the studios of poets and artists. How often do we hear about conversations or interactions in our mainstream institutions (education, or places of work) that invite people to consider their wholeness and human potential, and encourage them to follow the stirrings from the imaginal realm that are valued and listened to? Far from being a waste of time, creating space for our deeper relationship to the imaginal realm may well be critical for how humanity navigates its way through the global crisis. Our survival may well include being alive to dreaming. Indeed, dreams have the ability to signal potential directions for our growth and development, as well as warning of pending disasters.

In his fascinating book, *The Daemon*, Anthony Peake[39] retells some of the warning dreams, visions and premonitions of people who were booked on the maiden voyage of the *Titanic*. Some people heeded the warnings and cancelled the trip, others did not and perished, and some survived. I have been working with dreams long enough now to realise that they work far beyond the reductionist parameters of our rational minds. No doubt, there are people today having dreams and intuitions about the state and fate of the world, which act as *ominous warnings*. Jerome Bernstein[4] describes the many reports of people who on the day of the 9/11 attacks on the World Trade Center (WTC) and the Pentagon, experienced either premonitory dreams, spontaneous fantasies, synchronicities, sudden onsets of feeling unwell, or spontaneous feelings of dread. Bernstein provides one touching example, of a Fire Officer at the WTC, who had dreamt that one of the twin towers collapsed on top of him. Sadly, his dream came true after he had rescued children from the day care centre in one of the towers on the day of the attacks. I suspect his premonitory dream was the last thing on his mind as he was helping others. But what if we honoured the memory of this brave man and started to take our dreams more seriously, for example, if we spoke more openly about the state of the global ecological crisis and how it is impacting on our thoughts, feelings, behaviours, and our relationship to life as a whole? How might we share these experiences, and how might they inspire us to take transformative action? Alongside our conventional *think tanks*, where people use rational thought to find solutions to complex problems, perhaps we should also invest in forums for *dream incubation*, like those in the ancient world. It would recognise how the imaginal realm filters through various states of consciousness, opening us up to more complexity in our experiences, and providing new opportunities for regenerating meaning in life.[45]

Thankfully, there are still people and cultures today who value dreams and dreaming as an integral part of their social, cultural and spiritual rites, including healing methods, which bring deep connections to the ancestors and a rich sense of cosmology.[46] The ancient Greeks had a word for dreams that foretold illnesses, which were capable of revealing symptoms before they had even manifested in everyday life. The word is *prodromos*, which translates as that which *runs before*.[35] I would like to suggest that if we were truly interested in health, well-being and leaving a proud ecological legacy for future generations, then we would do well to wake up to the gifts that are seeded within our dreams and visions, which are awaiting incubation in our conscious awareness. Human wellness cannot flourish on a planet that is sick,[47] and lest we forget, it is humanity that is depleting the Earth's resources and creating a toxic legacy. Humanity has degraded its relationship to nature to such an extent that it has corroded our souls. Yet we have powerful myths that metaphorically underline the consequences of treating the sacred Earth with contempt. I am grateful to Jungian analyst and ecopsychologist Mary Jane Rust for telling me the story of Erysichthon.[48] Here's how I tell the story.

Sacred groves and the shadow

The ancient myth of Erysichthon offers us a warning about what happens to humans when they violate a sacred bond with Mother Earth. Erysichthon was a wealthy and arrogant man, who one day ordered his servants to accompany him to a sacred grove with the intention of harvesting the finest wood. Erysichthon led his men into woodland that belonged to the great goddess Demeter. As the group of men made their way into the dense canopy of trees, they soon came upon a mighty oak and Erysichthon immediately ordered his servants to cut down the tree. As the men took hold of their axes, there was a palpable sense of anxiety amongst them and they nervously avoided carrying out the task. They expressed their concerns about violating the sacred grove, and were frightened of incurring the wrath of Demeter. Erysichthon became impatient and mocked their superstitious beliefs, whilst grabbing an axe and swinging the sharp blade into the trunk. Then, as the mighty oak was being felled, dark red blood began to trickle from the damaged tree. The servants became more agitated, but Erysichthon continued until the job was done. He then ordered his men to take the bloodstained tree to his home. When news of Erysichthon's actions reached Demeter she put a curse on him – that his hunger will never be satisfied – no matter how much food he consumes. As the curse took hold of Erysichthon, he gradually sold everything he owned in an attempt to assuage his insatiable appetite. One day, in an act of desperation, he sold his daughter (Mestra) into slavery to a fisherman in a bid to make more money to feed his deep hunger. However, the god Poseidon learnt of Mestra's plight and took pity on her, giving her the power to change her form (shape shift), which enabled her to escape her bondage and return to her father. When Erysichthon learnt of his daughter's ability to morph into different forms, he took advantage of this and sold Mestra over and over again into slavery, and each time his daughter returned home. By this time Erysichthon's addiction had completely engulfed him, and nothing placated his desperate and destructive habit. Eventually, Erysichthon's hunger became so overwhelming that he ate himself.

Demeter's curse had amplified Erysichthon's greed and covetous nature to such an extent that he could no longer live in a balanced way. The myth reminds me of the Buddhist entity of the *hungry ghost* cited in the chapter, *Three Propositions for Deeper Living*. Indeed, Erysichthon's plight mirrors our relentless and unconscious assault on the natural world, which is devoid of any understanding of the Earth as a living sacrament and how to honour the sacred feminine. It is a stark illustration of the shadow linked to our modern consumer-based appetites. It is also a stark reminder of the cost of abandoning a holistic vision.

As Jung's dream of the round stone and wholeness suggests, we must abandon the ideology of separation and destruction and reclaim a vision for holistic living, focused on the creation of a shared future for all. David Spangler[49] says that we will only be able to re-imagine the world when we are able to re-imagine ourselves. However, to awaken to our full potential, we must commit to a process of transformative living. For example, our dreams may well be prodromal, that is, they may well be predicting the fate of the world and our disavowed human potential, unless we act. Indigenous cultures reveal to us the value of a close relationship with nature, animals, the ancestors, and the wisdom in dreaming. This wisdom does not separate the world into imaginary and real, but rather, considers it to be a soulful reflection, which is inclusive of a connection to the imaginal realm. Indeed, the way the industrial world has steamrollered the sacred sites of indigenous cultures reveals how far removed modern people are from the living mystery connected to the Earth and our own natures.[50]

I find the dream work of Arny Mindell[50] to be most illuminating. His fluid approach to the imaginal realm includes our night-time dreams, but also our dreams while we are awake in our daily lives. For example, he encourages us to be open to our multi-sensory experiences and relate fully to our impulses or encounters and find out about them. Mindell points out that even random fantasies are revealing tendencies that connect to our life energies, which are seeking expression in some way. This might seem irrational to many today, but the world is beset with problems because the irrational has no meaningful way of being expressed, and so ferments in the collective shadow.[51] But, as Debbie Ford[52] says, living our dreams means we commit to becoming warriors, which includes having the courage to face the shadow. Working with the shadow is integral for the activation of the Transformocene Age, connected to personal and planetary healing.

Exercise: Eureka (I have found it)

- Reflect for a moment on the state of the modern world from the perspective of your soul.

- Notice how the bureaucratic and technocratic world is impacting on your life (IT, work, consensus rules, institutionalised norms, etc.).
    - Where are you enchanted by the bureaucratic and technocratic world?
    - Where are you disenchanted by the bureaucratic and technocratic world?
    - Reflect inwardly and ask your soul what 'it' needs beyond the bureaucratic and technocratic world?

- Allow yourself to daydream for a while and take some time to connect with your soul first (before any bureaucratic or technocractic needs).
    - Breathe and feel connected to your body.
    - Take your awareness to your heart.
    - Notice how you connect with your inner nature (e.g. visually, feelings, sounds, movements, etc.).
    - Notice how you connect with other people and other species (e.g. meaningful relationships and connections, etc.).
    - Notice how you connect with the natural world (e.g. being in the elements, sensory connections, etc.).

- Imagine your soulful experience leading you to eureka (I have found it). It might be an image, word, feeling, thought, insight etc.

- Let eureka find expression in some way, by drawing, writing a poem or dancing etc.

- How does eureka support your soulful expression and bring more balance to your bureaucratic and technocratic world?

PART TWO: THE REDEMPTIVE QUEST

The Prisoner[1]

It is an impossible thought
but he walked in of his own volition
put on his chains
and declared his own judgement.

In exchange he would be loved
by his fellow prisoners –
his denial of freedom
shouted with praise from rooftops.

How industrious in the workshops
as he sewed his own funeral shroud
washed his sins daily in laundry,
fashioned wire to make safe his gaol.

Eschewed escape refused parole
embraced his inmate's warm security
hated the morning birds their flight
never more dreamed beyond the gates.

Visited chapel to be reassured of damnation
looked forward to hell beyond
assumed no forgiveness or release
loved the courtyard of limitation –

Here and here alone…
did he find what he sought?
Comfort from the cell of freedom
safety from the terror of reality?

Each night a warm bed
the proximity of other fools,
food to assuage the other hunger
distraction to hide the unbearable skies;

that brought him here
the haunting inner voice
that irritating other choice
shut away; buried deep.

The prisoner smiles
in shaving mirror,
happy at last in blissful routine,
despised by his own soul.

Redemption is not an end point; it's a beginning. When we step out of the shadows of our shallow egocentricities, we can start to connect to the 'world of the soul' and the 'soul of the world'. In this way, redemption isn't only personal; it's also transpersonal and ecological.

The Redemptive Quest

Rites of passage

The activation of the Transformocene is dependent upon a holistic vision that inspires and encourages the exploration and expression of our full human potential. Before a new vision can be considered and enacted, humanity will have to realise that the degrading ideologies underpinning the old epoch are now redundant, and we will have to deal with the dysfunctional beliefs and practices that have shored up our social systems.[2] Two heart-sinking examples of the old worldview materialised when this book was near completion. On Tuesday 28th March 2017, Donald Trump signed a Presidential order that revived the coal industry in America, reversing former president Obama's commitment to the 2015 Paris Agreement to reduce carbon emissions. Trump is keen to help American miners return to work by ending the "war on coal".[3] Yet, as the human and natural worlds slip further into a deepening crisis year on year, we have not even begun to calculate the impact of unleashing even more carbon into the atmosphere. The paradox is mind numbing; Trump's desire to end the so-called 'war on coal' is in reality *declaring war on life*. Trump then signed another executive order on Friday 28th April 2017 ending restrictions to drill for oil and gas off the US coast. Trump's mantra is to "unleash American energy".[4] If these actions were not worrying enough, on the 1st June 2017, Trump withdrew the US from the Paris Climate Agreement.[5] If Trump thought that his misguided actions would send a powerful message to the rest of the world that climate change denial is ok, he miscalculated the reaction of other nations who steadfastly honoured the Paris accord. This is an indicator that humanity is beginning to wake up to the consequences of our degrading activities, which have contributed to the Anthropocene. But we have not even begun to calculate the destructive impact on nature, let alone our hearts and souls.

We are not only destroying our relationship to the Earth, we are also killing of a part of ourselves.[6] Worsening planetary conditions are now mirroring back to us the impact of our objective attitudes and destructive behaviours towards life as a whole. We have yet to realise an important connection: that our degrading of the natural world is a consequence of squandering our human potential. For example, secular institutions and societal norms have ignored the life-affirming and growth-promoting sources of transpersonal practices (technologies of transformation), which have inspired humanity for thousands of years by reminding us that we are connected to a living and numinous mystery. The *redemptive quest* that is needed in the world today starts with acknowledging how our dissociation from nature is a contributing factor in our current ecological crisis and underpins the simmering spiritual crisis in humanity.[7] The scale of the anxiety and grief to come will no doubt be captured in statements like: "I can't believe it's happening", which will reveal how our habitual and casual expectations of life carrying on as normal (permanence) are shocked into the reality of *what is happening* (impermanence). It is here that modern societal rites and rituals are needed, which can initiate and prepare us for transitions and transformations, as practised in indigenous cultures.[8]

It is the chasm between our modern over-developed egocentricities and our under-developed human potential where our redemptive quest begins in earnest, through inner work. A student of Carl Jung, Maurice Nicoll,[9] was saying 65 years ago that the notion of psycho-spiritual change means we must be prepared to transform ourselves. Renewed visions for living will have to include conscious engagement of *shadow work* as part of the transformative process.[10] If we are sincere in our interest to evolve a more productive relationship to life, we will have to address the split-off and unprocessed thoughts and feelings that are contributing to the divisions, fragmentations and projections making up so much of our psychic lives today. In this way, shadow work is a prerequisite for a more holistic vision for living, bringing a more creative approach to our inner and outer work in the world. Rather than being an additional burden, along with all the other pressures in our lives, shadow work actually provides us with more energy. In this way, the energy gained from our recycled projections become available for more creative uses. Such a realisation has parallels in the world of physics.

Vision quests and questions

In his discussions on entropy (second law of thermodynamics), physicist and psychologist Arny Mindell[11] notes how energy becomes depleted when it is locked in a 'closed system'. We can understand this in relation to the Sun, which is constantly losing energy (heat), and will one day extinguish and die. The same process occurs when we take fossil fuels from the Earth for energy use, because these are finite resources, which will eventually run out. Mindell explains that similar energy loss can happen when we are locked in a closed system in our ways of living. For example, Maurice Nicoll[12] notes that when human beings live *mechanistically* it increases entropy and consequently our life energies begin to stagnate, which increases the chances of experiencing depression etc.

Nicoll was emphatic that living more 'consciously' creates energy. And so, working to decrease entropy in our human lives releases psycho-spiritual energies that add creativity and zest for living. It is here that Arny Mindell's[11] innovative blend of physics, depth psychology and spirituality is at the leading edge of working consciously with our unprocessed internal and relational dynamics, especially with regard to entropy and energetics.

Mindell draws our attention to an imaginative thought experiment conceived by physicist Clark Maxwell, who proposed the idea of two rooms (one hot, the other cold) with a door open between the rooms. When the door between the two rooms is left open, the heat from the warm room gradually dissipates, and the temperature between the two rooms eventually becomes more or less equal. But Mindell informs us that Maxwell introduced a new variable into his thought experiment in the guise of an imaginary figure that could either open or close the door. This means that there is now an opportunity to regulate the temperature exchanges between the two rooms, depending on whether the door is open or closed. This imaginative figure became known as *Maxwell's Demon*, and it can be applied to working with our psycho-spiritual energies, which Mindell wisely correlates with the use of 'awareness' e.g. when doing shadow work.

Arny Mindell's[11] *Process Work* approach to psycho-spiritual energy recycling is an important dynamic in the emergence of the Transformocene Age. His conceptualisation of how our multi-sensory channels of perception and expression reflect a composite of our energetic input and output is most helpful (e.g. seeing, feeling, hearing, touching, and tasting, smelling and moving etc.). We can understand his multi-channelled approach to psycho-spiritual entropy in the following way. Imagine if upon awakening one morning you felt low in mood, but in the night you recall having had a dream of singing in a choir, which was uplifting. Then you reflect on the feelings of low mood and realise that they are connected to feeling lonely and isolated, which is in stark contrast to the dream of singing in a choir, where you were involved in a process of creative expression and relatedness with other people. It is not too much of a stretch to understand how singing in a choir would lead to an energetic 'state' change. In this way, Mindell describes *switching channels* as a way of decreasing entropy, which in our example would be a shift from waking up *feeling low in mood and isolated* to being *more uplifted when singing with others* in a choir. When we start to work with our inner and outer processes, we are opening ourselves to the imaginal realm in a way that is not dissimilar to the vision quests of indigenous people, where encounters with visionary states and energies is a way of connecting with spiritual power.[10]

Engaging in such transformative processes is a key part of our redemptive quest in this time of global crisis. It is here that I develop further the use of metaphor from part one of this book. For example, the idea of *awakening* is itself a metaphor, indicating how a transition from 'sleep' is used in spiritual traditions, myths and folk literature, which is powerfully linked to transformative processes.[13] In this way, redemption in the Transformocene is a process of collective soul retrieval. If we are in any doubt about the wise promptings from the soul in times of uncertainty and danger we can learn from the case material presented by Jung. He once worked with a businessman who was eager to sign a contract, but at the time was not fully aware of how shady the deal was. The businessman dreamt that he was about to sign the paperwork, but noticed that his hands were soiled. It was then that he listened more deeply to the wisdom of the unconscious and reflected on his involvement in the deal.[14] This dream typifies the small acts of redemption that 'awaken' us and lead us back to the soul.

Each morning as we look in the mirror and groom our preferred identity, we have the opportunity to tend to the shadow in our ritual reflections. Shadow work loosens the grip of the ego's perceived rectitude, which is hygiene for the soul.

———————

CHAPTER FIVE

Global Crisis and the Unexamined Shadow

———————

Overview

In this chapter I make a connection between our unexamined shadows and the state of the world today. Our redemptive quest for wholeness will only be activated once we start reclaiming our shadow projections. I argue that the shadow has been neglected in our personal and collective lives, due to an overinvestment in one-dimensional and hyper-rational attitudes that are rife in the modern world. I argue that without a clear understanding of the way the shadow operates behind the scenes in our hyper-rational world, we run the risk of using reason to explain all our behaviours, which is dangerous. In this chapter I identify how personal, institutional and social aspects of the shadow need to be confronted. Shadow work is a key component in shifting mainstream cultural attitudes and behaviours, which is pivotal for activating a shift in consciousness. It is through the process of reflecting on our unconscious prejudices and projections, that Jung's insight hits the mark: that 80% of the shadow is pure gold. A neglected and unprocessed shadow is problematic to society, and whilst it is not evil, when left unattended, negative projections can strengthen. Therefore transforming our relationship to the shadow connects us to a rich seam of wisdom, while negating the propagation of evil seeds. In this way, shadow work is the foundation for redeeming our souls in the Transformocene Age.

The shadow of revelation

Action to avert the global crisis depends on a *mind* and *heart* shift in people's relationship to the planet. According to Johan Rockström[1] a new form of integrated science is needed, one that draws together a host of academic disciplines, along with representatives from business, politics, and the public in order to bring about transformation in societies. This is an excellent proposition, but I would add that this new form of integrated science would need to be open to the imaginal realm, and be responsive to diverse ways of knowing, including indigenous wisdom and the sacred feminine, etc. Scientists, academics, business people and politicians will need to become embodied agents of transformation if they have aspirations to lead us out of the Anthropocene into the Transformocene Age. Such leaders must *walk their talk*, which means that the various solutions for change discussed between specialists must be accompanied by a commitment to working on wholeness, both inwardly and outwardly. Furthermore, any such integrated approach will need to review the impact of the reductionist, materialist, objective and one-dimensional mindsets that have contributed to the problems we are facing today. Leaders in the Transformocene Age cannot be tethered to the destructive ideologies, attitudes and behaviours of the old world.

I have already spoken about the legacy of Cartesian reductionism, which led to a disastrous separation between mind and matter, and of humans from the environment. The result of our one-sided scientism and technocracy has now cast a long shadow over the modern world, creating a blind spot that needs addressing. It recognises that our technologies and science have immense potential for good and harm.[2] The task of transformation in this time of global crisis will require a fresh look at the foundations of our modern technocracy, which, in the case of economics alone, is mostly focused on income generation and *Gross Domestic Product*, driven by our consumer-based and one-dimensional lifestyles. Clearly, something is wrong with our economic, political, and social infrastructures that have the capacity to serve the greater good, but which have been diverted into self-serving structures focused on wealth creation that financially rewards a minority of people at the expense of the global majority, other species and the planet. Theodore Roszak[3] reminds us that it is highly irrational for a species to destroy the habitats upon which it depends for survival, yet this is exactly what we are doing, economically, technologically and politically.

The question of living more holistically means we will have to re-examine what we have been doing to the world with the knowledge that we have generated. For example, one of the 20th century's greatest physicists, Albert Einstein, once said that if he had his time again, he would be a plumber.[4] This headline grabbing statement gives some indication of Einstein's reaction to the way his scientific breakthrough was used to produce weapons of mass destruction, which have given humanity the means of creating hell on Earth. Science has given us complex capabilities like atomic power, artificial intelligence, and genetic engineering, but history has shown us that ground-breaking discoveries not only bring a promise of progress, they also have a sinister side.[5] The point is, *science as we know it* is based on a set of objective and testable methods, but as Stephen Buhner[6] reminds us, it has no means of generating empathy and love, which are also of great value to humanity. Instead, we have a socio-political world that is increasingly driven by the lowest common denominators of power, fame and greed.

Because altruism and compassion are not the cornerstones of modern societies, we are left catching up with the consequences of the various 'genies' that we have let out of bottles, with scant regard for the consequences. J. Robert Oppenheimer, Director of the Los Alamos scientific laboratory, pondered deeply the moral questions about the creation and use of the atom bomb. In his reflections on the interface between science and society, he spoke about his own academic discipline, physics, saying that its practitioners have known 'sin'.[4] It is an extraordinary exclamation, one that acknowledges the incalculable suffering it has inflicted on people, other species and the Earth. Added to this is the on-going threat of nuclear weapon use today, which primes our imaginations to fear the worst when tensions mount between superpowers. In the final analysis, these weapons of mass destruction offer no real security to anyone. This has been more than evident in the year 2017, where concerns about nuclear war are starting to surface in the collective once again.

It is interesting that Oppenheimer used the word 'sin' to describe his profession's contribution to the creation of the nuclear bomb, which I believe is exactly the right word to describe our misplaced trust in these destructive weapons. Pope Francis also used the word sin to describe our destructive attitude to the environment, where escalating levels of eco-destruction and erosion of biodiversity are the result of selfish and irresponsible behaviours.[7] Environmental degradation is a problem that belongs to us all, and the wise words of Jesus remind us to resist projecting our shadows when he says: let those without sin cast the first stone (John 8:7). It means transforming our own behaviours before judging others. The word 'sin' has religious connotations and has fallen out of favour in the modern world, but interestingly its root meaning simply refers to those actions that have *missed the mark*, in that they have been harmful to self, others, or the Earth in some way. Conversely *metanoia* (repentance) is a soulful response to sin, where we ensure that our actions *hit the mark*, and we actively engage in a process of change in our hearts and in our behaviours.[8] In the true sense of the word, recognising that we have *sinned* means redoubling our efforts to commit to wholesale transformation, not some minor adaptation that makes no real impact. For example, once the grim reality of the consequences of nuclear weapons use was known, Einstein swiftly set up the *Emergency Committee of Atomic Scientists* to explore alternative ways of resolving conflicts.[4]

We now live in the shadow of potential nuclear annihilation, and with all the nuclear weapons stockpiled underground, humanity would not survive if a maverick politician with the hate and fury of Hitler decided to misuse that power.[9] It underlines Jung's point that to be whole we will also need to integrate the shadow side of our personal experiences, but we also need to be watchful of any escalating shadow projections in the collective, socially or politically. The neglected shadow is an enduring problem, and we appear to lack the deep motivation necessary to do the work. We could say the trials connected to the neglected shadow are part of our collective myth.

In the modern world we may think that we have outgrown the myths of our ancestors, but we would do well to remember that ancient cultures on every continent had myths or fairy tales about the shadow side of life, and the nature of good-evil.[10] These stories helped our ancestors understand forces that are capable of working through us, which can wreak havoc in our lives, and for this reason the forces of good-evil are moral as well as mythical. Patrick Harpur[11] discusses the imaginative patterns found in myths, pointing out how they can help us deal with the very real struggles of daily life. One myth that fires the imagination is the story of Prometheus, set in Ancient Greece. The myth describes how the gods decided to create new life forms on Earth, including creatures of the land, sea and air. All the newly formed creatures were considered equal, and the Titan brothers, Epimetheus and Prometheus, were tasked with ensuring that all the species were equipped to survive, except that Epimetheus forgot to endow humans with any qualities at all. Prometheus felt sorry for the humans, and without gaining permission he took wisdom from Athena, fire from Hephaestus, and then instructed humans in the methods of science and the arts. Prometheus acted out of compassion, but he was severely punished by Zeus for giving humans access to knowledge that belonged to the gods. As a consequence he had Prometheus bound to a stake in a mountainous region, where an eagle would tear out his liver every morning. The liver would grow back each day, only for this gruesome scene to be repeated daily for a period of 30 years. Prometheus was eventually rescued by Heracles, but it was not only Prometheus who was punished for his indiscretion; humanity also suffered for this transgression,[12] as the story of Pandora reveals.

Pandora's paradox

Zeus believed that humanity should be punished for accepting the illicit gifts of knowledge and fire from Prometheus, because this knowledge was not his to give. Zeus commanded Hephaestus to create a woman of great beauty in his forge, and when she emerged, Athena instructed her in the ways of weaving, Aphrodite gave her grace and passion, and Hermes endowed her with the gift of communication. Zeus named this beautiful woman Pandora, because a host of gods (pan) had endowed her with gifts (dora). Finally, before releasing Pandora amongst the people, Zeus gave her one final gift, a jar (pithos), which he ordered her not to open under any circumstances. Zeus sent Pandora to the brother of Prometheus, Epimetheus, who upon seeing this beautiful woman was smitten and fell deeply in love with her. One day Pandora's curiosity got the better of her and she took the jar that Zeus gave her and cracked the lid open. To her surprise all manner of evils and sickness spewed out of the jar, which was released into the world. When Pandora realised what had happened, she closed the lid as quickly as possible, and in doing so she managed to contain the spirit, Elpis, which means hope.[12,13] Zeus, who knew all along that her curiosity would get the better of her, had tricked Pandora. For me, the myth of Prometheus and Pandora has three interlocking meanings, which we can reflect upon. The first is that what is concealed eventually gets revealed. Second, we cannot always put back what has been unleashed; therefore we need to use our knowledge and wisdom alongside our imagination and curiosity, to reflect on how we can grow in spiritual awareness. Third, it is up to each of us to do the required inner work to restore a sense of hopefulness. It is fitting that Pandora re-sealed the jar and managed to contain the spirit of hope, which reminds me of the process of alchemical transformation, which also happens in a hermetically sealed container (e.g. inner work). The moral of Pandora's story is not about how she was set up by Zeus to unleash his punishment on humanity for accepting stolen knowledge. Rather, Pandora is an agent of revelation, who brings humanity into relationship with the consequences of gaining such knowledge, and the inner work required to live hopefully and evolve wise courses of action. There are striking parallels between Pandora and Eve, who brought humanity into a conscious relationship with the reality of opposites, good-evil.

Reflecting on the myths of Prometheus and Pandora from the perspective of recognising hope as a gift, the stories have great importance for how we harness our resources to face the unknown and take action.[14] Vaclav Havel speaks about hope, not from the perspective of wishful thinking, but about living with *convictions*, so that whatever activities in life we are engaged in they actually make sense to us.[15] It suggests that we need to cultivate awareness and take responsibility for our actions and their consequences, which underlines the importance of doing inner work (*spirit of hope*). If we apply the myth of Pandora to our world today we have the task of facing the reality of the eco-destruction we have unleashed in the world, as well as finding a deeper conviction to do the right thing by living consciously and creating a future of hope. We have to move beyond our passive existence as acquisitive consumers,[16] which simply perpetuates the growth of individualism, selfishness and greed.[17] We can observe these collective irrational forces at work in our lumbering response to climate change.

The economic forces that bankroll the technocracy have created a collective shadow, based on control, fear and greed. Where is the hope (and the love)? The myth of Pandora reveals that hope is contained *within* and it suggests the need for inner work, with each of us taking responsibility for the projections from our disavowed shadows. Carolyn Baker[18] examines the impact of our personal and collective shadows and their contribution to the global crisis, and suggests that by working with the shadow we discover our transformative potential, and the deep healing associated with the 'Dark Gold' within. Remember, Jung is reported to have said that 80% of the shadow is pure gold,[19] but we must take the trouble to turn these base projections into the alchemy of transformation. The danger of neglecting and not processing our shadows means we are at the mercy of unconscious forces working within us. As Helen Luke[20] says, things gain power when they are repressed.

The importance of shadow work in the emergence of a new planetary culture involves what William Irwin Thompson[21] refers to as the development of sensitivity towards others. This is an important point, which indicates a reciprocal relationship between reclaiming our shadow projections and living in the world with more love and compassion.[5] It is undeniable that working with the shadow is uncomfortable, because the shadow is the arch-maintainer of *self-other* distortions, which only perpetuates further division. Therefore, catching our shadow projections at work is an essential first step for creating greater compassion towards self and other. This is where the spirit of hope comes alive (as inner work). For proof of the power of the shadow, look at the escalating levels of political, social, and religious polarisations in the world today. It is not only situations of *hot contempt* that reveal the shadow, but also in times of *cold indifference* towards others and life in general.

During the time I was writing this book, I read a column in *The Guardian* newspaper about empathy and the need for social connectedness.[22] The article reported an incident that happened one evening in a northern English town, where a woman fell over whilst crossing the road. As the woman lay prone on the ground, an oncoming bus drove carefully around her before continuing on its way. Then, two more cars managed to avoid hitting her, before a fourth car actually drove straight over the young woman, which resulted in her death. It starkly illustrates why the Biblical parable of the *Good Samaritan* is such a powerful story for awakening compassion, concern and care. Yet, how many of us have walked past a problem or made judgements about a situation and thought "I don't want to get involved" or "it's not my issue". Shadow work is about coming clean with the reality of our inner world, acknowledging the prejudices and projections that are operating within us, without dissolving into self-loathing. We simply make a commitment to acknowledge our prejudices and projections, and resolve to be more understanding and compassionate towards others (and ourselves). This is where *hope* becomes an active component of positive change and transformation. Hope is dynamic and active, like the guiding spirit, Elpis (in the myth of Pandora), who can inspire new possibilities and affirmative actions. We need hope to help us create firm foundations, where our actions are productive and orientated towards a shift in consciousness that works for the greater good.

Another story in the same *The Guardian* article revealed an incident where a lone engineer was stabbed at a London underground station whilst trying to stop a man cutting off another person's head. As this grisly scene was unfolding some bystanders took out their phones and filmed the event.[22] The author was calling for more empathy in the world as a means of creating a firm foundation for society, but the article also highlighted research showing a rise in narcissistic behaviours. The myth of Narcissus is a perfect story to illustrate how the cultivation of awareness requires deep reflection, not the shallow variety that led to his death. Narcissus became so absorbed by his superficial reflection in a lake, and he was unaware that he was slowly sinking into the water, and he eventually drowned.[23] It is a narrative that warns us of the dangers of ignoring the depths that can claim us if we only skim the surface of life in vainglorious ways. Returning to the distressing stories reported in *The Guardian* (above), they appear to reflect the growing dissociation in the world today, exacerbated by a rise in individualism, whose cumulative impacts: spiritual, ecological, economic, social, political and psychological, are an impediment to collective transformation.[19]

Even our highly prized scientific culture is not immune from narcissism. Swiss immunologist Bruno Lemaitre warns that the current obsession with researchers publishing in high-impact journals is actually leading to narcissistic behaviours in the scientific community. The rewards are access to influential professional communities, which increases the opportunities for grant awards or becoming peer reviewers for high-impact journals. He also believes that the quest to be an authority on a particular subject reflects a desire to be noticed, and in some cases become a media celebrity.[24] Further evidence of the shadow operating in the scientific community came to light when in 2009 a researcher conducted a meta-analysis of 21 previous studies on the subject of misconduct in research. The analysis was dependent on scientists admitting they had manipulated or falsified data, and the findings revealed that 2% of scientists said that they had done so.[25] Of course the figure could be higher. The moral position stated here is, *scientific objectivity* is not immune from the *subjective shadow*. Why is it that in our mainstream institutions (schools, universities and places of work etc.) there is no teaching or training about how to work with personal and collective shadows? Interestingly, it is through such neglect that the shadow flourishes.

The complexities of this era require each and every one of us to live deeply and process our shadows. To do this, we will need to radically reappraise life. William Irwin Thompson[5] stresses the importance of individual shadow work, with the emphasis on learning to cultivate tolerance and compassion towards other people's shadows. It does not mean that we excuse anti-social behaviours; rather we become more skilled at recognising when shadow projections are at work, in ourselves, in others, in our political, social and corporate institutions. Then, we are more able to act to help bring about cultures of transformation.

The technocratic shadow

Today, humanity is caught in the grip of a shadow epidemic. We have arrived at this point for one simple reason: our political and social infrastructures are based on the idea that rationality will always triumph. Yet, whilst we can agree that human beings are emotional and temperamental, we are asleep collectively to the deeper processes working within us. We can see this clearly in the way the Nazis manipulated the German people in the 1930s. The unexamined shadow is very much active in our lives today, personally and collectively. We have objectified life through industrialisation and the commoditisation of the natural world, which has cast a long shadow. Neglect of the shadow is what obscures our relationship to wholeness. Just watch or listen to the mainstream news from the perspective of a *shadow at work*; it is instructive. Our news bulletins feed us endless streams of information about war, murder, and sometimes about ecological destruction etc., but the media never raises the problematic question that we are all complicit in destroying the Earth, wiping out other species at an alarming rate, or always pointing to the bad guys 'out there', but what about 'in here'?

Theodore Roszak[3] believes that technologists, industrialists and developers are leading the destruction of the world (I would add politicians and financiers). At the beginning of this chapter, I said we will need leaders from all areas of civic life to inspire and mobilise a change of mind and heart in the collective, to motivate us to engage in behaviours that help one another, other species, and the world. But where is the leadership for such transformation? The challenging realisation for anyone interested in activating the Transformocene is that there are no real indications that our civic leaders are even aware of the transformative potential of doing shadow work. Therefore, leadership has to come from the grassroots, via people who are invested in making changes in our ways of living. For example, as well as doing our own shadow work, we could also work with trusted friends to strengthen our commitment through a process of *shadow sharing*, where we speak about how we are working to reclaim our projections. It means we are invested in recycling our precious life energy and putting it to good use. In addition, we could reflect on the shadow side of consumerism and make a commitment to buying less non-essential 'stuff'. This would mean including the interests of the planet alongside our personal interests.

As we know, Western societies produce and consume goods with in-built obsolescence, requiring endless upgrades or frequent replacement. This mechanisation shapes our everyday lives, and we need to find a way to redress the imbalances we are creating in the world through how we live. For those of us interested in wholeness, this shadow work is twofold; first, we have to work on our personal shadows in relation to our repressed experiences; second, we have to examine where we are contributing to a technocratic shadow, which undermines our humanness and our collective relationship to life as a whole. Look at the complexity and morality of modern economics and commerce, with some multinational businesses practising aggressive tax evasion. We have to ask ourselves: would a multinational company that aggressively avoids paying tax (in order to gain maximum profit) really be committed to safeguarding the planet? Obviously, the answer is a resounding no, for the simple reason, if such organisations are intent upon avoiding their contribution to the maintenance of societies where they make their profits, they are likely to be equally as self-interested when it comes to the needs of the planet. This is the shady side of the one-dimensional technocracy at work. In addition, there are corporations invested in maintaining the status quo, many of whom actively fund climate change denial.

It is always dispiriting when corporations act in unscrupulous or selfish ways, but these one-dimensional organisations appear unable to consider the world beyond their profit ledgers. In 1972 Theodore Roszak[3] warned about the rise of business mergers that were not only multinational, but which were also *trans-ideological*.

His words are almost prophetic in the context of corporate power and trade agreements in the 21st century. In these early years of the new millennium, 200 of the world's leading businesses have as much financial clout as the collective economic value of 180 countries. The economic leverage of these companies plays a major role in determining the rate and pace of global trade, finance, and technological development, all of which are having a high ecological impact.[26]

At the time of writing this book a contentious piece of trade legislation between member states in the European Union and the United States of America, called the Transatlantic Trade and Investment Partnership (TTIP), was under investigation by the press. Philip Inman[27] says that such deals in the past were a fair way of regulating trade and safeguarding business investments. However, grave concerns were levied against the proposed TTIP agreement, which led to questions about the possible negative impacts on public services (particularly health services), as well as the rights of workers, and the regulations that protect the environment. Inman points out that the real bone of contention in the proposed trade legislation was in the area of resolving trade disputes, which could be arbitrated outside of the civil courts. It transpired that the TTIP proposal included an Investor-State Dispute Settlement (ISDS) clause, which would allow foreign businesses or investors the right to sue a government if their trade or investments were harmed or compromised. For example, Inman mentions the case of a tobacco giant bringing a lawsuit against a government for its decision to introduce a policy of plain cigarette packaging. Essentially, ISDS would have allowed corporations to undermine the ability of sovereign states to regulate and uphold laws that are in the best interests of citizens.

In the worst case, the potential legal costs to a government in a trade dispute with a wealthy multinational corporation could be astronomical. Nation states risk putting the financial interests of large corporations ahead of citizens, so that trade disputes could result in a country's financial assets being diverted from social projects into legal fees. In a world where the economy dominates, such *trans-ideological* trade deals indicate moral blind spots where the shadow lies dormant and undisturbed. The reason why the European and United States TTIP negotiations ultimately floundered was because enough activists lodged their concerns with their respective governments, but the reality is that more trade deals will be negotiated in the future, and citizens will need to be diligent and ready to challenge the attempts of corporations to put their rights above the well-being of citizens.[28] Whilst business and political leaders grease the wheels of capitalism, the world slips into a deepening crisis year on year. The state of the planet always appears to take second place to economic interests on the world stage. Is this not the height of irrationality?

Our work begins with raising awareness of the worst effects of our reckless pursuit of a global industrial economy, and its devastating impacts upon people and ecological systems.[17] For those people who are concerned about living in balance and in relationship with the natural world, working with the shadow of the technocracy is a key area of raising consciousness. Jungian analyst Adolf Guggenbühl-Craig[29] notes the importance of ensuring that political and business leaders and decision makers have integrity and empathy for others. It is up to each person to be aware of the unconscious processes at work in self and society e.g. greed, power and control etc., which is where the shadow is free to work. An extreme example of ruthless and unrestrained ambition is found in the words of Hermann Göring, who, in the early days of the *National Socialist Party* in Germany, along with his friend Ernst Roehm, was instrumental in forming the brownshirt stormtroopers. In 1934, in what came known as 'the night of the long knives', Göring saw his friend Roehm and other party members murdered, because they were considered a threat to the Party. He coldly recounted to the psychiatrist who interviewed him after his capture at the end of the Second World War that he was ambitious and had no regrets about his 'friends' being eliminated.[30] We may protest and say that the Nazis were different to us, but the point is, how prepared are we to acknowledge our own ruthlessness, ambitions, or lack of concern for the welfare of others, other species and the planet?

The whole point of doing shadow work is to cultivate awareness, to understand that we have choices in life and are free to examine societal norms, prejudices, or unwitting recruitment into some jaundiced political ideology or other. The shadow leaks out in what we might think are the most respectable of places. For example, we have all heard examples of religious preachers who direct fire and brimstone rhetoric at the behaviours of wrongdoers, only later to get caught doing the very acts they seek to purge in others. You do not have to be a psychotherapist to see how distorted our inner compulsions can be in relation to our outer behaviours. Such examples serve to illustrate the chasm between the everyday moralising ego and the shadow energies in the unconscious. Debbie Ford[31] speaks about the need to face up to the lies we are living, and allow the truth of our situation to emerge safely, including any dichotomies and conflicting polarities operating within us, such as right-wrong, good-bad, or our likes-dislikes. In this way, shadow work is deeply reflective and potentially illuminating, helping to facilitate new points of growth in self-other awareness. Indeed, the Greco-Roman meaning of the word 'reflection' is *parhesia*, truth telling.[19] None of us are perfect, and shadow work is not about being perfect. Rather, it is concerned with the cultivation of self-awareness, which is capable of noticing when we are caught in the grip of an attitude or behaviour that is harmful to self, other or planet in some way.

As well as being honest, we also need to be kind to others (and ourselves), especially when the shadow is unexpectedly projected. We need to cultivate relationships where we encourage each other to grow in awareness. In this way we can muster the courage to explore the realities of our inner and outer worlds, including how our perceptions or projections influence our actions in the world, or how we respond to the social norms and consensus opinions in the collective.

German people in the 1930s were seduced by Hitler's rhetoric and messianic message of political salvation. The majority of citizens did not question the misinformation about Jewish people, who were used as scapegoats and were falsely accused of causing Germany's problems. Whenever we find ourselves making judgements about what is happening in the outside world, we also need to be willing to look within and do inner work. Awareness work demands that you cannot have one without the other. For example, Debbie Ford[31] says that most people have difficulty imagining that they could be a murderer, or have similar traits to a person like Hitler, and she is right, as I found out when I encountered the depth of my own shadow in the midst of a spiritual crisis in 1986.

The serpent in the shadow

Shadow material reflects those repressed and unprocessed feelings and experiences that have been disowned, but it is through the process of doing shadow work that we can start to become whole. Jung said that people who divert their precious life energies into being *normal* are creating restrictive conditions that can work against their unique human potential and flourishing.[32] This provocative statement contains a deep truth: how can it be possible to explore and live our full human potential if we are adapting and modifying ourselves to rigidly fit in with others or social norms all the time? Of course, there is a balance to be struck in terms of the need for social skills and having a sense of social responsibility, but if we never explore the boundaries between our inner world and our unique human potential, we will always be committed to living in the shadows. Part of the journey of awakening is to bring to light the unconscious complexities that are shaping our lives. In my book, *The Unselfish Spirit*, I wrote an autobiographical account of my journey through a spiritual crisis, which I encountered during my time living in a Tibetan Buddhist Monastery in the mid 1980s. I wrote about the impact of my spiritual crisis, which was both luminous and ominous.

I will not reiterate the context of my spiritual crisis, which I have elaborated on elsewhere, but suffice it to say, it was a profound spiritual awakening that opened me to experiences of love, beauty and bliss that I had never encountered before, and which lasted just over two days. This mystical awakening was a total surprise, and the experience of love was so strong that it eclipsed my everyday ego, which then resulted in me being so open that my repressed shadow material started emerging unfettered. Years of unprocessed emotional pain and anger flooded my consciousness, exposing me to extremes, such as murderous thoughts and feelings, which were very frightening. It took every bit of psychic energy and resilience I could muster to endure the overwhelming panic, chaos and disorientation that was triggered on a constant basis. I could hardly function due to the power of the altered states that I was encountering and I thought I was possessed by evil. It was only years later, after studying Carl Jung, that I realised I had been possessed by the unconscious. At the time the only safe thought I had about my predicament was that I would rather take my own life than harm another person. Some years later I was very touched when I read that Jung once said that he would rather sacrifice his own life than commit murder.[32] When I was living in the monastery I met a psychologist, who used to visit regularly and was interested in mysticism and consciousness. When he heard that I was having difficulties he managed to get a message to me, inviting me to stay the weekend with him. I only saw him a few times, but he understood that I was experiencing an extreme transformational crisis, and he encouraged me to face the experience and work through it. His wise, compassionate and non-pathological attitude gave me enormous encouragement to carry on. I lived on social security benefits for two years, and gradually learnt how to manage these extreme impulses within me without any other support. It was the single most difficult task I have had to face in my life to date.

Ten years after my spiritual crisis, I became a student of process-oriented psychology, and over the course of a decade, I worked on the integration of my spiritual crisis as part of my individuation process, which included dealing with the shock and aftermath that I had endured for a decade. In one of my therapy sessions, I processed the murderous thoughts and feelings I had experienced, as well as the distress of having been through such an ordeal. I was still reacting to what I had experienced and felt a sense of alienation, particularly because such subjects are over the cultural edge. The therapist I was working with perceptively observed that I seemed to be evaluating myself more like a psychiatrist, rather than someone who was interested in growing and learning from the experience. This insight was a game-changer. I was invited to go deeper into the experience of murderousness and this resulted in a bodily experience of shaking, which led to an inner vision of a large venomous snake. When I amplified the movement I could feel a power in my body, which was accompanied by a rasping sound. As I have discussed in previous chapters, snakes are symbolic of *healing* (Apollo and Asklepios), including *transformation* (shedding of skin), and *mystical consciousness* (Shakti-Kundalini). As the session progressed, the therapist suggested that I link the serpentine energy I was experiencing to my growing edge, where I could start to *mother my impulses*, rather than react to them. It was the first time that I really started to understand how the spiritual crisis I had experienced was more like a shamanic initiation and a process of renewal. The therapist said it was as if the snake energy could be used to strike for my individuation, and break through old patterns that no longer served me (transformation). Although things did not change overnight, I started to be more direct in the way that I lived, gradually becoming more congruent with the transformative energies that had been activated within me many years ago. Indeed, I learnt a very deep lesson in that session: that the unattended shadow has incredible power, which is where the killer incubates.[33] And yet, as I have revealed above, the shadow is also a powerful ally for transformation, if we are willing and able to work with it.

Over the years I have reflected on how I managed my transformational crisis. The seminal book on spiritual emergency, by Stanislav and Christina Grof, was published a year after I had been through the worst of my experience, but it was reassuring to know that I had intuitively done all the things they suggest are necessary to take care of the situation. In addition, it was also helpful to read the chapter on Kundalini by Lee Sannella,[34] where he notes that the sensations of heat and vibrations that I experienced are common in these types of awakenings. Sannella also speaks about the dynamic nature of Kundalini awakening. In the early stages, some people may encounter hostile or angry experiences, but it is rare for these to be acted out. Psychic disequilibrium can result from awakening Kundalini energy as noted by Charles Breaux.[35] He describes the peaks and troughs of his own Kundalini awakening, and his gratitude to the pioneering work of Carl Jung for paving the way for a non-pathological understanding of the psyche during spiritual awakening.

I was always curious why such powerful and extreme impulses arose within me. I reasoned that my turbulent emotional life as a child would have contributed to my repressed anger (adoption, early trauma, only child, no extended family, rootless existence with no lasting friendships, emotionally disconnected and chronic childhood bedwetting). As a child I was dissociated and disorientated. Between the ages of 15 to 18, I appeared in court four times for offences ranging from theft, to threatening behaviour and possession of an offensive weapon. I also reasoned that my time in the British army (infantry) must have honed a killer instinct within me. But I have come to realise that when we meet the unconscious we need to be prepared to face all manner of *adversarial* and *beneficial* symbols and energies. Normative social values for standards of behaviour are valuable (civic order), but they can also be inhibiting (social oppression). However, when we enter the stream of the individuation process, we can expect to meet all manner of experiences that go beyond cultural norms, and then the issue becomes how we learn to integrate such experiences and *not act them out* unconsciously. Arny Mindell[36] says that such encounters can become allies, and these often become known during a time of crisis. He wisely points out that we need to develop knowledge and awareness of the spirit that has awoken within us, particularly as the raw experience may be persistent and powerful, but also lack intelligence, heart or feelings. This was certainly true in my case (these processes will be discussed in Chapter Eight).

It is easier to manage powerful inner processes when our ego structures are reasonably stable, enabling us to meet the contents of the unconscious as they arise, which are then integrated into new patterns of growth and individuation. But, in my case (as for many other people) the spiritual crisis overwhelmed my ego structure, which was eclipsed by the unconscious. It meant that the unconscious content was in the foreground of experience, whilst a shaky ego was hanging on for dear life in the background. The crisis took me to the limits of my ability to cope. The unconscious assault was unrelenting. Yet, the spiritual crisis took me deep into altered and extreme states of consciousness, which held the seeds of my vocation as I eventually became an occupational therapist in acute mental health settings and in a psychological therapies team. The eruption of shadow material was like a shamanic calling for me, which reveals an important point – that whilst such experiences may feel like the end of the world, from another perspective they are just the beginning, like a new dawn.

The urgency of shadow integration

My spiritual crisis catalysed in me a deep interest in exploring my occupational myth, which connects to living a transformative life path of individuation and wholeness. Whilst it was a monumental struggle I somehow managed to emerge from the experience renewed. The greatest challenge was not to identify with the violent and murderous impulses that were constantly arising within me, and over a period of around two years I had to continually manage the self-annihilating idea that I was evil incarnate. But, as mentioned above, I learnt a very important lesson, that I was possessed by the unconscious, not by evil. Psychological possession can occur when unconscious forces overwhelm the ego.[37] William Irwin Thompson[5] acknowledges that we cannot run from our own shadows, no matter how much we may loathe ourselves, and the real point of shadow work is that it is an invitation to get to know ourselves more deeply. Recently I came across an article in *Psychology Today* by Douglas Kenrick,[38] which reported people's homicidal fantasies. In a series of studies he found that the majority of the male and female research participants admitted to having at least one homicidal fantasy, which seems to underscore the need for better understanding of the dynamics of the shadow in the modern mind. It also reveals that we need to make a demarcation in our processes of gaining awareness, where we learn not to conflate the shadow with evil. The shadow is not evil,[39] despite the fact that the contents of our repressed experiences can be very unsavoury, frightening and even terrifying. During the process of individuation each person is confronted with their own task in this life, as we are called to wake up and be true to our deepest natures, like the shamans who undergo the rigours of initiation, and then bring something useful back for the collective.

Our personal myth becomes an occupational myth when we dig deep and start to put our transformative potential into action. I like to believe that my psycho-spiritual journey of awakening through a crisis and sharing the edgy parts of my transformative crisis may be useful to others in some way. It taps into another belief I have, that in this time of global crisis, we are all being confronted with a collective rite of passage and opportunity to transform. It is here that we will inevitably meet a collective growing edge, which will challenge us to transform our outmoded consensus reality, where we will be forced to face the collective shadow and our responses to climate change, ecological destruction, and rapid increases in species extinction etc. It means that we will not only have to work with our shadow projections onto others, but also other people's projections towards us. For example, Arny Mindell[36] invites us to live fluidly in relation to projections and asks us to imagine how other people may feel about us e.g. in either loving or hateful ways. He suggests meeting the power that accompanies such experiences in various multi-sensory ways (e.g. visually, feelings, or movement etc.), which means we can then process, recycle and use the available energy wisely. This is such a wonderful example of using the imagination creatively to deal with inner tensions and transform outer relations (see the discussion on entropy in the introduction to part two). The following story underlines the power of shadow work, and how it enabled a woman to understand the destructive and creative potential of encountering the dark feminine.

I am on a steering group for a charity that works to empower people who have experienced *spiritually transformative experiences*. In a meeting I was telling the team about my new book, when Jeannet, a colleague (who is also on the steering committee) shared a recent experience of the dark feminine. During an ayahuasca workshop in March 2017 she had a visceral experience, which she described as "absolute terror". Her body started shaking violently and she let out screams from the pit of her stomach. The experience was a mystery to her, but she speculated that it connected to a body memory of an operation she had had as a child, which involved drilling into her skull. A week after the ayahuasca ceremony she was driving her car when she suddenly felt a sense of panic at being in her body. She decided to process this fearful experience at a *Holotropic Breathwork* workshop (a few months later). At the workshop she was able to reconnect with the fear, which she described as "being engulfed by a wave of undifferentiated terror". She continued with the breathwork and in the following session connected with the memory of a friend and close colleague who had hung himself a few years ago. She remembered how his face had been altered by the manner of his death. This image resonated with the sense of terror she was experiencing, which somehow mirrored her own self-destructive impulses. She inwardly felt the energy associated with the Hindu goddess Kali, whose destructive potential naturally evokes fear. It led her to recall a breathwork session from the late 1990s, where she encountered Kali as a magnificent, numinous, and totally impersonal force. In the session she experienced a sense of disembodiment and of being suspended in empty space, still with her thoughts and feelings, but no longer able to communicate with others or act in the world. It was as though she had killed herself, she thought. These experiences were terrifying when they happened; yet, the encounter with the Dark feminine gave Jeannet an appreciation of the destructive power of Kali, as a dynamic aspect of her shadow. On previous occasions she had experienced this destructive force as a life-threatening 'psychic attack', whereas now, she views working with unprocessed shadow material as actually deepening our connection to living. She learnt that what appears to be overwhelming and destructive also has creative potential: "I found that I could switch from seeing it one way or another, which was interesting and helpful." Jeannet's story reveals the importance of the dark feminine as a way of connecting to the transformative potential of processing our marginalised experiences and becoming more embodied.

Living a transformative life in the modern world means we will have to examine our personal and collective experiences (as well as reflecting on the morals and ethics that guide a global technocracy). It means we will need to be more committed to finding new ways of creating a relationship to life as a whole, inclusive of the shadow. At the present time our social institutions seem incapable of facilitating such a transformative shift, as most of them are bound too tightly to the status quo. However, failure to deal with the shadow side of our global predicament will be costly. Today, we constantly hear about the *bad guys* who are always *out there* (projection), but rarely do we hear about people who are working on their growing edges and doing the work *in here* (reflection). Jung[40] rightly said that the things that we ignore in ourselves filter into our reactions and behaviours towards others. The question is what do we do with such a realisation at a collective level? First, we should not catastrophise the human condition just because we have a shadow; indeed, the shadow helps us to grow in moral awareness and love.[41] Without shadow work, our consciousness will remain polarised and dualistic, for example in the way that we project good-evil onto other people and events. Yet, William Irwin Thompson[5] suggests that fear and terror, which informs our ideas of evil, may be a useful way of understanding the shady constellations that are unfolding in the world at this time.

We may not like the archaic word 'evil', due to its antiquated and religious tone, but it is certainly a human construct that helps to explain actions or events that cross agreed moral boundaries. Moreover, whilst the shadow itself is not evil, it is our disavowed individual and collective shadows where the seeds of evil are propagated. We ignore this reality at our peril. We need to be prepared for shadow projections to get out of hand when scapegoats are sought for collective problems. It is at such times that collective attitudes and actions can quickly crystallise into acts of evil. Meeting people who have been on the receiving end of such collective hatred is highly instructive. It helps us generate awareness of how quickly the shadow can get out of hand, particularly in these troubled times.

The Auschwitz death march

In the summer of 2015 I was staying in the picturesque market town of Hay-on-Wye (UK), where I was interviewed about my book at the international literature festival, which takes place every summer. My wife and I were staying in accommodation for two nights, and it was on the morning of our departure that we met an elderly couple that had arrived the evening before, Thomas and Peggy Buergenthal. Over breakfast we struck up a lively conversation, and it transpired that Tom was being interviewed about his book, *A Lucky Child*.[42] When I asked Tom what his book was about, he told us that it was about how he survived the Nazi death camp, Auschwitz, as a young boy. Tom also told us about his career and how he eventually went on to study law and became an international judge at The Hague. I was spellbound by Tom's story and disappointed that we had to leave Hay-on-Wye that day, as I would have liked to attend his talk. After a long conversation we said our goodbyes to Tom and Peggy, and I said that I would read his book on my return home, which I did.

The book is a heart-rending account of the terror inflicted by the Nazis on European Jews and other persecuted groups of people at that time, which resulted in the sinister climax of the Holocaust. The book is full of huge emotional twists and turns that dramatically illustrate how Tom and his family were dragged into a living hell. Prior to his incarceration in the concentration camp, Tom recounts a curious story that links to the title of his book. His mother, accompanied by a friend, went to visit a famous psychic. Tom's mother took off her wedding ring, so she did not give away any outward clues about her life. The psychic went on to tell her that she had a husband and a child, and that her son would come through the events that were before them, and she said he was: *a lucky child*. The word *lucky* does seem out of place when considered against the suffering, degradation, and losses experienced by Tom and his family. Yet, to survive Auschwitz as a 10- boy Tom was indeed incredibly lucky.

One day in Auschwitz, Tom describes in his book how he saw his mother behind the electric fence in the women's compound, and she also saw Tom. One can only imagine the impact of mother and son seeing each other alive in different compounds of a death camp. Sadly, Tom's father died in a concentration camp before the liberation. The magnitude of Tom's horrendous experiences is hard to imagine. For example, he took part in one of the infamous Auschwitz death marches when advancing Allied forces forced the Nazis to evacuate the concentration camp. The prisoners were force-marched by the SS for days in the ice-cold conditions of mid-winter in an attempt to preserve their slave labour.[43] Many people died in the freezing cold conditions, or were murdered by the SS if they were unable to keep up with the pace of the march. Eventually Tom was liberated and he managed to survive the Nazi killing machine, as did his mother, and they were eventually reunited after a long search. Tom's description about the reunion with his mother is deeply emotional and it represents a glimmer of light in the shadow of unimaginable cruelty and hatred. Tom also writes about a Norwegian man he met in the concentration camp called Odd Nansen, who had taken care of him. After the war Nansen wrote about his experiences in the camp, including the story about *little Tommy*, who he called *Angel Raphael of the Revier* (Revier means infirmary).

A few years after the war, Tom and his mother were invited to a conference where Nansen was presenting a paper and he spoke about the need to treat German refugees with empathy. The focus of the conference was on peace and dignity, which had a profound impact on Tom's eventual vocation as a lawyer and international judge, where he became concerned with upholding justice and human rights. Tom's experiences in the death camps inspired his commitment to help others suffering at the hands of persecutors. As he says at the end of his book, the Holocaust is a tragedy for the whole of humanity, not only Jewish people.

We must never forget the atrocities of history and be diligent about crimes against humanity, as well as the crimes against other species and the planet, which are being committed today. The collective shadow can quickly come to the fore when conditions in society change. Take the steep rise in anti-immigration rhetoric and racist behaviour after the UK EU referendum in 2016, which was marginally won by the 'Leave' campaign. The referendum unleashed a surge of shadow projections towards people from other countries, now living in the UK. It points to the need to be vigilant, especially in a world of instant communications, where it is becoming easier for extreme ideologies to reach large groups of people. For example, research has shown how extreme groups can manipulate rankings in search engines, through multiple 'clicks' on specific hyperlinks to strengthen optimisation. Searches linked to terms like Muslims, Jews, the Holocaust, and Hitler are in many cases connected to right wing and extremist groups.[44] The shadow is not confined to a particular group of people, as we each possess a personal shadow, but the collective shadow can be found lurking in any social and institutional context. Marie Louise Von Franz[45] warns us that when the personal shadow is not integrated, it is where the collective shadow enters.

Process-oriented psychologist Arlene Audergon[46] has worked internationally with communities, where conflicts have devastated people's lives. She speaks about the need to face the 'demons' that have impacted us, individually, communally, and globally, revealing that healing and awareness can be cultivated if we are willing to face the difficult dynamics that all too often lie submerged in consciousness. Her message is much needed in our volatile world today, especially to help us understand how 'terror' is propagated through tactics that dehumanise groups, which then become normalised and lead to further desensitisation. I believe that we cannot evolve as a species without educating ourselves about the power of the collective shadow and its consequences. It is critical to helping us develop greater understanding about the ways that evil can be seeded in the shade of our neglected prejudices. The reality of the Transformocene is that our collective predicament is adversarial, and it will take deep courage and resolve to face the global mess we have created. Yet it is through such rites of passage that deep transformation happens.

Exercise: Sacred shadow

- Take time to reflect on a particular social group that you have a reaction to. Notice how they arouse strong feelings in you, such as anger, irritation, dislike, or even hatred.

- Imagine the above negative thoughts and feelings being turned into a short 10 minute film clip. What is the title of the film? What is the key message in the film? Write these words down.

- Look at what you have written for the title and key message. Find one word that encapsulates the quality of the negative projection you are making. Underline the word.

- Now, reclaim your projection and imagine a symbol of positive change arising within you (e.g. a symbol that is the opposite of the negative word).

- Explore the qualities of this transformative symbol and notice how it could inspire you to make a new film about the group, one that shifts your attitude towards them.

- What is the title of the new film? What is its key message? Write these words down.

- Compare the two films. What have they taught you?

Understanding how evil is seeded, propagated, grown and harvested is a pressing question for humanity today. Such reflections begin 'in here', not 'out there'. In which case, as we shall sow, so shall we reap?

CHAPTER SIX

The Veil of Evil

Overview

The discussion in this chapter focuses on the meaning of evil and how it is an emotive word reserved for malevolent actions. Evil is a human construct, benchmarked by certain attitudes, values, and behaviours intended to do serious harm to others. In this chapter I ask, could humanity's destructive actions towards the natural world and other species be considered evil? I point out that our collective neglect of the ecological crisis, while also being aware of it, is tantamount to an act of ecocide. In this time of global crisis we need to reconsider the moral and ethical basis for many of our actions towards the natural world. I argue that tackling the issue of evil today requires honest appraisal of our complicity in acts of eco-destruction, which requires awareness of evil both 'out there' and 'in here'. I point out that most cultures have myths that represent the tensions between good-evil, where facing adversarial circumstances is often linked to spiritual awakening. Confronting the reality of evil is part of our collective wake-up call today, and creative participation in personal and planetary transformation is part of our redemptive quest.

The myth of evil and evil's myth

Carl Jung[1] wrote that the modern world is caught in the grip of evil, for which we seem to have no imaginative response. He meant that we have debunked ancient myths as mere superstitions, without realising the subtle and profound levels of wisdom they convey. Not only do myths inform us about our ways of living and doing,[2] they are a part of our human experience, and reside in the depths of the unconscious, where they repeatedly appear (in various forms) in our dreams, visions and yearnings.[3] And so, myths of good-evil are eternal conundrums, not mere abstractions or existential curiosities. The realities of good-evil tend to reappear in successive generations with regularity. The question is, why? It is an issue that no one can answer adequately, but when we listen to people who have encountered near-death experiences, we learn that there is a metaphysical dimension to good-evil, which involves us. Neurosurgeon Eben Alexander[4] shares his experience of the afterlife and says that while good prevails more than evil on Earth, it is because we have free will that evil happens. Our purpose on Earth is not to amass wealth or pursue fame; it is to open our hearts to the Divine and live with compassion and love. It is a mythic and metaphysical representation for how our life energies could be used on Earth, aligned with a sacrament of wholeness. It is the opposite of our current fragmented ways of living that make up modern consciousness. Worryingly, the prevailing attitude in the modern world is that people imagine they are free from the ancient struggles between good-evil.[5]

The combination of a one-sided egocentricity and a neglected shadow in the modern world are complementary elements of our dissociated experience of consciousness, which, if left unattended, will undoubtedly give rise to more acts of evil happening in the world. But, what do we mean by the word evil in a modern context? Rollo Romig,[6] writing in *The New Yorker*, drew on the work of various writers and noted that evil has been discussed in relation to *natural*, *metaphysical* and *moral* causes. For example, earthquakes or other disasters have often been described as *natural* or *metaphysical* evils, whereas *moral* evil is usually reserved for times when people commit atrocities, which provide a marker that alerts us to the seriousness of the crime. Moral evils are determined by malevolent acts, where people are intent upon inflicting grievous harm. They reflect a particular type of behaviour, which is directed with the sole purpose of impacting negatively on others. William Irwin Thompson[7] makes an important point when he says that the destruction of ecosystems and the biosphere is an '*evil*' that we urgently need to tackle today, particularly in our efforts to engage in a process of collective transformation on the planet.[8] This is an important point on two counts: first, if naturally occurring ecological disasters are considered natural evils, then it follows that those human activities contributing to worsening ecological conditions could be seen as evil. For example, in the ways they influence and amplify the worsening effects of climate change. Second, now that we are fully aware of the extent to which human activities are destroying ecosystems, we cannot avoid the fact that we are intentionally causing harm to other people, other species and nature as a whole. We may not like the idea that we are participating in acts of moral evil, but this could be a powerful way of reflecting back to us the impact of our destructive attitudes and behaviours, which could initiate and inspire transformational change. Jung[1] reminds us of the confession of St Paul, who said: *The evil which I would not, that I do*, is a meditation that could help us reflect on our actions in the world today.

Part of the wake-up call for humanity today is to understand the global crisis is our problem. It means we will undoubtedly have to confront the evils we have done, or are doing, as well as the evils that are done in our name. Jung[9] believed that each of us has the potential for both good-evil within, and for evil to be addressed it will require a radically different attitude from conventional life. He suggests that we will need to enter into a process of spiritual renewal to arrive at a new orientation for living.[10] Indeed, Paul Levy[11] says that the reason we struggle with understanding our potential for evil is because we find it hard to imagine how we are intimately connected to it. This echoes with Jung's view that our avoidant attitude to *doing* the required inner work is what actually stop us from confronting evil within.[12] I think this is a central issue in terms of how humanity can be encouraged to wake up and develop greater awareness and cultivate a new culture of consciousness, based on an honest assessment of who we are as a species. Jung[13] made it abundantly clear that his personal and professional interest was in the cultivation of wholeness, rather than simply being good. He also said that the only sane way to address the reality of evil is through the cultivation of *self-knowledge*.[13] Interestingly, theologian and activist Matthew Fox[14] says that *good* is not the opposite of evil, rather it is the *sacred*, and that facing up to evil is part of our spiritual work. I take this to mean that encountering evil and understanding it is a key part of our spiritual development.

We know that greed and avarice are not conducive for our spiritual development, or for society. For example, look at the impact on public confidence when politicians or financiers act in self-interested ways. What checks and balances are there in our social institutions to guide behaviours for the greater good? Jeffrey Russell[15] cites a college professor in the 1980s who advised students at a business school not to feel bad about being greedy. This attitude of entitlement was rife in a decade of excess, where a *yuppie culture* flourished, normalising and celebrating self-aggrandisement and unfettered moneymaking. It was a mindset that was undoubtedly present in the 2008 sub-prime banking debacle. The practice of selling mortgages to low waged American citizens, in the knowledge that a hike in interest rates would render their customers homeless, was symptomatic of a culture of excessive profiteering and self-interest. The individuals were seduced into buying mortgages that consequently left them homeless and impoverished. Similarly, many of the companies and countries that purchased the mortgage debt in good faith, as a viable financial investment, were also victims of the deceit that masqueraded as business.[16] Such insidious self-interest sows the seeds of evil.[17]

It is now painfully evident how institutionalised selfish behaviours are not only anti-social; they are immoral and actually erode cultural values and attitudes for the worse. The 2008 financial crash is symptomatic of our outmoded technocracy, where reductionist markers govern the economic drivers for growth and profit. For example, across the world, the key measure for progress amongst governments, academics, the media, and the UN is based on a single indicator for prosperity, *Gross Domestic Product* (GDP). It is a measure of wealth, which is used in preference to other non-financial variables. But there are more holistic ways of considering prosperity, where people and the planet could flourish.[16] Interestingly, GDP is not even a fair measure of how wealth is distributed in society, as seen in a Bank of England assessment, which looked at the value of National GDP across 12 regions in the UK. Only London and the South East were financially better off than before the 2008 financial crash. The mistaken idea that GDP means the same for everyone was starkly illustrated when a learned academic was giving a talk in the North of England before the 2016 Brexit referendum; he was warning people of the negative impact on GDP if the UK left the EU. Then, unexpectedly a woman in the audience shouted out: "That's your bloody GDP, not ours."[18] Since the 2008 financial crash the austerity measures imposed on people and communities have had a big impact. For example, since 2010 the number of people sleeping rough on UK streets has doubled.[19]

The 2008 sub-prime banking fiasco highlights the shadowy practices of the financial world today, where a sense of entitlement drove some employees to bring whole countries to the brink of collapse. The celebration of wealth creates desperate imbalances, such as the eight men who possess greater wealth than half the world's population.[20] However, the metric of the so-called 1% of the world's wealthiest people is more nuanced than we were led to believe. Financial comparisons have been made using Western earnings in a global context, which has taken into account the cheaper cost of living in poorer countries. It turns out that people earning £35,000 or more in the Western world are actually in the global 1%. Even a person on a low income of £7,000 per annum still ranks in the world's richest 15%.[21] That said, year on year the gulf between the world's rich and poor is widening and much more needs to be done to tackle global poverty and inequality.

Prophets of profit and doom

The 2008 financial crash was more than a banking debacle; it was a revelation that exposed the deeply entrenched greed that lies at the heart of modern capitalism. At the time of editing the penultimate draft of this book in February 2017, US President Donald Trump announced his plans to deregulate the financial safeguards placed on Wall Street.[22] Should we be worried? The answer is an emphatic 'yes'. It sends a green light to sharp-practising profiteers who want to get rich at any cost. We have evidence of such behaviours in the actions of financial traders who worked for banks at the time of the 2008 crash, which was catalysed by the collapse of Lehman Brothers. We also learn that financial traders in the city of London were involved in Libor rigging, manipulating and fixing lending rates in a system that was open to abuse. Banks headhunted 'talented' traders who were tasked with making as much money as possible for their bosses. The case of Tom Hayes is a good example of a trader who was prosecuted and jailed for his part in the 2008 financial meltdown, yet he was employed solely because of his ability to work at the edge of risky transactions. He said that the volume of money he made was his only key performance indicator, and the yardstick by which his efforts would be judged. He spoke about his dishonest actions in a dishonest system.[23]

A more holistic outlook for how finances are used in the modern world would seek a return to 'sacred economics', where life is seen as more than a commodity to be exploited, which results in unsustainable competition and the delusion of unending growth.[24] New economic models that focus on justice and sustainability are emerging,[25] which is a welcome sign. But I contend that these models will only be effective if we truly understand how the shadow operates in our transactional world. Since 2008 the shadow side of the financial world – rampant profiteering, greed and self-interest – have exposed a deep contempt for the welfare of others. Incidentally, the austerity measures that followed the 2008 crash have coincided with a rise in right-wing politics, which has resulted in cold and callous rhetoric and behaviours, particularly in the UK and USA (shadow projections). We can also see such hardening of attitudes being propagated in certain parts of the media.

A provocative social commentator who used to write for a UK national newspaper claimed that she did not care about the plight of human beings caught up in the European refugee crisis, even if it included news about dead bodies floating in the sea.[26] Similarly, a newspaper column reporting on the 2016 USA presidential preliminaries quoted Donald Trump calling Hilary Clinton *the devil*.[27] Presumably he was trying to make the point that she is evil. However, pointing to evil *out there* is part of the shadow problem that exists under the surface of modern consciousness. The remedy is to consider where evil exists *in here*, as noted by Jung[9] who also spoke about the need to confront the wrongs that we have thought, intended, or done. Otherwise we are at the mercy of the unacknowledged and unprocessed shadow.[28] It is here that the seeds of evil are germinated and propagated in our projections. Humanity appears to be slipping into a state of *peak shadow*, meaning our lack of inner work is now catalysing an escalation of shadow projections that will continue to spill over into our collective egocentric lives with devastating consequences, unless we act to remedy the malaise. It is an issue that is already starting to resonate in the collective. In February 2017 *The Guardian* newspaper reported that the books of Hannah Arendt, including *The Banality of Evil*, have become surprise bestsellers.[29] It points to a growing concern about the types of negative behaviours that are taking root in the world.

As we have seen, the work of Carl Jung first drew our attention to the parallels between myths and lived experiences. One such myth that reflects the destruction and madness of the Third Reich is captured in the story of Wotan. It is well known that Hitler was an admirer of the anti-Semitic composer Richard Wagner, particularly the four operatic dramas that make up *Der Ring des Nibelungen*, which chronicles the wanderings of Wotan. Hitler was keen for his SS officers to watch Wagner's opera, *The Ring Cycle*, which he believed represented a mythic connection to the Germanic spirit, but also conveyed a quest for knowledge and power (represented by the Ring). We begin to understand how Hitler inflated the importance of the Wotan myth to his life, shortly after German troops had annexed Austria. Hitler was addressing the adoring crowds from a balcony on March 13th 1938, basking in the adulation of his many admirers. He then looked upwards into the sky and had a vision of Wotan looking down at him, who was also pointing towards the East. Hitler interpreted this as approval of his intended plans to attack Russia.[30] It is clear that Hitler over-identified with the archetype of Wotan. Jung had already warned that over-identification with an archetype can have disastrous consequences, due to the possibility of psychic inflation. In this regard Hitler was hooked, for we learn that when he travelled incognito he used the alias, *Herr Wolf*, and it is no coincidence that the Wolf is another name for Wotan.[31] Hitler also referred to the SS as his Wolf pack[32] and he named his bunker, located on the eastern front, the *Wolf's Lair*.[33] In a fascinating twist at the end of the Ring cycle, *The Twilight of the Gods*, Valhalla is ablaze, in much the same way that Hitler's *Third Reich* was reduced to a smouldering ruin in the last days of the war. Hitler's over-identification with the archetype of Wotan seeped into the collective consciousness of the German people, who lapped up this mythic representation of the German spirit. As Jung noted, this was a collective over-compensation for the national humiliation following the First World War.[34]

The question we have to ask ourselves today is, what safeguards are in place to protect us from such destructive behaviours manifesting again? We have to be diligent of political wannabes who use manipulative rhetoric to blame *others* for the state of things. If we need a modern day example of how scapegoats are used, we only need to consider the threats and malice that were unleashed in the UK following the *Brexit* referendum, where law abiding people who had legitimately settled in Britain were subjected to racist abuse and even assault by some UK citizens. How far were these anti-social behaviours given legitimacy by lowbrow negative political campaigners, who tapped into a shadowy underbelly in the UK, puncturing the myth of British tolerance and fair play? If Brexit has taught us one thing, it is that it requires very little effort to mobilise intolerance (and in some cases hatred) in a country that is considered civilised. A UK Government-backed report that explored community cohesion, by Louise Casey, found 62,518 alleged hate crimes had been reported in England and Wales between 2015-16, a 19% increase from the previous year.[35] It supports the notion that if we scratch beneath the surface of any person or society a shadowy world will surface. The question is, how do we transform such a reality into a potential that serves the greater good? This question is set to become more prominent. For example, George Monbiot[36] points out that the political attitude of President Donald Trump and his denial of climate change could create the conditions for increases in armed conflict, that is, if countries put national interests above the greater good of the world. He goes on to say that humanity needs to imagine a new future, not one tainted by the past. Increases in world population and greater pressures on planetary resources, such as sources of energy, arable land

and fresh water, may well become the flashpoints of future conflict. If we think this is simply scaremongering, a brief look at Hitler's Nazi ideology shows how the collective shadow can become mobilised for national interests.

Hitler's dream

Before the Second World War, Hitler had wanted more land for the German people so they could live healthy lives. Timothy Snyder[37] discussed Hitler's fantasy of creating an ecological habitat (*Lebensraum*), or space to live for the German people, which has subtle, but nonetheless uncomfortable parallels with the ecological state of the world we are living in today. Hermann Göring said the *Third Reich* had no qualms about taking over foreign lands to feed German citizens, even if it meant people from other countries starving.[38] Snyder[37] points out that we need to be careful of our projections, for if we start entertaining the notion that we are victims of some sort of global conspiracy, we are moving closer to Hitler's worldview, where someone is to blame for the problems we are experiencing (scapegoat). In essence, Snyder is warning that our collective failure to take responsibility for worsening climate change may cause us to project our shadows onto some group or other for causing the global crisis. It will take a great deal of collective restraint and soul searching by a critical mass of people to start reclaiming our prejudices and projections as we start to work for peace on the planet.

History has shown us exactly what happens when toxic prejudices take root in the collective and are propagated as truth, and there is every possibility it could happen again. We all have a personal shadow, and the shadow also has a collective dimension, which means it can be manipulated and mobilised. The distressing images of emaciated prisoners in the concentration camps of the Bosnian war in the 1990s are a reminder that a modern European country can quickly descend into chaos, where atrocities are committed in the name of historical grievances. In the case of Adolf Hitler, he writes in *Mein Kampf*[39] that his beliefs were based on his *völkish* (folk) concept, which separated races into categories of superior and inferior. Hitler believed his folk concept was aligned with Nature's operations, and he envisioned a German race of human beings who were superior to others, and who would be masters over others and world resources. Later these ideas would feed into a pseudo-scientific racial theory. The Holocaust is a stark reminder of a shadow projection that resulted in the murder of millions of human beings who were deemed flawed when measured against the psychosis of Nazi ideology. Hitler's ideology was born in the trenches of the First World War, where he first had intimations that he had a destiny to fulfil.

One night in 1917, Hitler was stationed in the Somme and was sleeping in a trench when he had a suffocating dream that tons of earth and hot metal were falling on him. He woke up in a terrified state and ran from the bunker into the night to catch his breath and recover from his nightmare. Suddenly, the bunker from which he fled was hit by artillery fire, killing all his comrades. Such a powerful synchronous event fed Hitler's belief that he had been saved for a greater fate.[40] However, it has also been suggested that the dream may have been a prophetic warning of his future path of annihilation,[30] where his unbounded hatred eventually led to mass murder and widespread destruction for millions of people. Yet, in *Mein Kampf*[39] Hitler wrote about his time living in Vienna in poverty as a painter for five years. He was already harbouring negative thoughts about Marxism and Judaism. Hitler's anti-Semitism grew stronger after World War One and he started using defamatory language when speaking about Jewish people. He writes that initially he had to separate reason from sentiment to clarify his anti-Semitism, but as with all corrupted shadow projections, his sentiments fell in line with his twisted reasoning. What we see in Hitler's writings is a prejudice and projection that develops gradually, until it reaches a crescendo, where he demonises Jewish people as sub-human, evil and the cause of all Germany's problems. But Hitler was not alone in his hatred of the Jews. A prominent theologian of the time, Gerhard Kittel, also condemned Jews for being degenerate.[41]

The tragedy of the German people under the Nazis was how their psyches were manipulated and their visionary energies were mobilised by an arch-propagandist (Hitler had been the propaganda officer of the right wing political organisation, the *German Workers Party*, before he created the Nazi party). Hitler promised the German people a renewed sense of power, respect, order and authority, rather than post World War One humiliation.[12] Feelings of humiliation would have been close to Hitler at a personal level; we discover that his alcoholic father would regularly beat him as a child. But we also learn that the young Hitler was also a church chorister, and he harboured aspirations to become a Catholic priest.[42] Indeed, whilst it is important to not play down Hitler's malevolent attitudes and actions, the evil, which was seeded in the disavowed collective shadow, was not all Adolf Hitler's; it also belonged to all the people who supported him. This is illustrated by the fact that by the end of the Second World War in 1945, Hitler's book *Mein Kampf* had sold 12 million copies. Approximately 90% of the German people supported Hitler and his Nazi party.[43]

Hitler's persecution of Jewish people and other groups also reveals how the established professions and institutions in Germany were complicit in propagating the shadow of Nazism, for example, through the collusion of professions, such as law, medicine, and the military.[44] It is almost incomprehensible that the extermination of millions of Jewish people and others could have happened on such an industrial scale, and in such a systematic and orderly way, without the full involvement of the German social infrastructure. Yet it must not be forgotten, in the context of all this, that anti-Semitism was rife throughout Europe in the early 20th century, at the time of Hitler's rise.[12] The level of dissociation among the German people reveals the extent to which evil gradually became normalised. A leading Nazi, Adolf Eichmann, described his role in the mass extermination of fellow humans as *just doing his job*.[45] The example of the Nazis' rise to power shows us how shadow projections, if left unattended, can fester and crystallise into evil acts (see the book, *The Lucifer Effect*). It underlines the importance of doing shadow work in this time of global crisis.[46]

For German people who were psychologically aware of what was happening in their country, it was difficult to function in everyday life. Jungian analyst Max Zeller[47] says that he changed every item of clothing whenever he returned home from an outing in the German city where he lived. It is a graphic portrayal of a powerful need to be separated from the poisonous atmosphere that permeated all aspects of civic life. What Zeller encountered on the streets of Nazi Germany was the mass influence of the *collective shadow*. Jung noted around the time of the mid 1930s that Germany was already starting to be possessed by a collective psychosis,[34] revealing how psychic corruption is gradual and insidious. It is worth reiterating the point by Debbie Ford,[48] that in the process of doing shadow work, we may find that we have similar traits to Hitler. And this is a critical point: if we think Hitler was a one-off 'monster', or not human, we miss the point that his distorted views started out as a vehement dislike of other groups, and the more these prejudices were reinforced, the more he believed them. Indeed, Mary Harrell[49] recounts a story she heard about a person who was in analysis, and the person said that their analytical work would be finished once they had met the *Hitler within*. Of course, shadow work is a key factor in the process of individuation (like it is in alchemy), and the focus of the work is about becoming whole and exploring ways to align with the sacred, where we can begin to count our blessings and live a more enlightened existence. However, as a species we have not got to grips with our collective psycho-spiritual potential.

Shadow work is an integral part of becoming whole, where we own our projections, rather than *the other* becoming a convenient, objectified scapegoat, who ends up shouldering a burden that is not theirs to carry. Our job is to learn how our everyday life is a series of projections, which includes the shadow that is constantly flickering in our attitudes and actions. When we are caught up in deeply entrenched projections, which may be linked to our repressed or unexamined experiences, such as hurt, fear, malice, or hatred (from our personal unconscious), it is a cue for awareness work. When we address the energy bound to our shadows' projections and use it in the service of individuation it becomes transformative. The salutary lesson in the case of Adolf Hitler is that he invested in his prejudices and he acted them out with devastating consequences. He is epitomised as the embodiment of evil,[42] but we should never forget that each of us has the seed for similar potential to grow in us and become enacted.

Evil, the crucible of transformation

Working regularly on our shadow projections is like hygiene for the soul, because it makes a real difference to our cultivation of awareness, especially when we willingly confront our prejudices. As stated in the previous chapter, if the shadow is left unattended or unprocessed, our repressed experiences can become fixed, and if these prejudices or distortions are constantly endorsed or reinforced (internally and/or externally), the shadow becomes more and more crystallised as it forms into a more complex problem. A repressed and unexamined shadow, accompanied by a shallow and ineffective egocentricity, propagates the seeds of evil, which may eventually become rooted in our consciousness. But, if we hold to the idea that we can be transformed by working with our potential and growth, we can redress our one-sided egocentricity, through inner work, dreams and synchronous events. Jungian analyst Max Zellar,[47] who was living in Germany when Hitler invited Mussolini to visit Berlin, tells of one such serendipitous event. The Nazi leader decided to pull out all the stops to make sure the visit was a monumental success in terms of representing a cohesive fascist ideology to the masses. Hitler decreed that on the day of the parade all meetings and entertainment in the city were to be suspended and citizens were encouraged to line the streets in a show of support. However, on the same day as his parade, Hitler found out that a group of psychoanalysts had invited the Swiss psychiatrist and psychologist Carl Jung to deliver a lecture on the same day as his Nazi extravaganza.

Despite his autocratic ruling, Hitler thought it would be rude to cancel the eminent psychiatrist's lecture, particularly as it had been arranged before his fascist parade. The turn of events becomes even more extraordinary when we find out that Jung's lecture was to take place at the same time and on the very same route as Hitler's motorcade, which passed the window of the room where Jung was lecturing. On the day Jung was giving his talk the deafening sound of German citizens and their enthusiastic cries of support for Hitler and Mussolini grew louder as the procession drew closer to the building where Jung was addressing his audience. The sound became so loud that Jung actually stopped speaking, and stood in silence, waiting until he was once again audible. He then said in a measured tone, that "world history" had just passed beneath the window. The contrast between Jung and Hitler could not be starker. Jung was committed to working with the potential in his shadow as a creative act, discovering what it takes to be whole, whilst Hitler was possessed by the shadow, which eventually resulted in evil acts of destruction that affected the lives of millions. If this synchronous event teaches us one thing, it is how willingly the masses in Munich joined the hysteria whipped up by the collective shadow, which was orchestrated by a charismatic leader caught in the delusional grip of being a saviour. Later, in his role as Fuhrer, his megalomania was increasingly fuelled by daily injections of the drug *Eukadol*, which induces euphoric states.[50] Hitler was a complete mess and he made a mess of the world. It is a warning to all nations to put in place safeguards so that collective consciousness cannot be stirred by the lowest common denominator, which is a failure of the collective imagination.

We always have opportunities to redeem our consciousness from the grip of shadow projections. For example, Jungian analyst John Sanford[51] suggests that there are probably very few people who have not had a fantasy of wishing a person dead, which he says may simply be a way of fantasising about having more space in our lives, or the need to take time out from a relationship that has become too burdensome. Such fantasies, whilst unpleasant, are a contextual response to feeling trapped, oppressed, being in an abusive relationship or a deadening situation. This is very different to the example of Heinrich Himmler, who became head of the notorious SS, the politicised and militaristic wing of the Nazi regime. Himmler actively pursued his dream of annihilating innocent people, as revealed in archive footage. He also spoke about the *horrors* to come.[52] Himmler had never seen military action and he had no idea of the devastating impact that taking another person's life can have on the soul. One day he decided to visit one of his infamous death squads (*einsatzgruppen*), who were in the throes of murdering a hundred Jews by firing squad. Himmler almost fainted at the sight of the slaughter before his eyes, which made him feel quite unwell. He also became aware of similar reports of the traumatic impact that taking part in the killings was having on some of the soldiers in his death squads, with many of them reporting psychological and somatic symptoms (Himmler also reported having constant stomach problems). To remedy this, Himmler ordered his men to socialise in the evenings to strengthen their sense of camaraderie. He also sent out a startling memo to his generals and senior officers, thanking his "decent" SS soldiers for taking part in such a "difficult duty" (killing operations). The words of William Irwin Thompson[8] ring true when he speaks about ideologists who are capable of invoking noble reasons for the horrors that they perpetrate. In the case of Himmler his twisted attempts to rationalise mass murder illustrate how such evil atrocities are exercised via a shallow egocentricity[53] with no moral compass. Himmler's dissociation is evident in the way that he could not bear the visceral reaction to slaughter, which was his bodily response to the evil he ordered others to commit.

Lifting the veil of evil

Actions that are labelled good-evil evoke strong feelings in people, and whether we like it or not, our emotional lives are bound to mythic narratives, where these terms are deeply rooted. Myths of good-evil not only reflect moral scenarios and judgements, they also help our everyday consciousness to make distinctions between different courses of action (and their consequences). Rather than being outmoded and outdated, myths and fairy tales that portray the tensions between good-evil play an important role in the collective, providing a range of symbolic scenarios, which allow us to reflect and counter the one-dimensional mode of consciousness so prevalent in today's modern society. Stephen Larsen[54] helpfully explains that evil in myths often functions as an *activating principle*, bringing about a powerful dynamic that catalyses change. In other words, as Sanford[51] points out, people rarely feel motivated to engage with deeper questions about consciousness until events force the issue. In this way, evil jolts us into taking consciousness seriously, and as a consequence we have opportunities to take action, to grow and develop. Waking up to the evil we have thought, done or intended is only remedied by the sacred quest of redeeming our souls.

Jungian analyst Lillian Frey-Rohn[55] believes that humanity needs to connect with the highest virtues possible when confronting the adversarial nature of evil, in order not to succumb to it. Whilst this is an important point, we also have to put evil in its place, which is a test of our psycho-spiritual development. William Irwin Thompson[7] suggests that in order for a new conscious outlook to emerge, the traditional representation and polarisation of good-evil, such as found in representations of Satan and Christ, needs to be reviewed. I believe Thompson is correct on this important point for the following reason: good-evil are actualities that we have to encounter in our processes of psycho-spiritual awakening. These ancient stories are metaphors for how we approach the inner drama of transformation. All too often the 'Devil' is considered *out there*, and such externalising allows for projections to be directed at others, who then become known as the *evildoers*.[49] We need a more honest and nuanced understanding of the meaning of evil as an adversarial encounter, one that can spur us on to work for wholeness. For example, the powerful Western myth of Christ and Satan clearly identifies that they are contradictory forces,[56] where Satan is viewed as an adversary who tests our spiritual evolution. We can see this dynamic in the drama of Satan testing Jesus in the desert. As soon as Satan realises he has no hold on Jesus, he is told: "*get thee behind me*". It clearly shows that Satan has been put in his place, otherwise why would Jesus suggest that a potentially lethal adversary stand behind him? It also reveals a deep level of 'knowing' that can be activated via such adversarial encounters, for example, when Jesus advises us to: "Resist not evil" (Matthew: 5:39). It points to a necessary and unavoidable encounter that deepens our sacred quest. Let us not forget Jung's psycho-spiritual mantra, which goes something along the lines of: *that which is resisted, persists*.

Satan is a useful mythological figure to help us understand the root meaning of adversary, or one who is in opposition (*śtn*). In the Hebrew Bible, according to Pagels,[57] Satan is referred to as God's obedient servant. So we have to consider that the adverse circumstances we meet in life may be part of our growth and development, where we are tasked with not only objectifying evil, but also dealing with the seeds of evil that reside within us. For example, Pagels[57] points out that in the *Gospel of Phillip* (from the Nag Hammadi library) people are advised to look at their evil impulses within their actions, which if met, and not acted upon, can create shifts in awareness and understanding. A wonderful example of this is found in Jung's[58] book *Answer to Job*. The Biblical story of Job illustrates the adversarial nature of good-evil, when Satan takes God to one side and questions the faith of his most upright and moral servant (Job). Satan suggests to God that if Job was put under pressure and duress, he would probably buckle and his faith would waiver. God agrees to let Satan test Job, on the condition that he does not kill him. Satan quickly sets to work and he unleashes all manner of horrors onto Job, including boils, the loss of family, friends and fortune. Poor Job has no idea what fate has befallen him, but under the most terrible circumstances he does not lose his faith; in fact he grows in wisdom and awareness. Jung interprets God's willingness to let Satan test Job as a sign that God is unconscious, and that Job's ability to endure such adversity is recognition that transformation of consciousness on the human plane is possible. Jung believed that Job's growth in spiritual awareness also helps God wake up and become whole. It is an interpretation that is not without controversy.

In his book *Answer to Job*, Jung exemplifies the relationship between a supposedly unconscious God and Job's dawning Self-realisation, which connects to an emergent transpersonal consciousness. However, it is unlikely that the story is dealing with an unconscious God; it is more likely to be a mythic representation revealing how humanity can grow spiritually in the face of adversity (Satan being the adversary). John Sanford[53] makes an important observation that Jung overlooked, in that he (Jung) made no distinction between *natural evil* (such as disastrous events or calamities that happen), and other forms of evil, such as *moral or psychological evil*, which are reflected in people's actions. Sanford illustrates his point by quoting the Biblical prophet Isaiah, who speaks about God having the power to make peace and create evil, which Sanford explains is a reference to the occurrence of natural evil, not moral or psychological evil. In terms of Job's experience, Sanford says the Biblical *Book of Job* is a reflection on how God's faithful servant endures and manages suffering (as a natural evil); it is not concerned with how or why human beings do evil acts. Sanford regards Job as an excellent role model for how to adopt a sacred attitude in the face of adversity. The story of Job's encounter provides us with a useful mythic representation of how he holds to wholeness without splitting and projection. We can see this in the way he faces the *natural evil* that plagues him with great resilience and equanimity, but also in the way he does not *act out* and commit moral evil because of his plight. The drama is deeply mythic and indicative of the fortitude and faith required in psycho-spiritual awakening. Yet it is a patriarchal myth, and as Jung points out, it is Sophia who is missing from the drama, but interestingly, it is Job who awakens through her and gains a deeper insight (wisdom) into the sacred function of the *dark night of the soul*.

Sanford reminds us that human beings are capable of making distinctions between the natural evils that befall us as distinct from the moral and psychological evils we are capable of committing. Yet Jung has to be credited for initiating a discussion about the sacred polarities of good-evil and how they pertain to human consciousness and awakening to the transpersonal realm in the modern world. Jung also teaches us that questions of good-evil may have more to do with evolving our consciousness beyond duality, which is a view that can be found in Eastern philosophy and in the evolutionary psychology of

Gurdjieff.[59] In the Judeo-Christian tradition the question of good-evil appears to be about free will and the choices human beings make in life. Reiterating the point made in Chapter Three, Elaine Pagels[60] reminds us that in the mythical story of Adam and Eve, God advised the couple not to eat from the tree of knowledge of good-evil, but when they did eat the forbidden fruit their eyes were opened and they noticed that they were naked, which indicates that the act of receiving knowledge of good-evil was also an awakening of self-consciousness. The issue of free will in this regard can be seen in another reference to a tree from the New Testament, when Jesus speaks about a tree being recognised by its fruit (Matthew 6:44). I believe these stories point to an *original myth* where our actions and consciousness are linked to possibilities of *doing* good-evil, which also underlines the importance of exercising free will as part of our connection to being whole. In other words, humanity either grows spirituality through meeting adversity, or lives in fear of it and succumbs to it, which reveals that our cumulative actions in life are the fruits of how we have lived (good-evil). It takes courage to face the shadow and also acknowledgement of the evil we are capable of doing, or have done, which can then be transformed through awareness to assist our evolutionary progress, both individually and collectively.[61] But where shall we turn for help?

The depth psychological approach practised by Carl Jung and other practitioners of wholeness, such as transpersonal therapists, have shown us that creative approaches to complex matters in the psyche can be illuminating. Therefore, the importance of cultivating deeper levels of awareness cannot be emphasised enough. As I have explained in Chapter Two, we live in a culture that has discredited and disregarded the wisdom in the psyche. But this does not mean that the wisdom is lost. There is a Grimm's fairy tale called Fitcher's Bird, which is an excellent example of how we can understand and tackle complex matters in the world and in our psyches. It is a story that captures the mythic struggles of liberation and it graphically represents a powerful use of the imagination to illustrate how wisdom and empowerment emerge from adversity. I first came across the story when I was a student of psychotherapy, and later found it in a book by Donald Kalsched.[62] Here's how I tell the story.

Fitcher's Bird

There was a wizard who lived in a forest and he would often travel to distant villages disguised as a beggar in search of young maidens. One day, on his travels, the wizard knocked on the door of a house occupied by a man and his three daughters. The wizard asked for food and the oldest daughter brought him some bread with outstretched arms, whereupon the wizard grabbed her hands and tossed her into a large basket strapped to his back and ran off at great speed. The wizard took the oldest daughter to his house, deep inside the dense forest. The house was beautiful and the wizard said to the young woman that she would have everything she needed to live a happy life. Then he said he had to go away for a few days and gave the young woman a set of keys for the house, but he showed her one key to a particular door in the house and explained that if she entered that room it would result in grave consequences. He also gave her an egg and said that she should carry this with her at all times and not lose it. The young woman agreed to follow the wizard's instructions, and after he had departed she explored all the rooms in the house, which were full of great riches. Then she came to the forbidden room, and curiosity got the better of her as she unlocked the door and entered inside. The sight before her filled the young woman with horror, for in the centre of the room was a chopping board with a large axe, and next to it was a giant basin full of blood and human body parts. In a state of panic she accidentally dropped the egg into the basin and it was stained with blood. No matter how hard she tried to remove the marks of blood from the egg, the stains would not go away. Eventually the wizard returned from his trip and he immediately asked the young woman for the keys and the egg. As soon as he saw the stained egg he knew she had broken her promise. Without hesitation he dragged her off to the room, and she knew the fate that awaited her.

Eventually, the wizard assumed another disguise and returned to the house where the father and two remaining daughters lived. He used his deceitful ploy once again and tricked the middle daughter into giving him some bread and then he abducted her. The wizard told the middle daughter that he would be leaving for a few days and gave her a set of keys and a pristine egg, and once again he explained the rules. The middle daughter explored the house and eventually curiosity got the better of her as she entered the forbidden room, which led to the same tragic fate as her older sister. The wizard remembered that there was still another daughter in the house, and once again he disguised himself as a beggar and ran away with her after she offered him some bread. When they arrived at the wizard's house the same routine unfolded, with the wizard explaining the rules about the keys and egg. Once the wizard had left the home, the youngest daughter decided to put the egg in a safe place and then explored the house. She eventually came across the forbidden room, and upon entering was shocked to see her two dismembered sisters, who suddenly started to heal. They then, set about planning their freedom. Only then did the youngest daughter pick up her egg, which had not been stained, and when the wizard returned he asked to see the keys and egg, and he was delighted to see the egg was not marked. She then agreed to marry the wizard and they made plans for their wedding, but her real intentions were focused on liberation, and eventually the sisters outwitted the wizard (adversary).

In the story two symbols are dominant, the keys and the egg. Keys allow entry to locked spaces, that is, they grant access. However, in the case of the forbidden room the key is given to the young women, as a test, unbeknown to them. Ordinarily, to be given a key and then denied access to a room is a mixed message that would arouse suspicion. But this is a fairy tale, and it provides opportunities for imagination and reflection. For example, in the case of the first two daughters, they agree to the wizard's terms, but they also follow their curiosity and inquisitiveness without any active reflection, whereas the last daughter has a measure of discernment, and through her awareness she is able to break the wizard's rules and survive. Interestingly, the youngest daughter places the egg out of harm's way for safekeeping. Kalsched reminds us that the egg is a fairly universal and important symbol in myths for generating new life. It means that it is a potent image for incubating our human potential, wholeness and living creatively. It is also the symbol of resurrection of new life and hope in the religious celebration of Easter. The youngest daughter has the foresight to separate her potential for growth (egg) from the traumatic reality in the forbidden room. This separation enabled her to develop a level of discernment that supported her inner awareness and outer actions, which led to her freedom.

Incubating wisdom

The mythical themes and wisdom in Fitcher's Bird resonate with a dream reported by a study participant in Scott Sparrow's[63] research. The participant recounted a dream she had aged six, which occurred the evening before Easter Sunday. In the young girl's dream Jesus appeared to her in the living room. As the dream unfolds, the girl's father, brother and stepmother were sitting in the kitchen, and she ran to tell them that Jesus was in the living room, whereupon the family quickly got up from their seats to have a look, but Jesus was nowhere to be seen. The family returned to the kitchen, but once again, Jesus appeared to the little girl in the living room, and again she ran into the kitchen excitedly to inform the family that Jesus had returned, but they simply mocked her. Disappointed, the girl left the kitchen, but Jesus came to her once more and told her that only she could see him. The dream took a sinister turn when Jesus told the little girl to follow him into the kitchen, and he reassured her that they would not be seen by her parents, who were preparing Easter eggs for the next day. She saw that the eggs being prepared for her were laced with poison. Horrified, the little girl panicked and felt very sad. Jesus warned her not to eat the Easter eggs the next day. When she awoke in the morning the little girl remembered her dream and completely surprised her parents by refusing to eat the Easter eggs given to her.

As an adult the research participant reflected upon the dream and the wisdom in its message. It transpired that her father was extremely abusive, both physically and verbally. The dreamer said that throughout her time growing up, the dream had helped her see how damaged her parents were, and the powerful symbolism of the parents poisoning the egg gave her the confidence to know nothing was wrong with her. Indeed, the dream is congruent with Kalsched's[62] analysis above. The little girl saw that the poisoned egg was a warning that all was not well in her home life, and she trusted the guidance of Jesus in her dream, which revealed a level of awareness that helped her preserve a sense of wholeness. In a way, her dream was deeply symbolic of the Easter message – transformation.

We all have incredible opportunities to transform difficult and complex situations in life. As we have seen, Jung had a fierce commitment to exploring and working with his inner life, against the prevailing reductionism found in the 20th century, where he discovered the importance of myths, fairy tales and dreams, which act as creative templates for our human potential, growth and wholeness. Jung[10] spoke about the need for a spirit that makes us whole (Holy) in times of uncertainty. In a similar vein, Theodore Roszak[64] noted how our mystical traditions in these challenging times have withdrawn into contemplation and have become largely ineffective in helping the world find an effective response to evil. It suggests that in the modern world we have little guidance for renewed ways of transforming polarities, such as good-evil, which has created a vacuum in collective consciousness, leaving us vulnerable to charlatans. Furthermore, Roszak[65] warns us of the need to be discerning in relation to the teachings of phoney gurus, messiahs, and entrepreneurs who exploit troubled souls and who are working against the human spirit, pointing out that some of these people are no better than big corporations in their quest for money and fame. The challenge of personal and planetary transformation is a radical proposition and it requires us to enter deeply into complex realities of our one-sided technocracy. The issues of good-evil are calling for us to look within as a creative response to our evolutionary potential, where we can create communities,[66] which are based on deep awareness and the guiding principles of love and awareness.[15]

Returning to the symbolism of Fitcher's Bird, we have a myth that is also helpful for understanding the dynamics at work in this time of global crisis. For example, there is a powerful wizard who is abducting young women to satisfy his own desires, which are similar to the unrestrained patriarchal attitudes that have wreaked havoc in people's lives today, as well as destroying the Earth through technologies that have objectified life and alienated people from the planet. The story has a weak and ineffectual father, who represents the missing positive masculine energies, which if awakened, would not allow such abuses to be consistently repeated. There is also a missing mother, which indicates the absence of wise feminine influence, similar to the repression of the feminine energies in our society today. However, the growth of awareness and wisdom (*Sophia*) is represented in the youngest daughter, who has cultivated discernment, which allows her to expose the corrupted motives of the wizard, and a grim reality that was previously hidden. The young daughter is symbolic of a resurgent feminine wisdom that is re-emerging in the world today. She is able to witness the horrors that have gone on in the room before her, but she wisely protects her human potential amidst the carnage of the situation she finds herself in. It is a good example of how feminine awareness grows and heals when it follows its own instinct and potential (like the new life in the egg), rather than the patriarchal rules (represented by the wizard).

Matthew Fox[14] questions why societies have not invested more in ways of helping people to explore and understand the inner world, and how to deal with complex issues such as good-evil, thereby promoting experiences of spiritual renewal that go beyond dualities. It is a call to embrace a sacrament of living. According to Jung[9] when our consciousness is awoken, it is an act of creation, where ancient wisdom is born anew. It means that we have to honour the process of birth, which is the domain of the sacred feminine. It also means that when the ancient is born anew, we are making a conscious connection to our human heritage and our ancestors. As Marie Louise Von Franz[67] says, in order to deal with evil, we need to be connected to knowledge that understands higher states of consciousness. The myths of our ancestors give us clues about the inner and outer work required to face adversity, which is connected to our collective spiritual awakening. If we are emboldened to co-create the Transformocene, it means we will need to redeem a soulful relationship to the ancestors.

Exercise: The adversarial edge

- What thoughts and feelings are evoked when you reflect on the evil 'out there', in the world today?

- If our lifestyles and intentional actions are contributing to ecocide and destruction in the world, where is evil 'in here'?

- In what ways are we all complicit in turning away from the plight of vulnerable people affected by a warming climate, or ignoring the impact of species extinction, and the destruction of ecosystems?

- If your lifestyle is contributing to the eco-destruction happening in the world today, how are you part of the problem in the world?

- How could the above reflection impact on your lifestyle, thoughts, feelings and behaviours?

- In what ways does the above reflection help you wake up to your *part share* (participation) in the destruction of ecosystems, species extinction, and the impact on human communities?

- If the Earth is our life-support system (which is in crisis), how is the global crisis your spiritual crisis?

- What will you do to make a difference in the world?

An ancestral shadow permeates human existence. In the modern world it is the untold story of our species' struggle to live in peace and harmony. Next time we cry for the world, let us feel the closeness of the ancestors in each one of our tears.

CHAPTER SEVEN

Echoes of the Ancestors

Overview

In this chapter I explore the role of the ancestors as an important part of our collective awakening. I discuss how we all carry a biological link to the ancestors in our DNA, and how the wounds and wonders of our forebears have shaped our species. Jung pointed out that the trajectory of human evolution continues, with each successive generation contributing to collective knowledge that is stored in the collective unconscious. I discuss how the ancestral lineage is also a numinous connection to our collective human heritage, where figures from the past are active in the imaginal realm, and can manifest in our dreams and visions etc. In this way, I explore how ancestral knowledge is a rich storehouse that humanity can draw on to develop knowledge and wisdom. In this chapter I explore the salutary lesson that we are all future ancestors, and how this realisation has the potential to inspire us to honour those who have lived before us, as well as those who will live after us. A deep connection to our place in an ancestral lineage could inspire our actions in the Transformocene, building on our ancestors' achievements, as well as co-creating new opportunities for living in harmony with all life. Part of our redemptive quest is to learn from the ancestors, in the knowledge that we too are becoming future ancestors. It brings us into a deeper relationship with our species' evolutionary trajectory, to work for the greater good and leave a legacy of hope.

The spirit of the depths

If ever humanity needed a reminder of the importance of connecting to our visionary energies to bring forth a new myth in the collective, now is the time. We only have to reflect on world events today and observe the fast-track route to destruction that is happening in our collective ways of living. Our modern consciousness is either ignorant of, or actively ignoring, millennia of accumulated wisdom from our shared human heritage, which includes relating to life as a living sacrament. We have arrived at a critical point in terms of our evolutionary and transformational potential, one that is calling for a renewed connection to the numinous.[1]

Theologian Rudolf Otto[2] spoke about the importance of the numinous as an experience of the sacred, or the Holy, which is present in all spiritual traditions and cultures. The numinous opens up human consciousness to a living mystery, which can be experienced as either a *luminous*, peaceful or meditative presence, or an *ominous* encounter that is full of dread or foreboding. It is a natural experience of the sacred which is not owned by any spiritual tradition, and when it appears it can awaken us to the presence of the Holy, which brings us into relationship with our wholeness. In this way, the numinous reveals a spiritual connectedness and deep sense of belonging, which can create bonds in our collective efforts towards transformation,[3] and psycho-spiritual renewal. The numinous is the *royal road to mystical experience*. It activates revelatory and transformational experiences in consciousness, which deepen our connection to the sacred.

The numinous, then, is a profound representation of transpersonal consciousness. It was Carl Jung who first made the important connection between the numinous and the archetypes in the collective unconscious, and how such sacred encounters can awaken a renewed commitment to wholeness (*individuation*). It must be remembered that archetypal symbols, images and figures are configurations and patterns of human experiences that have been created, added to, and inherited by successive generations from our ancestors to the present. In this way, the collective unconscious is an archaic storehouse that reflects the evolutionary heritage of all our ancestors' mental and spiritual endeavours,[4] which also influenced Jung's work.[5] It transpires that when Jung finished working on his academic book, *Transformations and Symbols of the Libido*, he realised that it had activated his own unconscious process to such an extent that he started to record his deep explorations in his *Red Book*. It was his own process of inner work which helped him to realise that working with the unconscious was vital for remedying and renewing a deeper connection to his soul. The ancient Greek term, *physician heal thyself,* was not lost on this doctor of the soul. Indeed, Jung took the art of psycho-spiritual healing to a whole new level in the Western world when he explored the depths of his own experiences. Jung the medical psychiatrist, the psychologist, alchemist and shaman responded to the call from the deep at a time when humanity was becoming more absorbed in a mechanistic consciousness and increasingly experienced a loss of soul. Subsequently, Jung's work resonated with many people who intuitively knew that he was addressing an important issue that was evidently missing from the modern world. The reason why Jung's ideas have stood the test of time is because his work reflects congruence between different levels of consciousness from the surface to the deep.

The call of the deep

In his *Red Book*, Jung records and reflects upon his deep encounters with the personal and collective unconscious. Interestingly, the book contains no information about his family, marriage or everyday concerns. Indeed, the opposite is true: his *Red Book* is a chronicle of a journey into the world of the soul, which is animated by myths, symbols and figures from human history.[5] Jung's explorations exemplify the archetypal journey from the everyday self to a greater *Self-realisation*, which is born from the creative interface between the personal ego and a wider transpersonal consciousness.[6] Jung's experiential journey into the unconscious was ground breaking, in that it led to the re-emergence of methods for soul retrieval in the collective, which continue to flourish to this day in Jungian and transpersonal based therapies. These deep approaches to the psyche are in stark contrast to our modern one-dimensional mode of consciousness, which is dominated by consumer-based and technological interests. Jung's inner work led him to connect with a collective human heritage, via the wealth of resources found in the collective unconscious. He called his approach to wholeness *individuation*, simply because it honours the depth of the individual, whose origins are not separate from life as a whole, as found in the Latin word *individuus*, meaning not *divisible*.[7]

The process of individuation means that we are inspired and committed to work with symbols, images and figures arising from the unconscious, which can help us connect to a deeper path in life, where our talents, skills, gifts and passions are directed in the service of wholeness and undivided action. Jung's depth approach to consciousness is highly relevant today, because it assists people to reconnect with a vision of wholeness that is not bound to a technocratic and increasingly artificial existence.[8] Jung's own inner explorations and his work with others helped to demonstrate the unique qualities that each individual possesses, and how these gifts need to be lived in our outer work as an authentic expression of our individuation, life purpose, and wholeness. The unique process of individuation underlines the myriad ways people can imagine the world, amongst all the many other ways that the world can be imagined.[9] Thus, our individual paths in life are unique and it is up to each of us to find a connection to wholeness through inner exploration and *active imagination*, which is then directed in life through outer expression and *imaginative action*. This inner-outer process of imaginative living is the co-creative challenge facing each of us at this threshold, as we turn the threat of the *Anthropocene* into the dynamic era of the *Transformocene*.

In daily life, Jung discovered that not only was he working on the contents of the unconscious, as part of his inner work, but that the unconscious was also working on him.[5] As Patrick Harpur[10] says, one of the figures that came to Jung was *Philemon*, who was like an inner *spiritual mentor* for him. Through his interactions with Philemon, Jung learned that we could forge a relationship to the ancestors, including people from our bloodline or cultural heritage, as well as influential figures from history, or indeed those who come to us in visions and dreams. These figures can be incredible sources of inspiration, which can help awaken our hearts and souls to wholeness. In this way, the ancestors can inspire transformative action: encouraging us to *be* and *do* the best we can in this short life, not only for the sake of the dead, but also the living and the unborn. It is this connection to ancient knowledge and wisdom that can act as a creative catalyst in terms of spiritual renewal.[11] An important message that comes out of Jung's inner work is the notion that we are all connected to ancestors (via the collective unconscious), and yet their presence can haunt us, because modern lifestyles have contributed to a widening gulf between the living and the dead.[5] The modern world has a diminished relationship to the ancestors compared to the traditions found in ancient and indigenous cultures, who have maintained a connection to the sacred, where there is no separation between humanity, spirit and nature.[12] However, as the following case vignette demonstrates, the modern mind may be closer to the ancestors than we give credit.

The blood of the ancestors

In my practice as a holistic coach I worked with a deeply spiritual woman who came to see me after attending a shamanic workshop where she had a powerful experience that connected her with her ancestors. Prior to the workshop she had endured "a lifetime" of nocturnal spiritual intrusions several times a year, where she had been prodded awake, and on one occasion had experienced a feeling of being pulled out of bed. These night-time disturbances became more intense in 2013. She felt that the shamanic work would help her understand why this was happening and what she could do about it, so she prayed to the spirit world for help. During the shamanic workshop she followed the trance-like rhythm of the drumbeat and suddenly encountered hundreds of her Jewish ancestors in a state of semi-consciousness. They were stuck in a kind of limbo and were somehow unable to move on without assistance. All the people were Russian (the country of her grandfather) and had died of hunger and in pogroms. She was greeted by them wailing "Is it you?" and "Have you come to help?" She turned to the gathering crowd of spirits before her and announced, "I am Jaakov's granddaughter", which led them to rush towards her crying and wailing, longing for release. With the sustaining rhythm of the drumbeat, she sang them up to heaven, willing them onwards and as they streamed past her their souls were released.

When we started our holistic coaching work together, we picked up the thread of her ancestral work and she felt that they still wanted something from her. We made a space in the room for the ancestors to be present and my client spoke to them (it transpired that they were mostly men). On the shamanic weekend, the ancestors had mostly been women and children. She started to cry and said, "I feel for them". In our third week of working together we continued working with her ancestors, but it was more or less immediately after the session, as she was cycling home, that she had a heavy nosebleed, which was so intense that passing cars slowed down, and eventually one of the vehicles stopped and offered to help my client. I was unaware of the nosebleed until she discussed it in the next session and we explored the meaning of blood to the work we were doing. This proved to be a turning point. My client's associations to blood included its "life-giving" properties, as well as it being "oxygenating" and helping to "remove impurities". The link to blood provided a vital connection to my client's ancestors, when she said: "They not only wanted to be remembered, but they want to live fully and pass on their love, knowledge and experience to and through their descendants."

In the final session my client produced a photograph of her grandfather, *Jaakov Prelooker*, and other ancestors from the past. The acknowledgement of her family lineage was bringing them into consciousness. It was this bloodline connection that honoured the link between her ancestors and relatives who are alive today, particularly her grandchildren. She spoke about her feelings of wanting to tell her grandchildren stories about their ancestors, so that they get to know them, and most importantly to not forget them. In this way the ancestors will be remembered. She described the impact of the ancestral work as a sort of "undoing of a deeply held tension" and that "I feel less driven, more steady and grounded". My client already had a deep spiritual connection in her life, which has given her a very real sense of knowing where she comes from and where she belongs. She spoke about how the ancestors had evoked a sense of love, which has resulted in a "greater connection to all creation in a non-personal way". She said, "I love my fellow humans, nature, animals and everything". Furthermore, she said that her ancestors would have a great sense of gratitude and relief, knowing that their story will be heard, which will hopefully inspire other people to honour and remember their ancestors. She summed up the meaning of the nosebleed to her ancestral work as follows: "It's the feeling of the ancestors in your blood that is important, more so than remembering their names." After our holistic coaching work had ended, my client said to me: "I have a feeling the ancestors want to speak through me. I feel I have a duty to listen and let their creativity live through me, and I through them." The work we did together chimed with the work of the great author, Herman Hesse,[13] who wrote about listening to the whispers in the blood, concerning the quality of relationship between the living and the dead, and what we could learn from such rich contact and connections.

The above vignette is a touching representation of a woman's reconnection to her ancestral bloodline. Michael Owen[14] says that our ancestral and archetypal links are represented as a form of *dreaming* in the collective unconscious, and each successive generation takes that dream forward. It is a deeper reminder of the importance of lineage. In his book, *Memories, Dreams, Reflections,* Jung[15] wrote about continuing to grapple with the unanswered questions and unfinished work of the ancestors. It echoes the worldviews found in indigenous cultures, where the ancestors are just as important as each living generation. Vine Deloria, Jr,[16] a Dakota Sioux elder, speaks about his tribe's tradition where the future welfare of the people is always considered important, especially when they involve decisions that affect the collective. This includes reflecting upon the possible impact of actions that are carried out in the present, and how these may affect the tribe seven generations ahead of time. It is not only collective actions that focus the mind in Sioux culture, but also the personal responsibilities that each member of the tribe carries in terms of living a good life and not bringing shame on the family name or ancestral lineage.

Indigenous tribes and cultures have consistently spoken about the need for humanity to live in balance and harmony with nature, based on a sacred, reverential, and responsible relationship to the land. Books such as *Wisdom of the Elders* by David Suzuki and Peter Knudtson[17] leave us in no doubt about the conflicting worldviews of people who have grown up in modern materialist societies and those who have remained connected to their native cultural heritages. For example, the Hopi Indian tradition warns about the consequences of treating the Earth as a material object, instead of something alive and sacred. In short, modern technologies are continuing to push humanity out of balance with nature, for the sole reason that people in the modern world are desperately out of touch with deeper ways of living. How might a reconnection to the archetypes and ancestors help us live more harmoniously with one another, other species and with nature as a whole? A surprising and innovative answer could be found in the idea that we start to consider ourselves as 'future ancestors'. It could help us understand and connect with the responsibility we have to remedy the mistakes of the past, with a commitment to leave a legacy for the future.

We are all ancestors in training

In 2014 I met Mark Wentworth through a mutual friend and we soon found that we had much in common, particularly in relation to Jungian psychology and spirituality. Mark trained with Jungian analyst Roger Woolger and he eventually became one of Roger's assistants, working on his ancestral healing workshops. When I asked Mark about what the ancestors meant to him, he replied, "They just want us to be fulfilled and happy". I asked Mark why our contentment was so important to the ancestors, and he said that *our existence is the answer to their prayers*: "Someone, somewhere in the past prayed and hoped for someone just like you to be born." He gave the example of the struggle for women's emancipation and how women have been repressed by a dominant patriarchy, which has stifled their intelligence, freedom and self-determination. Yet, since the Suffragettes there have been generations of women who have fought for equality, dignity and respect that continues to this day. It helped me to appreciate how we all play an important part in the continuity of the human story. This idea resonated with my conception of occupational myths and how our personal journeys play an important role in the collective unfolding of our actions, which are connected to our species' soulful potential and spiritual trajectories. We are all threads in the great tapestry of life.

Around the same time that he was working with Roger Woolger, Mark attended a shamanic workshop focusing on how to assist others at the time of their death. Mark describes an experience that powerfully represents how the imaginal realm can deepen our vocational connection to what we do in life. In one of the workshop exercises, guided by the tempo of the shamanic drumbeat, he had a visionary experience of a figure standing by his feet. It was unlike any experience he had ever had in his life. The figure was a powerful female presence and he had the sense that he needed to bow down with his forehead touching the floor. The figure appeared black with flashes of red and as she opened her mouth she let out an unearthly scream, which sounded like it had "come from beyond". As soon as the scream subsided, the figure preceded to projectile vomit dead bodies on to the floor, which formed into neat piles at the feet of all the workshop participants. Mark went on to say, "She looked at me with a steely gaze and said *these are your dead – deal with them*." He then found himself with this figure looking down on the world and just above the Earth there appeared to be cloud-like formations and she said: "These clouds are groups of ancestors who are not at peace. The Earth's atmosphere is polluted, but the etheric world is also toxic, full of lost and unhappy ancestors – and that is your work."

The following week Mark was visited in his dreams by all manner of dispossessed groups, including murderers and prostitutes, all asking for help. They were not violent or aggressive, yet they were pleading with him. Mark said to me the only way he can frame and understand what this healing journey means to him, is that it is a form of service, where he is working for humanity's past, present and future. He turned to me and said: "We are all ancestors in training." I was so intrigued by this statement that I asked Mark to explain what he meant. He went on to say: "When I work with people I ask them to consider their legacy and how they would like to be remembered by their family and future generations. For example, people's ancestral lineage can include the profession to which they belonged. The ancestors are available to us at any time and they are such an incredible and untapped resource." Mark gave an example of professional ancestry linked to the death of his mentor Roger Woolger, who came to him after he died and encouraged Mark to follow his own path and develop his practice as a colour therapist.

Mark's workshops take him all over the world, where he combines ancestral work and colour therapy. He has even taken a group to Auschwitz, where he worked with the ancestors, remembering the lives of the inmates before they were murdered. The group also worked with the camp guards. The message I took from Mark about such horrific historic events is that all the ancestors need to be considered, whatever they have done in life. It is what makes ancestral work such deep healing for those who have passed away and also for those who are living. Mark speaks about his work as a duty and responsibility to humanity, ensuring the ancestors are acknowledged and heard. Yet Mark also spoke about the paradox of his work, because working with the dead enriches and deepens our connection to the past and at the same time encourages us to reconnect with living purposeful, meaningful lives here on Earth. Mark says his work enriches him as a human being and he describes it as "a flowering of consciousness". The conversation ended with Mark reiterating a point he had made at the start of our discussion: "You are the one your ancestors and descendants are waiting for." This statement has strong resonances with how I understand my own role in connecting to the ancestors.

The serpents breathe

I consider Carl Jung to be one of my ancestors. His theoretical and therapeutic approach has had a major impact on my adult life at both an intellectual and dreaming level. It has been noted in many indigenous African cultures that when ancestors have passed over to the spirit realm, they can act as channels of communication between the living and the divine, connecting with people via dreams.[18] I feel such a connection with Jung. Before I became a student of psychotherapy in 1996, I had a very short, but nonetheless awe-inspiring, dream of a powerful looking black snake. Then, without any warning, a pure white snake emerged from the mouth of the black snake. I knew the dream was archetypal and the only association I had to the dream was that it pointed to a process of transformation. I found a promising connection to the dream in a book by Arny Mindell,[19] *Dreambody*, where he analyses the Grimms' folk tale, *The White Snake*. In summary, the tale represents a pattern of individuation and it involves a servant who brings food to a king every day, but the meal is always covered and concealed. One day, out of curiosity, the servant lifts the lid from the platter, and on the plate is a white snake. The servant eats a little bit of the white snake and straight away finds that he can hear and understand animal communications.

The servant's ability to hear the communications of animals enables him to recruit the services of various animals to help him find a ring that the Queen had lost. With the help of his new allies, the servant finds the lost ring, which earns him his freedom. His newfound freedom and spiritual connection to animals also help him to find the lost ring of a princess who lived in another kingdom, and eventually they fall in love. Interestingly, the ring is a symbol of wholeness, which is represented twice in the story. First, the man's induction into the shamanic world of animal communications enables him to find the Queen's ring, where he is liberated from his role of servitude. Second, he uses his shamanic gift to find another ring, one that has been lost by a princess in a distant land, with whom he falls in love. The man's journey into wholeness is intimately connected with the integration of the feminine.

Mindell discusses how eating and digesting the white snake gives access to a consciousness that is mediumistic, which requires us to be willing to enter into a relationship with the imaginal. The serpent represents an induction into altered states of consciousness, which hold great potential for transformation. The white snake is symbolic of how we are capable of communing with the spirits in nature, in water, wind and plants etc., which could inspire us to bring forth a renewed consciousness and culture, where we live in balance and wholeness with all life and the universe.[20] We have many examples of people who have devoted their lives to working with consciousness and the process of awakening and action, for example in the works of Carl Jung. Similarly, the work of Arny Mindell is fluidly aligned with the imaginal realm, and his method of doing *process work* is contingent upon accessing the living unconscious through inner *dynamics, relational connections, conflicts* and *world work*. In this way, the insights that arise from working creatively between consensus reality and the imaginal realm become *grist for the mill* of integration and transformation.

Mindell's[19] book, *Dreambody*, was one of the first books I read about process-oriented psychology, or process work, and it led me into an understanding of how to appreciate the living unconscious. Central to this transformative approach to living is via our own inner work, and in my case the serpent dream was a potent symbol that deepened my sense of initiation and vocation. However, it was only after the publication of Jung's[11] *Red Book* that I saw my black snake–white snake dream in a new light. In January 1914, at a time when Europe was descending into a catastrophic war, Jung had a vision of a black snake winding its way up a wooden cross and entering into the body of a crucified figure, eventually emerging from the figure's mouth, totally transformed into a white snake. I thought that the parallels between Jung's vision and my dream were interesting, which exemplified the meaning that transformation has to be *embodied*. It is for this reason that I believe Arny Mindell's work on the *Dreambody* is a major contribution to our understanding of the imaginal in the context of a greater *embodied* transpersonal reality (including dreams, body work, relationships and world work, etc.).

The figure in Jung's vision was crucified, which represents a symbolic death of the personal (bodily) ego. Death is then followed by the dynamic transformation of the black snake, into a white snake, which happens within the body, which is where the birth of the transpersonal Self takes place. My black snake–white snake dream indicated that the dynamic processes associated with archetypal symbols of transformation had been activated, but this was only a prelude to the deeper work of embodiment that was needed. Individuation is a gradual path of awakening, which happens over a lifetime through cultivating a meaningful connection to the imaginal realm. It is this deep symbolic connection to life that informs the occupational myth that guides our actions.

At the level of the dreaming we are always being '*called*'. But whether we choose to embrace a path of individuation depends on how we view our personal lives in relation to our transpersonal potential. My black snake–white snake dream called me to a path of individuation, and it has been a symbolic point of reference for my embodied process of transformation for many years. I have purposely avoided a dualistic interpretation of this powerful symbol, for example I never say black snake and white snake. This suggests an *either/or* reality, rather than a *both/and* understanding. In a similar way, Chungliang Al Huang[21] explains that in the Chinese language *yin-yang* is one word: a unified (non-dual) expression of wholeness. The evocative symbol of *yin-yang* interweaves the opposites into 'one', where each part contains a representation of the opposite. If we apply this ancient Chinese symbolism to other polarisations in life, such as good-evil, we are confronted with the challenge of transformation, which is about understanding how parts contribute to the whole. For example, in Jung's vision of the black snake–white snake, both are needed for an embodied and activated transformation to occur. Similarly, spiritual seekers confronted with questions and contexts of good-evil, realise that adverse conditions 'test' our sacred resolve, which become *increments of integration* in our quest for wholeness. Such encounters connect us with the numinous and opportunities for experiences of wholeness that transcend polarities. And so, my understanding of the black snakewhite snake dream acts an inspirational template for an embodied awakening to wholeness. The purpose of such 'big dreams' is to help awaken us to the whole.

Dreaming big

Big dreams are divine inspiration. If we evaluate sacred dreams by the standards of modern one-dimensional ego-consciousness, we are more than likely to arrive at superficial understandings and overlook the deeper calling to live a transformational life. It is no surprise that the ancient Greeks had a god of dreaming, the winged figure of *Morpheus*. The name of this *god of the imagination* is perfect, because the word *morph* refers to a changing form, and it is here that the dream world is like a shamanic reality, where we can shape shift and work with the trans*form*ing power of the imaginal realm. Big dreams and visions bring us into contact with the mythic world of transformation and spiritual awakening. Patrick Harpur[9] suggests that our worldviews also represent an actual myth in which we are immersed. This is an important point, as myths are not antiquated or quaint stories that have been made redundant by the cool logic of our modern world. Far from it: myths are hot and dynamic and they enrich our existence by virtue of their transformative narratives that can connect to our own mythic journeys. The myth that is crying out to be lived today is a myth of wholeness; it is a call for a soul-enriching narrative that inspires our minds, hearts, and souls to live transformative lives. The mythic quest is about living authentically and having the courage to face adversarial challenges along the way. We can imagine, and be inspired by, the mythic journeys of our ancestors, which have contributed to the psycho-spiritual resources we can all draw upon. We all have access to archetypal symbols in the collective unconscious, which bring us into connection with the mystery of the numinous, bringing forth a deep mythical connection to life.

Myths are about making connections, and for this reason Brian Swimme and Thomas Berry[22] call for a greater understanding of the well-being between species, based on ethics, governance and education, which resonates with a deeper sense of enchantment that connects with a mystery in life. Jungian analyst Erich Neumann[23] speaks about mystical anthropology and how human beings are also homo mysticus because of our openness to numinous encounters, where the ego is brought into contact with a greater transpersonal-Self. This mystery acts as a creative catalyst in the transformation of consciousness, where numinous encounters are the lifeblood of the individuation process. For Neumann this mystical understanding of life involves a reciprocal relationship between the *numinous within the human*, and the *human within the numinous*. In this way, transforming consciousness connects to the fulfilment of our psycho-spiritual potential, forging a productive relationship between the ego and our Self-realisation, which is energised by the numinous processes at work within us. Indeed, it is this mystical connection that is so vital to our understanding of Jung's conception of the mythic function.[3] Myths help us to work with and go beyond polarities, such as rigid ideas of good-evil. We learn that such polarities are part of a process of integration that subsumes them into a path of wholeness, rather than division. Such a transformative process is critical for evolving consciousness in this time of global crisis. Finding a mythic connection to the ancestors is also a vital part of our spiritual work. It helps us to find the threads that run through our human heritage, which can serve as a potent reminder to make the most of our short incarnation on planet Earth. We may also find mysterious threads in our lived experiences that connect to deep memories and past lives, and unexpected connections to ancestral spirits.

Jungian analyst Roger Woolger,[24] in his book *Other Lives, Other Selves*, quotes Plato who spoke about the *act of remembering*, suggesting that if we can recall one event, we are capable of remembering any other event. Woolger's therapeutic work was predicated on the understanding that we all have deep memories, including those from the early stages of this life, via *in utero* experiences, and even past lives. I have every respect for the powerful workings of memory. I recall a family holiday in Spain, when I was out walking with my two nieces, Lucia, who at the time was nine, and Rachel, who was ten. We came across a friendly Welsh Border collie, and I said to the girls, let's make up a name for the dog. I quietly thought to myself the name *Taffy*, because of the Welsh connection. I was stunned when Lucia said the dog should be called Taffy. I asked her why she had chosen that name and she did not know; in fact she thought she had said something wrong when I questioned her about it. Rachel lives in England, but Lucia is Spanish and English is her second language. She had no idea what the word *Taffy* meant let alone where it came from. However, later that evening I was reflecting on the above experience, and I had a faint memory of a conversation with the children two years earlier, when I mentioned to them that our neighbour's nickname is *Taffy*, because he is Welsh. The fact that a nine-year-old Spanish girl can remember a brief conversation in English from when she was seven years old, without any repetition or encoding of those words into her long-term memory, is fascinating. Yet, such feats of memory recall set the scene for a more dramatic account from a child's memory of a previous life.

The living and the dead

Academics from the University of Virginia have amassed 2,500 case studies of young children who are able to describe events that led to their deaths in a previous life. For example, Michael Jawar[25] published an article on the subject in *Psychology Today*. He cites a case of young boy named James, who kept having nightmares and post-traumatic symptoms related to Second World War fighter planes, which were linked to a 'boat' called *Natoma*. James recounted how the plane was hit by enemy fire in the engine, causing an explosion, which resulted in the plane crashing into the sea. James also mentioned the name of a man who witnessed the crash, called Jack Larson. James' father did some research and he discovered that there was an American aircraft carrier in WWII called *USS Natoma*, and during operations in the battle of Iwo Jima, one pilot had been lost, whose name happened to be James Hudson. The pilot who flew next to Hudson on the day of the fatal crash was Jack Larson, and all the details of the crash that the little boy described were accurate. It would appear that we are capable of connecting with memories from past lives, but these memories typically fade by the time children reach six years.[25] These documented accounts raise complex questions about what such memories mean, which if supported, could bring a deeper understanding of experiences that may be impacting on us in this life. Perhaps distant memories of past lives, or of our ancestors, are revealing dimensions of conscious experience that could be meaningful to our collective growth and development. For example, Ervin Laszlo's research into the *Akashic Field*[26] may help to contextualise such experiences, in terms of transpersonal phenomena, revealing how an interconnected consciousness encompasses non-local information, which reaches across space and time. Such examples could inspire us to take the imaginal realm seriously.

It is up to each of us to choose whether we want to open our minds to the symbolic, visionary and dreamlike world of the imaginal. As discussed in Chapter Two, our modern mindset prizes hyper-rationalism, and views facts, proof and evidence as the highest form of knowing. Yet, this has choked our human potential by throttling any meaningful relationship to the imaginal realm. It has resulted in a form of schooling that is driven by facts and testing, and avoids the deeper questions in life. The result is a society dominated by shallow materialism and egocentrism, which (in the worst case) is focused on consumer-based lifestyles and behaviours that are killing us, as well as killing other species and the Earth (e.g. the Sixth mass extinction). Our modern superficial and consumer-based lifestyles amount to millions of acts of ecocide every day, and we are all complicit. We have to ask ourselves, if everything is ok, why are so many younger people self-harming in the Western world? Why are we witnessing escalating levels of intolerance and hatred? When will we face up to the collective cynicism and arrogance (such as found in the worldview of scientism) that breeds a deep contempt for genuine experiences that connect people to a living mystery? Why are we so content with the status quo? Why are we not asking ourselves and each other, what does it mean to live a transformative life?

Part of the response to these questions is that we have to participate in processes of transformation to understand its benefit to our lives and consciousness. Yet it is demanding work and it takes a deep willingness and commitment to enter onto the path of individuation, which is not only for our benefit, but also for our species' benefit as a whole. If we think such a sentiment is a flight of fancy, we would do well to consider the fact that unprocessed trauma is transmitted trans-generationally. Psychologist Molly Castelloe[27] writes about the sorts of complex issues that are unable to be confronted by one generation and are then passed on to the next. She posits that this type of *unfinished business* is transmitted unconsciously to the next generation, where it becomes active at the level of our dreams. It validates Jung's position, and it underlines the importance of trans-generational healing, where the effects of the ancestors are closer than we imagine.

The modern psyche is in danger of losing a deeper connection to the trans-formative imperatives that have served our species well for thousands of years. We neglect the ancient and archetypal forces in our collective experiences of consciousness at our peril. In this regard, Jung can be seen as an elder, whose devotion to working with the depths of his own experiences was able to guide modern people back to the soul through a journey of personal and transpersonal redemption. In his life, Jung used the full spectrum of the imagination to engage his conscious potential, which was *de facto* soul work. In his *Red Book*, Jung[11] revealed that inner work is like a *hidden practice*, which he advised should be done secretly, and done for the sake of the dead. The *Red Book* is where we witness how Jung engaged in an intimate relationship with the ancestors who guided him. If humanity is intent upon finding ways of working for the greater good, we must be willing to enter the world of what I call the *ancestral shadow*, which is deeper, older and more neglected than the individual and collective shadows that are being unleashed in the world today. The *ancestral shadow* must be howling and weeping for the trans-generational repetition compulsions that continue to drive our reckless actions in the world today.

The *ancestral shadow* is where we learn the lessons from the past, and see how our fate is intimately bound to a trans-generational spirit, teaching us that we need to clear up the problems from the past, which intrude on the present. In this way, ancestral memories and awakenings from past-life experiences can inspire us to learn historical lessons, and live with deeper meaning and purpose today. For example, Arny Mindell[28] reminds us of our species' great diversity and all the people (past and present) who have endured and worked through social complexities linked to different abilities, sexual preferences, and altered states of consciousness etc. He says that the memories of people's struggles need to be honoured, because change happens in the collective when people have the courage to live the *truth of who they are.* It sharpens the question about the importance of understanding the truth of who we are, even if this runs contrary to social conventions.

We have only survived as a species because of the ingenuity and efforts of our ancestors and they are still present in our imaginings and dreams, where our kindred connections are revealed.[29] From this perspective, we can understand the words of Matthew Fox[30] who refers to the ancestors as "luminaries", beings of light who can inspire our imaginations, as well as providing us with energy and courage. How we connect to the ancestors is unique to each person, and in the following story I share a session I did with a friend who made a connection to the ancestors, which was important to her work in bringing greater transparency to spiritually transformative experiences.

Emerging with pride

I did a piece of work with a friend and colleague at a time when she was organising an international event to honour people's processes of spiritual emergence in the collective. The campaign was exhilarating, and it also brought opportunities to deal with her outmoded beliefs, such as inner criticism. We agreed to work together for three coaching sessions to explore how her inner and outer realities could be more fully aligned. We did a vector walk in a local park and before we started the session, she turned to me and said: "I feel like I'm about to leave the birth canal and it's scary…but it's now time to emerge into adulthood and step into my power." In the park she was drawn to a willow tree, with its low-hanging branches offering a veil of protection and hidden power. As we stood under the willow, I asked my friend what she wanted to let go of. She knew it connected to releasing limiting beliefs that held her back. I suggested she go dreamy and explore how nature was connecting with her. Then, right in front of her she noticed a willow branch with a coiled thread of dead, wispy bark attached to it. She said it looked like it was "holding on for dear life, for stability and protection". She was confused about whether it was better for it to hang on, or let go. I asked my friend to enter into the reality of the dead bark and she noticed two options. It could either fall off (die), allowing opportunities for new growth, or it could remain connected to the tree and be 'safe', but different, although this option would not lead to death and rebirth. She reasoned that the only option was to let go and risk 'death' in order to be 'reborn'. Throughout this part of the process I felt heaviness in my heart.

We moved on to the next phase of the vector walk and I asked her what was it she was seeking to connect to, what wanted to be born? My friend went dreamy again, and after a short while she felt drawn to the entrance of the park, where a concrete ball on a firm foundation had caught her eye. She said: "I'm giving birth to a solid, huge project, which is painful, but bearable." She sat on the huge ball – as if giving birth – and almost immediately felt that the structure was supporting her, bringing a sense of lightness and energy. It was like death and rebirth happening simultaneously. It reminded her of a vision she had once had in Brazil of flying over the world and spreading love. My friend reconnected to her core vision of healing divisions in the world, in a grounded and unified way, where she is *emerging proud*.

We moved on to the final part of the vector walk and I asked what support she needed for this birth to happen. My friend went into a dreamy state and an ancient tree with new budding growth caught her eye. As we walked towards the tree, she felt an energetic pull, which was also grounded. Standing in front of the tree, she had a sense of her feet being in the Earth, intertwined with the roots, growing down and connecting to wisdom. I asked: "Is there a message for you in this experience?" My friend replied: "Trust", which was about letting go of the hidden safety and protection represented by the willow tree at the beginning of the vector walk. In a gesture of trust, my friend touched the old bark on the tree, and felt a connection to the ancestors, which was also a connection to 'truth'. The connection to the ancestors led to a mixed emotional reaction. She was in a deep state of flow, while simultaneously feeling sadness connected to the tree. It was then that a message from the tree came to her: "Don't forget about us." It was a powerful connection to the ancestors, and the realisation that when the *ancients* and *nature* are unacknowledged we become hungry, both physically and spiritually malnourished. I had the sense that my friend was being nourished through her connection to the ancestors in the natural world, and I said: "While your feet are grounded in the Earth, notice how you connect to the new growth on the bark before you." She went further with her connection to the tree and suddenly said: "Oh, did you see that?" I replied: "No, but I trust you did!" My friend went on to explain what she had just seen:

> "I saw a light emanating from the tree; it was as if the tree (ancestors) were trying to highlight their message. It started with a fuzzy energy around the new budding growth on the tree trunk, then quickly the light expanded and it encapsulated the whole trunk. It was reminiscent of how these energies were portrayed in the film *The Celestine Prophecy*, like a spotlight making everything else fade into the background."

My friend said that she had a strong realisation that she needed to speak the truth for the ancestors – to honour that. And so, she walked a *songline* between the ancient tree and the concrete ball, to deepen the connection she was making to *trust* and *truth*, but as she was walking away, with her back to the tree, she started to feel wobbly, which connected to self-judgement and the fear of social judgement. We worked on her inner critic and also supported her vision. Gradually she dropped any sense of judgement and started to trust the process, and the truth in her conviction to live it. As soon as we reached a natural point of resolution in the work, a bird perched high up in the ancestor tree crapped from above, and it landed right in the middle of my friend's crown chakra. It was a shimmering green colour. The only thing I could say to my friend in that moment was: "You've just been anointed." We rolled on the grass laughing. It was such a wonderfully synchronous moment. But I am reminded that excrement has a symbolic connection to the divine, in the way that it fertilises and nourishes new growth.[29] We spoke about the session and how it links to the manifestation of her vision, and she said to me: "I will never give up; if I tried to stop my soul would die."

My friend's determination to live her vision made me think about the nature of the *daimon* and the *amor fati* – the love of our fate. When we are attuned to the spirit of the ancestors we are opened up to a greater depth of consciousness and *calling*, which can inspire us to co-create the Transformocene. In doing so it brings us closer to the realm of the daimon.

Exercise: We are all ancestors in training

- Reflect on the state of the world today (economic, ecological, social and political etc.).

- What might the ancestors make of the world in this time of global crisis?

- What group of wise ancestors would you call upon for help?
  - What would you ask them?

- Imagine this group of wise ancestors sharing their wisdom with you.
  - What would they say?

- Now, imagine yourself becoming a future ancestor – an ancestor in training
  - How would you begin to live more wisely today?

If 'eudaimonia' is to be blessed, then what does this say about the wholesale neglect of the daimon in the modern world? If we feel a lack of blessings in our lives, it is an opportunity to enter into a deeper dialogue with the soul.

CHAPTER EIGHT

Daimons and the Amor Fati

Overview

In this chapter I discuss the role and function of the ancient Greek spiritual entity called the daimon, which helps us awaken at a soul level, stirring us to explore and express our true character in life. I explore how our connection to the daimon is an important part of our redemptive quest. The daimon activates our potential for awakening consciousness through dreams, visions, hunches and synchronicities. Integrating daimonic inspirations requires depth, discernment and determination, which can bring us into a closer relationship with the divine. It also requires discipline (as a disciple of truth). In this way, bringing forth our *true character* and meeting our *fate* can make life a blessing, or *eudaimonia*. Working with the daimon leads to a deep sense of vocation, exemplified in the lives of people like Socrates and Jung. The daimon brings opportunities for creative living, which means having the courage and trust to live authentically and wisely. I argue that *eudaimonia* (to be blessed) is the result of transformational ways of living, where the shadow needs to be integrated to avoid corrupting our daimonic potential. Working with the daimon is a powerful way of meeting our *growing edges*, which catalyses the awakening and redeeming of the human soul in relation to the *anima mundi*, the soul of the world, contributing to the Transformocene.

Eudaimonia

As a species we have arrived at a threshold in terms of our evolutionary journey. Even 40 years ago William Irwin Thompson[1] was discussing the tension between the apocalyptic threats of industrial destruction versus millennial opportunities. Now that we have entered the 21st century we have yet to shift out of our outmoded ways of living and co-create a renewed sense of destiny as planetary citizens. Thompson notes that these tensions are also being played out between the 'diachronic' movements of ego and the 'synchronic' emergence of a spiritual consciousness, which is connected to the *daimon*.[2] The daimonic realm may well have an important part to play in our understanding of wholeness. For example, Anthony Peake[3] draws on knowledge from ancient Greek mystery cults, and informs us that our everyday self (*eidolon*) is unenlightened. However, when we experience a spark of divinity within, it enables us to make a soulful connection to a *Higher Self* (*daimon*). The *daimon* is a complex phenomenon, but its animating qualities as a sacred power can inspire human consciousness and behaviours through an awakened sense of awe. Patrick Harpur[4] says that when we encounter the daimon it can be absorbing or compelling, probably because it touches into deep religious awe and "daimonic dread",[5] as it did for our ancestors. This sense of awe and dread connects us to a living mystery and the sacred power of the numinous.[5] In ancient Greek religion daimons were identified as guiding spirits[6] and an important part of life was to develop a constructive relationship to the daimon.[7]

Patrick Harpur[8] tells us that as Christianity became more popular the spirits, such as the genii (daimons) and nymphs of the old world, were replaced with the Virgin Mary at ancient sacred springs and Holy wells. At one level this was a continuation of a sacred connection to the natural world, however, at a deeper level, it was a separation from pagan ideas[9] and a sacred relationship to nature. People in the ancient world had a sacramental connection to the Earth, where forests and trees, as well as rivers and rocks, were the dwelling places of spirits (*genii loci*). In 2015 I attended a Buddhist Fire Puja (a ritual ceremony) in beautiful north Norfolk woodlands, and the Tibetan monk who conducted the ceremony, Lama Karma Samten, made offerings to the local deities. It was heartwarming and spiritually enlivening to be part of a ritual that creates a sacred bond with nature, where the *spirits of the place* arc honoured. However, the daimon is not just a spirit that is connected to nature; it has a powerful role to play in awakening us at a soul level. It opens us up to the numinous, where we encounter moments of awe, which can be beautiful and compelling (*mysterium fascinens*), or dreadful and terrifying (*mysterium tremendum*).

Rudolf Otto[5] originally coined the term numinous to describe an experience of the Holy. He noticed how unremarkable people (spiritually speaking) could also possess a quality of character that has the force of a daimon. For example, Adolf Hitler comes to mind as a person who believed it was his destiny to restore Germany to greatness, which was reinforced (in his mind) by a series of uncanny signs, such as surviving an explosion in the First World War, and other later attempts to kill him. We also have verbatim reports from people who were close to Hitler during his time as *Fuhrer* of the *Third Reich*, and they painted a picture of him as a megalomaniac, who believed he was divinely appointed to lead his country into a new era.[10] Yet, Hitler failed to learn the lessons of what it means to encounter the daimonic, which, as we shall see later in this chapter, is connected to the activation of our psycho-spiritual potential. In short, the daimon is an animating spirit that awakens the soul, and brings forth opportunities for us to develop our true character and meet our fate. The art of working with the daimon is to learn the lesson of humility and wholeness, which goes beyond polarities of good-evil or dark-light. The numinous quality in the daimonic presence brings us into relationship with a sense of life's mystery, which also becomes a liminal threshold that opens us up to a process of transforming consciousness. Hitler made the error of forging ahead with his plans, but they were fuelled by deep prejudices and the more he invested in his ideas, the more he became ensnared in a vice-like grip of evil, ultimately unleashing what Rudolf Otto[5] refers to as a *mysterium horrendum* in the world. Patrick Harpur[8] illustrates the importance of cultivating self-knowledge and awareness to distinguish between *daimonic* (potential) and *demonic* (possession), without which we lack the ability to discern the forces that are at work in our inner lives.

As Arny Mindell[11] points out, recovering a sense of soul and wholeness is an ancient human endeavour, which also includes understanding the 'demons' that scare us. For example, we have tangible representations of the demons that possess us, which are connected to our disavowed shadow energies in the personal and collective consciousness. While these demons may be threatening to our sense of orderliness, the energy they bring is also regenerative. Mindell adds that when each of us struggles with our personal demons we are doing 'worldwork', because when we explore the energies behind our crazy experiences, perversions and sufferings etc., these are also collective issues. It is here that Mindell makes an important connection to processes of growth and renewal, between the norms that shape our sociocultural realities in the outer world, and the inner world of our latent demons. I can certainly attest to the dynamic and edgy nature of meeting inner demons, linked to my personal encounter with the shadow when I was overcome with murderous feelings during a period of spiritual emergency. Such experiences are over the cultural edge, but I can safely say I am not the only person who has had such an encounter. The more important point to pick up on is Mindell's[11] observation that becoming a warrior means to meet the power of the adversary and turn it into an ally, which not only assists in a shift of identity, but also re-channels the energy into serving society and the world.

Hitler misused the numinous power of the daimon with disastrous consequences because he did not work with his inner demons (prejudice and hatred). Yet he, like anyone else, could have worked to transform his shallow egocentricity and disavowed shadow into a path of wholeness and individuation. I am reminded of the synchronous moment in Berlin when Jung was speaking on the day of Hitler's parade (see Chapter Six). Hitler and Jung were two daimonic characters. However, Hitler was in the grip of *unconscious forces, which possessed him*, whereas Jung was *processing the unconscious forces that guided him*, and the gulf between the different realities of these two men needs no further explanation. From a moral perspective, the Berlin synchronicity discussed in Chapter Six underlines the importance of free will: that there is always an alternative path to take in life. However, we also need a modicum of awareness to know when something needs to change. Theodore Roszak[9] alludes to how we harness and work with the energies of the daimon. He speaks about the *hinterland* between the *divine* and the *diabolical*, which we require awareness of, particularly when we are exploring and exercising our sacred life energies.

History shows us that we have continually undermined our connection to the daimon as a spiritual power in this world, and we have countless examples of *warnings* and *wonders* initiated by people who were full of daimonic character; for example Socrates is a well-known luminary. He had a productive relationship to his daimon, which helped guide him, and Socrates played a very influential role in the development of Greek philosophy. When daimonic and numinous energies are awoken within us they can inspire feelings of awe, as well as opening us up to the imaginal realm, which can inspire and motivate our actions.[7,4] How we choose to engage with this dynamic and daimonic potential is a matter of free will and our preparedness to meet our fate.

An important ancient Greek philosopher (and mystic-shaman) named Empedocles spoke about transcendental matters and how human beings could be inspired to reflect upon the ways they live their lives, especially by adjustments to live in ways that minimise strife. Empedocles emphasised the importance of connecting to the divine at a soul level (through the daimon), which plays an important role in bringing forth identity and character.[12] The daimonic character is not interested in superficial living; rather, the intentions, volitions and actions associated with the daimon go beyond the usual concerns of mundane existence. But it needs to be pointed out that working with daimonic energy takes courage. The work can often be burdensome, particularly because the process involves living authentically, developing wisdom and cultivating humility as we move through life,[13] which can be witnessed in the life of daimonic characters, such as Jung. The divine connection to daimons brings a creative spark, for example Socrates emphasised the importance of examining life in relation to goodness and virtue. His questioning approach to human existence is captured by his student Plato in the Socratic dialogues, which marks an important development in Greek philosophy. Socrates had known the daimon that accompanied him since he was a child, and he forged a productive relationship with this spirit throughout his life.[14] Socrates also valued dreams and acknowledged the oracle at Delphi.[15] These are deep spiritual resources, which can inspire our own transformative paths of awakening.

Another Greek philosopher, Aristotle (who came to prominence after Socrates and Plato), believed that the main purpose of human life and actions (*telos*) was to achieve *eudaimonia*, which is often translated as happiness. Yet, *eudaimonia* more accurately means *well-spirited*, and Baird Callicott[16] offers two additional meanings for how *well-spirited* can be interpreted, which were in use around the time of Aristotle. The first concerns whether a person's character or soul was in a good state; the second, Callicott informs us, was a more 'superstitious' belief, which means that a person was well-spirited because of a benign relationship to a spirit guide (daimon). There is an important distinction in these two representations of *eudaimonia*. The first is a more self-contained idea of soul and character, whereas the second reflects a divine-human interface between a person and a spirit guide. It is clear that in the modern world the former interpretation would be more palatable than the latter, due to its more rational and non-metaphysical stance. Yet, the latter reveals a relationship between the human and the sacred realm, which is what we appear to have lost in the modern technological era.

A contemporary interpretation for *eudaimonia* could be best summed up as *human flourishing*, or to be blessed.[16] The question is what does it mean to live a blessed life in a spiritual context? We have a hint of this from the teachings of Jesus in the Beatitudes, or the Sermon on the Mount,[17] particularly when Jesus says that we are blessed *if we know what we are doing*, but *if we do not know what we are doing* we are cursed (Luke 6:5). It means that blessings are not conferred upon us for any other reason than our ability to live in accord with spiritual depth, which then informs our actions in life. In this way, to be blessed means that we know what we are doing with our life energies and the directions we are taking. To be blessed is deep soul work. For example, Jesus says we must be prepared to be poor in spirit (*humble*); to mourn, as in compassion (*suffering with*); to be meek (*gentle*); to be hungry and thirsty (*committed*); to be merciful (*kind*); to be peacemakers (*loving*); and be able to face persecution and falseness (*deep faith*). The truth of these teachings is only found in the extent to which they filter into our consciousness[18] and into our actions. The *Beatitudes* are the beating heart of soulful ways of living.

Soul work

It is clear that in the modern world we have rationalised the human psyche to the point where we now question the validity of the soul, divine inspiration and spirit guides. Yet, because our one-sided modern ego-consciousness does not believe in the soul or spiritual realities, it does not mean they do not exist. For example, a typical Jungian view of the daimon and the soul is that they need each other to flourish.[19] Indeed, as Rollo May[15] says, it is easy for people to lose themselves in our industrial or technological world, where time and energy is invested into constructing lifestyles that evade the daimonic. The result of this collective disconnection at a soul level is all too familiar to anyone who works as a depth-orientated therapist or coach. It reveals a society that is crying out for a deeper engagement with the world of the psyche. When people do engage with soul work, it opens new life-lines, where vital energies can be harnessed, which can be transforming and liberating.[20] The daimonic world brings people to a boundary between the human and the divine, a liminal threshold that brings opportunities for creative interactions, where we co-create with the inspiration that is given to us from the imaginal realm.

If we recall the philosophy of wholeness advocated by Parmenides in Chapter Two, we realise that the interface between human reason and divine inspiration is not an either/or matter; it is both/and. Socrates is a good example of a *eudaimonic* person, in that he remained faithful to his true calling in life, but his unorthodox approach unsettled the authorities to such an extent that they made him take his own life by drinking poison. Socrates accepted his fate, and on his deathbed he asked that an offering be made to Asklepios, who as we remember from Chapter Two was the son of Apollo and a god of incubation and healing. In life and in death, Socrates did not compromise his vocation as a philosopher; indeed, he embraced a path that focused on the love of wisdom and knowledge. This is the type of spirited character that emerges via a productive relationship with the daimon. It is no surprise that the ancient Greek meaning for the word daimon has such a close association to the word fate,[15] and Carl Jung also acknowledged the importance of this link.[21]

To meet our fate means that we need to be discerning and ethical in the life-decisions we make, particularly in the way that vital energies inform life choices. Again, Carl Jung is a great example of someone who was a *congruent eudaimonic person*, which is evident in his drive and commitment to help humanity reconnect to the long forgotten and neglected world of the *anima mundi*, the soul of the world. James Hillman[22] reminds us of another ancient Greek philosopher, Heraclitus, who coined the phrase, *ethos anthropoi daimon*, which roughly translates: *character is fate*. Therefore, the true *eudaimonic* person is someone who is able to meet life and manifest their destiny (as a blessing), including the task of facing adversarial encounters, for example, between good-evil. A key quality associated with the *eudaimonic* person is that they actively meet their fate and use their free will, discernment and discipline to cultivate their true character, rather than being swept along in a maelstrom of unconscious projections, as in the case of Hitler and his supporters. The deep, soulful and sacred connections that underpin the daimonic journey into wholeness[7] are captured in the phrase used by Friedrich Nietzsche, the *amor fati*, or the *love of your fate*, which is a state of living imbued with great spiritual virtue.

Fate for the *eudaimonic* person is not some passive existence, where we are helpless in the face of life's unexpected twists and turns, nor is it concerned with some predetermined end point. Rather, it is a deep process of discovery that is centred on recovering a sense of wholeness. Therefore, working with our fate is soul work, where we are *alive to living fully*. It means we are orientated and committed to drawing on all the resources at our disposal: our dreams, inspirations, hunches, and synchronicities, as well as our gifts, talents and passions, which are directed in the service of the greater good. The love of our fate also means that we are prepared to enter into the unknown, where at times we follow the light of reason, and at others we enter the darkness, which enables us to grow in self-knowledge and avoid the destructive powers of the unconscious (shadow work). It is in this darkness that we connect to the depth of the soul, and it is where we discover a more active relationship to the daimon.[13] Therefore, working with the daimon means cultivating a quality of discernment, which ensures that all we encounter in our *soul work* becomes a *crucible of emancipation*. In this way, the *eudaimonic enterprise* is where our blessings are brought forth through deep inner work. This point is emphasised in the life of Carl Jung.

Jung's daimon

In true *eudaimonic* style, Carl Jung fused his interest in scientific rationality with a deep exploration of the irrational and mysterious forces that had captivated him from an early age. Jung went beyond the boundaries of Western reason and met his fate as he descended the depths of the psyche without any worldly guides or gurus. He encountered and struggled with the contents of the psyche arising within him, such as emotions and visions that were overpowering, as well as using creative impulses that were inspired by his inner work.[23] Jung describes these encounters with the unconscious as an assault, yet his determination to enter the world of the psyche was unwavering, and he felt that the task was connected to a higher purpose, which he felt *called and compelled* to master.[24] It is no surprise that the ancient Greeks considered the daimon to be a power that brings inspiration to the poet, artist and spiritual seeker etc. This is how the daimon leads people to discover their unique *signature* in life, which is connected to the expression of true character. It is through such deep and creative engagement of our human potential that we are encouraged to change outmoded beliefs and ways of living, as we enter a transformative life path.[25] We become inspired to live the truth of our existence, where we discover the unique gifts and talents we possess, which also contribute to the greater good.

Jung[24] realised that he was gripped by a daimon that was informing his visionary work, which resulted in him having to catch up with the insights that were coming to him. He became aware of this daimonic presence after he noticed an inner voice that was different from his own, which was almost prophetic.[26] The figure came to be known as *Philemon*. Jung first saw Philemon in a dream, flying in the sky with wings that resembled a kingfisher.[27] Jung was a visionary who understood that his journey of individuation was also in service to the greater good. What made Jung's approach to soul work so interesting and important were his phenomenal intellect and scientific mind, as well as his appreciation of cultural myths, and how meaningful coincidences can resonate between our inner and outer worlds. For example, one day Jung was painting his dream of *Philemon* using the bright colours of the kingfisher for the wings. He took a short break from painting and went for a walk in his garden, when he suddenly came across a dead kingfisher. Jung was only too aware how rare kingfishers were in his locality; in fact it would be a half-century before he would see another one near his home. He took the kingfisher experience as a synchronicity or meaningful coincidence, where an event in the outer world corresponds with an inner process, which confirmed for him that he was on the right track. It is fitting that his own connection to the daimon in the figure of Philemon resonated with the discovery of a dead (wounded) kingfisher bird.

Jungian analyst Robert Johnson[28] reminds us of the story about the *Fisher King*, which is predominantly concerned with wounded masculinity, and linked to the legend of King Arthur and his knights. The *Fisher King* has a deep wound that will only begin to heal when the right question is asked ("what is it that ails thee?"), which not only catalyses a process of bodily healing; it also restores and replenishes the Earth, which has also become depleted. Such stories encourage us to understand the nature of the spiritual 'quest', which concerns the right 'questions' that pertain to the soul and the journey into wholeness.[29] The story has resonances for our time that Johnson[28] links to the wounding connected to masculine power, which dominated 20th century science and individuality. These developments opened up new opportunities for humanity, but at a great cost soulfully and ecologically. It prompts us to pause and ponder the questions that are meaningful for the collective healing quest in this time of global crisis. The story of the *Fisher King* is relevant to Jung's inner journey, simply because he was concerned with asking the right questions about the life of the soul and our feelings in the troubled times we are living. In this regard, Philemon was invaluable to Jung.

Philemon instructed Jung on the ways of cultivating a proper relationship to his soul, to the ancestors and the daimons.[30] Indeed, Philemon enabled Jung to understand that the psyche has a life of its own, which he incorporated in his inner work and in his work with others.[24] The beauty of Jung's journey of individuation is that he recognised he was connected to daimonic energies.[23] It took great courage for Jung to find a new way of working with the depths of the psyche arising within him, which became a process he referred to as active imagination. This deep method of doing inner work became a highly creative process, with various channels of expression, such as painting and movement etc. The *genius* in Jung's discovery of active imagination is that the method brings us into direct contact with the living unconscious, which enables new states of consciousness to emerge. But this discovery only came about because Jung recognised the *real genius* at work, the daimon. Indeed, the Latin translation of daimon is *genii*, and as Rollo May[15] informs us, it comes from the Latin root meaning *genius* or *genere*, to generate. Genius (daimon) was recognised in the ancient Roman religion as a spiritual guide that helps bring forth a latent talent. The beauty of genius, in the true sense of the word, is that it is initiated by the daimon or spirit guide, who provides us with inspiration, and it is our task to discern its meaning, particularly through those insights or revelations that may not always be obvious. James Hillman[22] says no person *is* or *can be* identified as a genius, as its qualities are more associated with divine inspiration which comes to us in numinous signs, urges, hunches or dreams etc.

A powerful example of a daimonic encounter is told by Patrick Harper,[31] recounting the dream of a young boy, who lived around the time of William Shakespeare's premiere of *Macbeth* in 1606. At school the young boy told his teacher about his dream, which revealed that one day he would be King of England. The young boy was severely punished for uttering such nonsense, yet as it turned out, four decades later, just as King Charles (I) was ousted from the throne and put to death, young Oliver Cromwell's dream was not far from becoming a reality. In 1653 Cromwell became the Lord Protector of England, a Head of State, which is not quite King of England, but it was certainly the most powerful position in the land. Dreams and synchronicities are uncanny, and the gift of Jung and his depth approach to working with the psyche is to reawaken us to the knowledge and wisdom that could temper the modern obsession with hyper-rationalism. We can learn so much from people who have undergone long trainings in Jungian, transpersonal, spiritual or indigenous traditions. I consider myself fortunate to have friends who have served as 'apprentices' in such traditions.

I first met my friend Nick Hurn in the mid 1980s, around the time when he first started using a Native American ceremonial pipe. It was a ritual that helped Nick to connect to life and all beings. Nick's use of the Native American ceremonial pipe reflects his deep interest in this tradition, which includes a long-term relationship with a shaman-mystic from the Pueblo and Ute tribes, Joseph, who is also known as *Beautiful Painted Arrow*. Nick told me that in the Native American tradition the whole point of shamanic training is to "awaken and develop visionary capacities". He spent 20 years studying and learning the ways of Native American ceremony, which included taking part in Sun Dances every year for 12 years. The Sun Dance involves four days of fasting and ritual dancing. Gradually the physical exertion induces altered states of consciousness, deepening the participant's connection to visionary energies.

Nick says that taking part in this ceremony facilitates a relationship with the *outer landscape*, which resonates with and alters the *inner landscape*. When Nick attended his first ceremony with *Beautiful Painted Arrow*, he had a series of visions that predicted he would eventually run and lead his own Sun Dances, which he now does, as well as running traditional sweat lodges. When I spoke to Nick he elaborated further on the importance of the Native American tradition in which he trained: "The native people understand how to work consciously with the forces of nature. They can alter what happens in the natural world, for example *Beautiful Painted Arrow* had to be able to call rain when conditions on the land were too arid. The visionary ceremonies are a way of connecting with the forces of nature." As Nick spoke I was reminded of the often-told story of the Taoist Rainmaker, in which a shaman is called into a village that had not had rain for many days. As the Taoist-shaman enters the village it is evident to him that the inhabitants of the village are in a chaotic state of mind. The shaman then makes a request for a hut, along with a request that he is not to be disturbed. He then proceeds to sit within the chaotic atmosphere of the village and do inner work until a natural state of order returns, whereupon it starts to rain. What I learn from such shamanic stories is that they are reminding us that we are not helpless in the chaos of this world. I recall a particular time in my life when I was embroiled in a conflict and how a synchronicity with a kingfisher shifted my life direction in unexpected ways. Rather than sharing the details of the event that initiated this period of self-exploration, I shall emphasise how it turned into an initiation. It was a time of deep learning for me that underlined the importance of living in wholeness, and how opportunities for growth are ever present in our lives, which can connect us to the call of the daimon.

Kingfisher spirit

Some years ago I contacted Nick to ask if he would facilitate a pipe ceremony with me. I wanted to find inspiration to approach a relationship difficulty that had arisen in my life. The conflict uncovered a deep vulnerability within me, and I initially struggled to deal with the situation. It was an unexpected life event that breached my well-crafted personal boundaries. It became impossible for me to ignore the situation and consequently I felt compelled to act. Like many people, I do not relish conflict, but I realised that if I avoided this situation I would not be living authentically. However, facing up to the task exposed me to fears and anxieties that had been lying dormant in my psyche for years. I also learnt how life-events challenge us to be real and authentic, allowing us to develop our true character (daimonic potential), which can inspire our life-path and help us to meet our fate. In this instance, I was enmeshed in a relationship dynamic and soon realised that I had limited resources to deal with it effectively. At the time I was floundering in my ability to respond to the situation, but it also presented me with a range of transformative possibilities. I was able to explore and cultivate new skills that enabled me to live in empowered and enlivened ways. When the daimon awakens we are often caught between the pull of consensus reality and the call of the soul.

When I met Nick to do the pipe ceremony, I told him about my predicament as we drove to a beautiful local nature reserve. We then walked for some time along the narrow waterways until we found the right spot. We sat near the edge of a waterway and prepared ourselves, and Nick asked permission from the *Spirit of the place* for a sign that it would be acceptable for us to do the ceremony. A split second later, a kingfisher dived in the water about 1.5 metres in front of where we were sitting, and in a flash it flew out of the water with a small fish in its beak. I was astounded, as the kingfisher ally was a deeply synchronous and symbolic confirmation for me. Nick and I were both satisfied that this was a meaningful sign to proceed with the ceremony. Nick prepared the pipe, joining the *female bowl* to the *male stem*, which creates an altar and becomes a sacramental vessel for the ceremony. I then focused my intentions and prayers as I held the pipe bowl next to my heart, where I called on and invoked the spirits to help me find inspiration and courage. We then smoked the sacred tobacco, which carried my prayers and intentions to the four directions. Nick offered a sacred song as a way of saying thanks.

I went home and meditated on the spirit of the kingfisher as a shamanic ally, hoping that it would guide me. I also knew that the kingfisher is an arch predator, which hunts using stealth and speed. It made me think about our indigenous sisters and brothers who enter into shamanic relationships with animal spirit guides. I decided to explore the strengths associated with kingfisher-like speed, directness and precision in all my interactions. These qualities were not part of my usual everyday ways of relating, but I reasoned that if I used them skilfully and compassionately, they could support me to become more empowered in my relationships. At times I felt uncertain and uneasy about my new attitude and communication style, but there was also something exciting about these new behaviours, where I was awakening new possibilities for living. I was a bit anxious at times, but I was also determined to take this opportunity to grow. Prior to these new developments, I had also (synchronously) enrolled on an online course, exploring ways of working with relationship dynamics. The course provided me with wonderful conversations and ideas about working with new patterns in human relationships, emphasising facilitation skills and how to resolve conflicts. Interestingly, the relationship issue I was in, also resolved to the satisfaction of all involved.

From the moment of the kingfisher synchronicity, it was like I was compelled to live more authentically. It ignited a dramatic shift in my attitudes, behaviours and relationships. In many ways, the events at this time were like an unexpected rite of passage, calling me to live more congruently in relation to my psycho-spiritual development. It was a potent time of self-exploration and my life-direction changed as a result of this life event. Looking back, it is evident that my past social conditioning (and traumas) had resulted in behaviour patterns, where I was prone to adapting myself. For example, I had developed an unhelpful habit of not always expressing my true feelings, when it would have been more honest to do so. In essence, I had become ensnared in a placation trap of my own making, where I was more invested in 'keeping the peace' rather than upsetting others. In reality this was driven by not knowing how to represent myself congruently in conflicted relationships. Interestingly, I find the wisdom in the story of the Fisher King an apt representation for how we can address the wounds that many of us are carrying today. We are living in a time where deep healing is being called for, where each of us is tasked with finding the answers to the right questions in our lives, such as: 'What is it that ails thee?' Only then can we start to heal. My kingfisher encounter chimes with Jung's experience of finding a dead kingfisher in his garden when he was painting Philemon (his inner guide), which took him into a deeper relationship with this daimon. If we take heed of the signs and synchronicities that accompany our everyday experiences in life, we may also find unexpected opportunities for healing and psycho-spiritual awakening.

If we are truly interested in the love of our fate – the *Amor Fati* – it is through the daimon that we are brought into a deeper relationship with our true character. For example, working with our daimonic potential encourages a deeper response to life events, which is underpinned by a commitment to become a whole person. Jungian and transpersonal psychologies are contemporary approaches that inspire us to embrace such soulful and holistic ways of living, which are much needed in the world today. In Chapter Eleven, I touch upon the work of Abraham Maslow and his observations about human development in relation to Hierarchy of Need. Maslow helps us to understand the impact of deficiencies in terms of our human development, and also how we can support physical, psychological, social and spiritual growth. It is instructive that the Greek meaning of the word hierarchy is derived from the words *heiros* (sacred) *archein* (leader), which implies a spiritual emphasis.[32] Therefore, the word hierarchy is concerned with the activation and expression of our deepest potentials as a process of awakening to the sacred. If we include the daimon in our understanding of hierarchy, we realise that we are being led into a deeper and more sacred relationship with life.

W.B. Yeats[33] wrote in his book, *A Vision*, that when the creativity of the daimon flows through our life events and passions it could lead to a unity of being, which connects to our fate and destiny. Indeed, the hallmark of a daimonic character is that they are true to their deepest calling and life path. This message continues to inspire me to be true to who I am in all that I do, which also connects to the coaching work that I do with people. The following vignette reflects some coaching sessions I did with a woman who had come to a point in her life where she wanted to take a new creative direction, but noticed some inner resistance. She had done a lot of work on herself over the years, which meant we could travel fast and deep.

_____ **Tango killer** _____

A woman came to me for coaching to explore her 'writer's block'. It soon transpired that her obstacle connected to a dichotomy between writing about professional matters, and following her personal interests in writing about shamanism. On the surface the dilemma seemed to be an either/or predicament, but as we went deeper into my client's creative process we discovered inner dynamics that were self-sabotaging and connected to a fear of being seen. In one of our sessions we returned to the question about the writing she wants to do, and we explored the creative edge that was emerging. My client said how frustrating it is when she is preparing to write, only to find that she then begins compulsively seeking out any distraction, such as housework. She said to me that she knows she is "running away" from the creative expression she craves. As she was speaking my client was gesticulating and making energetic movements that corresponded with running away. I suggested we amplify the movement energy and literally "run with it" to find out what it is like to run away. We playfully began running around the room but very quickly my client noticed feelings arising, which she described as "grief" and an overwhelming sense of futility. There was a palpable sense of sadness in my client at this point, and I had the impulse to ask if she would like a hand to hold. She appreciated the gesture, saying it created an important feeling of connection for her.

My client reflected, and took more time to feel deeply into the experience of grief. She then started to speak about the experience, whilst making movements with her arms that flowed up and down the front of her body like those of tai chi, and her hands expressed gestures similar to Indian Yoga Mudra. It seemed as if my client was making some energetic connection between above and below, which she said felt more integrated. I thought this might be a good moment to ask her about what she had been "running away from?" She reflected on a familiar feeling of fearfulness around "being seen" and a lack of safety. The connection I had offered her earlier (holding hands) had stabilised the flight/collapse response, and resulted in her feeling "rooted in the Earth", like a tree. I turned the question around and asked her: "What are you running to?" This was a prompt to go deeper, and she literally felt her awareness of being rooted in the Earth taking her further down into it, where she had a visual and felt a sense of entering a "crystal cave". She described it as a connection to Gaia. Throughout this time she had continued making the tai chi and Mudra hand movements, which combined with the crystal cave experience and seemed to enhance the energetic flow in her arms and hands, now full of numinous energy. She described the experience as "going deep" (below) and "connecting out wide" (above). It was powerful witnessing this unfolding process of integration, which was also very enlivening. However, in the midst of speaking about this process of energetic and creative flow my client noticed a sensation in her throat that was restrictive and tightening up. I suggested we find out more about this.

My client was happy to proceed to find out if the restriction in her voice was connected to the self-sabotage pattern in her creative writing. I suggested a way forward and I knelt down (to reduce my presence), offering my wrist, and inviting my client to create the same choking restriction on my arm that she had felt in her throat. She took my wrist and started to squeeze it, and with a little encouragement she increased the strength in her grip, and it was at this point she noticed feelings of panic and anger. She also said that she could feel the pulse in my wrist beating strongly. She began pulling hard at my arm and said that she wanted to "uproot me". I resisted this attempt and questioned the motives of the part of her pulling away. She then abruptly loosened her grip and collapsed on the floor, curled up in a foetal position. I thanked her for showing the 'strangler', and she remained curled up on the floor, saying she now felt like a "seed" in the Earth (new growth and potential). My client said that it was a safe space and clasped her hands together, saying the process was about "making a connection", not only to herself, but also to others. Following on from this, she reached out again to hold my hand and we made the 'self-other connection' more visible and real.

In our discussion, we went back to the process of how her creativity comes from the heart, but is frequently sabotaged. She said the *strangler* is like a "psycho-killer", and we made room for this energy to be represented as a 'role'.

We found out that the self-destructive motives of the strangler are actually linked to an old self-protection system, linked to a fear of being seen (existing), but we also learnt that the 'protector' also prevents true connection to self and other. Now that this powerful energetic/destructive force had been made *visible* it brought an awareness of the underlying process. We deduced that when the 'psycho-killer' is free to roam in the unconscious, its natural default position is predisposed towards self-sabotage, which keeps my client 'safe' but also 'stuck' in disconnection. We spoke about the possibilities of consciously transforming this (now) available energy into the seeding of her creative potential. In the session that followed, my client used her voice to take an authoritative lead in our dramatic representation of her process, where she was able to relate to all parts of her inner world (integrating the psycho-killer energy).

She found a sense of *containment* and *flow* in the experience, which she described as being "like the firm banks of a river, which enabled the water to flow within it". In a spirit of fluidity, she bowed to the 'psycho-killer' and acknowledged its former protective function, and then she invited it to take a new role, joining her and creating new energetic opportunities, speaking out and making new connections for living. She explored, embodied and expressed her creative responses to the process, which turned into Tango moves, where she became free to lead or follow. As the process of integration continued, she spoke about a "new creative dance", where new patterns for living (structure) are free to morph and flow (fluidity). It was deeply touching to witness the 'psycho-killer', who was formerly a saboteur and inhibitor, now included in the creative dance leading to emancipation.

The coaching sessions created deep opportunities for discovering the creative edge, between my client's inner work as *active imagination*, and her outer work as *imaginative action*. The process brought to *conscious awareness* my client's *unconscious dynamics*, which were causing her to 'run away' from her creative potential. Understanding these inner dynamics also enabled her to find a conscious connection about what she is 'running to'. The work with this client reveals how the imaginal realm brings deep and numinous connections in our quest for wholeness. The collective significance and meaning in this work is illustrative of the powerful inner dynamics that can curtail our creative potential. Yet, when they are fully represented they point the way for a redemptive quest of soulful renewal. My client feedback to me the impact of the work we did, which has been deeply transformative for her. She says that the process of embodying and integrating the self-sabotaging 'psycho-killer' has brought more awareness about her inner and outer dynamics, which has now freed up some exuberant energy to 'dance'. It is a creative connection that is bringing new enthusiasm for writing, but also in her connections to others. She went on to say: "It is impossible to dance Tango alone!" The work with my client also illustrates an important interconnection, between the processes of our individual awakening, which can then be expressed in the outer world to counter the collective nullification and neglect of our transpersonal potential. This dynamic is at the heart of our collective growing edge in this time of *psychic stagnation* and *planetary degradation*.

Each of us has the opportunity to consciously engage in a creative process of working towards *eudaimonia*,[7] which is where we are blessed. This is an important observation for the crisis-ridden times we are living in today, inspiring us to bring forth our potential. At the heart of the daimonic encounter is imaginative work, where the *creative urge* to live in wholeness bring us to a *creative edge* and we meet the limits of our fears, passions, impulses and preoccupations. Indeed, daimonic energies bring us into a deep connection for living, through a co-creative relationship[19] with the sacred, which informs our path of wisdom and transformation. Rollo May[15] speaks about the creative imperative within the daimonic encounter, which is always seeking to be expressed, and Patrick Harpur[31] believes our potential is wasted if the daimon is not encountered, because it has a significant impact on our imaginative lives and souls. One of the *Vital Signs* noted in our collective response to the global crisis is the restoration of our connection to the daimons.[34] It is pleasing to see contemporary ecotherapy approaches acknowledging the daimon and the importance of eudaimonia in relation to cultivating and fulfilling our potential. It is the cultivation of such a spirited and meaningful connection to the natural world which brings home to us the importance of living ethically and sustainably.[35] It means being open to a process of awakening that may be beyond our current ways of knowing.

Sometimes we are awoken in the most unexpected ways. Arny Mindell is someone who models deep awareness into everyday action, through working creatively with life's complexities and synchronicities. As a contemporary figure, Arny Mindell would be someone I consider to be eudaimonic. In his wonderful book *The Shaman's Body*, he writes about a woman who was living in New York and was told by her spirit guide to go to the main international airport, where someone would give her the money to buy a plane ticket. After a few hours' waiting at the airport she was given the money and her spirit guide told her to buy a ticket to Zurich. When she arrived in Switzerland her guide told her to randomly open a phone book and place her finger on a name, and then ring them. The number happened to be Arny Mindell's Zurich office, where he was working as a Jungian analyst. Within an hour the woman was sitting in his office. She told him that her spirit guide was telling him he had to write books. Ten years after this unconventional meeting, Arny published his first book, *Dreambody*.[11] He has now written 20 books that have been translated into numerous languages.

We can no longer overlook the mystical connection to visions, dreams, myths and synchronicities, which bring our consciousness into relationship with the imaginal realm, either in the depths of sleep, or in the reveries of the waking state. For example, dreaming is where we can get used to meeting the reality of the imaginal, which is still one of the most powerful means of initiation accessible to us in the modern world.[8] In this way, the daimonic character is a driving force of the Transformocene, where our blessings, or *eudaimonia*, can contribute to the co-creation of a sustainable and improved future. What is more, if we fail to take heed of the daimon's call in this life, we are sure to be reminded of it when we die.

Exercise: Eudaimonia

- The daimon acts like a divine spark (an animating spirit) that is activated in our souls, and helps to bring forth our true character.

- Where are you being called to authenticity?
  ○ What pre-occupations are percolating within you?
  ○ What Big Dreams are awakening within you?
  ○ What synchronous events (meaningful coincidences) are manifesting in your life?
  ○ What visionary possibilities arise within you?
  ○ What socio-political reactions are activated in you for a 'just' world?

- How can you honour the sacred urges within you in your daily life?

- What life contexts or situations bring you into alignment with your wholeness?

- What can you do today to honour your sense of soul as part of the soul of the world?

- How is the sacred being activated in your life as part of your true character and calling?

PART THREE: THE EMANCIPATORY EDGE

Philosopher[1]

That's more like it!
The measure of an alchemist...
let's not struggle with syntax,
these are words hammered in the fires of life
not nice or agreeable
sweetly spiritual.

These are the muscles
of life's work and discipline
the conflicts of heaven and hell
the ravages of pleasure and pain
the frustrations of hope and dream
all goes into the alchemy!

It has always been this way
I work!

There is no end to that
no comfortable harbour
in which to pray and plead
I live!

This body so tired
this heart ravaged
this mind stretched

and the soul
god bless it

still willing before death!

When we realise that our attitudes and actions can create 'hell' or 'heaven' on Earth, we arrive at a 'creative edge'. Enlightenment is a deep commitment to live in freedom and love. In the Transformocene Age, emancipation is a co-creative force.

INTRODUCTION TO PART THREE

The Emancipatory Edge

Visionary energies and edges

Tipping points are edges that morph into new realities, which can be promising and/or challenging. For example, in this book I have proposed that the Anthropocene could become the tipping point for the Transformocene, revealing that humanity can no longer invest in a myopic materialist and hyper-rational worldview. As we have learnt in the previous chapters, our global collective reality is full of dynamic, complex and unpredictable tipping points that threaten to push us 'over the edge'. The ecological crisis and our psychological, social and economic responses to it are a major tipping point at this time,[2] which means that we will need to double our efforts to prepare ourselves for deep change. It means creating a focus for living in wholeness, so that our 'collective edges' are managed through our inner and outer work: physically, psychologically, socially, soulfully, spiritually, ecologically and cosmologically. Nothing short of a renewed vision for living, one that promotes wholeness in action, will tackle the toxic legacy of our collective neglect, which is layered in the geological record (Anthropocene). It means that we have a deep responsibility to co-create a sustainable future, where global well-being is linked to 'social virtue' in three overlapping ways, as noted by Professor Tim O'Riordan.[3] 1) *Esteem* (e.g. personal awakening, justice and rights); 2) *Security* (e.g. safety, health, employment and community); 3) *Responsibility* (e.g. others, future generations, the planet, morality and spirituality). These three spheres of influence connect to awakening at an individual and collective level of consciousness. For example, in the pioneering work of Ervin Laszlo[4] we learn that because the cosmos is interconnected and non-local, our awakening to a transpersonal dimension of consciousness brings more sensitivity and responsibility towards life in our relations with people, animals and plants etc.

It is through our conscious connection to a process of awakening that a 'contemplative consciousness' reveals our primary relationship to a non-dual reality (wholeness). In this way, Lawrence Freeman[5] views such a shift as a vital tipping point for a new spiritual consciousness to emerge, one that embraces diversity, but which is wholly connected to unity. The focus on interconnectivity and interdependence underlines the possibilities for evolving an eco-consciousness that is also metaphysical.[6] Such a perspective highlights the need to reconnect with wisdom traditions that put wholeness first. Our species has a wealth of ancient spiritual lineages that understand the deep value of ritual and initiation, which could be coupled to the cultivation of deep ecological awareness.[7] We have an opportunity to embrace a collective tipping point that brings forth awareness of life's subtle interconnectedness (e.g. through non-locality and synchronicity), where our visionary energies are aligned with the imaginal realm. For example, Veronica Goodchild[8] considers Jung's work to be a *songline* between the world of dreams and a non-local soul, where we can also come into contact with mystical entities such as daimons and angels. She points out that such a connection with the imaginal realm can energise our lives in terms of bringing healing and intuition, which is like a shamanic reality.

The invitation to reacquaint us with the imaginal realm, as put forward by Goodchild,[8] cannot be approached from an objective point of view, which has been the dominant mode of consciousness in the Western world for the past few hundred years. Therefore, the tipping point in consciousness that will help facilitate a shift into wholeness is based on a more subjective and qualitative relationship to our imaginative resources, as a source of deep spiritual inspiration. Goodchild[8] reminds us that such encounters can include an interpretive 'as if' approach to our subtle and symbolic experiences, but she also points out that the work *actually* brings us into connection with a mystical reality. For example, pioneer of transpersonal consciousness studies Stanislav Grof[9] shares stories of working at the growing edge of consensus reality (tipping points), where people's deep transformative potentials reveal how the 'impossible' *can* happen. However, due to our modern hyper-rational minds there is so much scepticism in the world today towards what Grof[9] calls "non-ordinary realities", yet it is curious that a *Time Magazine* survey found 69% of American respondents declared a belief in angels, with 32% reporting direct encounters with these spirits.[10] It is my conviction that hyper-rationalism has made people reluctant to talk about phenomena broadly connected to the imaginal realm, due to fear of ridicule or actual discrimination. We have tangible evidence of such discriminatory attitudes, when a woman shared her visionary experiences of the afterlife with a doctor following a near-death experience, and ended up being sectioned in a psychiatric hospital.[11] Such occurrences are what Arny Mindell[12] calls our collective *City Shadows*. The woman's experience above highlights the level of cultural dissociation from direct spiritual experiences.

Visionary actions

We have tangible evidence of such non-ordinary encounters in people's near-death experiences (NDEs). Programme Director for the Scientific and Medical

Network, David Lorimer,[13] speaks about the initiatory processes that accompany visionary NDEs, which more often than not catalyse a process of spiritual engagement when people return to their Earthly existence. Lorimer discusses the impact of the *life review* in NDEs, and how people report experiences of feeling the emotional impact of their actions towards others. It points to a holographic reality, where 'unitive consciousness' is more than speculative. In fact, such experiences raise serious questions about morals and actions in our world, individually, institutionally and socially. David Lorimer's[13] emphasis on "empathetic resonance" lies at the heart of how we can raise our vibrational and energetic resources for living and growing. It points to the value of acknowledging what we do in the world will be reflected back to us at death. If such knowledge were more widely known, it could initiate greater awareness of compassionate reflection and action in daily life that benefits our collective spiritual awakening. Being sectioned in a psychiatric hospital for sharing a profound vision of *Divine love* reveals how much work there is to be done on Earth.

In his book *Memories, Dreams, Reflections*, Carl Jung[14] shares his visionary experiences following a heart attack in 1944. The period during and immediately after his heart attack resulted in experiences of expanded consciousness, including seeing the Earth from space, and entering a cosmic rock temple (located within a meteorite), where he met an Indian man meditating. Jung described the experience as being as if he had been stripped of his Earthly identity. He experienced an overview of his life, and while he was in the cosmic temple he met his Earthly doctor who told him to return to Earth (which Jung tried to resist). In his visionary state Jung became very worried about his doctor and had a premonition that he was in danger of dying. When Jung recovered from his heart attack, he learnt that he was the last patient to be treated by his doctor, who suddenly contracted septicaemia and died. Jung also speaks about his visionary epiphanies in the NDE as being joyful and enchanting, where both *light* and *angels* were present. During his recovery, Jung's nurse told him about a bright glow that had surrounded him, which is something she had seen many times around people when they are dying. Jung also saw a blue-coloured halo around her head. All that Jung describes is not out of place from a mystical perspective, for example references to angels during processes of awakening in consciousness are well represented in Alchemical and Kabbalistic traditions.[15,16] Indeed, I once heard an old Talmud saying that angels even encourage blades of grass to grow. I played with this idea and thought, if this was so, perhaps the same must apply to us?

When we honour the subtleties of the imaginal realm we need to be discerning. For example, there are very real examples of both helpful and harmful experiences connected to the angelic realm,[10] which means that the vibrations and motivations that accompany our intentions for living are of great importance. It points to the need for our inner and outer work to be directed towards love and serving the greater good, which are the types of resonant actions that are needed to bring forth the Transformocene. It is here that we can align with what Thomas Berry[17] calls *The Great Work*, which is a dream for an improved world, fuelled by a "mythic vision" that inspires transformative action. Veronica Goodchild[8] speaks about visionary ways of knowing as a vibrant relationship between the cosmos and our Self-realisation, which is linked to transpersonal consciousness. It puts into context the work of Kingsley Dennis,[18] who refers to people interested in co-creating a new era of consciousness as *The Phoenix Generation*, which means they are interested in cultivating a world of connection and compassion.

Humanity has an opportunity to engage in collective transformation, which will bring us to an emancipatory edge. For example, if we are emboldened to 'wake up' we will have to navigate the contrasting realities of *transpersonal* consciousness, versus the robotic drift into a *transhuman* reality, where we are in danger of squandering our soulful potential. If we are in any doubt about the threats posed by a technocracy devoid of soul, the prospect of 'killer robots' are already on the horizon, unless we act fast. In an open letter to the United Nations (August 2017), 116 leaders in the field of artificial intelligence expressed their concern about the 'Pandora's box' that could be opened if *murdering machines* are allowed to be developed.[19] Interestingly, it takes a mythic description (Pandora's box) to help scientists convey the seriousness of their concerns about the rise of such lethal technologies. Such is the power of myth.

Our Earthly existence is intimately bound to the web of life. What we do in thought, word, and deed has Akashic resonance. The mystery of death reveals karmic reverberations in the life review. We do, therefore we evolve.

CHAPTER NINE

Life and Death Transitions

Overview

In this chapter I explore research findings from people's near-death experiences, which expose the limiting ideologies that serve our current one-dimensional consensus reality. I discuss how near-death experiences reveal a sacred reality, where interconnectedness, divine light, angelic encounters and the life review unveil important life lessons about living in love, not fear. For example, insights from people's life reviews inform us that they experienced the emotional impact of their actions on others, revealing the deep consequences and reverberations of their actions in life. These spiritually transformative experiences often initiate new life directions once people return to their Earthly existence, knowing that they have life lessons to learn. These changes can include a renewal of identity and action with spiritual significance, particularly being more loving and compassionate in the world. It puts under the microscope what we are doing with our vital life energies in this time of global crisis. These spiritual revelations contrast with the drift into a high-tech world that is increasingly soulless. I point out that the Transformocene confronts us with two competing realities, which brings the human soul to an emancipatory edge, between *transhumanism* and *transpersonalism*.

Life review

Daimonic energy brings a dynamic focus to the process of individuation and our journey to wholeness, but of course we have to play our part in awakening at a soul level. We may well think that individuation is a pointless task, and why bother? However, individuation is concerned with psycho-spiritual awakening and the quest to live a meaningful life, which is not some arbitrary pursuit; rather, it is recognition that the call to transformation is an essential life task. Our *transformative imperative* is revealed in the *Myth of Er*, an ancient account of a near-death experience told by Socrates and then Plato, about a soldier named Er, who died in battle. In the afterlife he saw the souls of the dead who were witnessing the consequences of their actions, linked to the life choices they had made and the quality of the character they had developed. Er noticed that each soul had a guardian spirit (daimon). He was sent back to Earth to resume his life and share with the living his account of the afterlife. It is a message that continues to this day, through modern people's life-changing near-death experiences. It is a persistent call from the spirit world to renewal and transformation.

Stephen Levine[1] likens deep change and transformation to a process of dying to outmoded habits and limiting ways of being. He asks, what would we do if we only had one year to live? It is a great question. When we live deep transformative lives it is '*as if*' we are dying to our outmoded worldviews and behaviours, which then makes way for changes, including new patterns of growth and development. In this way, death is central to the process of individuation,[2] which aligns us with our full human potential as an *individual*, as well as being connected to the universe as a whole, *undivided*. The notion of 'dying' before physical death was an ancient spiritual practice in Greece (see Chapter Two), based on the recognition of the need for preparation for this life stage. For example, Socrates advocated that an awareness of dying should permeate all the ways we are occupied in life.[1] In the modern world we do not reflect enough on death, and how it could enrich our ways of living. This great journey into the unknown has troubled philosophers since ancient times. Whilst nobody is 100% sure what happens when we die, reports from people who have had near-death encounters are quite intriguing and revealing.

The phenomenon of people, who have experienced 'clinical deaths' and are then resuscitated, provides us with a glimpse of what an experience of the afterlife could mean. For example, research across seventeen institutions in the UK and USA over a four-year period, tracked 2,000 people who had had a cardiac arrest (and had been pronounced clinically dead). The medical teams were able to resuscitate and revive 16% of people, and managed to interview 101 patients, out of which around half the group could remember something about their experience. People reported experiencing terror, fear, violence and persecution or bliss, pleasantness, bright light and seeing deceased family members.[3] One thing is for sure: these people's experiences were not all sweetness and light. Indeed, the reported experiences chime with Buddhist teachings that say the state of mind at the time of death is important as we prepare to leave the *Bardo* of this incarnation. It illustrates the point that we are advised to prepare for death, and paradoxically, this preparedness can itself be a very healing process. Doing a life review before we die is not only a powerful way of reflecting on our attitudes, values, purpose and meaning; it may also have deeper consequences about who we are, and the lives we are living.

A doctoral thesis and book by Penny Sartori[4] report that life reviews are a recurring theme in the near-death state, where people find out that there are important lessons they have yet to learn, or life-tasks to be fulfilled. The question is, why would any of us want to wait until we are confronted with our physical death to find out that we still have valuable life lessons to learn, or life-tasks to fulfil as part of our awakening? Stephen Levine[1] suggests that carrying out a *life review* whilst we are alive gives us the opportunity to cultivate such awareness, whilst also becoming more grateful and forgiving (of self and other). Indeed, the life review could be a useful way of inspiring or initiating change in collective consciousness, which could help us to engage more deeply with the life we are living, before we actually die. For example, Sartori[4] reports patients' near-death experiences who say they were exposed to a reality where all life is part of an *interconnected whole*. Such experiences have the power to shift attitudes and behaviours towards being more consciously loving, kind and peaceful. Reporter Pierre Jovanovic[5] provides two interesting examples from near-death experiences. One was a priest who had lost his devotion and was just going through the motions in his ministry. However, his life review revealed to him that his everyday actions on Earth mattered, and after his encounter with death he changed his behaviour and became a more loving and devoted priest. The other example was a preacher who realised that he needed to change his attitude after he saw the consequences of his actions in his life review. He realised he had been poisoning the minds of his congregation by continually warning that they would go to hell, scaring them rather than making his ministry a sacrament of love.

A salutary lesson for us all is that people who have encountered near-death experiences often make radical changes in their attitudes, values and behaviours when they return to everyday life. For the priests (above) their life reviews revealed to them the consequences of their attitudes and behaviours, which became powerful catalysts for initiating transformation. Sometimes people's life reviews showed them that their work in the world was not complete, whereas others were told that they were on the right path.[5] A key point for many people after their NDE is that the boundaries of *life as they knew it* had been expanded,[6] which led them to live more consciously on their return to Earth. Physician Larry Dossey[6] recounts a story of a university researcher who had a near-death experience when she was a young woman, and then she had a similar experience whilst engaging in an everyday activity, where she experienced a sense of *oneness* and *light* whilst addressing a gathering of people. She went on to research this phenomenon and collected 102 case reports of people who had had similar transformational encounters. Interestingly the people she talked to had been engaged in diverse activities such as rest, prayer, meditation, driving, flying, dreaming, conversation, work and leisure activities at the time of their transpersonal experiences. It transpired that these expansive encounters engendered feelings of renewal in these people, which brought them a greater sense of meaning and purpose in their lives. These transpersonal experiences are available to all of us, and they have been extensively documented in the literature over the past five decades.[7]

Interwoven karma

Jody Long[8] reports on a review of 319 people who had had near-death experiences, and one of the most significant catalysts for change was the life review. The findings revealed that the life review was carried out in a loving, compassionate and non-judgmental atmosphere, showing people the consequences of their actions in life, and how their actions reverberated in the lives of others. It is not too dissimilar to the experience of Scrooge in the story, *A Christmas Carol.* The moral lesson of the life review seems to indicate that love, compassion and forgiveness are major lessons to be learnt in life. Becoming more loving and compassionate towards life as a whole (not just to our family and friends) is cultivated through deep reflections about purpose and meaning in life, and how our actions have been helpful or harmful to others.[4] The life review underlines the importance of working on the shadow in this life.

In one account of a life review, a person was accompanied by a cloaked and bearded figure, whose non-judgmental presence helped her gain a balanced perspective on her actions. She saw her life as a tapestry and within the woven stitches were all the events from her life.[8] She asked the figure why there were so many loose threads on the tapestry, to which he replied that it was not complete yet. This example resonates with the idea of karma (from Hinduism), where the fruits of our actions in this life (and past lives) can ripen, presenting us with pleasant or unpleasant consequences, depending on the quality of our prior actions. The tapestry gave this woman a rich perspective for understanding the greater patterning of events and actions that were interconnected throughout her life. Here, we can also see links to the Hindu spiritual practice of tantra, which according to William Irwin Thompson[9] literally means *threading* and *weaving* material. It suggests that a spiritual perspective for living can help us to live in awareness of the *interwoven matrix* of life, and how we are intimately bound to the *whole* in all that we do. In the Myth of Er, Er's travels in the afterlife included witnessing the *Three Fates* (daughters of the goddess) who are spinning the *Spindle of Necessity*, which is revolving before the ranks of departed souls.[10] These examples suggest that we could develop a spiritual practice in life that is based upon a clear understanding that we have free will over the patterns of behaviour we weave. It is instructive to note that to weave is highly symbolic of a creative process,[11] which begs the reflective question: what we are weaving in our lives in terms of our attitudes and behaviours? The life review from near-death experiences seems to be teaching us that life is far more sacred, interconnected and nuanced than we have been led to believe. For example, in the dogma of scientism we are told that life is a process of blind evolutionary unfolding. Such a worldview has resulted in a spiritual blindspot in our understanding of life.

Scientism is unable to explain the deeper meanings associated with near-death experiences, yet systems theory and complexity science could be used as a starting point to explore such matters, particularly as they offer a more holistic understanding of life's patterns and interconnections. Stephen Buhner[12] informs us that the word *complexity* is derived from the Greek *plecko*, meaning to *interweave*, *plait* or *twine*, and Michael Meade[13] speaks about wisdom and sense of knowing, which comes through the discovery of the intricate threads of our fate, including all of the entanglements that make up our destinies. For example, after his near-death experience, neurosurgeon Eben Alexander[14] speaks about the "golden thread" that connects us to the sacred. It underlines the importance of understanding the realities we are weaving, particularly in relation to our lived human potential. The life review reveals that what we are creating with our life energies has strong resonances with the idea of our karmic imprints and potential. The real fallacy in our technocratic world is our ignorance of the deeper layers of existence, particularly in connection to spirituality and mysticism as revealed through NDEs. People's near-death experiences could be used to inspire a collective wake-up call for how we use our precious life energies and the co-creation of a more loving world. Therefore, picking up the thread of how we live our lives is not so much determined by a grand theory, which seeks to explain the meaning of life; rather, the life review seems to be pointing towards a prescient understanding about how our *actions* determine *meaning in life*, especially when they are directed in the service of the greater good.[7]

We have a very graphic portrayal of the depths that can be revealed when we are forced into a life review whilst we are alive. The psychiatrist at Nuremberg, Douglas Kelley, who was responsible for the welfare of the Nazi hierarchy captured at the end of the Second World War, reported how the highest ranking SS officer in captivity, Ernst Kaltenbrunner, collapsed when the sheer brutality of his crimes were revealed. His past had caught up with him. During the Nazi reign of terror he had been part of the war machine that inflicted unimaginable horror on millions of people. Yet, the psychiatrist observed how this scar-faced and stern looking soldier, who gave the impression of having a tough persona, simply cracked under the weight of being held to account for his callous actions. He was frequently seen sobbing and weeping and he could not come to terms with facing the consequences of his actions as the Nuremberg Trial drew closer. Furthermore, when other top-ranking Nazis were shown films of the slaughter in their concentration camps, many of them covered their eyes, or could not watch the projections of their ideology in action. Many were heard crying in their cells the night after the films had been shown.[15] These are extreme events, but we have all acted in ways that we are not proud of, and which may have been harmful to others, other species and the planet. Confronting who we are, and what we have become through our actions, is not an easy thing to face. But it seems that there is no escape from such reflections, if not in this life, then certainly at the time of our physical deaths.

Death is the great awakener and if, as Jesus says in the Bible, a tree shall be known by its fruits (Matthew 7:16) how we navigate *meaning in life* is probably the most important factor when directing our life energies. For example, Jung viewed his heart attack in 1944 as a symbolic death, and he became resolute about following his deepest calling in life. Interestingly, he did not invest much energy in regret or guilt about past mistakes; he single-mindedly got on with cultivating a life, in which wholeness was his *raison d'être*. At the time of his heart attack, one of his students was also very ill and close to death, and one night the student dreamt that Jung appeared to her, saying that he was not going to die, and he advised her that she should also get back into her body.[16] I never take such accounts at face value, and I wondered why Jung would pop up in a student's dream and give her such explicit instructions to live, which happened at a time when he was also at the crossroads between life and death. Of course, each person who has a dream must decide on the meaning of that dream, but when a teacher and student are at a shared threshold, in this case, the edge between life and death, it adds an interesting dynamic to our discussion about cultivating meaning in life. Jung and his student were both committed to the process of wholeness and individuation, which promotes the realisation that there are still psycho-spiritual tasks to be fulfilled.

Each person has unique gifts, talents and skills that could bring more love and wholeness to the world, and the life review seems to be underlining the importance of living closer to our unfolding life potentials. A very touching story is told by David la Chapelle[17] who writes about working with a dying man who had cancer in the brain. He would often massage the man's neck to help him become more comfortable. One day la Chapelle said he slipped into a dream like state during the massage, where he visualised himself and the man standing in a swathe of light. From this vantage point they observed the murky energy of the material world in the distance, and the man turned to la Chapelle and spoke about the light that comes when love is manifest in our actions. It is a beautiful synchronicity, connected to a shared spiritual experience.

For millennia human beings have been pondering the questions of *who am I?* What is the meaning of life? What should I be doing? The important lesson from research into near-death experiences is that we do not have to wait until we die before we start finding out what our lives mean. We can begin opening up to a greater purpose for living by having a life review whilst we are alive, and asking ourselves if we are living in accord with our deepest potential. For example, are we really content with the way we are using our precious life energies? The great spiritual teacher Jiddu Krishnamurti[18] used to say, do not work in a job if you do not love it. Propositions like these can be both exciting and threatening, because they make us question what we are doing with our lives, or they inspire us to meet challenges (like my relationship conflict in Chapter Eight). We may need to face uncomfortable questions, such as: are we totally consumed with work just to make our way up the corporate ladder of *success*, or are we stuck in a dead-end existence due to fear, etc.? The path of transformation begins the moment we start questioning what is important to us in terms of our wholeness, where we are emboldened to engage more deeply with questions about life purpose and meaning. It makes no difference how complex our lives have become, or even the extent to which we have been conforming or adapting to the status quo, because there are always opportunities to reconnect with wholeness and redeem ourselves at a soul level. The point is we can always access the imaginal realm to inspire us with new possibilities for healing and change. It means that we start to work with the great myth that James Hillman[19] calls our *real biography*, e.g. discovering who we really are, as the following case vignette illustrates.

A Dervish who was in a whirl

I once worked with a middle-aged man who had not worked for two and a half years, since separating from his wife. We explored his life situation in the context of holistic coaching. As a father of three children, he was struggling with his daily responsibilities and was getting into a pattern of avoidance. In fact, he said on our first meeting: "I feel fearful and crushed by the weight of my inability to meet my responsibilities." He said that he needed to recalibrate his life direction and break out of the fear that was dominating his existence. We worked together for six sessions, and early on in our work my client could not shift out of the habit of looking back over his life. He repeatedly wanted to speak about old themes and patterns, which seemed to be keeping him stuck in a rut. Gradually, we managed to turn the focus to the present and direct his energies to what he wanted to do with his life, rather than resurrect the tired stories of self-defeat. We used a variety of methods to access his deeper interests, such as dream figures, movement and bodywork, as well as active visualisations.

In one of his inner work sessions my client was working imaginatively on connecting to a place on the Earth, a sacred spot that had deep spiritual resonance and power for him. It was a beautiful nature reserve, and as he spoke about how he connected to the *Spirit* of that place, he had a spontaneous reflection about the spiritual tradition to which he belonged. He said he was getting tired of the social constructs and spiritual hierarchy in his community, with members appearing to be competitive about each other's spiritual practices, which he was finding suffocating. Something had changed for him, because his early connections to this spiritual tradition were like he had: "reconnected to the beautiful innocence of childhood". Interestingly, the visualisation work (linked to the nature reserve) re-awoke an innate spiritual spark, a 'joic dc vivre', and a realisation that this divine connection needed to be represented more fully in his life.

Interestingly my client felt quite vulnerable when he reflected on the connection to a divine spark, the 'joie de vivre', as it seemed to herald a potent time for change. The coaching journey began by cultivating a more wholesome relationship to his masculine energy. He had grown up with a strong and deeply spiritual mother who was a great inspiration to him, and his family life had taught him the importance of empathy and emotional intelligence. His parents were both very nurturing, and whilst he had a very clear understanding of what the feminine meant, he felt a bit lost about the nature of his masculine identity and direction, although he spoke about his grandfather who was a great male role model for him. Our work together enabled him to explore the interface between manifesting a spiritual direction (with all his vulnerabilities), and a deeper exploration of his masculinity.

We started to explore what a renewed direction would mean for his life. We went deeply into his process, which posed questions for him about how he might gradually integrate some of the insights gained from our sessions into his daily life. Then, in week five, my client spoke about a powerful dream he had had. Until this point he had not been remembering any dreams. The dream was powerful and it took place in a church, where he was sitting behind a screen, which was located near the altar. His dad, brother, and a male priest (all men) were near the altar discussing who would be delivering a eulogy. Only then did it dawn on my client that he was witnessing the preparations for his own funeral. In the dream he was still alive, but he also knew that he had a terminal disease. Despite the intense drama and revelations that were unfolding in the dream sequence, he said to me that he was completely at peace. However, when the men at the altar stopped talking about the eulogy he started to experience a rising sense of panic, particularly when he realised that he was going to be killed before the funeral took place.

Still sitting behind the screen, he started thinking: "Are they absolutely sure there is not a cure, and should I not be allowed to die naturally?" In a state of panic he ran from behind the screen, pushing past all the people who were now starting to file into the church to attend his funeral service. Interestingly, the only face he remembered passing in the crowd was his dad's. At the back of the church he found the Vestry, and as he ran into the room he firmly slammed the door shut, and then he slumped against a table and blacked out. It is interesting that masculine figures are represented quite strongly in the dream. Also, the *altar* is where the sacrificial feast is prepared, and it must be remembered that the *Eucharist* is a deeply symbolic ritual of transformation, from death into new life, i.e. it is an *altering* experience. In addition, the drama in the dream is connected to strong *altered states of consciousness*, which included the prospect of death, panic, and blacking out.

After my client had recounted the dream, I asked him: "What is it that needs to die?" and he replied: "I need to die to fear, panic and running away." The eulogy was never read in the dream, so I suggested that he used the rest of the coaching session to write a eulogy for the symbolic death that was needed. This led to a powerful process of transformation and he was in floods of tears as he read aloud to me the eulogy he had just written (directly after recounting the dream). What followed next was quite unexpected: my client came to the last session in week six and told me that he had spontaneously started writing poetry, despite never having written a poem in his life. It was like something had ignited his vital energies, and he was alive to living. In the last session we pieced together all the key points from our work, and it transpired that writing poetry enabled my client to connect to a creative spark, where he could encounter his raw and honest self. He realised that his previous fear of responsibility was connected to being dishonest with himself.

These revelations put into perspective why the dream of death and dying was so potent in terms of his transformative potential, because it was connected to him being more authentic and true to who he is as a living, dynamic, creative and whole person.

Poetry gave my client new opportunities to experiment safely with his identity. It enabled him to explore new parameters for his emerging masculinity, which was not only connected to his vulnerability but also to his spirituality, and he felt renewed and strengthened. He started to pick up his responsibilities in daily life with regard to family and work. He changed old redundant patterns for living that were no longer needed. His everyday actions were also connected to how he lived his spiritual life: "I am no longer driven by the idea that I need to be holy in the eyes of others, I am just happy *doing* and *being* good in my life."

The vignette above reveals how dreams and creative approaches to living can inform our life reviews whilst we are alive, which can activate powerful processes of change and transformation. It reflects the courage needed to live authentically in daily life, and enter into a deeper journey of living. Stephen Levine[1] says that the way we face our death is a reflection of how we have lived our lives. When we are open to visions, dreams and synchronicities from the imaginal realm, we have an opportunity to align with the numinous and sacred dimension, which brings a wider context of the transpersonal into our lives. Our work is to weave together the threads of our life pattern, where the physical, social and spiritual strands of our lived potentials are the *warp and weft* that create new opportunities for transformation in our life and consciousness. In the modern world, so much of our life energy is channelled into work, economic pursuits and consumer-based activities. If we are not careful the subtle and sacramental realms are increasingly neglected. But it seems to be the case that if we cut ourselves off from the numinous, we live well below the threshold of our full potential, and consequently we are cut off from living with a greater sense of wholeness. Near-death experiences or powerful dreams about death (like the one above) are a salutary reminder of the importance of living our transpersonal potential.

Doing and the evolutionary edge

As we have seen, the life review is important because it gives us a very clear message that what we do in this life matters, and if the point of life is to wake up and be more loving and compassionate, then it means we have an opportunity to better understand the impact of our ways of *doing* and *being*. If the life review in the near-death experience can lead to a profound spiritual awakening, then *why wait until we are at death's door* to understand the lessons we need to learn in life? Imagine if a critical mass of people started doing life reviews with the emphasis on co-creating an improved future through changing hearts, minds and behaviours. It would embolden us to trust that our activities of daily living, such as self-care, work and leisure can revolutionise our lives, especially when we connect *doing at depth* to transformative practices, such as karma yoga, which advocates using everyday activities as a path of service. Transformative living is based on the idea that our inner work complements our outer work, which means that *technologies of transformation* (mindfulness, yoga, and dream work etc.) are central to the expression of our lived potential. Can we imagine a world where our social institutions invest in wholeness and help cultivate successive generations to be planetary citizens? For example, the act of doing dream and shadow work, or mindfulness meditation, yoga, rituals and prayer bring forth a new vibration for living, based on the cultivation of love and compassion that serves the greater good?

Technologies of transformation are an important accompaniment to our high technologies and tool use. It should remind us that we need to remain diligent in a world of *high-tech* innovations, where we see them for what they are, simply tools to help us live. We would do well to reacquaint ourselves with early Greek philosophy, which emphasised metaphysics of technology,[20] where technical nous was not separate from a natural order. Today, we have the misguided idea that technology is a uniquely human endeavour. It is becoming increasingly clear to me that investing in technologies of transformation would bring a counterbalance to the world of unrestrained high-tech developments, which are driving the modern world at breakneck speed. We need to temper the idea that all technology is good, which means reflecting on and questioning what we are doing in terms of our occupational potentials and evolutionary trajectories as a species. We are now entering a new technological era of artificial intelligence, and a critical question is: will our quest, to become *masters of high technology*, *imprison* or *emancipate* us? We cannot fully appraise this question without considering our relationship to the *imaginal realm*, which paradoxically requires the integration of technologies of transformation. Remaining oblivious of the metaphysics of technology will have serious consequences for what we do next as a species.

Doing is pivotal in terms of human evolutionary adaptation and our collective heritage is packed with examples of how we have used tools and technologies to adapt and transform our lives, such as the early hunter-gatherers, who made fine axe heads from large lumps of flint. It takes imagination to craft (*techne*) a lump of flint into a decorated tool.[21] Then, around 10,000 years ago our ancestors made a great innovative leap when we shifted to agricultural based living, where our species (once again) made a major adaptation and developed tools and technologies. The more recent Industrial Revolution about 200 years ago led to a monumental shift in how we lived, for example, when mechanisation led to more people working in factories and being organised into shifts.[7] Today, we are living in a high-tech world that is driven by information technologies, where new technological innovations are rapidly propelling us into uncharted territories. This is nothing new, as technological advances have always shifted the boundaries between *what we do* and *how we live*. However, the scale, rate and pace of technological shifts at this time are fraught with complexities and we will have to remain vigilant about the impact these innovations have on our hearts, minds and behaviours. I remember watching science programmes in the early 1970s, when technological progress was always projected as a future of increased leisure, with labour saving devices creating the fantasy that people would have more free time. Forty-five years on, it turns out that life has become more busy and relentless with information technologies dominating our lives for better or worse.

Homo diabolus

Like all future projections, we may fantasise and enjoy speculating about the Utopian technological dream that will somehow set us free, but the reality always seems to be less than ideal. While technologies understandably bring great benefits, they also create *more* work. For example, communication devices have transformed information exchange, but an office worker who is bombarded by emails every day is under constant pressure, compounded by the desire to check personal emails and social media accounts. The dream of having more time has evaporated into a culture where nobody can switch off, which is fast becoming the curse of modern living. It is recognised that modern lifestyles are so pressurised that millions of working days are lost to stress, and it is a trend that has been exacerbated by information technologies.[22] Jung[23] spoke about the paradox of material scientists and philosophers who triumphantly report that superstitions have no place in the modern world, but they fail to notice the demons that are being created in our machine technologies. He liked to quote the ancient saying, that haste is the work of the Devil: *omni festinatio ex parte diablo est*.

It remains to be seen, what this relentless race for techno-innovation and 'improvement' means for the future. We have glimpses of the changes that are on the horizon. A 300-page report by the American Bank, Merrill Lynch, in 2015 outlined the potential impact of robotic technologies, which warns of a steep rise in job losses. One person was quoted in the article, predicting that the rise in artificial intelligence would allow people to have more time to play.[24] However, as we have seen from past projections about the future, this sort of rhetoric is simply misplaced wishful thinking. The evidence seems to point to the opposite trend: more stress.[22] My concern is that human beings will become more tightly bound to a technocracy that is already spiritually bankrupt. This is the price we pay when we neglect our human potential and fail to wake up to the materialist and technological onslaught that is draining the life from our souls. A fascinating article appeared in *The Guardian* newspaper in December 2016 written by Mark Boyle, who made the decision to renounce the use of complex technology in his home (washing machine, phone, laptop, fridge, TV, music and gas etc.). He points out that our modern cultures fuel technological developments in a devilish pact, which are having a destructive impact on humans and nature, and so he decided he wanted his soul back.[25] The underlying myth in Boyle's story is the tussle between 'devilish' technologies and the reclamation of his human soul. For this to be a both/and, rather than either/or reality will require much soul searching by all of us.

Mythic language helps us to articulate problems because the metaphors used are often loaded with cultural power. For example, when human behaviours are described as our *worst* or *best angels*[26] they convey a mythic reality, which can be used by people who do not necessarily believe in angels. Yet, these ideas have resonance for one reason: they describe a mythic world that is linked to lived actualities. We will be increasingly confronted with such powerful mythic representations the more our high-tech world begins to impact us, particularly as we wrestle with ideas about what it means to be human. If we doubt the pernicious invasion of modern technologies in human life, we already have evidence of companies who track every movement of their employees through electronic devices used in their place of work. It is the beginning of a human-robot interface that is set to escalate.[27] I had a recent experience of such corporate surveillance (as a consumer), which was quite amusing. I sometimes use an online bookseller to purchase books, and one day I was sent an email with a recommendation for a book, and I was told the selection was based on my browsing history. They were absolutely correct; I was very interested in the book they recommended, not least for the reason that I had actually written it!

In the not too distant future there will be highly sophisticated algorithms used to triangulate information about all of us, where there will be no ambiguity, like suggesting an author purchases their own book. This is a good moment to pause and reflect. Our surveillance technologies are undoubtedly very sophisticated, but compared to the holographic reverberations we encounter in near-death experiences, they are paltry. In fact, our modern obsession with surveillance (Big Brother) could be a perfect reminder for us – about what to expect when we die – where *everything* we have *done*, are currently *doing*, or intend *doing* is recorded (as revealed in the life review). Then, the full consequences of our actions in life are revealed to us. High-tech surveillance might remind us to stop and think about what we are doing with our lives, especially the consequences for how we are using modern technologies. We need to reflect deeply on these issues because cyber space is beginning to enter our lives powerfully, for better or worse. We only need to consider the recent examples of information technology used by the Brexit (leave) campaign in the UK, and Donald Trump's election campaign in the US to be concerned. It emerged that an analytics company used algorithms to trawl through prospective voters' online data, gauging their lifestyles and emotional reactions etc.[28] Such unfettered access to our collective profiles, which detail our psychological and social interests, our 'likes' and 'dislikes', is *de facto* a 'thumbs up' for a new era of technological propaganda and manipulation. The mindless drift into a new high-tech era is full of danger, particularly if we lose our soulful connection to life.

Homo roboticus

The language that philosophers and scientists use today to refer to certain aspects of human biological functioning suggests we are gradually adopting a machine metaphor for understanding who we are. For example, Nicholas Carr[29] points out that in the 20th century our brains' neural activities were repeatedly referred to as *hardwired* in much the same way that computer chip circuitry is described. Such analogies corrupt our understanding of who we are as sentient beings. Language has power, and the narratives of science and technology are among the most powerful in the 21st century. We need to question the metaphor that suggests our brains are simply hardwired machines, because we are far more magnificent and fluid than that. Think about the placebo response, which was discussed in Chapter Two. Using a less mysterious example to illustrate the point, Nicholas Carr[29] discusses the role and functions of *neuroplasticity*, which reveals how the brain is a fluid and dynamic system that is far more impressive than a machine. He cites the work of Pascual-Leone who taught piano to two groups. One group actually practised playing the piano for two hours a day over a five-day period, whereas the other group simply imagined doing piano practice over the same period. The same changes were recorded in the brains of participants from both groups, which shows the incredible power and influence of the imagination. It is often said in the world of neuroscience that: *neurons that fire together, wire together*. However, if we consider the role of the imagination in our species' flourishing, we could say that: *images that grow together flow together*. It underscores the importance of the imagination to human functioning.

We urgently need to question the use of language that ties us into myths of the machine. My concern is that this issue is going to become more pronounced as technocratic advances rapidly unfold in the 21st century. Human beings are now entering a world of technology that I believe we are ill prepared to face. The combination of artificial intelligence and robotics are about to propel us into a whole new era of technological transformation.[30] One of the hallmarks of our current technological progression is that products, like smart phones, are designed with built-in obsolescence. But are we prepared to accept that many of our human skills may soon become obsolete in the workplace? For example, Katie Allen[31] reported in *The Guardian* newspaper that the chief economist for the Bank of England has warned that 15 million jobs in the UK are potentially threatened by future robotic technologies. Others rightly argue robots or artificial intelligence cannot do workplace skills involving negotiation, creativity and empathy, yet.[30] Who can say how robot technologies will 'evolve', or how humanity will 'devolve' with these new innovations? However, we desperately need to take stock of the ways our current uses of information technology are about to impact us.

Information technology and the *World Wide Web* have spawned a global culture that is increasingly networked, and it has rightly been suggested that we need checks and balances to ensure that these technologies do not dominate our lives.[32] Nicholas Carr[29] says that the 'Net' has spawned a swathe of innovations that are probably ranked amongst the most highly powerful technologies ever produced, which is altering the mind of our species. These are strong words, but we need to heed them. The warning chimes with a similar concern made by neuroscientist Susan Greenfield[33] who also commented on the monumental changes that are afoot, and how these powerful technologies will be impacting humanity. She speaks about the potential vulnerabilities of the *self*, and the boundaries between our embodied human-world (*in here*) when it blurs with the cyber-world (*out there*). She rightly points out that our self-concept is largely cultivated within social contexts and she cautions that the current information revolution is set to have a far greater impact on our lives than the Industrial Revolution. This statement should make us sit up and take notice, for we are in the midst of a major technological revolution, one that will undoubtedly confront us with major dilemmas.

Humanity's over-reliance on computational systems means that artificial intelligence increasingly plays a part in how we acquire knowledge, and as a consequence human intelligence may well become more atrophied.[29] The problem with the current rise of technologies such as smart phones is that they are subsumed into the economic machinations of the technocracy, where we as *consumers* are propelled into a world of endless upgrades that end up *consuming* us, and worryingly, appear to make us less smart. Nicholas Carr[29] draws on various studies which point to trends that show how online activity leads to shallow reading, rushed thinking, and patchy learning. These are major issues that are about to impact all of our lives. For example, Yuval Harari's book, *Homo Deus*, suggests that the bio-tech revolution will lead to a new world order of machine intelligence, where human intelligence will be out-paced, and less importance will be placed on human consciousness.[34] At this moment in time nobody really knows the impact of the next technological revolution, but one thing is absolutely clear, the technocracy has never valued or invested in the flourishing of human potential and consciousness. Think about it: people like Jung and disciplines like transpersonal psychology have always been on the edge of mainstream consensus reality, and we lose sight of this point at our peril. It is my view that Jungian and transpersonal approaches to consciousness could well save humanity from the mindless capitulation of our most cherished asset, the soul. The sharp drift into the world of robotics is simply the next increment in our wholesale abandonment of a soulful and intelligent connection to the imaginal realm.

Cyborgs and the soul

At the time of writing this book, articles started appearing in the quality press following the story of a computer program that beat a human grand master at the fiendishly complex game called Go. The computer program won four games to the human's one. The company that built the computer program is called *Deep Mind* and its game-winning success is based on a process of learning by trial and error, called *deep reinforcement*.[35] The program has developed the capacity to learn through the use of algorithms and artificially created networks that mimic the workings of human neurons in the brain. Then in February 2017 an artificial intelligence machine named *Liberatus* beat four of the best poker players in the world. Worryingly, the machine had learnt how to simulate a 'bluff', thereby confounding its human competitors.[36] These are examples of the type of rapid technological advances that are revolutionising life today, which will eventually 'evolve' to do tasks such as diagnosing illnesses and managing power grids.[37] The rapid rise of such technologies in the modern world is resulting in humans having to keep up. But, as a species how much thought are we giving to such technological development, especially where the operating spaces between the human and machine worlds are already becoming more integrated? How will humanity adapt to robotics and AI? This is a very serious question.

The levels of automation and electronic interconnectivity are growing exponentially. However, the complexities of this new reality mean it is very difficult to show how such systems arrive at decisions, especially those that use artificial intelligence and deep learning. This is especially worrying when we learn that the algorithms used in these systems are prone to creating errors.[38] Tech companies are developing and using such systems today, which raise serious questions about how this unpredictability will be managed. For example, a recent article reported on developments between different AI systems, and how they would interact in a game that involved gathering a supply of apples. When there were plenty of apples the AI systems cooperated, but when the amount of apples reduced there was more conflict.[39] Our insatiable desire to adapt and accommodate the machine world suggests we need to give more thought to addressing such coding problems at the design stage.[40] Moreover, it has to be asked, who is making the decisions about the way such technologies are being embedded in modern societies? And, an even more pressing question has to be: who is authoring the 'moral code' in the world of AI?[41] Make no mistake about it, the next technological revolution, which is already underway, will have far-reaching implications for what it means to be a human being, including the way we live and work.

Artificial intelligence already has the capability to outstrip the human mind in terms of data storage and computational speed, and yet we have only scratched the surface in terms of the way humans and machines are set to interact. As I have stated previously, I am not against science and technology, but I am saying that we are unprepared for the technologies that are about to be unleashed. Anthropologist and futurologist Genevieve Bell works at Intel, and she makes an interesting point, that there are different cultural reactions to robots. For example, Bell points to Japan where there is a more welcoming and imaginative attitude to robots. She uses the example of Masahiro Mori's book, *Buddha in the Robot*, and how he thought robot technology could become our best "angel". She leaves us in no doubt that robots are simply technologies that reflect the capabilities that we humans have given them when they were created.[42] The benign attitude towards robots in Japan is the result of a post Second World War emphasis on technologies of pacifism[43] as well as the influence of Shinto religion, where spirits (*tamashii*) inhabit the natural world (of rocks and trees, etc.), and this pantheistic perspective also includes the world of computers and robots.[44] However, it is my belief that robotics will lead to a clash of cultures, which will bring to the surface many of the problems discussed in this book, such as science-soul and good-evil, etc. Therefore, the subject of such high-tech advances is intimately connected to the discussion about human beings' connection to a spiritual reality and the imaginal realm (as we shall see below).

Science is an internationally recognised approach for acquiring knowledge, and its practitioners are part of an international culture, guided by methodologies that are recognised and replicable worldwide. However, I recently watched a documentary[45] that showed a group of scientists involved in the field of artificial intelligence and robotics. One of the scientists, Professor Hiroshi Ishiguro, had built a life size replica robot of himself and he spoke about how he would like to have a conversation with this android about the nature of the soul. First, we must remember that as far as traditional science is concerned the soul does not exist. But Ishiguro seems more allied to a cultural-pantheistic view of consciousness that resonates with contemporary neuroscience views, which hypothesises that *consciousness is everywhere* (see Chapter One). Far from being an idle curiosity, the research by Ishiguro may well tap into a complex issue about the nature of consciousness and the soul, which will confront humanity very soon.

Today, technology is *transnational* and research in countries, such as Japan (one of the leading countries in robotics), will undoubtedly filter out into the wider world. It is possible that we will be confronted with questions about whether robots are soul-centred or not. If it turns out that the answer is 'yes', then it raises further questions about pantheistic understandings of consciousness, and what a robotic soul is, as distinct from or similar to a human soul. The question may seem irrelevant to some, but if we contextualise the issue further, we find that the field of robotics is slowly taking us a step closer to *transhumanism*, and we need to be very clear about what is at stake. Transhumanism is an ideology that is based on science and technology, which seeks to *enhance* human biology in terms of physical and psychological capabilities. In this way, the human-robot fusion of transhumanism also brings us a step closer to the hubris of us becoming the Creators of life (see Chapter One). For example, Professor Hiroshi Ishiguro believes the goal of humanity is to become robots. But, we need to ask ourselves, why should a clever technician – whose professional interest is making robots – be the spokesperson for humanity about its collective destiny, goal, or purpose? A cultural difference aside, the BBC programme[45] highlighted an important issue for me, revealing that humanity has no coherent understanding of the collective meaning linked to our shared odyssey into the world of robotics. The drift into transhumanism will concern anyone with the capacity for reflection about the deeper questions concerning the soul and what it is to be human.

Since Japan appears to be positively embracing robotics, it is only right that we examine the shadow side of its culture. Professor Hiroshi Ishiguro's desire to talk with a robot about the nature of the soul is troubling when we learn that Japan has a suicide rate 60% higher than the worldwide average.[46] In 2012, the number of people who committed suicide was a staggering 29,442. Coupled to this, Japanese youth are losing interest in forming intimate and sexual relationships with each other, a phenomenon which the Japanese media refer to as *sekkusu shin ai shokogun*, or 'celibacy syndrome'.[47] It has also been noted that some people are starting to form intimate relationships with robots. I do not wish to single out Japan as the only country that has such social problems; I am simply pointing out that in a country that has embraced robotic technologies there are clear indications that all is not well beneath the surface. If the fantasy of transhumanism is investing in the idea of enhancing human biological capabilities, will it have the ability to tackle suicidal impulses, which paradoxically may well be the result of a culture that is already one of the most mechanised on the planet? However, these important questions should not overlook the important benefits that robot technologies have already brought to people who have been paralysed, and are helping them walk again.[48]

Technological innovations will present us with breakthroughs that are uplifting and brilliant, alongside ideas that are challenging, such as the scientist who is desperate to upload the contents of his brain (memories and experiences) into a computer,[45] which he describes as a quest for *immortality*. The myth of Narcissus is not out of place here. But, if we think this is the work of one zealous individual, we learn that there are serious sums of money underpinning research in this area, and it is believed that uploading the contents of our brains into computers is only a few years away from becoming a reality.[49] Transhumanists are seeking to merge human consciousness with machines, and we need to make sure that we do not exacerbate our existing state of *collective dissociation* by moving towards a cyborg reality unthinkingly. In contrast, transpersonalists (inspired by pioneers such as Jung, Maslow and Grof etc.) are working to expand human consciousness by means of technologies of transformation, where the focus is concerned with *soulful interconnection*. The question is, which realities will we be drawn to, and why? And, if we are interested in furthering high-tech innovations, how will we integrate technologies of transformation, so that we do not further erode the life of the soul?

Transhuman or transpersonal?

Where is the accountability for the high-tech knowledge that is being created in the name of humanity? It is abundantly clear that each adaptation – between the human and machine worlds – is gradually taking us further and further away from the roots of what it means to be human (the soul). It calls for a consensus about the *meaning* of transhumanism. It raises serious questions about the evolutionary interface between the human soul and the rise of robotic technologies. For example, a US company is now making machines with the intention of *obviating* human employees in the food industry, and another post-futurist commentator is suggesting that by 2025 humanity will face difficult questions about work and roles for many people in a robotic-based economy and society.[50] Artificial intelligence is one of the new technologies that will revolutionise human life. However, whilst it has been suggested that technological intelligence appears to be outstripping biological intelligence,[51] the comparison is only valid at a computational level, that is, in terms of comparisons with memory, technical problem solving and speed of information processing etc. Let us not lose sight of the fact that human intelligence is much more than computational; it is also emotional, musical, ecological, spiritual, occupational and kinaesthetic etc.[7] Human intelligence also connects to the imaginal realm, which nourishes the soul and enables our imaginations to flourish.

Professor of Statistical Science at Oxford University Peter Donnelly[52] is chair of the Royal Society working group on machine learning (artificial intelligence), and he is calling for a debate on the subject. He points out that our *attitudes* towards machine learning will determine whether these technologies become our friends or foes. It is a reasonable question, but it never ceases to surprise me that the discussions and debates about advanced technologies, such as artificial intelligence and robotics, do not seem to consider what might be lost in terms of our human development. For example, do these debates ever consider our collective transpersonal potential and what this could mean for our species' ongoing evolutionary trajectory, via technologies of transformation? It is a serious issue, because every advance in artificial intelligence and robot technologies brings the operational spaces between human and machine worlds closer together. I argue strongly that a transhumanist 'merger' undermines our transpersonal potential and also our connection to the soul. It was philosopher Gilbert Ryle who spoke about '*the ghost in the machine*' as a metaphor for discussing the soul-human interface. Of course, humans are not machines, but as we drift deeper into a world of robotics, our lives will become more and more *part of the machine*. In such a world of soulless technology, will the 'ghost' *haunt* us, or will our relationship to it be eroded and eventually lost from our vocabularies (and experiences) altogether?

We need a collective approach to living that emphasises a greater level of techno-soul stewardship. Our high-tech advances need to be moderated and complemented by *technologies of transformation*, which connect us to the soul, via dreams, vision quests, walking labyrinths, shadow work, and mindfulness etc. The technological challenges before us are twofold: first, we need to consider the broader implications of high-tech innovations and how they serve humanity and the planet; second, we need a concerted effort in all of our social institutions to evolve our human potential through technologies of transformation. It is not an either/or proposition, but rather a both/and opportunity. It will allow us to co-create an evolutionary path that blends high-tech developments alongside our sacred heritage, where we can support the next stage of our unfolding human potential without compromising our wholeness. To move beyond a one-sided technocracy, we will have to craft (*techne*) a way of life that is sacramental and which keeps us intimately connected to the biotic community of which we are a part. How successful we are will depend on our responses to the deep questions about our technological heritage and its future place in our lives. The question of the soul at this point in our evolutionary journey is not a peripheral issue; it is being highlighted by transhumanism, which puts it at the centre of who we are, and who we are becoming as a species. Matthew Fox[53] is absolutely correct in my view, when he asserts that we need to make decisions and take actions that weave wholeness into the tapestry of the cosmos, of which we are an integral part. We should not underestimate the importance of our full human potential, and how it is given evolutionary expression when it connects to the light in our souls.[17] This is part of our transpersonal heritage.

One thing seems clear: the more we align our consciousness with a technocratic evolution, the more we are in danger of losing our connection to a depth of living, which will make it harder for each successive generation to reclaim the deeper levels of consciousness where our soul resides. In his *Red Book*, Jung[54] wrote about modern humans' habit of living superficially, and how such a surface approach to everyday life results in people becoming shadows, rather than whole. We have been destroying the planet to such an extent that we are only now waking up to the prospect that we may have left it too late. An article in *The Guardian* newspaper[55] titled: "What have we done?" reflects the sort of reactions that are set to become more widespread, especially as we wake up to the scale of our destructive behaviours towards the environment, ecology and climate. The article discusses the likely rise in syndromes of human distress, which corresponds to the ongoing stress being placed upon ecosystems. This is an issue I have discussed elsewhere.[7]

In the absence of any other meaningful way of mobilising hope, we might be seduced by the idea that high-tech companies are our salvation. However, big tech giants of Silicon Valley (for example) thrive on *disrupting* the status quo[56] in order to make way for a new world. But what is the guiding vision for these disrupters? Tech journalist Jamie Bartlett has investigated the *Secrets of Silicon Valley* in a BBC documentary and found that it was an analytics company (using sophisticated algorithms) that was the beating heart of Donald Trump's successful presidential campaign.[57] It transpires that they paid social media companies millions of dollars to access their influential platforms of human connectivity. We should never forget that high-tech companies and their *disruptive* social agendas are funded by venture capital, which means these businesses are also wedded to the economic status quo. It is a salutary reminder for us to question what *disruption* actually means, before all manner of unexpected genies are 'let out of the bottle'. There is no doubt about it; we have to *do* something radical to meet the challenges that are already upon us. Susan Greenfield[33] poses questions for humanity to consider, such as: what sorts of issues are important in our lives? What is common to us as a species? And, what it is about life (as we know it) that is most important to preserve?

One of the greatest contributions a human being can make in the world at this time of global crisis is to realise the impact of our actions in this life and how they can connect us to the deepest part of our being, which we feel in our hearts and souls.[19] It helps us to appreciate how our actions are rippling and reverberating in the lives of others. Jean Giono[58] gives us a beautiful reminder of the gentle and pervasive power of human action. In his very moving book *The Man Who Planted Trees*, there is a brief section about the exceptional qualities of people who are motivated by kindness and generosity, which is cultivated through unselfish activities over many years. In effect, such people leave a legacy in the world without ever seeking reward for their labours of love. It speaks volumes about the often-repeated mantra that actions speak louder than words. It is the essence of deep compassion that is interwoven in our actions, which can be cultivated through technologies of transformation. The Transformocene is dependent on humanity making a connection to the world of the soul, which underlines the importance of understanding the contrasting worldviews of transhumanism and transpersonalism.

Exercise: Life review

- Think about the trajectory of your life to date. Bring to mind the positive actions that you have done in your life.
  - What is your reaction to the consequences of your actions?

- Now, bring to mind the sorts of actions that seem to have had little or no consequences in the world, for example engaging in seemingly mundane activities, e.g. washing up or commuting to work etc.
  - Are you content with using your life energies as if these activities were a mere chore?

- Finally, bring to mind the negative actions you have done in your life.
  - What is your reaction to the consequences of your actions?

- On balance, how would you sum up the quality of your existence, based on what you have done with your life to date?

- What changes or adjustments to your ways of knowing, being, and doing will you make as a result of this mini life review? For example, in relation to:
  - Identity
  - Attitudes
  - Behaviours
  - Social networks
  - Political alliances
  - Spiritual practices
  - Ecological awareness

- How do the above changes or adjustments connect to the daimon exercise (in the previous chapter), in terms of bringing forth your true character?

- What life lessons are you inspired to learn before you die?

The inner work of 'active imagination' is complemented by the outer work of 'imaginative action'. These deep connections to the imaginal realm are like living alchemy, where both divine and mundane tasks can 'ignite' the sacramental 'flow' of individuation.

CHAPTER TEN

Active Imagination and Imaginative Action

Overview

In this chapter I discuss *active imagination*, as conceived by Jung, which resonates with a deep occupation-focused approach that I conceptualise as *imaginative action*. I suggest that the dynamic interaction between these different uses of our imaginative capacities brings us into direct relationship with the imaginal realm. It is here that we can make a soulful connection to life, which enables us to engage and express our full human potential. I discuss how doing inner and outer work connects us to archetypal occupations, bringing forth greater depth in our ways of living and transformative actions. Our connection to the imaginal realm helps us discover our innate indigenous wisdom and the 'songlines' that are vibrating and resonating throughout life. I point out that this kind of soul work is where we find our own 'song', aligning us with the *anima mundi*, the soul of the world. It is through such harmonious connections that the Transformocene revives our *joie de vivre* and a renewed resonance for living. Our *active imaginations* and *imaginative actions* not only connect us to the imaginal realm; they lead to vibrational and emancipatory vocations in all that we do. Our inner and outer work is where the emancipatory edge of the Transformocene is engaged and enacted.

The unselfish spirit at work

Our everyday ways of doing carry immeasurable potential and opportunities, inspiring transformational shifts that can help tackle the global crisis before us. David Spangler[1] believes our behaviours and actions are like *incarnations*, where we manifest particular qualities in our ways of living. Making the most of all that we do, as a continuous process of incarnation, means that we need to be alert to what we are creating in life. It requires a deeper quality of awareness to understand that what we are crafting today becomes a legacy for tomorrow's generation, and it underlines the idea that what we do in our lives is not only for ourselves.[2] The poem by D.H. Lawrence, about the '*things*' we humans make, touches on the theme of how our actions can be infused with the numinous, which he links to the awakened hands of a creator, meaning someone who is able to craft an object that is aglow with living warmth.[3] The creative links between the imagination and our transformative actions are also expressions of the *spiritual power of doing*. It means that what we do in the world is part of our evolutionary emergence.

For David Spangler[1] words such as *emergence*, *renewal* and *creativity* are verbs, meaning they connect to a quality of being alive and active. He points out that everyday life is full of transformative potential, with opportunities to nourish our connection to the imaginal and the sacred, through doing. Buckminster Fuller[4] understood the power of such actions when he reflected upon his identity, saying that he knew he was not a category, or a thing (noun), but that he seemed to be a *verb*, and it was this realisation that alerted him to an evolutionary process of unfolding, where all life exists as part of an integral whole. Fuller understood that life's unfolding also included a connection to the sacred, and that 'God' (or the Great Spirit) is also a *verb*.[5] Fuller's ideas resonate with the accounts from near-death experiences, when the impact of an individual's actions are reflected back in the life review, revealing that whatever we do is interwoven in the lives of others, for better or worse. Therefore, a 21st century trajectory of transformation is to realise that we live in a sacred cosmos, one that is dynamic and constantly reverberating.

Recognition of this deeper connection to life through doing also brings us into relationship with the archetypes that are acting through us, where our actions connect to our deepest nature at a soul level. Jung has been an invaluable guide in helping us to understand the importance of soulwork in modern times, especially through the creation of meaningful relationships with the unconscious, the archetypes, collective myths and fairy tales, where our connection to shared symbols, dream figures, or life experiences is revealed. For example, the archetypes that have evolved alongside our collective actions and ways of doing, I call *archetypal occupations* (doing with depth). Such experiences in our everyday actions bring a deep connection to life, which manifests as a sense of flow (and sometimes timelessness) in our daily activities, aligning us holistically in body, mind and soul. This is how our ways of doing can bring forth our spiritual potential. It means whenever we engage in activities with depth, it can feel like we are participating in a sacrament or even a prayer. For this reason, it is important that we take time to find our gifts, talents, skills, creativity and passions and *do what we love* in our everyday lives, which then deepens our connection to living.

When the archetypes are activated through our ways of doing, our actions are literally awe-inspiring, and this is especially true when we are connected to a spirit of compassion, altruism, love, equanimity and peace etc. It means that what we *do* in our homes, our places of work and our communities can have real significance for how we engage our collective potential. Perhaps a modern spiritual mantra that sums up our transformative potential to act could be:

we do, therefore we evolve – soulfully and spiritually.[6] In this time of global crisis we are all being called to dig deep and work together for the greater good, and to co-create an improved future for all. The dynamic potential within our daily activities connects us to our deepest *occupational myth*, which can be expressed through a process of *occupational intelligence*. In this way, our co-creative actions are pivotal for actualising our occupational and transpersonal potential (doing and being), as a process of individuation (wholeness).[6] Arny Mindell[7] is correct in my opinion, when he says that unless we are connected to something greater and more infinite, our ways of 'doing' simply deplete us. Similarly, Jung's occupational engagement reveals how his process of individuation was inclusive of a certain quality of action that was connected deeply to his ways of living.

Jung's Red Book and tower

Jung's[8] *Red Book*, which he crafted in the years 1914-30, provides a deep insight into his process of individuation, which he said was a most difficult task. The *Red Book* bears testimony to the intense preoccupations that accompanied his inner work, and how his journey into the imaginal realm led to a constant stream of fantasies from the unconscious that not only captivated him, but held him captive.[9] Through the process of doing active imagination and recording his inner work, Jung[8] began to realise that the *Red Book* – important as it was to him – could only take him so far, and that the reflective process that he was capturing on paper and in words was not real enough for him. Jung had a hunch that something else was required to take the process of individuation deeper and further, which would enable a fuller expression of the archetypal material he was encountering. He had arrived at a point where he needed to go beyond active imagination, which turned into what I call a deeper expression of his *occupational myth*, where doing became a core part of his unfolding path of individuation.[6]

Jung the explorer of the imaginal realm turned his attention to creative action, which enabled his *inner work* to be more aligned to his *outer work*, thereby bringing forth a sense of *occupational congruence* in his process of individuation. Daily occupations need to be seen for the depth that they bring to our processes of spiritual awakening, which runs counter to the oft-repeated saying: *we are not human doings, we are human beings.* The modern temperament that trivialises doing represents a very superficial understanding of human action, and it underestimates the significance of how our daily occupations bring depth of meaning and purpose to our ways of living.[6] We are co-creators in a dynamic and unfolding universe that reverberates through motions, momentums and actions. In this way, we find a deeper connection to *doing* in Jung's question, when he asks: *what do we do with the unconscious?*[9] It means that as we *wake up* to questions about *who we are*, we naturally encounter opportunities that deepen our ways of living, as noted by Ram Dass[10] who says that when consciousness is evolved, it reflects greater coherences between our ways of *doing* and *being*.[6]

Jung's process of 'doing' took a significant turn when he purchased some land on the upper shores of Lake Zurich at a place called Bollingen, where he built a tower. Jung eventually came to realise that at Bollingen his self-expression and Self-realisation were intimately connected, and he could become *what he was*, *what he is*, and *what he will be*.[9] The tower was not built in an ego-driven way; in fact, we know from Jung[9] that its construction gradually emerged through a process of *dreaming* and *doing with depth*. The design of the tower had a reciprocal relationship to Jung's individuation process, in that he felt as though the emerging stone tower was symbolic of a rebirth.[9] The question is: *what was being born anew* in Jung? He described the way his work with the *living unconscious* informed the dreamlike construction of the tower, which reveals to us the resonances and reverberations between his inner work and his outer work. He trusted that the unconscious is always *doing something* to help us grow on our journey of wholeness. In this way, Jung[11] actually lived out a deep realisation, which emphasised that the psyche is alive within us, and we each need to discover our personal paths of revelation, or what he called the *undiscovered way*. When Jung completed the tower he had a revelation, noticing that all of the various parts of the building belonged together, which not only represented a symbol of psychic wholeness, it is where he discovered a deep connection to living.[6] The tower was so important to his growth and individuation that he spoke about how his life's work would not have emerged without this deep connection to the land.[9] At Bollingen Jung expressed himself simply and symbolically in all of his actions, taking great care in the way he lived.[12] His occupational focus at the tower was based on living naturally, and he enjoyed cooking simple meals, chopping wood, carrying out repairs, and making carvings in stone, etc.[13,14]

When we consider what *doing* means to the journey of individuation, we can see that for Jung the tower was a form of sacred expression: he said that working with stone was like making a "confession".[9] This statement is like a Koan, for what does it mean to make a *confession in stone*? Koans are questions or riddles that do not make sense in conventional terms (and cannot be answered logically). In this way, Zen masters help students shift out of their logical mind to awaken, so they break through the binds of everyday reality.[15] The Koan is a brilliant representation of how the irrational is used imaginatively in action. Returning to Jung's confession in stone, we know that he was inspired by alchemy, and his construction work using *Earthly stone* at Bollingen was also a form of spiritual expression. Interestingly, the alchemical process of working with stone is connected to a release of the divine spirit.[16] It is curious that one of Jung's last known dreams before he died was of a large stone circle, which to him was a symbol of wholeness. It is at Bollingen that we can see the creative interface between Jung's uses of *active imagination*, where he *dreams the dream forward*, and connects this to an occupation-focused approach, which I have conceptualised as *imaginative action*. This is where the wisdom from the dream is engaged, enacted and integrated in everyday life. It underlines the important relationship between images arising in our imaginations[17] and our imaginative capacity to use these as part of our occupational and transpersonal journey into wholeness, or individuation.

For Jung, working with stone was both symbolically and occupationally connected to his process of individuation at an archetypal level. The critical point is that Jung recognised how archetypes enable adaptation, because they function as a system that is ready for action, as well as being connected to emotions and images.[18] I have referred to Jung's depth of engagement at Bollingen as a good example of an *archetypal occupation*,[14] which sums up how the power of *doing with depth* contributes to our spiritual growth and expression. Engagement of our archetypal occupations requires two key elements; first is the use of *active imagination* (inner work), where our processes of individuation are directed towards increased awareness and Self-realisation. Second is the need to engage *imaginative action* (outer work), where we express our processes of individuation in the world. I would like to share a part of my own synchronistic experience that happened at Jung's Bollingen tower during a pilgrimage I made to Switzerland in honour of Jung, one of my professional ancestors.

_____ **Boundaries and Bollingen** _____

Soon after retiring from my life as a university lecturer and academic, I decided to visit the Jung Institute, as well the graves of Jung, and his close colleagues Marie Louise Von Franz and Barbara Hannah in Zurich. It is hard to put into words what such a pilgrimage means, especially when visiting the places where these highly innovative and pioneering people crafted their relationship with the imaginal realm. It seemed to me that my trip to Zurich was as much about the inner pilgrimage I was making, as it was about paying my respects to these inspirational people. One part of the pilgrimage that I was looking forward to was a trip to the upper part of Lake Zurich to get a glimpse of Jung's famous tower at Bollingen. The journey to the tower proved to be more complex than I had realised. It involved a train ride to a nearby town and then having to hire a bicycle to make the rest of the journey. I had looked at a map and managed to get a sense of where the tower was in relation to local landmarks and amenities. It was a beautiful sunny day when I made my journey to Bollingen, and the train and bicycle rides were very enjoyable. As I cycled around the stony track near to the edge of Lake Zurich, I eventually found what I thought were the gates of Bollingen, and there were two cars parked outside the perimeter fence. I was disappointed that I could not see the tower from the track, as the building was totally obscured by the surrounding trees and dense canopy of leaves. I was tempted to enter the gates and make my way to the tower and introduce myself. However, I decided against doing this, as I was very aware that the tower was a private residence and a retreat used by the Jung family. It was not a museum and I felt that it was very important to respect these boundaries.

I sat on a small patch of grass outside the perimeter fence and spent some time reflecting on the work that Jung had done on this site. It was frustrating not to be able to see the tower, but I had seen photos and I knew enough about Jung's work at Bollingen to bring my imagination into play. I simply allowed myself to feel my relationship to this place, and whilst I was not able to see the building it somehow made the situation more mysterious and intriguing. Whilst I was sitting on the grass reflecting and contemplating, a small bird emerged from the hedge in front of me; it then flew to the inside of the perimeter gate and started to pull at a short bit of string attached to the wire gate, before eventually flying off. My immediate and literal thought was that the bird was looking for nesting material (string), but my symbolic associations soon kicked in and I played with the idea that it was a synchronous sign that the gates would eventually open. I am sure Jung would have approved of my symbolic interpretation, and so I decided to stay longer. After sitting quietly for about 10 minutes I saw someone coming to the gate from the tower. I stood up and introduced myself in English and it transpired that the person was a builder who spoke some English and he was doing some work at Bollingen. I explained that I had come from the UK to see the tower and in a very generous and open manner he told me to come with him to meet a relative of Jung's who was still in the building. It turned out to be one of Jung's grandsons, who kindly allowed me to walk around the outside of the building and also to spend some time in the courtyard. It was far more than I ever expected, and I thanked him deeply for letting me take time to look at the building and the carvings made by his grandfather. I spoke to him about the impact of Jung's work on my life. It was a very special experience.

Eventually I left the grounds of Bollingen accompanied by Jung's grandson and as we walked to the perimeter gate he pointed me in the direction of an affordable restaurant nearby, where I could buy lunch. As I ate a refreshing salad overlooking a tiny church in a field near Lake Zurich, I reflected on the inner meaning of my visit to Bollingen. First, I thought about the little bird pulling the string at the gate and saw this as a synchronicity, a form of symbolic communication, which I imagined would say something along the lines of: 'trust the process and be patient'. Second, the doors of Bollingen unexpectedly opened, and it brought me into a more intimate connection with the work of Jung and one of his grandsons. I recalled all that I had read about his experiences at the tower, and the meaning it had for him, without which his life's work would not have come into being. My pilgrimage to Lake Zurich and the unexpected entry into Bollingen gave me fresh impetus to consider my life direction and the next stage of my life's work following my retirement from academia. The opening of the perimeter gate and the doorway into Bollingen stimulated my imagination about new opportunities that were beckoning; for example, at the time of my visit, I was already deeply engaged in the process of writing this book, which coincidentally is about the imaginal realm.

My conceptualisation of human occupation being connected to deep processes of *imaginative action* is about channelling our visions, dreams, and pre-occupations into something tangible as part of our journey of individuation. I take the view that if individuation means anything in this time of global crisis, it must not only connect to the life-tasks of each individual, but that each individual has to understand their connection to an undivided whole, and then make a commitment to work for the greater good in the world. It means that individuation becomes an expression of our commitment to draw upon our deepest capacities to work for the 'collective' in compassionate, cooperative and co-creative ways. After my pilgrimage to Bollingen, I deepened my reflections and made a commitment to work more creatively (i.e. in a shamanistic way), which inspired me to continue finding ways of weaving the imaginal into my holistic coaching practice.

Pre-occupation and emancipation

My trip to Bollingen was a pilgrimage of the soul, but to illustrate how soul work is about working with all sides of our experience, I would like to share a dream that occurred the night I returned to my hotel in Zurich. In the dream I was visiting a couple and they immediately started recounting all the bad things I had done in my life. The husband was particularly aggressive, saying: "This is the Mick Collins who writes about human potential, but he is a bad man." In the dream I was frozen and could not respond to the critical accusation. I was unable to defend myself. When I woke up in the morning, I immediately started processing the dream, as I knew it was an important counterpoint to the wonderful experience of entering the private world of Bollingen the previous day. I reflected on Jung as one of my professional ancestors, and how he would not be interested in labelling people as good or bad. Jung was interested in awakening. My dream led to a mini life review. I decided to do some active imagination and entered into an imaginative and dreamlike conversation with Jung. He was stern and pointed out that my dream was revealing a complex that was not only silencing me, but if left unattended, it would impede how I work with my unfolding potential. He said: "You are overly identified with your past misdeeds [criminal convictions etc.] and this is squandering how you are engaging your life energies today." He went on: "You cannot change the past, but you can change your attitude to it – wake up – *the complex* is the real criminal here; it is 'stealing' your vital energy." The final message in my imaginative interaction with Jung was unequivocal: "This dream is your deathwalk; you must die to the unconscious drama within you, otherwise the haunting shadow that stalks your soul will kill your potential."

This is how the unconscious works: for every moment of illumination or damnation, there will be a compensatory response in the psyche that points to the real task of living wholeness. In my case the dream was reflecting an inner critic linked to my shadow actions. It highlights the difference in awareness, between the realities of us *having* complexes, or whether complexes *have us*. Our path of individuation is based on knowing the *former*, and working with the *latter*. Such inner work necessitates being honest about who we are, and this is paramount today if humanity is interested in transforming collective consciousness. In my case, the dream revealed how all the bad things I have done in my life are alive within me, and unless I understand the deeper lesson from these experiences (including self-forgiveness), they perpetuate inner fragmentation. My trip to Zurich taught me a valuable lesson about the way our good-bad actions impact the soul. It helped me understand the deeper meanings connected to the mini life review, where psychic fragmentation can be healed via processes of integration (wholeness). Such experiences are entry points that reconnect us with the sacred, which is not bound by opposites (good-bad). These encounters are like the process of purification in alchemy, and integrating them is important for our awakening.

At this time of great global change, we simply cannot modify our existence with minor adaptations. We need an occupational shift that engages our visionary energies (in the service of wholeness) and brings them into action, which enables us to realise a wider spectrum of possibilities for how we live. Theodore Roszak[19] has written about the importance of our human potential and how growth and transformation are promoted through finding a sense of heartfelt purpose in life. Roszak speaks about the loss of myth and mystery in the modern world, compared to previous times, where people's qualities of lived experience were linked to the sacred. Today, we need to examine our pre-occupations and bring them into conscious awareness.[2] In this way, we can become more aware of the ideas that are percolating within us, meaning we can be more discerning about the various courses of action we take in life, and how we can cultivate greater wholeness. In my work with people as a holistic coach I have found that the pre-occupations that regularly come to the surface are questions about identity (who am I?), as well as thoughts about meaning and purpose in life (what have I done, and what am I doing?).

Pre-occupations are fascinating because they can be used as access points that connect us to the imaginal realm. They represent contact with a liminal threshold between our everyday conscious mind and the flickering, or fired-up, potential found in our musings, visions, dreams, imaginings and actions. Indeed, the images and feelings percolating from the unconscious reveal what the soul is doing.[20] In this way, Jung viewed the unconscious as an equal partner in the process of individuation and he spoke about how he would often let his hands do some creative work, so that he could reflect on what the unconscious was seeking to express,[21] such is the power of *activity* and *doing* for revealing our latent potential for psycho-spiritual growth. Visionary and imaginal energies are the soul's creative expression, which can be crafted through the use of our intuitions, imaginings and pre-occupations, which can then be woven into our everyday occupational engagement as a form of soul work. Patrick Harpur[22] proposes any occupations that are inspired by the imagination can become rituals, imbued with the sacred. Harpur[23] also speaks about the enduring curiosity of human beings, and that our most compelling interests are linked to *archetypal pre-occupations*, which imagine, speculate, and question how life has evolved.

As noted above, I have approached the question of archetypes and doing from a different perspective, which focuses on the ways we can actually engage a deeper quality of meaning, purpose, and potential through our daily actions as *archetypal occupations*, which brings forth a connection to our occupational myth. It is deep work, where our imaginative actions serve the process of individuation.

Our occupational myths evolve through the interactions that occur between our everyday ego-consciousness and the unconscious. Occupational myths have an archetypal resonance, because they bring forth a greater range of possibilities for developing awareness, where our unique talents, skills, gifts, ideas and passions serve our paths of wholeness and the greater good. Our work is to ensure that we live as congruently as possible, to make sure we are connected to our personal and transpersonal potential, and that we do not become overly fixated on the one-sided technocracy that dominates mainstream consensus reality. The following story illustrates the courage of a person whose deep sense of vocation was ever present in the midst of an adverse life event.

_____ **The spirit in the stroke** _____

I recently learnt that an old friend had had a stroke, which was then complicated by a life-threatening situation that thankfully managed to resolve itself. When I visited my friend we spoke about how he was managing the symptoms of the stroke. He and his wife are both healers and eventually the subject turned to healing. At one point in the conversation I asked my friend about certain hypnotic healing techniques he had used in the past, and he offered to do a demonstration on me. It was the most wonderful experience, accompanied by a palpable spiritual presence in the room, which I felt on the crown of my head. After spending some time integrating the experience I offered to do a simple process of visualisation for my friend. He prepared himself by lying on the floor and as my friend's breathing became slow and rhythmic, his bodily tensions gradually lessened. I suggested that he visualise something that might be helpful for him while in this relaxed state. Then, a short while later he experienced a few shakes that started moving from the base of his neck up through his head. It was accompanied by an experience of a purple wave, which rose up from the soles of his feet and moved up through his body. He described it as a profound healing experience, saying it was an 'aha' moment, where he felt reconnected to the universe.

The next morning my friend's wife sent me an email saying her husband had had a dream of being in South India, where he was a well-respected grandfather, surrounded by lots of smiling children. He was teaching the children the wisdom of the elders and forefathers. It made me think about our reciprocal healing experiences from the previous day, and how the three of us had created a special atmosphere. I wondered if the healing energy we shared had activated something in my friend, which was calling him to deepen his healing journey. We agreed to meet a few days later to discuss the dream. My friend said it was rare for him to have such a dream, which prompted me to ask what the symbolism in the dream meant for him. He said that it was like having a connection to wisdom, which was now ready to come out and be expressed.

My friend explained his associations to the various parts of the dream. For example, 'India' represents a society that is overtly spiritual, which is deeply integrated in the culture and people's lifestyles. He went on to speak about the 'happy children' and how their joy was connected to receiving spiritual nourishment. The children had a meaningful relationship to an elder, which brought them into contact with the wisdom of the ancients. I asked my friend what the 'ancestors' in the dream meant to him, and he said that they are in tune with nature. He pointed out that the ancestors are *connected* to the universe, which helps to remind us that we are all connected. Finally, I asked him what being a 'well-respected grandfather' means? He reflected deeply on this point and eventually said: "It means that I intuitively know what to say, be, and do." I was curious about what such a statement could mean to him in his everyday life, here and now. Once again, he reflected on the question and said: "It's ok for me to come out now." He went on to speak about the importance of being true to who he is: "As a doctor I had to shut down lots of who I was, particularly my interest in alternative medicine."

The conversation was unfolding in ways that neither of us expected. I have known my friend for 30 years and I had not heard him speak about his work in such depth before. It was a beautiful conversation. In fact, I had never heard him speak about the following stories in all the years I have known him. He worked as a hospital anaesthetist and revealed to me that on many occasions when he was working in operating theatres he would have an intuition that something was not quite right with his patients. His first response in such situations was to always check that the anaesthetic equipment was ok. He said it is hard to explain what happened next, but when checking the equipment he would see a glowing light surrounding a specific bit of equipment, which seemed to be alerting him to check for any problems in those areas. The glowing light was always correct and he would rapidly make any necessary adjustments, which on many occasions was potentially lifesaving. He said to me: "It's not easy to comprehend or explain how this glowing light works, but I have always found it important to pay attention to these intuitions and signals."

It was fascinating speaking to my friend about his deep intuition and the spiritual connection to his work, which complemented his conventional medical expertise. This was particularly evident when he used hypnosis, not anaesthetics, to put people to sleep before their operations. He said that on many occasions an image would appear before him; for example, a rose was quite common, which he took as a sign that he and the patient were *connected* at a level of shared consciousness. Then he would say to the patient: "What colour are the roses?" He was always assured that the connection between them was good if the patient responded without hesitation. The operation could then proceed. He also pointed out that people rarely needed postoperative medication for recovery if they had had hypnosis. He said that: "We need to trust our inner resources for healing." It was also evident that my friend was now calling upon those same inner resources, as he navigated his journey of healing and recovery through his stroke.

One unexpected development in my friend's healing journey happened when his wife said how much she would like to go back to India again one day, but somehow she had thought that their long-haul travel days were over. But interestingly, my friend's dream had also awoken his interest in visiting India again. I learnt the next day that my friend set out to renew his passport. Because he and his wife were both deeply interested in alternative healing, they were planning a trip to a hotel that specialised in Ayurveda medicine in South India. Talking about the trip led to my friend becoming more animated in conversation, particularly because the adventure chimed with the growth-promoting tendencies indicated in his dream. A subtle shift was now taking place, as he became less focused on the deficits connected to his stroke, and more invested in holistic healing connected to his path of eldership. Interestingly, the shift that was happening in my friend also benefited his wife. Both were now re-aligning to their shared interest in healing and growth, not coping with deficits. It is a transformational story that is as subtle as it is magical. Confirmation of this new lease of life came in the guise of another dream, where my friend's grandfather was teaching him how to plant potatoes. The symbolism in the dream seemed to be pointing to 'eldership' and 'wisdom', linked to the seeding and growth of new potential.

Deep vocations

Theodore Roszak called the value and meaning of our working lives into question years ago when he noticed that so much of what we do is tied into industries that are destroying the environment.[24] In a similar vein, James Hillman[20] argued that our working lives are so tethered to the economic status quo, that even if we had alternative ideas about *doing* or *being*, the cultural-fiscal consensus in which we earn our living makes it difficult to accommodate our unique potential for wholeness, and this is where we could easily forfeit our birthright. For this reason, it is imperative that our social institutions start to recognise the importance of our connection to the symbolic and imaginal forces that can awaken our visionary energies, which incubate and stimulate our evolutionary development. Such visionary energies are the lifeblood that brings deep meaning and purpose in all that we do.

If we want our daily occupations to contribute to cultivating new ways of doing, it will involve *undoing* many of our current limiting ideas about how we live and work.[2] We need to find ways of becoming more permeable to images and knowledge, arising from the collective unconscious via dreams, visions, inspirations and synchronous events.[2] Such a proposition is not new. For example, the ancient Greek philosopher Heraclitus lamented that most of the people he met in life acted as if they were asleep. The statement challenges us to live more fully and deeply, rather than skimming across the surface of life. What is being called for is a deeper alignment between our visionary energies and our active participation, so we can engage in a quest for wholeness that

Theodore Roszak[19] refers to as *doing-power*. Roszak[24] highlights the danger to humanity if we just allow ourselves to drift into a *vocational vacuum*, compared to responding to self-discovery and the expression of our *natural vocations*, through the deep calling from within (*vocāre*). Thus, for our visionary energies to be crafted in life-affirming ways, our imaginations are central to the task of enacting our vocations in life.[25] It naturally follows that an important part of our collective work at this time is to question what it means to be a human being and to *re-imagine* what *doing* means to the human enterprise.

I have already spoken about the need for humanity to develop a greater occupational coherence between the *inner work* and *outer work* we do, with a particular focus on the integration of our personal and transpersonal potential. This is like an alchemy of doing that brings about a shift in consciousness,[6] where we are awake to manifesting wholeness.[26] Jung[8] advocated that we create a relationship to the *spirit of the depths* (*geist der tiefe*), via our individuating dreams and actions, which create new pathways for living. He also spoke about not being swayed too readily by the *spirit of the times* (*zeitgeist*),[21] or the shifting sands of everyday consensus reality. Thus, the quality of our inner work is dependent upon staying alive to *visionary energies*, which can then be engaged as outer work in our everyday activities.[19] In this way, our *creative acts of doing* are also representative of transformative vocations,[19] which reverberate in our inner and outer lives as a force for co-creation in an interconnected world. We could call it a *cosmic action vibration*. It's like the idea in chaos theory, where the flapping wings of a butterfly in South America impact on the weather in Europe.

Physician Larry Dossey[27] writes about how at the subtlest level we occupy an interconnected and *non-local* universe, where nothing is separate. For example, people's feelings and thoughts can connect, even when they are a great distance from each other. The impact of our actions on one another is a deep meditation for living: *what we do in and to the world, we do to each other and ourselves*. Such ideas chime with some of the ground-breaking ideas from the world of quantum physics, such as Jung's concept of synchronicity and Ervin Laszlo's idea of the Akashic field. These revelations of interconnectivity could inspire us to *cooperate* in our ways of living, not *compete*. For example, David la Chapelle[28] writes about the *potlatches*, where the First Nation peoples of North America would share resources between them, generating great social and spiritual cohesion within the tribes. Any contemporary shift in consciousness has to understand the interconnectedness between the local and non-local effects of our actions both in and on the world.

Turn on, tune in and take action

Modern people may have difficulty accepting the idea of non-local actions, yet Edgar Mitchell[29] speaks about the importance of our *emergent potentials* that are expressed within daily life contexts. As we saw from the life reviews reported by people who have encountered near death experiences, the impacts of our actions on each other, other species and the planet are enmeshed. It reveals how the idea of *occupational entanglement* is intimately linked to our *occupational potential*. Indeed, we could say that a quantum leap is needed to bring forth a new level of awareness that goes beyond, or through (*trans*) established ways of knowing and being, which takes us into new patterns of transformative doing. Living in a world that we know is interconnected at a subtle level could inspire a deep change in behaviour, where we understand that what we do to others and the world, we do to ourselves. What would it be like if each of us, our communities and institutions promoted a more holistic relationship to nature and life as a whole, which inspired us to live more generous, kinder and loving lives? It is through such a shift in our intentions and actions that we can become eco-participants in life, where an improved future is co-created in all that we do. It means that we have to rediscover the indigenous nature, which resides in the heart of our human heritage.

A very touching example of the lesson of indigenous wisdom and a deeper connection to life, to the land and to one another is provided by Paul Kingsnorth[30] who recounts his experiences of spending time with the Lani tribe in West Papua Highlands. He tells a story of climbing a mountain ridge that was also covered by a vast ancient rainforest, and he speaks about how the Lani sang songs of gratitude to the forest, which is fully alive. The songs were a way of reflecting the tribe's deep sense of belonging with the land, and often the forest 'sang' back. It fits with the indigenous ways of knowing, where nature is alive and communicative. Kingsnorth is correct when he says that modern people have two typical responses to nature's song. The first is indulging in *sentimentality*, and the second is dismissing it as *superstition*. It is here that we return to the relationship between the imaginal realm and our dreams. Indigenous wisdom understands that everything is connected to a living reality, which also comes to us through night-time dreams[31] and waking visions, in which the spirits of nature (plants, animals, elements of the land) communicate with the dreamer, and often a song is given, which can be used for healing. This deep receptivity only happens because indigenous people know that nature and all life forms can speak to us, and through us; that is, if we are tuned in to the living world and are prepared to listen. Jung[32] noted that 'nature' no longer appears to communicate with modern people; however, it seems like it is humanity who no longer wishes to communicate with nature and the plant world. But this does not mean we are unable to make such a connection (see the excellent YouTube film, *The Animal Communicator*).

It has been recognised that a deep emotional connection to life can happen when people receive a song in a dream. Garfield[33] talks about research into sacred songs that have come to Native Americans, for example, from singing trees or crows etc. The Native Americans protect their songs by composing obscure lyrics and phrases, so that the message remains private. These songs are also obtained during vision quests and they forge a very powerful connection to our spiritual nature. The songs are sung when a person is embarking on a serious endeavour, or when confronted by danger, which enables them to make a connection to a spiritual force. Similarly, in traditional ceremonies, the 'songs' of plants are used by healers, and each human being is recognised as having a 'song', which connects to the deepest part of their being, or soul.[34] Indeed, indigenous wisdom says that the discovery of a song in the soul brings forth a sacred alignment to the beating rhythm of the heart.[35] The following vignette tells the story of a woman who was seeking to make a change in her life after years of living in the shadow of old self-destructive patterns. Neither she, nor I, were prepared for the song that emerged in the last session of our work together.

A song of freedom

I worked with a client over a number of sessions and we focused on breaking the binds of internal oppression, which had affected her life for many years. The work we did enabled her to understand the internal structures that were disempowering her. The last session we did was a vector walk and the work was very powerful, so much so, that even her recollections of our work (for this vignette) tapped into her body memory of the empowered feelings that were linked to the session.

It was the first time that my client had done a vector walk and she did not know what to expect. The session took place at the client's home, in the back garden, and I asked her to consider what she was ready to let go of in her life, and I encouraged her to experience the natural world as if she were in the dreamtime, to *look*, *see*, and *feel* if anything caught her attention. She noticed a small thyme bush, which she felt was staring at her. It was not a comfortable connection, and as she started walking towards the bush she suddenly stopped. She said that she felt fear taking over her body; she froze and felt as if her legs wouldn't move any more. She said that she was afraid of the bush, which she described as ugly. We acknowledged that what she wanted to give up was a disempowered connection to fear, which was felt in her bodily experience, which made it clear to her the extent of the internalised oppression we had been working on in the previous sessions. After the session I went to my library and looked up the mythic associations to thyme, and one of its uses in early Roman times was in purification rites.[36] This seemed like the perfect symbol for the journey my client was about to take.

The next stage of the process involved focusing on the connection and direction of my client's transformative process. I asked her to see what aspects of nature were calling to her and as she turned around, she felt relieved when a tree caught her attention. The tree appeared to have a light around it. It was like the tree was calling to her, welcoming her with open arms. She felt a strong sense of hope and gratefulness as she walked towards it, noticing that her steps were getting faster and tears of happiness welled up from deep inside her. She said that she felt so happy, a happiness that can be compared to a hostage who has been saved, which she described as a powerful and beautiful experience. As she walked towards the tree she had the feeling of becoming 'one' with it, blending into it and soaking up all the information she was getting from this deep connection with nature. She said: "It felt like a gift had been given to me, a veil had been lifted and I could see the light."

The final part of the vector involved, once again, engaging with nature and waiting for a connection to happen. This time, the focus was upon the path that was calling her. She noticed at this point the garden looked different; it was more *tranquil* and *peaceful*. Suddenly she was drawn to birds flying over the roof of her house. The birds brought a sudden feeling of freedom, which made her feel complete, content, and she experienced a sudden burst of joy and happiness. She said that she felt like a little girl, who was happy and wanted to sing and dance. She said: "I have to sing and I have to dance!" The song that came to her was, "Birds of freedom knocking at my door!" It is a song that has stayed with her since she did the work.

My client said that the song that came to her on her vector walk was a breakthrough in her finding her own voice. It transpired that singing was important to her for a long time, and whilst she was really good at copying other people's vocals, the lack of her own distinct style was frustrating and confusing to her. The vector walk unlocked something within my client and she suddenly connected to her own unique singing voice. In fact, she says that: "It feels like I have finally connected to the innermost part of my being, which was hidden. It is like my soul was hiding, and as scared of being seen. But now it feels like I have opened the door and I have access to it, and this has been such a great gift to me." My client spoke about how she now sings from the soul, and how her voice is genuine, which brings a deep connection to her real self. Since the vector walk she has written a number of songs.

My client revealed that her old fears, what she referred to as "the deep ones", have now left her, like they have simply vanished. She went on to say: "I feel freed from a heavy burden, I am lighter, much more flexible and the horizon now seems clearer. I also feel braver, like I could do anything, in fact everything is possible." Indeed, my client revealed how nature itself can help us connect to the deeper parts of our own being, and like her, everyone has a song in their hearts, which reverberates through thoughts, actions and in the world.[37]

The above vignette shows that old patterns can be shifted when we pay attention to the deeper yearnings from the soul, where our song is waiting to be sung. But first we have to have the discipline to stop investing in our worries and negative pre-occupations, and start to take time listening to the Earth and to the soul, which is facilitated by opening up to our dreams and the imaginal realm. It is here that our direct encounters with subtle energies are the 'songlines of our souls', where we become co-participants in an emerging myth.[38] It is where each of us has to find a way back to nature, which is not separate from our deeper nature. David Abram[39] sums up the subtle connection between *nature's song* and the way that it finds expression in the melody of the human voice, where our speech is as much the wind flowing through the human body, as it is the physical characteristics that enable our vocal vibrations to form sounds. In this way, human communication is made rich and varied by the voice, and it is one amongst many other rich and diverse ways that nature communes, which can include the pheromones that enable insects to connect, or even the blossom on a tree that attracts wildlife.[39] The world is alive with rich and diverse forms of communication, which is an invitation to listen and feel a deeper connection to all the different voices from the Earth.

Understanding the breadth of nature's ways of communicating, says David Abram,[39] brings us back to the interweaving of the human senses and how they connect us to a sensual world. It emphasises why our empathetic natures need to be cultivated, so that we can listen and be responsive participants in a sentient world.[39] Humanity has yet to awaken to the subtle sensitivities of our sentient potential, and how we are interwoven in the tapestry of life. For inspiration about the intimate ways we are connected to the sentient world, and how nature is capable of registering and responding to our intentions and actions, I recommend the book, *The Secret Life of Plants*.[40] We need to cultivate a renewed relationship to life and the cosmos (or whole), which is not mechanistic, but recognises nature's songs, where all life vibrates and reverberates in relationships of interconnectivity.[28] It would equip us with the subtleness that can discern the whispers in nature's communications.

When we consider the importance of indigenous knowledge, as well as the spiritual heritages that have valued nature, it is clear that part of our evolutionary task is to understand how humanity is interwoven within an interconnected whole. It is a call for each of us to begin living in harmony with all life, and start connecting with the *Song of the Earth*.[41] A valiant response is needed to counter the trajectory that was unleashed by the raw power of the Industrial Revolution, which tore into nature and plundered its resources to support a *vision of conquest*. What we need today, more than ever, are enough people in the world to engage in *vision quests* to heal our dislocation from nature, which has left us isolated and lost.[42] It is our responsibility to re-animate our relationship to the natural world, as Jung[43] pointed out. He saw the consequences of humanity abandoning the sacred connection to the daimons, and he noticed that these spirits no longer inhabit the natural and sacred world of rivers, trees and rocks etc., yet their effects are felt more strongly in the unconscious.[22] Secular and scientific worldviews cast out spiritual phenomena such as the daimons, because they were considered irrational, implausible and impossible.[23] But, when we connect with the soul, we find a new resonance in our ways of living. No matter how derided the notion of the soul may be in the modern world, we know that it is through an animated relationship with nature that we are able to hear the *Song of the Earth*, which connects to the song in our hearts. This is the domain of the daimon, which animates the life of the soul and initiates a connection to the spirit. It is through the cultivation of such a sensitive relationship to the imaginal realm, where our subtle energies are activated, that our relationship to the Transformocene Age will be able to flourish.

Exercise: Finding your song

- Part one:
  - Find a place in nature and take time to tune into the natural world. When you are ready to start, think of a particular way of being or pattern of living that you are ready to let go of.
  - Scan your surroundings slowly (as if you were in a dreamy state), and notice if something catches your attention – it could be a natural object like a plant or bird. It could be a fabricated object, or even the breeze on your face, etc. – just trust the intuitive connection you have with it.
  - Walk slowly in the direction of the thing that caught your attention. Then open yourself to its quality (real and imagined). Ask yourself, how does this connect to the pattern of living or way of being you are ready to let go of?

- Part two:
  - Now think of something you want to connect with in your way of being or pattern of living, e.g. being more creative, or a social activist etc.
  - Again, scan your surroundings slowly (as if you were in a dreamy state), and notice if something catches your attention.
  - Walk slowly in the direction of the thing that caught your attention. Then open yourself to its quality (real and imagined). Ask yourself, how does this connect to the pattern of living or way of being you are seeking to connect to?

- Part three:
  - Open your heart to creating a meaningful connection to life and receiving help from the imaginal realm in your quest.
  - Again, scan your surroundings slowly (as if you were in a dreamy state), and notice if something catches your attention.
  - Walk slowly in the direction of the thing that caught your attention. Then open yourself to its quality (real and imagined). Notice how it brings a deeper connection between the imaginal realm and your soul.

- Part four:
  - Explore the real and imagined links in the discoveries you made in parts two and three of this exercise.
  - Walk slowly between the two places that inspired you in parts two and three. Open your heart and let a song come to you. It can be a song that you create, or a song that already exists.
  - What does this song bring to you in terms of new ways of being and patterns of living?
  - Sing your song a few times and find a connection that helps you live closer to your deeper potential and nature.

Daimonic fate is initiated in the soul, which becomes a deep catalyst for awakening. As our 'true character' comes to the fore, we naturally engage our angelic destiny. Spiritual awakening is a 'mystical occupation'.

CHAPTER ELEVEN

Daimonic Fate, Angelic Destiny

Overview

In this chapter I make a connection between our subtle energies (as found in the chakras), and our psycho-spiritual potential for growth (as noted by Abraham Maslow). Our subtle energies reveal how mystical phenomena are present in our bodies, and when linked to our psycho-spiritual potential can assist our spiritual awakening. I discuss how such awakening is important for regenerating a sacred connection to self, others, other species, and nature as a whole. I characterise the process of subtle and soulful awakening as *daimonic fate*, which is an authentic representation of our true character. I point out that this awakened soul energy connects to our *angelic destiny*, which expresses our spiritual potential in life. Representing our subtle energies in relation to the daimonic and angelic means that we have a mythic and tangible way of understanding how our dreams (soul work) link to an energetic vibration (spirit work). This is one example of how our psycho-spiritual activism brings us to an emancipatory edge, where we can co-create a sacred connection to life as a whole. It reveals the depth of our mythic engagement, which contributes to the Transformocene through inner and outer work.

The myth of sacred renewal

Humanity has an incredible opportunity to link our everyday actions to our spiritual development and help tackle the global challenges we are facing. We can become more empowered to start living as global citizens, actively participating in collective transformation through renewed *ways of doing and being*. Bringing about this *occupational shift* in our daily lives is paramount, because modern life is currently based on an unsustainable mode of consciousness. Collective change will happen when more of us start engaging these transformational actions at home, in our neighbourhoods and communities.[1]

The question is how can we be inspired to connect to a re-sacralised vision for living? Eco-philosopher Henryk Skolimowski[2] has highlighted the need for an eco-spiritual consciousness, one that inspires us to cultivate our interest in *transformative actions* through practices like eco-yoga, encouraging us to integrate eco-spiritual awareness into our everyday lifestyles to tackle the global crisis. Spiritual traditions such as yoga have much to offer humanity in terms of our transformative potential, especially in the ways that we make an adaptive response to climate change and co-create an improved and sustainable future. For example, the law of karma posits that our actions have consequences,[3] and this resonates with the findings from the life reviews that accompany NDEs. Such an understanding could encourage us to reflect deeply on the impact our lifestyles are having on the planet. Awareness of karma yoga could encourage us to cultivate an eco-spiritual response that is connected to *direct action* in relation to our daily routines, social engagements, and working lives, which can all become sacred activities. It is here that our thoughts and deeds are the basis for transforming so-called 'mundane activities' into a sacrament of living. Thus, karma yoga is a path of selfless action that leads to Self-realisation and liberation from the binds of our egocentric behaviours. In this way, our individual journeys of Self-realisation could be combined and strengthened by joining with other people who are also working to serve the greater good. Today, spiritual activism is vital for our collective development, and every human being alive could play a significant role in the emerging global shift, supporting and encouraging each other to bring more depth to what we do in life.

The *spiritual art of doing* is where some of our most potent opportunities for deep change and transformation can be found. But how do we harness the transformative potential that is ever-present in our daily actions? For example, think about those moments when you are engaged in activities where you feel at '*one*' with what you are doing, which may be accompanied by a deep sense of flow. Times like these are gifts in terms of our health and spiritual well-being. They reveal the deep potential for wholeness that we already possess, where a spiritual connection is revealed through our skills, talents, creativity and passions. It is a marvellous instance of how our daily occupational engagement is a source of living alchemy, aligning our attitudes, awareness and actions to spiritual inspiration and meaning in everyday life contexts.

Rainbow bridge and chakra-actions

The *occupational shift* that is being called for today – to meet the global crisis – is about a renewed relationship to *technologies of transformation* (such as yoga, tai chi, meditation, prayer or dream work etc.), which can help us to expand our consciousness and inspire new ways of living, connected to *doing with depth*. How we *bind together* (yoga) and co-create an improved future is set to become the great challenge of this era. As Professor Tim O'Riordan[4] says: "*sustainability is examining our humanness*", which means that the global crisis will test who we are as a species, particularly our collective resolve to be less greedy or selfish. The global crisis is a perfect storm that will examine our willingness and resolve to become more altruistic and compassionate in our everyday lives. In this way, karma yoga exemplifies how *technologies of transformation* can bring us into a deeper and more spiritually nourishing relationship in our ways of living. It is through such deep actions that we can transform outmoded modern consumer-based lifestyles (now being adopted by many non-Western cultures) into a living sacrament.

We have been treating the Earth's resources as a commodity for so long that we appear to have lost a sacred relationship to nature. To be sustainable, it is clear that humanity will need to do more in terms of our *outer adaptations*, such as reducing carbon emissions, using more renewable energy and recycling etc. But, in order to live more harmoniously with other species and nature, we will need to do more in terms of our *inner adaptations*, such as increasing our awareness and raising our conscious vibrations through technologies of transformation. The global crisis is a wake-up call for all of us to start co-creating a more just world, where the rights of all people, other species and nature are taken into equal consideration. Next time we go shopping for food, we might pause for a moment and spare a thought for the thousands of children who die every day due to poor nutrition and starvation.[5] Such a realisation could inspire us to do something different in our daily activities, such as cultivating awareness about the ways we produce food as a commodity, allied to insatiable consumer appetites and outrageous levels of waste, which will be put under the spotlight with an increasingly volotile climate. The global crisis will test our willingness to adapt and co-create a fair world for all, based on the realisation that the actions we take today will shape the world we live in tomorrow. We are living in a time where radical change is set to become the norm, and we will have to face the consequences of our actions and inactions. It is a call to live with more depth.

We can deepen our ways of living by acknowledging the coexistence of the 'material body' (physical) and the 'subtle body' (soul-spirit). It represents the wholeness that can emerge, between our *personal identity* and the *transpersonal Self*, which brings about an *occupational resonance* in our ways of *doing* and *being*, both locally and non-locally. In Chapter One I discussed Buddhist practices that connect to the rainbow body, which are based on tantric philosophy and meditations. The meaning of the word *tantra* is 'loom', and as we saw in Chapter Nine, this connects us to the metaphor of weaving. It helps us understand that the path of tantra is about unification, in that our actions weave a sacred thread that is allied to creative transformation and the evolution of consciousness.[6] As far back as 1932 parallels were being drawn between the tantric path of Kundalini yoga and the process of individuation, as conceived by Jung,[7] where both approaches require a commitment to transformation, as well as discipline and willingness to face issues that may surface.[8] The process of individuation is a path to wholeness, and in a similar way, Kundalini awakening reflects a holistic understanding,[3] which provides a cosmological connection to life.

The awakening of our psycho-spiritual potential occurs in the subtle body, which is represented in the tantric tradition through the energy centres known as chakras. It is through the chakras that we experience a greater connection between our Earthly incarnation and the sacred.[8] Anodea Judith has produced an excellent synthesis of the bodily chakra centres linked to Western psychological models.[6] I was particularly drawn to the way she integrated the work of psychologist Abraham Maslow, and his theoretical model *Hierarchy of Need*, as I had previously written about Maslow's ideas when I was researching the actualisation of psycho-spiritual potential through human occupations, or doing. A question that has interested me for many years is how we are occupied when we become conscious of the 'material body' interweaving with the 'subtle body', and the dynamic energies of awakening that are active within us. It inspired me to consult the literature and compile the *chakra-actions matrix*, as a way of further engaging opportunities in everyday living as a path of awakening, emancipation and service (see Table 1).

Table 1. The Rainbow Chakra-Actions Matrix

Chakra	*Muladhara*	*Svadhisthana*	*Manipura*	*Anahata*	*Vissudha*	*Ajna*	*Sahasrara*
	Root chakra at the base of the spine.	Sacral chakra at the navel.	Solar plexus chakra at the base of the sternum.	Heart chakra at the centre of the chest.	Throat chakra at the base of the front of the neck.	Third eye chakra at the centre between the eyebrows.	Crown chakra at the top of the skull.
Maslow	*Physiology* Survival, food & water etc.	*Safety* Stability & health etc.	*Belonging* Intimacy, family & friends etc.	*Esteem* Confidence & being a unique person etc.	*Self-actualising* Personal potential & growth etc.	*Transcending* Peak experiences & transpersonal potential etc.	*Transcending* Spiritual & transpersonal awakening etc.
Rainbow (light) Body	*Red*	*Orange*	*Yellow*	*Green*	*Indigo*	*Blue*	*Violet*
Everyday Actions	Grounding & taking care of the body. ***Trusting.***	Feelings of pleasure & pain. ***Generous.***	Growth in self-identity. ***Secure.***	Connecting to love & compassion. ***Positive.***	Evolving self, inclusive of a cosmic connection. ***Expressive.***	Inspiration & perception. ***Intuitive.***	Flow & wholeness. ***Connected.***
Shadow Actions	Anxiety & fear. ***Self-centred.***	Repression & guilt. ***Shallow.***	Shame & anger. ***Dogmatic.***	Grief & self-loathing. ***Alienated.***	Lies & deception. ***Cunning.***	Distortion & illusion. ***Confused.***	Attachment & envy. ***Doubtful.***
Sacred Actions	Lives with awareness of how the subtle & material bodily energies co-exist. ***Aligned.***	Does not waste vital energies & knows what activities support well-being. ***Empowered.***	Cares for self & others, including nature & other species. ***Emboldened.***	Lives with a more expansive connection to life as a mystery. ***Enlivened.***	Lives in abundance & able to express the truth about cosmic experiences. ***Co-creative.***	Transforms everyday life by putting visionary energies & wisdom into action. ***Imaginative.***	Participates in an interconnected cosmos where unity & divinity are integrated into daily life. ***Emancipated.***

Acknowledgements: Chitrabhanu (1979);[9] Judith (1996/2004);[6] Breaux (1989);[8] Paulson (2003);[3] Fox (2016);[10] Khalsa and O'Keefe (2016).[11]

As noted in Chapter One, Tibetan Buddhist monks refer to the awakened subtle energies in the chakra system as the *rainbow body*, and Anodea Judith[6] describes the colourful world of our conscious evolution as a "rainbow bridge". It is a developmental path, where technologies of transformation become part of a sacred quest, which enables us to make greater connections between our Earthly existence and our place in the cosmos. Arny Mindell[12] refers to the subtle processes of awareness in our bodies and nature, such as spiritual expression, altered states of consciousness and creativity that lead to experiences of oneness, as "Rainbow Medicine". In this way, the *rainbow* as a *bridge* and *medicine* encourages us to consider our full potential as whole human beings, and how our transcendent experiences become immanent in the context of our everyday lives and actions. The work is about cultivating our potential to be *heart* and *soul*-centred beings. Judith[6] asserts that the heart chakra (*Anahata*) is the point where each *individual* can experience an Earthly (*body*) and celestial (*divine*) connection, which inspires love in action, cultivated through right livelihood, relationships, and creativity.

Jung's[13] conversations with the Chief of the Taos Pueblos tribe, Mountain Lake, taught the psychologist how his people 'thought' with their hearts. It is no coincidence that most spiritual traditions consider the heart to be important in sacred activities, such as prayer, which transforms our relationship to living.[14,15,16,17] A Sufi saying compares being close to the divine, as if the *great beloved* (God) is kissing us on the inside of the heart. Simply imagining and feeling this tender and intimate connection with the divine (as a beautiful meditation) can bring our hearts into a powerful alignment with the sacred. Indeed, Henry Corbin calls the *heart* one of the centres of mystic physiology, which he describes as having a green light (see Table 1). It is through the heart that we are capable of transforming our relationship to the world, and healing ourselves, because the heart connects us to one another and to the cosmos through love. Indeed, Corbin[18] says that the heart is the temple where the angel resides, suggesting that subtle states of consciousness intersect here with our physical and temporal lives (hearts), which is interwoven with the divine (angelic).[19]

There appear to be many similarities between daimons and guardian angels.[20] Henry Corbin[21] explains that daimons are spirits that guide our souls, who accompany us throughout our lives, including the time of our deaths. They also act as witnesses (*testis*) and guardians (*custos*), whose *nous*, or intelligence, reflects the soulful aspect of each person. For me, the *daimonic* is where the 'spirit' is *activated* in our lives at a soul level, which initiates the meeting of our true character and fate. But these soulful promptings require that we learn from the depth of our experiences, rather like Jung's relationship to Philemon, which emerged from his deep encounters with the psyche. Indeed, this concurs with Patrick Harpur[22] who believes the daimon works at a soul level, and is active in the dark depths of the unconscious. When we work with such subtle and soulful energies it helps to have a narrative that can guide us. As we shall see, both the daimonic and angelic are mythic representations of *energetic actualities* that can inspire our psycho-spiritual development in life.

The myth of daimonic fate and angelic destiny

Humanity has a modern mythic narrative for awakening our subtle energies, which is represented in the life of Jung. He responded to the *call of the daimon*, by listening to the soulful promptings that were communicated in visions, dreams and intuitions etc. When the daimon is stirred into life and given expression, it is complemented by the angelic, which inspires us to actualise our spiritual destiny through the transformative actions we take in life. Thus, the *soulful daimon* is the counterpart of the *spiritual angel*, and they are dynamic energies that can help us express our true character, craft our destiny and meet our fate. It is a path of individuation and non-duality (undivided). It is how I approach my dream of a white snake emerging from a black snake's mouth, where they are representative of two dynamic and symbolic elements within a unitary process of transformation. Such symbolism helps us make a deep connection to the imaginal realm and appreciate what Henry Corbin[18] refers to as *"imaginative presence"*, i.e. where the heart is the temple of the angel which, I believe, is stimulated into action by the soulful and imaginative awakening of the daimon.[22]

The interweaving of the *daimonic soul* and the *angelic spirit* (which happens through the threads of our mythic imaginations) draws inspiration from the imaginal realm. The daimonic soul and the angelic spirit are literally the warp and weft of our sacred fate and destiny, weaving the Earthly and celestial threads that make up the tapestry of our life. In this way, we create a sacrament through our ways of living, thereby fulfilling our human potential as soulful and spiritual beings. Of course, it needs to be reiterated that meeting our *daimonic fate* and *angelic destiny* is a big responsibility. Such an undertaking means we will meet adversaries, both within and without, as well as tests that will often take us to our edges or limits of our ability to cope (remember Job from the Old Testament?). Henry Corbin[21] also reminds us we all have the potential to be fallen angels (demonic). We can see a clear example of where Hitler's *daimonic fate* was subsumed into a *demonic destiny*, rather than an *angelic destiny*. He became a 'fallen angel'. Instead of working on his inner shadow and his inner potential, Hitler became intoxicated by the idea of becoming a messianic saviour of the German people and the German people were clearly seeking a saviour at that time in history. It is a stark illustration of what can happen when we are collectively asleep (soulfully and spiritually).

Rather than working with the adversarial challenges in his life, Hitler fully embraced the adversary (Satan), destroying the lives of millions. It is a warning to humanity about the need to cultivate a transformative relationship between the *shadow* and the *sacred* in our Earthly activities and individuation. What we do every day matters enormously to our fate, and also to the fate of the world, as every action reverberates, not only in consensus reality, but also across time and space. The following dream illustrates the mysterious workings of an interconnected universe. Esther Robb was a prisoner in the Nazi concentration camp at Sobibor in the Second World War, and along with other inmates had decided to escape. The night before the breakout Esther had a dream of her mother, from whom she had been separated after her internment. But in the dream her mother knew she was planning to escape, and showed Esther an unusual looking barn. She told her daughter that she must find this place, and that she would be safe there. Although many of the escapees were killed in their bid for freedom, Esther managed to evade capture. Wounded and hungry, she spent days hiding and walking, until one day she miraculously saw the barn that her mother had shown her in the dream. She entered the wooden structure and to her utter amazement she found her brother hiding in the barn. Esther had presumed that the Nazis had killed him, but he had also managed to escape. The brother and sister spent nine months hiding in the barn, cared for by the farmer who brought them food and drink daily.[23]

The young woman presumably trusted the dream, because a central figure in it was her mother. Nobody knows how such intelligent actions work in the spiritual world of the imaginal realm, but we know that such occurrences happen. Carl Jung noted our powerful connection to the imaginal and the world of the psyche, and how it graces us with insights and inspiration to guide us. Indeed, it opens up opportunities for a closer connection to the divine that Henry Corbin[21] called the *mundus imaginalis*, where we encounter an *active intelligence* that is the *angel of humanity*.[18] This angel-intelligence is what can manifest when we work with the raw soulful potential of our *daimonic fate*, which then seeds transformations in consciousness, enabling our *angelic destiny* to flourish through intelligent and imaginative reflections and actions. Henry Corbin[18] suggests that when this *angel-intelligence* is awakened at the highest level, it is akin to a connection with the *Holy Spirit*, which brings revelatory knowledge. It is our choice (*free will*) to create a responsible relationship to the divine and become co-creators in working to fulfil the sacrament of our personal and transpersonal destinies. Such shifts are frequently found in the transformational narratives of people who have encountered NDEs.

The world we live in today has become highly sceptical of daimons and angels and other sacred phenomena, which cannot be proven by science. For example, there are some scientists who say that advances in neuroscience are making the idea and existence of spirits and souls seem ridiculous (scientism). They suggest that the next scientific frontier for humanity will require a new understanding of our identity, which will include debunking the *false myths* that have misled and trivialised our species.[24] Again, scientism's intolerance of a spiritual reality shows complete ignorance of our sacred heritage. Their reductionist dogma is attempting to align humanity with a factual understanding of life, based on material evidence. This is why the *lived experiences* of people's consensus and non-consensus spiritual realities need to be communicated, heard and taken seriously. The intolerant and overpowering mindset of scientism only forces people into silence. John Geiger[25] has investigated the subject of angels and he found that people's experiences of being helped by 'spirits' usually occurred in times of danger or stress. Geiger speculates that such experiences could be explained by neuroscience, when the right hemisphere of the brain (imaginative and creative responses) can activate, or switch on, an 'angel effect'. He argues that the rising numbers of Americans who are reporting angel experiences could be accounted for by a world that is increasingly crisis ridden. The question is, are angels exclusively brain-based phenomena, or do they represent a subtle level of reality?

Daimonic and angelic vibrations

I greatly admire former Apollo 14 astronaut and champion of consciousness studies Edgar Mitchell,[26] but he says that if *angels* or *beings of light* existed they would emit such high frequency energy levels that would be equal to the destructive power of a nuclear reactor. His statement underlines a cultural conundrum with regards to angels, and he favours explanations that situate such phenomena in a natural context, as opposed to the supernatural. We cannot prove that angels exist, but despite our best efforts to disprove them, they continue to manifest in people's lives, as they have done for thousands of years. Mitchell suggests that such realms, entities or energies are best explained as *metaphors*, which represent shared human experiences. However, I suggest that *myth* and *metaphor* are probably the best way we can communicate about spiritual phenomena that are real and difficult to prove. I am reminded of the energy sources in Tibetan monks (see Chapter One), who are able to generate inner heat, or *gTum-Mo*, through the activation of subtle body energies linked to tantric meditation practices. There is no mainstream physiological explanation for the levels of intense heat being generated by these meditation practitioners. Yet tantric methods are embedded in a cosmology, which is full of supernatural entities (Dakinis etc.). Similarly, in the near-death experience, people report colours unseen before, or they mention encounters with a pure white light (inclusive of flecks of gold),[27] which is different from any light experienced in their Earthly existence. In addition, the Tibetan Buddhist practice of dying involves preparation to meet the experience of clear light, which connects to an enlightened mind.[28] Until we have proof of the contrary, I uphold the view that these reported experiences reveal a 'supernatural' living mystery, which is subtly enfolded within a natural order.

Tibetan Buddhist spiritual practices go beyond our current understanding of physical laws concerning the regulation of bodily temperatures, metabolic activity and divine light. These findings have been largely overlooked by mainstream Western scientists, despite them corresponding to a system of subtle energetic potential (Kundalini), which has been known and practised for thousands of years. Indeed, Henry Corbin[18] speaks about the *mystical physiology* of the *subtle body*, and how these 'organs' function in relation to psycho-spiritual determinants. Interestingly, Tantric practice includes a dynamic relationship with 'deities', which helps meditators activate energies in the subtle body. However, many Western materialists would probably agree with Yuval Harari[29] that spiritual entities such as angels do not exist. Matthew Fox[10] highlights the prejudice of reductionists (the scientific shadow e.g. scientism), who are only interested in shoring up a certain view of reality. Again, we come up against a materialist belief system that dismisses alternative ways of knowing when it meets phenomena that cannot be explained by its methods. Yet daimons, angels and other sacred entities exist in every religion in some form or other as devas, djin, sprites or kachinas etc.,[30] and this points to the angelic realm being part of a collective mythic actuality, which links to our shared human experience of the sacred.[19] As noted in Chapter One, the focus of scientism is concerned with material explanations, but not sacred experiences. Yet, as a species, we may be overlooking an important spiritual connection that could align us to a greater sense of imagination and incarnation.[31] The real folly is trying to appraise the angelic realm using a materialist and reductionist mindset.

The creative connection between the daimonic and angelic realms, via dream and visionary work, opens us up to an intuitive and instinctual life, providing a quality of intelligence that animates our relationship to life as a whole.[32] Lorna Byrne,[33] who has communicated with angels all of her life, says that religious differences are of no concern to the angels. She describes a conversation she had with the *Archangel Michael* who told her that fewer and fewer people are communicating with the angels, and as a consequence a vast number of these spirits are *unoccupied*. As an occupational therapist (who is also interested in the angelic), this statement caught my attention. As we've seen, people who report encounters with angels, or beings of light, are often given messages that they still have tasks to complete in their Earthly existence.[34] A productive relationship between the *soulful daimon* and the *spiritual angel* could help us meet and fulfil our fate and destiny. For example, I wrote about a Benedictine monk, Brother Ralph, in my book, *The Unselfish Spirit*, after speaking to him at length about the angel who visited him in his prison cell one night, whilst he was serving a fourteen-year sentence for armed robbery. The angel had such an incredible impact on Brother Ralph that he knew his vocation was to become a monk, which he duly became. Brother Ralph's profound transformational experience one night in prison was just as dramatic as the one St Paul had on the road to Damascus. I am in no doubt that such spiritual forces are trying to guide us.

Journalist Pierre Jovanovic[34] became interested in angels after a *life or death* experience that he could not explain. He was driving along a highway in North

America, when, without any thoughts guiding his actions, he unexpectedly flung himself to one side of the car whilst a bullet simultaneously smashed through the windscreen and hit the spot where he had previously been sitting. When the police arrived at the scene Jovanovic was told that random sniper fire was a reasonably common occurrence in this particular area; however, the journalist's intuitive, instinctive or reactive response could not be explained. This mystery led him to investigate those lifesaving moments that are prompted by warnings, hunches, inner voices, dreams and premonitions, as well as meaningful coincidences that manifest unexpectedly, and which change the course of life events. Anthony Peake[20] reports how in 1956, W.E. Cox investigated 28 train accidents, comparing the number of passengers on the day of the crash to the volume of travellers on the six days that preceded the catastrophe. For example, one of the calculations he made (reported by Peake) was based on an accident that happened on 15th June 1952, where there was an 84% drop in the numbers of passengers travelling on the day of the train crash.

It is up to us if we wish to listen to these instinctive and intuitive experiences.[35] However, they may not conform to our cultural expectations. For example, Robert Moss[36] reports on an indigenous person who dreamt of their ancestors, and was surprised to find they were accompanied by angels and the figure of Jesus, who went on to reveal sacred land and places of power. The dreamer was shown places where the ancestors had previously performed ceremonial rites. This is a lovely example of how spiritual guides from mixed traditions function in the dreamtime, where they convey important information and ancestral knowledge. Clearly, there are no ideological divisions in the realm of the spirit. Perhaps we could break through our collective scepticism if we understood that the angelic realm could inspire us to live good lives and work for the greater good. It is a spiritual reality, one that is subtle and mostly hidden, but the impressive lives of spiritual practitioners like the Saints reveal the importance of such a sacred reality.[37]

The hidden work

In 1947 a young, newly ordained priest made a visit to the monastery of Franciscan Friar Padre Pio, with the intention of making a confession to this humble monk, who incidentally had attracted much interest from around the world after the stigmata, the wounds of Christ, appeared on his body at the start of his sacred vocation (supernatural occurence?). These signs remained with him for the rest of his life, only disappearing when he died. In the confession, which is a solemn and sacramental rite, Padre Pio told the newly ordained priest, Karol Wojtyla, that he would one day be Pope. Not only did the young priest become Pope John Paul II, the pontiff went on to canonise the deceased Padre Pio, 50 years later.[34] Saint Pio was blessed with the ability to read souls, as well as being able to bi-locate (manifest in spirit to assist other souls worldwide). Miracles have been reported through his works, and Jovanovic tells us that Saint Pio spoke and prayed to his guardian angel every day of his life. One day he was in the middle of listening to the solemn confession of another priest, when he suddenly rebuked the priest. Saint Pio informed the priest that he could see his guardian angel standing directly behind him and protecting him, and he urged the priest to *pray heartily* to his sacred guardian. Working with our guardian angels provides us with spiritual strength, as it did for Saint Pio who endured repeated attacks by negative spiritual entities night after night.[34] The case of Saint Pio echoes the trials and tests endured by the Old Testament character, Job, who grew spiritually wiser through the adverse encounters he endured. Indeed, spiritual practice is about engaging our full human potential, finding and fulfilling our life-tasks as we grow in trust. Then we commit to manifesting a more loving, compassionate and dedicated existence, which is directed towards working for the greater good in our everyday ways of doing.[32]

Physician Elizabeth Kubler-Ross was another shining example of a person with an active relationship with her guardian angel.[34] She emphasised one of the key messages that is at the heart of this chapter, that we all have a central task to fulfil in this life, as well to grow in love, wisdom and compassion. In her view, our lives should be lived as a prayer, which in her own life she expressed as a physician, and in her everyday activities, such as gardening or cooking. Indeed, it reiterates the point that through our everyday activities we can cultivate our rich psycho-spiritual potential for wholeness,[1] where we grow through experiences of awe, compassion, humility and gratitude. It underlines how our deep sense of vocation in life is activated in the soul,[38] and it is here that our *daimonic fate* is found through the expression of our true character, which is then actualised in everyday life as *angelic destiny*. James Hillman[38] uses the terms fate, destiny, and character in interchangeable ways, which seems to emphasise that '*whom*' *we become* in life is a matter of '*how*' we heed the call of the soul. It is where we embrace the challenge of finding out *what we are meant to be doing in life*, and how we give expression to our spiritual potential. Jungian analyst John Sanford[39] speaks about the courage and humility needed to work with one's fate, especially when the depth of our character begins to emerge.

The Greek word for character, *xaractēr*, means an imprint or stamp.[39] It indicates that character not only emerges through our deeds and actions[40] but also in our intentions in our ways of living. It suggests we need to be proficient in working with the instinctual as well as the rational.[41] In the early 1970s at a time when computers were in their infancy Jacob Bronowski[42] wrote a book, *The Ascent of Man*, where he describes human beings as a blend of *animal* and *angel*, which beautifully captures the material and spiritual realities of who we are as a species. In the book, Bronowski compares the human imagination to a "telescope in time", and yet even his extensive understanding of human evolution and the rise of our high-tech nous could not have foreseen that our species is entertaining ideas about becoming part *android*. The prospect of humanity drifting into an era of *Homo roboticus* challenges our ideas of developing character. Robotic technologies are confronting us with the reality of *cyborg innovations*, which could diminish our interest in *spiritual initiations*. These are set to be the sorts of tensions in our high-tech world, where our psycho-spiritual evolution is in danger of being eroded, rather than incorporated in our lives. Robotic technology could well propel us into an era where we become a blend of *animal* and *android*. Where this leaves our human-sacred potential, as a blend of *animal* and *angel*, is a troubling question.

The angelic realm is an ancient spiritual reality that cannot be airbrushed out of the human story, despite the attempts of scientism. We should not overlook the fact that angels have sparked the human imagination across the ages and across cultures,[43] and it happens because they and we are connected via the imaginal realm. The mythic actuality of angels may have a vital role to play in counterbalancing humanity's unconscious drift into a new dimension of machine-mindedness, one that we are currently ill prepared to face. In the coming years our imaginative lives will be increasingly challenged to understand the interplay of opposites that are at work in the world, such as good-bad, light-dark, placebo-nocebo, animal-angel, and animal-android, etc. These dualities are real and everpresent forces that are unconsciously being acted out daily. Matthew Fox and Rupert Sheldrake[44] have said in their book, *The Physics of Angels*, that each action we take cannot be undone, and everything we do contributes to a world of creative and destructive tendencies, where heaven and hell are not some far-off place; rather they become the mythic actuality of life itself. And so, in this time of global crisis, a mythic understanding of the value of *daimonic fate* and *angelic destiny* is a way of aligning our soulful and spiritual energies and actions in the service of the greater good. Yet we would be unwise to ignore the shadow side of the angelic, which is personified in the greed, materialism, and self-aggrandisement of the fallen angel Lucifer, who represents the misuse of power and knowledge, especially when they are aligned with our base instincts and behaviours of envy and hate, which are driven by arrogance and acquisitiveness. And so, the task working to bring forth character through *daimonic fate* and *angelic destiny* means developing qualities, such as wisdom, moral imagination, intellect, intuition, good heartedness, justice, service and love, where our lives are infused with spiritual energy and values.[44] We need to be bold in acknowledging the hidden world of subtle energies, daimons and angels.

US Senator Mark Kirk had an encounter with angels after experiencing a severe stroke and a near-death experience. He saw three angels by the side of his bed and they offered to take him with them, but he said he wanted to remain on Earth. After the event, the senator's spiritual faith deepened, but the reporter who wrote the article interpreted the angelic encounter as the result of oxygen deprivation on brain function.[45] This is the heart-sinking legacy of scientism.

We have to ask ourselves, are spiritually motivating encounters with angels or the supernatural only the result of an oxygen-deprived brain? One thing is certain: revelations from the imaginal realm present us with all manner of difficulties, especially if we are looking for hard evidence. For example, we learn that the 16th President of the United States of America and his wife Mary were interested in metaphysics, and attended séances, but they kept their interest in such matters discreet. There is controversy about the extent of President Abraham Lincoln's interest in the spirit world, but a Masters thesis on the subject points to evidence suggesting he was an active and willing participant.[46] The thesis also mentions a self-published book by Colonel Simon Kase, titled: *The Emancipation Proclamation, How, And By Whom It Was Given To President Lincoln In 1861*. Kase reports that psychic, Nettie Mainard, spoke to Lincoln and the angelic and supernatural information she shared with the President informed his conviction to abolish slavery. Whilst we shall never know the truth of this story, we would do well to keep an open mind about Lincoln's sensitivities to the imaginal realm, because the better-known dream he had foretelling his assassination did actually happen.[47] Again, was it oxygen deprivation that led President Lincoln to foresee how he was going to die? What if humanity were more attuned to the subtle workings of the imaginal realm? How would it change the way we live, if we woke up to the angelic as a source of guidance and inspiration? Such questions bring into focus the meaning of the emancipatory edge.

Angels of transformation

A very dear friend who I have known and respected for 25 years, who had an angelic experience that radically changed the course of his life, told the following story to me. He is a devoted family man and at the time of the following incident, he was working as a senior executive in a FTSE 100 company, and was taking a well-earned sailing holiday after negotiating a £1bn sales contract. Whilst on holiday he received a call informing him that his 83-year-old father had just been admitted to hospital with heart problems. Naturally, my friend cut short his holiday to be with his father, who had undergone two heart operations in an attempt to try and fit a stent. However, his condition had deteriorated and the family were preparing themselves for the worst. For the next five days and nights my friend spent all of his time at his father's bedside, and he described the experience as if he were "sailing at night". On the fifth day my friend spoke to his dad and they agreed that it would be good for him to travel home and see his wife and family, who lived 150 miles away. His father encouraged him to go home, but my friend said there was a palpable feeling of sadness in the room, and an unspoken understanding that they may not see each other again in this lifetime.

My friend went to a local car hire firm and picked up a vehicle to make the journey home, but before leaving, he made one more trip to the hospital to say goodbye to his mother and father. The final farewell was communicated in a fairly controlled way, with no mention of death or dying, but once again, a deep sense of emotion and pain pervaded the atmosphere in the room. As my friend was leaving the hospital room, he paused at the door, and turned for one last wave goodbye. My friend saw the resigned expression on his father's face, which was a clear acknowledgement that his son was leaving, but it was the look in his eyes that conveyed a deep longing that was beckoning him to stay, not only to be with him when he died, but also in eternity, like he was saying, "you can go, but I don't want you to go". My friend said the moment was completely openhearted, and the atmosphere was so powerful that all of his senses were fully focused and heightened. It was in this state of deep connection that my friend, who is not religious, saw two angels either side of his father. He could not believe what he had just seen, and he left the room in a somewhat bewildered state. Interestingly, people who experience near-death experiences have reported seeing angels after being resuscitated,[44] but in this instance, it was a family member who saw the angels around a dying relative.

He made his way to the car park and sat in the vehicle for a while to compose himself and to try and get his emotions in check before making the long journey home. As he left the hospital grounds he found himself snared in rush hour traffic, and all he could do was be patient. It was a short while later that he slowly approached a roundabout and was waiting for a car to pass, when for no reason, the other driver unleashed a barrage of abusive language, screaming at him and making threatening gestures. My friend recalls the other driver had demonic characteristics and his behaviours were full of hate. It was an inauspicious start to the journey that was expected to take four hours, but which became nine hours in the end, due to every road he took being blocked because of road works or excessive traffic. After 36 hours at home my friend was recalled to his father's bedside, being told he had only hours left, and he returned to the hospital (with his wife). His father passed away peacefully four days later.

My friend returned to his high-pressure job, but suddenly the work he had done for years, which he was very good at, no longer had any meaning for him and he started to question what he was doing with his life. He said that he wanted to live with more value. After three months he left his work, but the experience led to a breakdown, which eventually became a breakthrough, since over the course of a year he entered into a time of deep introspection, healing and rebuilding his life. It was a difficult time, and in the midst of the transformational process he was going through, he said it was as if he were seeing demons everywhere, in the form of callous attitudes and behaviours, as well as unnecessary environmental waste and disregard. It was a time of utter chaos for him, but as he worked through the process, he had a growing realisation that: "There is a choice: I can either see devils or angels". He also reflected on his own attitude towards life and how it had been corrected by death, after his experience of being so close to his father as he was dying, which had had a profound impact upon him. Today my friend works with young people and lives his life according to a set of core values; for example, in relationships he gives people respect, time, space and attention, as well as praise when he sees someone has done something that deserves positive feedback. In addition, his attitude also extends to caring for the environment.

This story is a wonderful example of how the choices we make can inspire us to awaken. My friend's experience of seeing angels at his father's deathbed informed his own symbolic death and renewal, as he shifted away from old patterns and attitudes that no longer served him. During his process of transformation (breakthrough rather than breakdown), he saw how attitudes and behaviours could be expressed demonically or angelically, and this realisation inspired him to live more congruently. He made a resolve to align his human potential to work for the greater good. The story chimes well with the work of Matthew Fox and Rupert Sheldrake[44] who speak about the "moral imagination", and how spiritual values can be inspired by the angelic.

The *mythic actuality* of an *angelic reality* challenges us to face our life-tasks, which has added potency in this time of global crisis. However, whilst the planetary crisis is amplifying our human struggles and conflicts, it also confronts us with spiritual opportunities to do the right thing and co-create a just world. If we enact such transformative possibilities, we are creating a sacramental vision that resonates energetically with the angelic.[44] Without such spiritual inspiration, what values will guide our actions for the greater good of humanity, other species and the planet? How will science inspire humanity to love and awaken our hearts? Which Randomised Control Studies will determine the next course of action for humanity to co-create a better world? Science has an important role in the creation of a productive future, yet we should not let *technicians* determine which aspects of our human heritage are the most important. The last 300 years of scientific exploration have led to some breath-taking discoveries (often revealed in dreams), but scientific knowledge and power have also contributed the means for evil to be enacted on a grand scale, for example, from the production of gas used in Nazi concentration camps (Zyklon B), to weapons of mass destruction, used in World War Two. We should be asking what myths are guiding the dogma of scientism and the maintenance of a one-dimensional technocracy, where along with creative innovations we also have growing levels of eco-destruction wrought by our industries.

Redeeming the soul, releasing the spirit

We need courage to question the possibility – that for all the cleverness in the world – humanity is not immune from slipping into a Faustian pact[44] in its pursuit of power and knowledge. As ever, the 'devil' is always in the detail; that is, if we care to look at the narratives that push the material dream of consumerism, or the lowbrow propaganda espoused by certain political parties in their quest for control. How we live in relation to fate, destiny and character is all a matter of myth, where the cultivation of deep stories can guide our actions. For example, I am sure we have all heard tales of redemption and inspiration that awaken our hearts and stir our souls, which are the kinds of shared stories we need in this time of global crisis. It is up to us to generate the narratives that will help us pull together and take affirmative action, in the knowledge that our collective efforts are reverberating positively in the world. It is a deep call to emancipatory action, inspiring us to raise our vibration and resonate with greater love and harmony in all that we do. We can no longer ignore the world 'out there', for it truly is 'in here'. Matthew Fox and Rupert Sheldrake[44] reflect on the 12th century mystic, Hildegard of Bingen, who spoke about the song of angels being sung throughout the cosmos, connecting us to a cosmic resonance and vibration. Such descriptions chime with indigenous wisdom, where myths of *spirits* and *songs* help people connect deeply with nature. If we cultivated the mythic actualities of our soulful potential (as *daimonic fate*) and spiritual awakening (as *angelic destiny*), we may be able to find the 'songs' that animate our existence and raise our collective vibrations in our ways of living and loving. As we've seen, near-death experiences and the life review show how our actions reverberate powerfully in the lives of others and the world, which is the seedbed of our karmic destiny. If we regarded what we do in the world as *daimonic fate* and *angelic destiny*, we could create a collective mythic actuality for the expression of our subtle energies to help co-create an improved and sustainable future.

The *spiritual power of doing* in the awakening of collective consciousness requires us to work deeply and soulfully on our paths of individuation (*daimonic fate*), as well as working together, by pooling our heart-energies, talents, skills, gifts and passions as spiritual expression (*angelic destiny*). This inner work and outer work could connect to the angel of the Earth, *Jimazen*,[48] as world work. Imagine if a critical mass of people connected their dreams, intentions, transformational energies, prayers and actions to *Jimazen*. It would harness the soulful work done by each of us (*daimonic fate*), with our spiritual potential (*angelic destiny*), to consider the Earth (Gaia) as sacred, and us as spiritual and planetary citizens. When we live soulful and spiritual lives in the world, our actions reverberate like we are numinous actors who also become numinous attractors in the sacred web of life. Working imaginatively with our visionary potential means our life energies can become transformative actions, and we become part of a co-creative force in our everyday lives (doing and being). As Debbie Ford[49] once said, our sense of service in the world is not helped if we play it small. I would add our sense of service is compromised if we are cut off from the soul and spirit that has guided our species in incalculable ways for millennia. This is a time for deep reflection and bold action, based on meeting our *daimonic fate* and expressing our *angelic destiny*. It involves participating in a living myth, one that is at the heart of a living mystery in an ever-unfolding cosmos. These mythic actualities bring us to the emancipatory edge of the sacred, where we are inspired to co-create the Transformocene Age.

Exercise: Daimonic fate and angelic destiny

- Refer back to Table 1 in this chapter and read all the columns and boxes.

- Each day make a commitment to explore one column (and all the boxes in that particular column), starting from the column on the left.

- Each day reflect on the written content in the boxes for the particular column you are focusing on.
  - How does the written content in the boxes inspire you to explore further the particular issues that are unique to your calling, character, and destiny?

- At the end of the seventh day reflect on how your intentions and actions are aligning with the co-creation of an improved and sustainable future.

The complementary worldviews of science and spirituality are more likely
to be understood once we have explored the shadows that divide them.
One obstacle to ecology of wholeness is the shadow bypass we call Woo Woo.

CHAPTER TWELVE

The Spiritual Art of Wu Wu

Overview

In this chapter I explore how the ecology movement could be at the leading edge of the Transformocene, but for this to happen more work needs to be done to tackle the split between science and spirituality. I argue that the hostile rhetoric from some scientism-minded people in the ecology movement towards those who are seeking to integrate spirituality is nothing more than a microcosm of what is happening in our social and institutional lives. I point out that spiritual and transpersonal traditions have been marginalised in society, at great cost to our species' development. I argue that the accusation of so-called '*Woo Woo*' towards spiritual and transpersonal realities is simply the shadow side of a culture of scientism at work. Yet, science and spirituality could act as complementary ways of knowing to assist us in deepening our relationship to the Earth and all life, leading to new understandings and patterns for living. Spirituality is subtle, energetic and experiential, whereas science explores, elucidates and explains; yet both require discipline and discernment. The reality of the global crisis means this is not a time to fragment into ideological squabbles. The Transformocene requires that we engage with an emancipatory edge, where we draw on the wisdom from the imaginal realm, coupled to holistic science.

From Woo Woo to Wu Wu

When *The Unselfish Spirit* was published in 2014, I heard through my networks that a fairly well-known person in the ecological movement had described my work as *Woo Woo*, which was a convenient way of categorising my work as either a flight of fantasy, or fake and flaky. Interestingly, my book was drawn on decades of inner work, years of formal training as a therapist, academic and coach, as well as research drawn from 20 years of writing peer-reviewed articles on the subject, including insights from my doctoral thesis. As an academic I have learnt to value well-crafted criticism, which accompanies the process of peer-review, and more often than not, improves an article prior to its publication. But I have come to the conclusion that the term *Woo Woo* is a short cut, used to keep mysticism and spirituality at the margins of a hyper-rational consensus reality. Such attitudes are more closely aligned with the dogma of scientism (see Chapter One). However, there are opportunities for science and mysticism to work much more productively together.

I have spent my professional career working in the context of the medical sciences. When I initially trained as an occupational therapist in the National Health Service (NHS), the subject of spirituality was not taken very seriously. From the very start of my career I published scholarly and research articles on spirituality and health (including case studies), but the subject was peripheral in the context of medical care. However, health practitioners today are aware of the tangible benefits that spirituality can bring to people's health, well-being, and recovery, which is not only evidence-based; it is now enshrined in the UK *Department of Health* policies, where all professionals working in the medical field are expected to have competencies in working with spirituality. It is a subject that I continue to teach in the *School of Health Sciences* at my local university. Conversely, there are no peer-reviewed articles in support of *Woo Woo*, which should alert us to the fact that we are dealing with an opinion, or worse, a shadow projection. This is not surprising as the shadow is so pervasive in the modern world and remains largely unaddressed in our collective lives. The neglected shadow is at the heart of humanity's adaptive potential at this time, and therefore it is no surprise that it exists in the ecological movement, especially in the *shady projections* of scientism.

The ecological movement has a great opportunity to work on the shadow projections that are flickering between secular scientism and spirituality. It could act as a microcosm for doing shadow work in the wider collective, and perhaps activate the transformative potential that is waiting to happen in the world at this time. How the ecological movement deals with the *shadow bypass* of *Woo Woo* could be a litmus test for society as a whole. Equating spirituality with *Woo Woo* comes from the reductionism advocated by scientism, which is shoring up an outmoded mindset. But it is worth remembering Jung's advice that 80% of the shadow is pure gold. If well-intentioned and good-hearted people in the ecological movement cannot reclaim and integrate shadow projections to help find a way forward (between rational science and spirituality), then what possibilities are there in the world at large? A classic example where the shadow of scientism is aligned with mainstream consciousness is found in cases where people experiencing life-transforming spiritual crisis are sectioned in psychiatric hospitals. Yet research shows that people transitioning through spiritual emergencies are having deep transformative encounters, where they experience life as an interconnected and ecological whole.[1] Referring to such experiences as *Woo Woo* is supporting a one-dimensional system that is complicit in labelling and oppressing our collective transpersonal potential in pathological ways. The polarity between scientism and spirituality presents us with an opportunity, a chance to find a way to draw on the best of both worlds. A deeper look at *Woo Woo* could lead to a surprising philosophical shift, one that points to a deeper integration of spirituality and science in the ecological movement.

Bron Taylor's[2] book *Dark Green Religion* makes a clear distinction between *Gaian spirituality*, which is mostly aligned with pantheism, and a metaphysics that is predominantly holistic and New Age. In contrast, *Gaian naturalism* is more aligned with mainstream science, as a way of relating to awe and wonder in the natural world. As well as the two Gaian perspectives above, Taylor notes there have also been strong eco-spiritual developments by prominent figures in the counterculture. For example, individuals who helped evolve transpersonal psychology (e.g. Stan Grof, Ralph Metzner, etc.) are also aligned with new paradigm science, as mentioned in the chapter 'Three Propositions for Deeper Living'. We need people to join together in a spirit of openness, to learn from one another about the various worldviews that unite and divide us,[3] where we can cultivate opportunities to enhance our awareness for a new vision of wholeness. This point will be discussed in relation to developments in the field of permaculture.

The philosophy of permaculture provides us with a helpful theoretical platform, revealing how a shadow bypass is being played out between supporters of a scientism, and advocates of spirituality. For example, one website I found supports a secular and scientific understanding of permaculture, expressing a concern about the movement being influenced by New Age spirituality (Woo Woo), which peddles all manner of 'snake oil'.[4] Once again, the patriarchal shadow side of scientism is evident, referring to the serpent as maligned and deviant, rather than a symbol of transformation (sacred feminine). However, the same website helpfully highlights the value of many permaculture design courses, which draw upon Abraham Maslow's model, *Hierarchy of Need*. Interestingly, I have written extensively about Maslow's work and how it contributed to the evolution of transpersonal psychology, which informed my research into human occupation and self-actualisation.[1] The transpersonal paradigm evolved through the efforts of highly qualified professionals and researchers who realised that it was self-limiting to ignore the full spectrum of human experiences and potential, which includes altered and expanded states of consciousness, meditation, mysticism, the sacred feminine, dream work and other spiritual phenomena.

The evolution of the transpersonal paradigm alerted modern humans to the reality that we live in an interconnected cosmos, where synergies between experiences in a world 'out there' have resonances with states of consciousness 'in here'. In this way, a transpersonal perspective has a valuable role to play in evolving our human consciousness to tackle the ecological crisis.[5] For example, the field-like experiences of a wider transpersonal consciousness resonate with the work of Arne Naess and his philosophy of *deep ecology*. It suggests that *deep ecology* needs a *deep self*, based on the understanding that if humanity had a more expansive self-connection to life, it would engender a more protective and caring stance towards the natural world.[6] Thus, transpersonal consciousness brings forth greater potential for humanity to engage in transformative actions, which are central to our evolutionary and co-creative potential, enacted through a process of living with depth (doing and being). This exemplifies the idea: *what we do to the world, we do to others, and to ourselves.*[1] We cannot underestimate the importance of what it means to live in an interconnected world, which calls for an openness to the transformative meanings found in synchronous experiences.

When I work with people I always take the position that I am entering their dream world, which means I am open to local and non-local experiences, as well as ordinary, non-ordinary and extra-ordinary happenings. The following story is a touching example of how synchronicities arrive unexpectedly, and yet they seem to go to the very heart of what is happening in our lives. The vignette also reveals how nature plays a part in our healing experiences.

Sleeping beauty

I was working with a woman in a secluded part of huge woodland, on an old wound that had been with her since she was a young girl. She said: "I don't want to die without having sorted this issue." The work included finding a way of letting go of old defences, represented by a dense and thorny thicket, which reminded us of the fairy story, Sleeping Beauty. It was evident that these old defences were no longer useful, as she contemplated new patterns and opportunities for living soulfully and in wholeness. The session was going well, but we both realised that something was inhibiting the work from going further. I suggested that she let nature 'flirt' with her and show us a spot that would represent the blockage. She saw a small and almost dead rhododendron trunk, which had a small clump of new leaves growing on it. As we stood looking at it, the woman noticed a small white feather meshed around one of the new leaves (I thought angel, but this is not her belief). She was dreaming into the symbolic meaning of the rhododendron leaves, which held two meanings for her: the dead wood (trunk) and the new life (leaves). By this time we had been in the woods for about 45 minutes uninterrupted, when suddenly a group of about 15 children arrived with their teachers on a nature walk. They were about the same age as the woman had been when she was traumatised as a young girl. What happened next was quite uncanny.

The children enthusiastically gathered around the rhododendron and asked what we were doing. I showed them the white feather stuck to the budding leaves and told them we were wondering why it was there. I asked them if they had any ideas. Immediately a flurry of hands shot into the air, with the children eager to share their insights. There were some wonderful contributions. One child said, "It means it's going to burst into lots of colours"; this wonderful comment resonated with the woman's re-emergent interest in art, and her re-discovery of using a palette of expressive colours. Another child said: "The feather is keeping the leaf warm", and curiously, one of the children said: "It means it's going to die". This last comment had quite an impact on me, as I strongly believe that the process of individuation is like a symbolic death of the old, so that the new can be born. The children's appearance at that moment and their contribution to the woman's process was stunning. I am always staggered when synchronicities like this happen. The woman reflected on this experience and said: "I was drawn to the tiny white feather that seemed to have woven itself in and around the leaf bud.

When the children arrived, their energy and enthusiasm confirmed what I had been feeling. I saw that my protective defences were like the feather, but its job had been done. As the new growth pushed through and the leaves unfurled, it would naturally blow away. I felt a strong re-connection to my natural creativity, which I have neglected over the years, but in the work I experienced it as a powerful life force within me."

In a follow-up session the woman spoke about having a difficulty with another family member who had expressed anger at her, which was upsetting and emotionally taxing. It became clear that due to her personal history, she had a tendency to avoid conflict. We worked on her ability to find a way to approach the relationship issue, so that she could communicate in a heartfelt way with the family member, whilst also supporting her own needs. As we worked, the woman began to feel quite emotional and said it felt like something was dragging down on her heart. I suggested that we represent the 'symptom maker' and she visualised this sensation of being dragged down as a hunched and hooded bitter old woman. I had an intuitive urge to remind her of the previous session, where 'Sleeping Beauty' was enclosed in a dense thicket (after a spell had been cast upon her). Suddenly the work became mythical and we agreed that I would play the role of her heart, and she would play the old woman (who in the fairy tale had also been the jealous queen). I knelt on the floor and presented my arm, asking, "See what it's like being the old bitter woman who is pulling your heart and dragging it down". She took hold of my outstretched arm and started pulling it. We interacted for a while, with me (her heart) protesting about being dragged down. The woman wondered what was going on, and I encouraged her to keep pulling, whilst focusing on her reactions to the experience. Suddenly, a shift happened and she said: "Wow, I had a feeling in my stomach like a bird being let out of a cage." She said her heart felt lighter and her body was shimmering with white and gold. She also reported a sense of feeling energetically taller. It was a numinous moment, where an archetypal story had come alive.

The next day she sent me a text saying that she had had a conversation with her relative, which had gone reasonably well. She also sent me a picture of a cactus in her home (protective thorns), which had synchronously flowered for the first time on the day we worked with the pulling sensation in her heart (flowering of new life and potential). Sleeping Beauty had awoken. She recounted to me afterwards: "The experience of being unburdened and opening up (the bird released), which happened through the mythical work, felt like the dense protective thicket around me had been cleared and I was free and unafraid to express my feelings. Later that evening I noticed that a single yellow flower had bloomed on the cactus plant on our kitchen windowsill. I felt the flower had been waiting for the right time to emerge, like the truth in my heart."

The work with the woman was deeply sensitive and it touched into a part of her personal history, which had dominated her life for too long. The emphasis of the work was to support her to break free from her childhood trauma. Even if I had the power to conjure up something that would have been helpful to the woman, I doubt whether I would have thought about 15 children joining our session and enthusiastically offering their wonderful energy, imaginations and insights. Of course, they did not know the real context of what we were working on, but that's not the issue (or maybe deep down they did – who knows?). The children were an amplification of the woman's inner process, and their joyful contribution was all the magic that was needed to confirm a liberating moment. Her process of growth is perfectly symbolised by the mythic story of Sleeping Beauty, and the synchronous flowering of the thorny cactus in her kitchen confirmed to her that transformation and emancipation are connected to imaginal possibilities and her lived potential.

We live in a world where we are all *occupationally entangled*, which means *what we do* in life has resonance and also reverberates in a *non-local* universe. It will be a revolutionary step for humanity to embrace the idea that the ways in which we are occupied in our everyday lives, physically, psychologically, socially, spiritually and ecologically can have an impact that goes beyond the local *time* and *space* where the actions took place.[6] The children turning up in the woods at just the right moment shows me that we are more connected than we know. It challenges us to wake up to the ethical and moral implications of our actions. It means training ourselves to become more conscious of how our actions connect to the lives of others. I would also add that the flowering cactus was highly symbolic of how the natural world can resonate with us (synchronistically) when we connect with our deeper nature.

The spirit in the Tao

A key message in my book, *The Unselfish Spirit* was 'we do, therefore we evolve' and this includes our spiritual development. It goes to the very heart of how we consider our human potential, and our growth and development as transpersonal beings. It underscores the importance of cultivating an intimate relationship with a universe as a whole, which is reflected through us, in our imaginations and actions,[7] inspiring us to evolve a greater eco-connection to life. As Ram Dass[8] says, all that we do is a mirror, which reflects back to us how evolved our consciousness is. If we consider our place in the natural world, we need to learn more about how we are not separate from nature. Indeed, we are interwoven with all life, which underscores the importance of a transpersonal perspective, revealing how we are part of a co-creative universe. The question then becomes, how can our co-creative efforts best contribute towards a sustainable and improved future? It is here that science and spirituality can work together, as advocated in the systems perspective discussed in Chapter One, where technological progress can be blended and balanced by spiritual growth and development.[9] The integration of systems science and spirituality is a first step to fostering a deeper and more holistic connection to tackling the global crisis before us. Indeed, the state of the planet will undoubtedly force humanity into new ways of thinking and acting, which includes a spiritual perspective.[10] However, it is my contention that systems thinking does not have a robust enough understanding of the *depth approaches* associated with the imaginal realm at this time. But we have the means to develop such links, particularly in disciplines like permaculture.

In permaculture we find ideas that are progressive and inclusive in terms of integrating systems approaches, spirituality, as well as learning from our ancestors,[11] which points to a guiding philosophy that is sensitive and understands the importance of interconnectivity. The co-founders of permaculture, Bill Mollison and David Holmgren, introduced ideas from indigenous cultures into their ways of understanding, observing, and working with the natural world.[12] In this way, it is only right and fair that the wisdom of indigenous cultures is honoured for the knowledge they have preserved, which is steeped in myth, spirituality and shamanic practices.[13] Moreover, in his *A Designer's Manual*, Mollison speaks about the resonances of *Taoism* in permaculture philosophy.[10] Taoism is a tradition that is deeply connected to esotericism. For example, in the commentary of the *Wen-Tzu* by the Taoist Sage Lao Tzu, he reveals his teachings on *Understanding the Mysteries*, which extol the virtues of adepts co-joining *Earthly* energies to a *Heavenly* mind, where inner nature merges with a light that is spiritual.[14] Joseph Campbell[15] says that *Taoism*, like many other Eastern traditions, helps people to develop a connection between a cosmic mystery and a mystery in our being.

It is through such *Taoist* links that the reductionist concept of *Woo Woo* could be transformed into a more holistic and credible philosophy of 'Wu Wu'. This is an issue that I discussed at the 2015 International Hay Festival of Literature when I was interviewed about my book, *The Unselfish Spirit*. I suggested that the ancient Chinese philosophy and *nature spirituality* of *Taoism* provide us with two interconnecting processes: *Wu Chi* points to a non-dual cosmos, a universe of *formlessness*, which also gives rise to *form*. For example, the unmanifest field of *Wu Chi* is where the opposites of yin-yang arise. We can align with this life force (Chi) through *Wu Wei*, where our ways of *doing* are an expression of action with *least effort*. In this way, 'Wu Wu' leads to a dynamic equilibrium between stillness and movement, where we are connected in wholeness in our ways of doing-being. It also brings a connection between Heaven-Earth. In addition, anyone reasonably acquainted with *Taoist* literature, such as the *I-Ching*, will know that in this philosophy there is a *Spirit* at work in nature.

I have been using the *I-Ching* as a means of spiritual reflection since 1984 and I have kept a record of all the times I have used it (except for the first time). This ancient *Taoist* text provides a symbolic connection to the imaginal realm, which inspires the human imagination to reflect on the cultivation of wisdom and a relationship to the spirit and the natural world. During a long process of working through a spiritual crisis, I was weary and struggling to cope with the unconscious forces that were activated within me. I consulted the I-Ching in the hope of gaining some inspiration to help me reflect on my desperate predicament. It was a time when I was very vulnerable and not long after a period when I had contemplated suicide. I used the three-coin method, where they are thrown together six times, and each coin will either land yang or yin side up. Each time I threw the coins all of them landed yang side up. I suspect the chances of throwing three coins, six times in succession, and getting heads every time (yang) would be quite rare. But, as I found out, the synchronistic guidance from the I-Ching was profound.

It transpired that the coins led to two readings (hexagrams) from sixty-four possibilities. The first reading was number one, *Creativity* (masculine, Heaven and yang), and the *moving lines* from the first hexagram led to the next hexagram, which was number two, *Receptivity* (feminine, Earth and yin). It was such a profound and synchronous reading that it led me to reflect on the spiritual potential I was seeking to integrate in my life. I was in quite a fragmented state, due to the impact of the spiritual crisis, but the I-Ching provided me with a way of envisioning a path of recovery and wholeness. It pointed to interplay between Heaven-Earth; masculine-feminine; creativity-receptivity etc. It instilled a deep sense of hope within me about the possibilities of becoming more aligned to wholeness, which enabled me to trust the path into the unknown that I was taking. It provided me with a meaningful connection to the imaginal realm, in that it helped me understand how we can be guided spiritually, via synchronous experiences, which bring a deeper sense of trust and connectedness to the process of recovering wholeness. It was a tipping point where I began to believe I could find a way through the chaos I was experiencing. It was a sort of confirmation to make room for the spirit, so that it can help. It is through the I-Ching that I had my early intimations about what it means to co-create and co-evolve with spirit. I learnt a valuable lesson about the real value of *Wu Wu* in the midst of a life and death struggle.

It is my firm belief that the next frontier in consciousness is the *emancipation of the human imagination*,[1] which connects to spiritual truths and inspires our actions to live with wisdom, compassion and intelligence. It means keeping an open mind, rather than dismissing spiritual phenomena as *Woo Woo*, or 'snake oil'. If we had an open mind, we might consider the *wisdom in the serpent*, as the ancients did. The story of mathematician Srinivasa Ramunjan (see Chapter Four) is a beautiful illustration of how the divine world brings knowledge to humanity. He spoke about how the Hindu Goddess Namagiri Lakshmi provided him with visions of mathematical knowledge, which inspired his work, and he felt that his vocation in life was to authenticate the mathematical formulas given to him. It was not only a vocation; it was a form of devotion, as if he were contemplating the face of God. His work was so ahead of its time. It powered disciplines such as artificial intelligence and astrophysics in the 1990s, which started to come to prominence 50 years after he had died.[16]

It comes as no surprise that in Hindu mythology the Goddess Lakshmi sits near the Hindu God Vishnu, who lies on the Divine Serpent *Adishesha*, who was present when the universe was created. Once again we find a mythical link to visionary revelations, which underlines the rich connection to the imaginal realm, where – as Joseph Campbell stated – the *manifest* world interacts with the *unmanifest.*[17] The materialist mindset that cries *Woo Woo* and 'snake oil' has no answers to how such mysterious ground breaking phenomena work, let alone how the imaginal realm acts as a powerful force for transformation in our lives. The story of Srinivasa Ramunjan is inspirational in the way he was devoted to the spirit, which he served, and in a reciprocal way, it helped him in his scientific endeavours. Such devotion is also a common feature in the lives of authentic spiritual practitioners. The following story reflects the gentleness and humility of a Benedictine monk, Brother Herbert, who lives and breathes spirituality. It is in the subtleness of his lived presence where he conveys a depth of kindness, which is the fruit of his spiritual practice. It is in the life of such a gentle soul that I see how simplicity and spirituality are vital to the emergence of the Transformocene.

The spiritual vocation of Brother Herbert Kaden

It is a privilege to be able to tell the story of a dear friend and Benedictine monk, Brother Herbert Kaden. When I first met him near the end of the 1990s, I had no idea that this peaceful monk had been through such extreme situations in his life. The following account is based on his book[18] and also my interviews with him on 13th and 14th December 2014 at Turvey Abbey, near Bedford, UK. In the first interview Herbert said to me: "My path to becoming a monk was not straight. It was all in God's hands." He said that he had a sense of vocation, and that one day "I must become a monk".

Herbert was born in Dresden, East Germany on 25th January 1921. His family's spiritual heritage was mixed, and it included Judaism on his mother's side, but she was baptised in the Lutheran Church at the request of his father's family. This arrangement was agreeable to both families. When Herbert was a small boy his mother and father separated. Herbert had a happy childhood growing up in Germany. However, his life was about to be turned upside down with the rise of Adolf Hitler's National Socialist Party. There are few people alive today who can say they saw Hitler in real life, but Herbert recounts the first time he saw the Nazi leader in the summer of 1932 during a vacation in Bavaria with his mother. They were staying in a small apartment and Hitler's sister had a house close by. One day Herbert heard dogs barking and, intrigued by the commotion, he ran into the road to see Hitler's two German shepherd dogs attacking a Doberman owned by a local couple. Hitler emerged, shouting: "Tie up the dogs." Although young, Herbert was aware that Hitler was a troublemaker. He turned to his mother and said: "I cannot hate him." He saw Hitler at close quarters on two more occasions. In my interview with Herbert I asked him about his compassionate outlook and he said: "When I was a child I realised that cleverness was not as valuable as wisdom. Valuing wisdom has been important to me throughout my life."

Hitler's eventual rise to power led to the boycott of Jewish shops and businesses. The ever-growing presence of Hitler's Storm Troopers also resulted in the worsening treatment of Jewish people and other marginalised groups. In his book about his lived experience at this time, Herbert recounts how: "At school, even though I was 'half-Jewish' and only 'half-Aryan', I was treated very well and with great kindness, both by the teachers and the boys. It may seem surprising, but one of my best friends was actually a leader in the Hitler Youth Movement... His name was Kaspar Pfau." Before Easter in 1938 Herbert's uncle invited him and his mother to come for a visit to England, where he told them that they must make preparations to leave Germany. Around that time their landlord in Germany reluctantly gave them notice to leave their home by 1st June 1938. They came to England, but Herbert's mother had to return to Germany shortly afterwards so they could emigrate legally (it was still possible to do this, but only just). She also sold her parents' house (who had died of natural causes in 1934 and 1935 respectively). The Gestapo officer who was assigned to watch her movements every day illustrates the threatening atmosphere that Herbert's mother faced during her return to Germany. On the first day he came in uniform, saying "Heil Hitler", but on the following days he arrived in civilian clothes, saying "Good Morning". It was a tense time, but Herbert was delighted when his mother returned to England on 2nd July. She managed to organise a container with all their possessions, but she had no money. She left Germany with ten marks.

Herbert and his mother were extremely close. They also shared artistic and spiritual interests (his mother studied art). When I interviewed Herbert, he remembered his mother having a German copy of Lao Tse's book the *Tao Te Ching* when he was a little boy. He did not read this book until many years later, but at that time he remembered thinking something was missing in European life in terms of our connection to the sacred. He had a feeling for the spiritual side of life, and at the young age of sixteen, he had a sense that he would not get married. His monastic temperament was quietly forming within him. His interest in Eastern spirituality continued and when he was a bit older his mother sent him a copy of *Confucianism and Taoism*, from a series of books called *Wisdom of the East*. These Eastern ideas changed Herbert's life and he recounts that *The Way* (*The Tao that cannot be named*), as espoused by Lao Tse, helped him to understand the meaning of 'God'. Herbert's mother was also interested in the work of the German mystic from the Middle Ages, Meister Eckhart. During our interview Herbert said: "My mother was a mystic." Of course, one of the abiding hallmarks of mystics is that they go through trials, aptly named, *the dark night of the soul*, which was a fate that Herbert would encounter.

Dark night of the soul

As Herbert and his mother were settling into life in England, Herbert secured a place at the Royal West of England School of Architecture, and his mother went to live and work in Cambridge. Whilst life in England was good to Herbert, Britain's relations with Germany were fracturing and the prospect of war loomed ominously. As a young German immigrant, Herbert was considered an 'enemy alien' and after the fall of France he was placed in a series of internment camps behind barbed wire with armed guards in towers. Herbert recalls the hunger he and the other German refugees experienced after a train journey up to the North of England. In the camp Herbert witnessed Orthodox Jews reciting their prayers and performing daily rituals; he saw someone have a complete breakdown, and how other people helped the internees by running seminars on topics such as using art as therapy, which Herbert found very interesting.

In his book Herbert writes that he noticed a conflict within him following his two months in the internment camps. Not only did he feel anger at being detained; he also felt that he had deserted all the others who had had to remain in the camp. He was released to work on a farm in the West Country (where he had worked before being interned). In 1942 Herbert went to live in Cambridge with his mother and he met friends who introduced him to Zen Buddhism, and around the same time his mother gave a talk on Meister Eckhart. Aged 24, Herbert sensed the deeper stirrings of a monastic vocation within him, but this idea was not yet fully formed or clear. He had close female friends, but something in him gently resisted any romantic involvement. Herbert continued to live with his mother in Cambridge until the end of the war. Interestingly, Herbert's mother earned money by typing Professor Ludwig Wittgenstein's manuscript *Tractatus*.

In 1946 Herbert returned to Bristol with a view to resuming his architectural studies, but he had become disengaged with the subject. He went to the Bristol Art School for the rest of the year. Around the same time he was also considering his spiritual path and eventually settled on becoming a Catholic. His thoughts for embracing Catholicism were based on the idea that: "If Meister Eckhart could be a Catholic, then I could too." He was received into the Catholic Church on 7th November 1950. An unexpected turn of events in 1951 focused Herbert's interest in a monastic vocation, when he was given an advert in a newspaper. A monastery (Prinknash Abbey in Gloucestershire) was looking for a potter. Herbert got the job and worked closely with Brother Gilbert in the glazing department. Herbert attended mass every morning and on Sundays he joined the monks for mass and breakfast. Now his vocation and desire to become a monk was becoming stronger. However, out of a desire to help the monastery he worked long hours and he was not eating properly. One day Herbert injured himself at work, breaking his hand in the clay press. Unable to do pottery, Herbert went to stay with his mother in Cambridge until his broken hand healed.

It transpired that Herbert was unwell and exhausted, but he was desperate to get back to the monastery. His mother became concerned and called the doctor, who thought Herbert would benefit from a psychiatric assessment. Upon hearing this Herbert quietly tried to slip away to the railway station so he could return to Prinknash Abbey. His mother managed to get Herbert back to the house and eventually a psychiatrist arrived with two magistrates. Herbert did not want to be treated by the psychiatrist, and consequently he was sectioned and taken to Fulbourn Hospital,

Cambridge, on 16th January 1952. Herbert said: "I was in complete revolt against being in there as I felt it was all wrong...the medication was making me feel worse. I would have been better to have been left in my previous state". When I interviewed Herbert about this episode in his life he said he felt: "This cannot be God's will". Herbert recounts one interesting coincidence that happened, as he walked into the admission ward at Fulbourn. He saw a large tin placed under a boiler to catch water drops and the label on the tin had the words "Benedict Peas". When Herbert was recounting this story I thought he said "Benedict's Peace", which made us laugh. But for Herbert, seeing the tin in the hospital that day simply reminded him of the Benedictine monastery where he longed to be.

It seemed like the hospital was the antithesis of the spiritual community he longed for. He was even denied Holy Communion by the Catholic Chaplain, which was the directive of the Bishop who had forbidden the Eucharist to be given to the 'insane'. Thankfully, the Chaplain managed to get this decision reversed. Herbert's medical treatment included insulin-induced comas and electroconvulsive therapy (ECT). He also participated with other patients in activities like art therapy, basket weaving and walks. Herbert learnt to channel his resistance and started to accept his stay in hospital. In my interview with him he recounted: "One beautiful warm day it was raining gently and I felt there was no need to rebel, this *is* God's will." He reflected further on this point, saying: "It taught me the importance of God's will – whatever it is, in whatever way it comes – to just accept it. Also, it taught me to see the good in what we often think of as bad." He was eventually discharged from hospital nine months later in October 1952.

After leaving hospital Herbert worked on a smallholding outside Cambridge owned by a woman called Mrs Collins and her daughter. One day Mrs Collins showed Herbert a newspaper picture of monks working in the harvest at Mount St Bernard's Abbey. She then told Herbert that she had dreamt of him becoming a monk. It was a dream that was to become a future reality for Herbert. From 1955 to 1971 Herbert worked in the gardens at St Edmund's House (Cambridge) and befriended many homeless people. The years continued to pass and eventually Herbert's mother passed away. A few months after his mother's death a family friend asked Herbert: "Didn't you want to become a monk?" and he recounts how he thought, "Yes, I did". He wrote to the Abbott of Prinknash Abbey and asked to be accepted as a brother. On 8th June 1972 he was clothed in the novice's habit and it has been his vocation ever since. Herbert reflects on his life of monastic work, contemplation and prayer at the end of his book, recounting the teaching of Jesus: "*The Kingdom of God is within you*". Herbert underlines the importance of making effort in our spiritual lives, which he does through his commitment to the teachings of Jesus, making them a living reality in his way of life. Herbert's lifelong love of wisdom is revealed in the following statement he made about living the teachings in the Gospels: "Good will, the thirst for righteousness and the will to work for it in our own lives".

The indomitable spirit

During my interviews with Brother Herbert he shared his poetic writings with me, which he had been composing for many decades. In 2011 he wrote: "There is something – far greater than all religions, and religions can only give a glimpse of it, an introductory course – God, Tao, Allah, Dharma, Om." Herbert's life exemplifies the discipline of spiritual development, especially the importance of oneness and interacting with all life as sacred. Brother Herbert wrote the following poem in 1983:

> *My Lord – you are ONE.*
> *Infinite, incomprehensible – yet close to us.*
> *Untouchable – yet within us.*
> *Invisible – yet we can see you in all things.*
> *Inaudible – yet we can hear you in all sounds.*
> *You are in light – you are in darkness.*
> *You are in life – you are in death.*
> *Life and death are one.*
> *Light and dark are one.*
> *Infinite and miniscule are one.*
> *Universe and atom are one.*
> *All above made by you.*
> *Kept in being by you.*
> *Taken back by you.*

In 2016 I attended a conference at Turvey Abbey, which was convened to explore our human and spiritual response to a world in crisis. At the event I happened to mention to another delegate that I hoped to have a chance to say hello to Brother Herbert. The person I was speaking to had also visited Turvey many times before and he told me the following story: one morning he saw the gentle old monk standing outside with bread feeding the birds, when suddenly a little wild bird flew onto Brother Herbert's hand and proceeded to eat the food that was being offered. It is a fitting image that conveys the peace and connection that can be communicated between species when the qualities of our doing and being are infused with love, compassion and care. I am reminded of the life of Saint Francis, a deeply humble friar, whose devotion to spirit also manifested an intimate connection to animals and the natural world. This is the spiritual art of Wu Wu. It reflects a profound understanding of life's interconnectedness in all that we do. It was Jesus who spoke about spiritual awareness in our actions: if we know what we do we are blessed, but if we *do* not know, then we are cursed and transgress the law. Perhaps the research findings from people's life reviews in NDEs help us appreciate this Biblical passage, where we learn how our actions ripple in the lives of others for better of worse.

Brother Herbert's story is full of examples about how his spiritual practice enabled him to integrate and transform the shadowy experiences of his life into a sacrament of living. We can learn from gentle and humble souls like

Brother Herbert – that life is full of opportunities for surrender and transformative action. It reminds me of the Sufi story (told to me by a friend) about a Holy person, who made a commitment to live peacefully, generously and prayerfully. Here's how I tell the tale: the angels were so impressed that they spoke to God about this saint, saying: "This Holy person should be granted the gift of miraculous powers." When the angels told the saint that God had granted her the gift of any miraculous power she was bemused and indifferent, but the angels said it is better that she has a say in the matter; otherwise a miraculous power will be given to her. She thought carefully for a while, and then said that she would like: "To do good without having knowledge of it". The angels then hatched a plan, and whenever the saint's shadow was behind her, or at her side, it would (if contacted) alleviate people's sorrow, ease pain and make nature flourish again. The saint went about her daily life as before, but unbeknown to her, the shadow she cast was life-affirming: it brought joy to people, made polluted waters fresh again, and brought fertility back to parched lands. The Divine flowed through her.

Similarly, when we do shadow work we flourish. Reclaiming our prejudices and projections heals the divisions in our hearts, in our relationships, and in our connection to nature and the world. A fertile imagination is essential for enabling humanity's collective potential to emerge, inspiring our efforts to co-create an improved future. We have incredible untapped psycho-spiritual resources for awakening our visionary energies, which could renew our relationship to life as a whole. The imagination is where we craft anew a planetary culture that reveres nature and puts into action a sacramental vision.

Where the light gets in

A long-time friend of mine, Anne, a Chi Kung teacher, grandmother and entrepreneur, shared with me an experience she had had during a Chi Kung session. Her instructor was leading a group of practitioners through an exercise, focusing on Wu Chi, which encourages the group to align their bodily movements with Chi energy. The exercise was accompanied by a guided visualisation, and during each in-breath the group were led through a process of energy expansion. Anne felt the energy intensifying inside her as the instructor encouraged the participants to imagine the Chi energy filling and flowing through their bodies. She felt the energy radiating within her. It continued to grow in intensity as the group progressed through the exercise, which was based on imagining the Chi energy going beyond their bodily boundaries to fill the room. However, when the instructor asked the group to go a step further, to imagine the Chi energy expanding into infinity, Anne noticed her resistance as she realised that: "I was scared to let my imagination go…I thought I might lose myself". But Anne has a keen interest in science, and it was her natural curiosity that enabled her to flow with the experience to find out what would happen.

She continued the exercise with her eyes closed and entered into an energetic connection of universal expansiveness. Then she suddenly became aware of a "sliver of light" that started from a narrow point above her heart, which gradually opened to a width of two inches at the centre, before tapering off to a fine point just below her navel. It was a light that she described as: "Clear, clean, whiter than white, and intense". She became deeply immersed in her experience, while simultaneously becoming aware that all the other participants in the room also had these slivers of light. In fact, she realised that everyone in the world had them. It was a realisation of "interconnectivity" that would catalyse a process of reflection for her that went beyond the Chi Kung class. She started musing on the idea that certain world leaders – those who are not known for their compassion – may have damaged their connection to the light. But, after careful consideration, she came to the conclusion that we all have access to this light, no matter who we are.

It became evident during my conversation with Anne that her curiosity, openness, connectivity, and love of diversity have deepened her sense of purpose in her unfolding life journey. Her ongoing vision into action, which I call an occupational myth, has made her more courageous and optimistic in the ways that she lives her truth: "I'm being myself…dropping fear". She described her unfolding journey in life as a creative process, and says that: "Since the white light experience I'm working more intuitively". She makes no reference to religion or New Age ideas in her work; rather the guiding principles in her life are: "To follow the language of experience…to just notice what I notice". I asked Anne: "What are you here to do on planet Earth?" She replied: "To help people access their deep wisdom, strength, and peace." This connects to her vision of bringing people together from diverse backgrounds and experiences, encouraging people to make connections with their bodily wisdom through 'free movement', inspired by Chi Kung. She is passionate about the possibilities of movement work that enables people to access the 'dynamic' qualities of being alive, while also encouraging the lived expression of love, compassion, connection, hope and optimism.

Cultivating a renewed relationship to all that we do in life can lead to deep processes of change. However, a vital first step in bringing forth our gifts, talents, passions and skills is to find something we love doing in daily life, something that is akin to devotion, which then becomes a way of expressing more love in the world. In this way, doing is at the very heart and soul of spiritual activism. It is a deeper participatory call, where selfless action not only serves the journey of Self-realisation, but also works for the greater good.

It is of great interest to me that two parallel processes are happening in the world at this time: the destruction of nature and an underinvestment in human potential. It is without question that human attitudes and behaviours have caused terrible destruction in the world, which is having a catastrophic impact on the Earth's ecosystems. But how many of us have sat down and thought about the erosion of our sacred human potential, which shows up in our dissociated relationship to the natural world? Our overinvestment in a hyper-rational and objective worldview has cut us off from the life-giving and life-sustaining world of the imaginal realm. As Arny Mindell[19] says, inner work helps us prepare to engage our outer work. Yet modern people have spurned some of the greatest sources (technologies of transformation, such as dream work and shamanism etc.), which enable us to develop a relationship to the imaginal realm. As the biography of Brother Herbert reveals, mystics live lightly on the Earth, intent upon cultivating humility, gratitude and a sense of service and love. The subtle energies guided by technologies of transformation bring us into a more sacred relationship in our ways of living.

Following his near-death experience, neurosurgeon Eben Alexander[20] realised the consequences of objectifying and manipulating the natural world, and he understood that the answer to our planetary problems was both spiritual and material. Perhaps a renewed fusion between science and spirituality is not only an integral part of our next evolutionary step; it may well be deeply connected to *Wu Wu* after all. This is the emancipatory edge that brings forth the spirit of the Transformocene.

Exercise: Numinous attractors

- Bring to mind all the different areas of your life and the roles that you occupy.
  - Family, job, institutions, social groups etc.

- Now, bring to mind a spiritual or soulful figure (alive, historical, or imagined), a figure that would support you to follow your deepest calling in life.
  - What qualities does this spiritual/soulful figure possess that resonate with you?
  - Imagine how this figure will help you in the next stage of your spiritual/soulful quest. Imagine what they would do to help you.
  - How does this relationship to the figure inspire you?
  - Where do you feel this connection to the figure in your body (e.g. heart, solar plexus, or hands, etc.)?
  - Notice the particular feeling quality or sensation that accompanies this bodily connection (e.g. is it warm, energised, or free, etc.).
  - Allow this feeling or sensation to flow freely and naturally throughout your body.

- Notice the numinous attraction between the spiritual/soulful figure and your bodily experience.

- Notice how this numinous connection resonates in your relationship to others and the world.

Do we ever examine the myths that imprison us, and do we ever take the time to explore the myths that could liberate us? The walls of our prisons are also the 'Zendo' of our awakening. We are all on death row, but some become warriors of the soul.

Rainbow Warriors

The only way out is through

My motivation and passion for writing this book was to chart a pathway from the Anthropocene to the Transformocene, outlining how our collective odyssey can be engaged in these tumultuous times. A central theme that unites the diverse range of subjects discussed in the book concerns the re-imagining of our relationship to wholeness, and how we can be inspired by the wisdom of the imaginal realm. It means re-activating a deeper, intuitive and experiential connection to life, which has been preserved in many indigenous cultures and the sacred feminine. These traditions run counter to the hyper-rationalism that has a firm grip on the modern imagination, which has also undermined our collective human development. Consequently, the global crisis before us is an epochal defining moment, where we are presented with an incredible opportunity to actualise our human potential and co-evolve sustainable relationships, where we care for the Earth and all the diverse species that live on the planet. The global crisis is a collective *night sea journey* for humanity, which is similar to the psycho-spiritual trials that confront an individual's passing through spiritual crisis. Such processes of awakening herald a breakthrough in consciousness, where we are freed from the binds or restrictions of a one-dimensional consensus reality. Jung reminded us long ago about the consequences of ignoring the unconscious, which leaves us at the mercy of the psychic underworld, but he also pointed out the deep wisdom in the collective unconscious, which is always available to us. A productive relationship with the collective unconscious also strengthens our connection to the imaginal realm.

An important first step in the emergence of the Transformocene is to shift awareness from the dominant Western worldview that propagates a *cult of individual satisfaction*, which is a prelude to a more profound *culture of collective awakening*. In this way, a key part of our redemptive quest at this time is to become agents of deep change, who are invested in the realities of interconnected living, and also honouring the resonances between the *human soul* and the *world soul.*[1] The emergence of a 21st century consciousness, which is invested in wholeness and the greater good, will bring us to an emancipatory edge. It is here that *technologies of transformation* help us to access the collective wisdom of our species' psycho-spiritual heritage (such as prayer, meditation, shamanism and dreamwork etc.), which guides and grounds our awakening. We need to trust that we can turn adversarial circumstances into pathways of redemption and emancipation. It is up to each of us to co-create the Transformocene and live at the vanguard of a collective shift in consciousness. Like the archetype of the Bodhisattva, our compassionate and wise actions can be expressed for the benefit of all sentient beings and the planet, where the *gift of life* is appreciated as a living sacrament. If we are in any doubt that such transformation is possible, the following story about an inmate on death row reveals how deep change stems from our intentions and willingness to act.

Shadows of redemption and emancipation

In *Finding Freedom: Writings from Death Row*, Jarvis Jay Masters[2] writes about being raised in foster care and sliding into a life of delinquent behaviour at an early age, resulting in time spent in locked institutions for youths. In his late teens Jarvis was not only angry and disaffected; his criminal activities escalated to armed robbery (although he never shot anyone). Eventually he was caught and in 1981 he was convicted and sent to San Quentin prison, aged 19. In prison he joined a gang, and then in 1985 he was implicated in a serious incident after a prison officer was murdered in the prison. The fatal attack took place on the second floor, but at the time it happened Jarvis was in a cell on the fourth floor. The accusation was that Jarvis provided the sharpened metal object used in the murder. Certain prisoners were suspected of actually killing the prison officer; however, three were eventually tried and Jarvis was the only one who received a death sentence. He has been on death row since 1990. Around this time Jarvis describes a recurrent nightmare that he had, where about 100 people are gathering outside the observation area surrounding the gas chamber, and they are watching his execution. Jarvis occupies a dual position in the dream: he is witnessing the event, whilst at the same time experiencing being strapped into place ready to die. Jarvis notes that there is communication between these two parts of his experience. Then, the gas is released into the chamber and Jarvis starts to choke. At the same time Jarvis is also floating above events and witnessing the scene. From the vantage of his witnessing self, Jarvis notices that he can see through the bodies of all the people present, and he can also see through his own hands. The only person he cannot see at this point is himself being gassed. He then wakes up.

In his book, Jarvis reflects on his situation, living on death row, and he muses on the idea that so many people never have the time to prepare for death, if for example, they die quickly in a fatal accident. But over time he has come to realise that what is going on in our hearts at the time of death is an important matter. It is a realisation that he shares with some of the other inmates in San Quentin and through his writings. He is concerned about the importance of being loving and compassionate in life. Jarvis speaks about the importance of prayer and joy, as well as taking responsibility for the consequences of our actions. Such an empathetic attitude has enabled him to take risks, to reach out and try and 'touch' the souls of fellow prisoners who have become hardened, due to life events. His reflection includes recognition that he has made mistakes in his life, but says that anyone can end up in difficult circumstances. But most impressively, he has managed to transform his anger into active compassion. Death row hardly seems the most conducive environment for such transformative potential to be realised, but this is what happened for him, and it is also a powerful teaching for us.

We should never forget that our *past transgressions* are also powerfully aligned to our *present transformations*. When we are inspired to renew our intentions and actions, we also become committed to a path of redemption and emancipation. The story of the great Tibetan yogi, Milarepa, serves as a powerful reminder that deep change is possible. In his early life Milarepa became embroiled in a life of black magic and murder, but he renounced his negative ways, and sought spiritual guidance from the great Buddhist teacher, Marpa. To help Milarepa purify his past misdeeds (karma) and cultivate discipline (become a disciple), Marpa told Milarepa to build a house out of stone, and when it was completed, he told Milarepa to take the house down and rebuild it in another location. This arrangement went on for years, and it had the effect of deepening Milarepa's sense of devotion and humility. These preparations (and purifications) created the right inner conditions for him to receive spiritual instruction from Marpa. It reminds me of the parable of the sower told by Jesus, who tells us that the seed needs good soil to grow (Mark 4:3). The story of Jarvis Jay Masters reveals a similar inner preparedness to live a transformative life.

When Jarvis was on trial for the murder of the prison officer, it transpired that a woman who was working on his case, Melody, gave Jarvis literature on how to meditate. She also encouraged him to practise meditation to help reduce the panic he was experiencing. It seemed to work; the meditation had a calming effect on him and it helped slow him down. It was during this period that he read an article about Buddhism in a magazine, synchronistically titled: *Life in Relation to Death*, by Lama Chagdud Tulku Rinpoche. At the foot of the article was an address, and he felt inspired to write a letter, to which he received a reply from a woman called Lisa, who offered to help Jarvis and also visited him regularly. The contact between them eventually led to Lisa visiting Jarvis with Lama Chagdud Tulku Rinpoche. Jarvis describes a very touching scene when he first meets the Lama, saying how he did not know how to greet him. Then, Jarvis bowed to the Lama, and the Lama returned the gesture.

Jarvis writes about how he likes the Lama, because he found out that he was a monk who had been through difficult experiences, and not only was he feisty and not scared of speaking his mind, he was also deeply compassionate.

Jarvis eventually took a vow of 'refuge' to live as a Buddhist. The Lama also conferred on him a tantric empowerment, initiating him into the practice of Tara, the female deity of active compassion. It is a spiritual practice designed to purify the heart and mind, in order to bring more compassion into the world. The Lama instructed Jarvis on the impermanence of life, and explained how this Earthly realm is full of suffering (samsara), where even people with wealth and riches are not immune to feeling imprisoned and leading miserable lives. The Lama said to Jarvis that the focus of his spiritual practice was to do no harm, to be helpful to others, and to be pure. Jarvis was also advised to reaffirm his spiritual vows daily, as well as confessing any thoughts or actions that were negative. In this way, he could then cultivate habits of mind, dedicating the beneficial merits of his virtuous actions to the well-being of others. In the afterword of Jarvis's book, Lama Chagdud Tulku Rinpoche speaks about how this diligent practitioner has learnt to cultivate a focus for his intentions and actions (in body, speech and mind), which reveals the goodness of his true nature and desire not to harm others.

Numinous attractors

The power of our hearts and minds to be receptive for rapid transformations should alert us to the possibilities for our awakening. Swami Kripananda[3] writes about a letter he read in an American magazine in 1981, which was written by an inmate who was incarcerated in a very tough US prison. The inmate describes how he had been cheated by a drug dealer in the prison, and in a fit of rage, he decided to take revenge. He obtained a sharp blade, and was making his way down the corridor towards the drug dealer's cell, when ahead of him he saw a group of prison visitors who were following a man dressed in orange clothes. It transpired that it was the famous Yogi Swami Muktananda who was scheduled to give a talk to the prisoners that day. Then, as the prisoner with the knife passed the group, he and the Swami looked into each other's eyes, and at that very moment the prisoner was overcome with a sensation that he described as love. His murderous rage evaporated and he turned and joined the group and listened to the Swami's talk, which lasted an hour. The Swami told the prisoners that through their thoughts and actions the hellish experience of prison life could be transformed into a place of paradise. The prisoner received a mantra from the Swami and he started to meditate regularly. It became his steadfast practice over many years, which enabled this angry man to transform the grim reality of his prison life from a place of desperation and being out of control, to the cultivation of being more calm and centred.

This story should leave us in no doubt about the power of the numinous by making contact with an awakened soul. The numinous brings us into communion with the *Holy Spirit*, which not only binds us in terms of a shared sacred heritage, but where we are also inspired to act as numinous attractors for each other. It reflects a deep connection to the sacred dimension of life in our relationship to our self, each other, other species and nature as a whole. The numinous awakens us to the sacred, which reverberates in our dreams, visionary energies and actions. Perhaps this is why a transformational story about a prisoner on death row is such a poignant reminder about our own awakening.

The inspirational story of Jarvis Jay Masters[2] who began his journey of psycho-spiritual transformation on death row is a prime example of a person who is inspired to open his heart and awaken consciousness. Extreme situations, such as the one faced by Jarvis, can either diminish us, or inspire us to find the courage to face our wholeness. He lives in a literal prison, caged and restricted in ways that few of us could contemplate, let alone comprehend, with the prospect of being told the time of death ever-present. But Jarvis's daily spiritual practice has opened his heart and mind in ways that can never be locked up by any institution. It is the opposite of the imprisoning reality that is underpinning our one-dimensional technocracy, where modern lives are increasingly subsumed into a world of techno-hypnosis. If we recall, philosophy in the ancient world often advocated the need to 'die' before our physical death (see Chapter Two). This was not a literal death; it was symbolic of a transformative imperative, where human potential is awakened and connects to a renewed sense of meaning and purpose in life. We are all on death row, but how many of us are devoted to opening our hearts and souls like Jarvis Jay Masters?

We know that when we are open to the mystery in life, the soul begins to thrive and the spirit starts to flourish. It seems that this deep sense of mystery, which has been missing for so long in the modern world, has been with us all along in our dreams, imaginations, synchronicities and visions. Now is the time to reawaken our connection to our sacred heritage and the gift of the imaginal realm, which spurs us on to live in wholeness. We should be aware that whatever we decide to do has consequences, for better or worse. The words of Hisamatsu Shin'ichi reflect this point, which goes something along the lines of: *If what you are doing appears ineffective, what could you do?*[4] The future is ours to create, and it may well be that the imaginal realm acts as a trusted guide for the future of humanity, as much as it has done in the past. The Native American prophecy of the *Warriors of the Rainbow* is a potent myth that could help mobilise collective inspiration and transformation at this time. The rainbow is the perfect symbol that reflects the realities of the seen and the unseen,[5] between the material and subtle world's, which makes it a bridge to the imaginal realm.

Rainbow warriors

The prophecy of the *Warriors of the Rainbow* appears to have its origins in the oral traditions of North American Indian tribes (Cree, Hopi, Zuni and Cherokee). It anticipates a time of decay and destruction, and a world affected by greed and war. It promises that the spiritual ancestors will return to the Earth to share their wisdom and inspire peace, equality and healing. It marks a time of spiritual resurgence, where people from all nations recognise that life is 'One', and how they rediscover the sacred unity that heals the Earth and one another. The prophecy chimes with myths from other cultures that point to a new era of sacred restoration.[6] The publication of the prophecy of the *Warriors of the Rainbow* is not without controversy, with suggestions that a version of the story (printed in 1962) was an attempt to spread the New Testament within Native American cultures.[7] I do not know the truth of this story, but it acts as a reminder to respect the wisdom from other cultures, and to learn from them with gratitude and respect.

It turns out that one of the authors of the 1962 book acknowledged that he had researched Hopi Indian prophecies, which, of course, are usually communicated within oral traditions.[6] The prophecy has inspired groups like Greenpeace, who have always named their ships *Rainbow Warrior*, as well as a hippie community called the *Rainbow Family*.[7] My interest in discussing the prophecy of the *Warriors of the Rainbow* is how it relates to the workings of the imaginal realm in this time of global crisis. It is interesting that the origins of this prophecy come from the Native American heritage, but its focus is concerned with events on a global scale, particularly a crisis that is impacting all humanity. It is fascinating that this prophecy has captured the imaginations of so many people in the modern world, which makes it doubly important that the cultural origin of this prophecy is honoured. It seems that the prophecy of the *Warriors of the Rainbow* is a message to humanity, in that, it is pointing to the need for a profound transformational shift in collective attitudes and behaviours. It is a sacramental vision that could inspire humanity to learn from the wisdom of our indigenous sisters and brothers, and how they have steadfastly honoured a connection to the imaginal realm.

The prophecy of the *Warriors of the Rainbow* points to a world where humanity celebrates diversity, and lives together in unity and harmony. It reflects a multidimensional representation of life, as distinct from our modern one-dimensional worldview today. Each of us can take responsibility for loosening the binds of a hyper-rational technocracy and begin to pave the way for more sacramental ways of living. I once heard a Native American Indian saying: *it is through the tears we shed that rainbows are created in our souls*. The question we might ask ourselves at this time is, will we shed tears of sorrow for the world we are losing, or will we shed tears of joy for the world we are healing and co-creating together? It suggests an emotional connection to life, allowing us to contribute to an emerging holistic worldview, where we *manifest rainbows* through our sacred actions (see Table 1, Chapter Eleven). To be motivated by the prophecy of the *Warriors of the Rainbow* is to understand the significance of the imaginal realm that can guide us. It also raises questions about our receptivity to subtle levels of reality that go beyond the worldview of mainstream consensus opinion. It is an invitation to honour the subtle worlds of the soul and spirit.

I would like to share an experience that happened to me after attending a film and workshop on mental health and shamanism. In January 2017 I attended the UK premiere of *Crazy Wise*, a documentary about psycho-spiritual crisis and how people's transformational processes are similar to shamanic crisis and awakening. After the film I was introduced to a friend of a friend, someone whom I had never met before (Chris). At one point in the conversation Chris said to me that an angel and a spirit guide were standing either side of me. Chris went on to share information with me that was both personal and accurate, particularly in connection to my research and writing linked to Jung. The meeting with Chris was very motivating and it spurred me on to keep writing about the imaginal realm. However, I am also aware that sharing such a story in a culture dominated by hyper-rationalism will undoubtedly fire up heated reactions from sceptics. But all I can do is report honestly and faithfully what happened. Remaining silent is how such experiences become marginalised, which is why my synchronous meeting with Chris emboldened me to share information about angels and daimons in this book.

Contact with the imaginal realm brings us alive in the most unexpected and unpredictable ways. Dreams, visions, synchronicities, spirit guides, daimons and angels are all ways that we can be guided to live in wholeness and become *warriors of the soul*. When we are awoken at a soul level, it activates a spiritual relationship to life, where we participate in a cosmos that is alive and animated. Such revelations inspire us to live more lightly on the Earth, to live in gratitude, compassion and forgiveness. It is here that a commitment to a *New Age* of enlightened living is based on serving the sacrament of wholeness, the very essence of Rainbow Living, where we are encouraged to embrace life opportunities that bring forth the fullness of our human potential. We can align our subtle energies for living through mythic actualities, which are inspired by prophecies such as the *Warriors of the Rainbow*. Like the rainbow, we are a spectrum of multi-dimensional energies (see Table 1, Chapter Eleven), which can be awoken when we pay homage to the wholeness that is our birthright. Here are some ways we can engage in the transformational shift that is gaining momentum at this time (doing-being):

• Using high technologies as a part of life, not a way of life.

• Honouring the ancestors, and also our legacy as future ancestors.

• Healing from self-other criticism and destruction (wounded transformers).

• Forgiving self-other for what has been done (and what we have failed to do).

- Opening to the imaginal realm by appreciating and working with dreams and visions.

- Trusting intuition, hunches and synchronicities.

- Finding a spiritual practice that is sustaining (technologies of transformation).

- Engaging daimonic fate and angelic destiny.

- Making time to do regular shadow work.

- Doing regular mini life reviews.

- Living with fluidity and multi-channelled awareness.

- Being committed to the individuation process.

- Exploring talents, skills, creativity and passions to work for the greater good (doing-being).

- Connecting with our occupational myth, occupational intelligence and potential.

- Making a positive difference at home and in our communities.

- Inspiring others through sacred actions, and becoming numinous attractors.

- Living at the 'edge' with imagination and boldness.

- Co-creating an improved future through kindness, generosity, love and compassion.

- Becoming warriors of the soul.

Tibetan Buddhist teacher Chögyam Trungpa[8] spoke about *The Sacred Path of the Warrior*, who is someone not preoccupied with egoic goals and concerns. Rather, the warrior is interested in generating awareness, compassion and the cultivation of wisdom, based on intelligent living, discernment and service. In this way, Trungpa tells us that the warrior is invested in healing and nurturing relationships to fellow humans, other species and nature. Similarly, Arny Mindell[9] says that the warrior knows how all our experiences in life are interwoven, which highlights the importance of understanding how thoughts, feelings and experiences are connected between self, other and world. Mindell also points out the importance of resolving our inner and outer conflicts, in ourselves, in our relationships and in our organisations.[10] The question is, will we heed the call to mobilise our *visionary energies* and align with a *visionary spirit* that seeds our transformative potential? How we respond to this question is a matter of how we understand the importance of *vision quests*, as important rites of passage for our individual and collective well-being. In Native American traditions, vision quests are synonymous with processes of spiritual awakening, which enable people to find strength, healing and freedom. The process includes facing fears, terrors and evils, which are important preparations that enable warriors to emerge from the shadows. Vision quests are also guided by prayer and fasting (technologies of transformation), which help create humble and receptive hearts that are open to the *unity* and *light* of the Great Spirit.[11]

We are living in a time where sacramental living and spiritual renewal are central to the expression of our human potential as a collective rite of passage, where we have a great opportunity to co-create an improved and sustainable future. In this book I have outlined the importance of the *imaginal realm* as a means of mythic activation and collective expression of our unexplored potentials. I have shared ideas about participating in a *redemptive quest*, where we retrieve our souls from the impacts and aftermath of a one-dimensional technocracy. I have proposed a method that brings us into connection with an *emancipatory edge*, which is a psycho-spiritual threshold for our personal and collective awakening. We can all play our part in a *vision quest* that awakens our visionary energies and connects us to a *visionary spirit*. This is the mythic actuality that gives birth to the Transformocene Age, which is ours to co-create. It starts *right here, right now* as love in action.

Exercise: Rainbow warrior

- Reflect on your imaginal journey in life to date. It could be a long-standing interest in following your dreams, a devotion to the arts, or shamanism etc. It could be connected to something you have read in this book.

- If the prophecy of the *Warriors of the Rainbow* is a call, or return to sacred living and wholeness, how is your relationship to the imaginal realm inspiring you to co-create an improved future?
  - In what ways are you a champion for equality?
  - In what ways are you an advocate for peace?
  - In what ways are you an example of empowerment?
  - In what ways are you contributing to healing in the world?
  - In what ways are you a steward for the Earth?

- **Active imagination**: How does the prophecy of the *Warriors of the Rainbow* inspire your connection to working with the imaginal realm in this time of global crisis?

- **Imaginative action**: How does the prophecy of the *Warriors of the Rainbow* deepen your resolve to act for collective transformation?

Glossary

Active imagination: A method developed by Carl Jung, where unconscious contents (e.g. found in dream images, body symptoms and even synchronicities) are integrated into conscious awareness.

Akasha: A Sanskrit word that refers to 'space', which is a cosmic field-like phenomenon (information and interconnectivity). Ervin Laszlo has developed the idea of an *Akashic field*, which includes references to quantum physics and transpersonal psychology.

Alchemy: A process of transforming base metals into gold. European alchemy existed in the Middle Ages, and while it was a precursor to the emergence of chemical science, the art of alchemy was also conceived as a psycho-spiritual practice. The alchemist transforms base human impulses into a quest for the philosopher's stone, and the realisation of this task is called the Magnus Opus, or Great Work. The transformational psychology of Carl Jung was inspired by alchemical writings.

Ancestor: Although we most often identify our ancestors as direct family and cultural descendants, we can broaden and deepen our understanding of the ancestors to include professional or inspirational figures. We can also have a sense of connection and kinship with other species and also through our relationship to nature and the Earth. The latter underlines our interconnected relationship to life as a whole.

Angel: A divine messenger, guardian and protector. Some cultures consider the divine messages we receive via dreams as angelic. The angelic realm is vibrational and light, and is not constrained by the material world, but angels can manifest in the material world. There are also fallen angels and we need to be wise and discerning when requesting angelic assistance.

Anthropocene: The eco-destructive habits of humanity are now layered in the Earth's geological record, evidenced by plastic and nuclear waste etc. At the end of 2017 the Anthropocene had not officially been confirmed.

Archetypes (Jungian): The archetypes manifest through images and symbols (as in dreams and fantasies), which are intimations of a greater archetypal reality that cannot be experienced in its entirety. Jungian archetypes are viewed as original patterns or behaviours that have evolved throughout human history. For example, cross-cultural roles linked to being a mother are easily recognisable. A good illustration of an archetype in action is found in the actions of birds constructing nests, where the structural pattern of the nest is consistent amongst all the birds of that species, despite never being shown how to construct such a nest.

Archetypal occupations: The individuating human being encounters what Jung described as the transcendent function, where the ego bears the tension of meeting unconscious processes. Archetypal occupations reflect deep levels of human reflection and action, where the meaning found in unconscious material (e.g. symbols, dreams, and symptoms) can be expressed and integrated in everyday activities or projects. These deep actions (doing) provide a transitional function in relation to new ways of being in daily life with transpersonal significance.

Chakras: There are seven subtle energy centres in the body that are not physical, but are represented at certain points on the body, from the base of the spine to the crown of the head (see Table 1, Chapter Eleven). There is one main central channel (Sushuma) that connects the seven chakras, as well as two accompanying channels (Ida and Pingala) that weave and intersect at each of the seven chakras. A network of subtle energy pathways called nadis also accompanies the chakra system.

Daimon: In Ancient Greece the daimon was a spirit or divine power that inspired human beings to wake up at a soul level, which connected to fulfilling their true potential and character. Therefore, the daimon functions as an intermediary between spiritual and material worlds. The daimon is a guide and is also associated with helping individuals to manifest genius, making this a divine gift, not a human attribute.

Deep ecology: An environmentally based philosophy developed by Arne Naess, which situates human beings within a greater ecological whole.

Evil: A term that is used to reflect *moral evils*, or human malevolent actions towards others, which lead to serious harm. This is distinct from *natural evils*, where destruction is the consequence of natural causes, such as earthquakes etc.

Imaginal realm: A sacred level of reality, which is revealed through visions, dreams, synchronicities and the angelic. The human imagination can connect with the imaginal realm as a soulful experience, which awakens our visionary energies.

Imaginative action: When processes emerging from active imagination (as conceived by Jung) are actualised in everyday life contexts. Imaginative action (conceptualised by the author) is based on having a close and intimate connection to the imaginal realm, which is expressed in our everyday ways of doing and living.

Indigenous: Originating from a particular place or region on Earth.

Individuation: A term used by Jung to capture the psycho-spiritual growth and development of individuals who are working with and integrating materials from the unconscious (via dreams, symbols, symptoms, conflicts and relationships). The path of individuation is connected to a lifelong quest for unity, in that the *individual* is *indivisible* from life's wholeness.

Koan: A paradoxical statement used in Zen Buddhism, which is an irrational riddle that cannot be solved by logic or reason. Koans are used to bypass the rational mind, which has limitations in its ability to bring about an awakened mind.

Kundalini: An experience that can occur as a result of regular meditation practice (and sometimes spontaneously). Within Indo-Buddhist philosophy Kundalini is referred to as the 'serpent power', and is a process that involves energy arising from the base of the spine to the crown of the head. Kundalini reflects an awakening of the feminine energy, Shakti, which unites with the masculine energy, Shiva, and involves a process of purification as the Divine awakens from deep within. In the Hindu and Buddhist traditions a teacher or Guru is a guide who helps the student manage the process, which can be very intense. Physical signs of Kundalini include subtle vibrations throughout the body, disorientated thoughts and bodily sensations of heat.

Mysticism: A connection to a divine mystery, which is deeply experiential, reflecting a direct and subjective encounter with the sacred.

Myth: Often portrayed as cultural stories and legends that reveal pearls of wisdom, for example, through narratives that help us understand adversarial encounters between light-dark etc. Whether we are aware of them or not, myths are always at work in our lives, where they represent metaphors for lived actualities (for example, all the ideas, fantasies and hopes that contribute to the *American Dream*). Therefore, becoming aware of our 'personal myth' is important for distinguishing our true path in life, from the collective norms and realities that surround us (e.g. the *American Dream*).

Near-death experience: An encounter that happens when people are close to death, or have momentarily been pronounced clinically dead. Upon revival, people report a variety of experiences that have been shown to be consistent across research studies. For example, people report travelling through a tunnel, meeting dead relatives, encountering beings of light, experiencing divine love and having a life review, etc. The experience usually precipitates a major transformation upon return to an Earthly existence.

Non-locality: A concept that emerged from quantum physics, where at a subatomic level, reality exists as a field and all phenomena are interconnected.

Numinous: The word numinous is derived from the Latin *numen*, which refers to the sacred and divine. The *numinous* was used by theologian Rudolf Otto in his landmark book *The Idea of the Holy*, which proposed a more holistic view of the sacred as being both beatific and wrathful. Carl Jung integrated the numinous into his psychology of individuation.

Occupational congruence: A process where our inner work aligns with our outer work. The idea of *occupational congruence* includes our abilities to respond to 'local' events and also to 'non-local' occurrences and information (e.g. synchronicity).

Occupational engagement: In a traditional 'local' sense, occupational engagement is the conscious and volitional act of doing, which is holistic (e.g. physical, psychological, social, spiritual and ecological). However, the author has expanded the idea of *occupational engagement* from a 'non-local' perspective, based on the realisation that what we do in the world is interconnected, and our actions have resonances in the world that connect beyond our everyday 'local' intentions. For example, we can see such instances in moments of synchronicity when the 'non-local' world intersects meaningfully with us.

Occupational entanglement: Where our actions in the world have 'local' and 'non-local' resonances. The findings from people's life reviews in the near-death experience reveal how we face the emotional consequences of our positive and negative actions, particularly in the way they impacted others. This is a key lesson for developing awareness about interconnectivity and the quality of our occupational engagement in life (e.g. what we do in the world, we do to ourselves).

Occupational intelligence: Where the engagement of our multi-chanelled capacities (visual, auditory, kinesthetic, feeling/emotional, olfactory, gustatory, and relational), are directed towards the expression of our psycho-spiritual potential. *Occupational intelligence* (as conceptualised by the author) is pivotal for enabling self-actualisation and individuation (doing and being). It complements and resonates with multiple intelligences as conceived by Howard Gardner, and also spiritual, emotional and ecological intelligence.

Occupational myth: Where the 'personal myths' that underpin our lived realities find expression in all that we do in life, via our attitudes, values, morals and behaviours, etc. *Occupational myths* are based on the recognition that what we 'do' in life can be inspired by our dreams, visions and synchronicities, which brings forth deeper vectors for living. It is here that meaning and purpose, as an expression of our occupational myth, connects to the deep engagement of our occupational potential.

Occupational resonance: Where the 'material body' (physical) resonates with the 'subtle body' (soul-spirit). Occupational resonance is the energetic connection between our *personal* and *transpersonal* potentials, which finds holistic expression through embodied action.

Occupational shift: Where our so-called ordinary or 'mundane activities' are integrated into a transformative life path, which gives expression to life as a living sacrament. In this way, our everyday 'personal occupations' contribute to a collective shift and transformation, through our alignment with the 'transpersonal'.

Occupational vectors: Based on the vector walk, as conceived by Arny Mindell. Occupational vectors are the realisation of all the various 'trajectories' that can inform our ways of doing in the world. For example, the vector walk can reveal how we are occupied in relation to different layers of experience, such as the demands of *consensus reality*, as well as the *dreaming level*, and a more integrated position, where we are aligned with *wholeness*, or the Tao.

Permaculture: A system of ecological design. It works with natural patterns in ecosystems that point to how we can live in harmony with nature and co-evolve sustainable ways of living.

Pre-occupation: A process of being absorbed or engaged with an idea or an actual task.

Sacrament: A symbol or experience that has mysterious or sacred significance.

Sacred feminine: A way of knowing the divine in the world, through Earth mysteries, intuition, dreams and the body etc.

Scientism: A dogma that believes science is the most important way of knowing. Practitioners of scientism are prone to passing judgement on other 'ways of knowing', which are often beyond their area of expertise.

Self: The self with a lower case (s) reflects personal experiences that are connected to ego, identity and personality. The Self with an upper case (S) reflects a more *transpersonal* level of experience (as noted by Jung), where a person (engaged in the process of individuation) connects to a wider experience of consciousness, life and the cosmos.

Shadow (Jungian): The shadow is made up of unprocessed experiences and feelings that reside in the personal unconscious. The shadow reliably manifests in our negative projections towards others. Shadow work is concerned with reclaiming these projections and using the available energy for our growth and development (individuation). The collective shadow can be represented through the example of the Nazi party, particularly in the ways they tapped into and mobilised unprocessed prejudices and resentments in the German population after the First World War.

Soul: The non-material and immortal quality within human beings (which is also the seat of emotions and character). The human soul is visceral, in that we can connect with it in moments of love and in dreams. The human soul also connects to the soul of the world (*anima mundi*), which is why we can experience soulful connections in the natural world.

Spirit: A metaphysical reality, where the sacred is expressed in connection to God, the Great Spirit, or associated guides and messengers, such as angels and other deities etc. It is a hidden reality that can be experienced in the natural world. Spirituality also reflects a vital force in life, and can connect to individuals' authentic selves (e.g. a spiritual person).

Tantra: A spiritual practice linked to Hinduism and Buddhism. It involves a detailed cosmology and intricate energetic systems associated with the subtle body (e.g. chakras).

Taoism: A Chinese spiritual and philosophical system, which is concerned with living in harmony and wholeness (Heaven and Earth). The most famous Taoist is Lao Tzu, who wrote the *Tao Te Ching*, which is how to live in accord with the Tao (way). Taoism has a strong mystical component, which is found in Taoist Yoga, as well as the path of divination, known as the I-Ching.

Technology: From the Greek techne, meaning *craft*. In the modern world technology is associated with tools and mechanics, but in the ancient world it included a metaphysical connection, in that all life is being creatively brought forth, including the natural world (e.g. birds constructing nests and beavers building dams etc.).

Technologies of transformation: As co-creators in life we craft (techne) our reality through what we do, but the metaphysical link to techne means that our high-tech world can be tempered by technologies of transformation, such as prayer, mindfulness, dream work and vision quests etc. These can help us remain aligned to the cosmos (in order and wholeness).

Transformocene: An eco-spiritual approach to planetary transformation developed by the author. The *Transformocene* is an attitudinal and behavioural shift that is committed to engaging a new consciousness to counter the destructive impacts of modern lifestyles on the Earth. It is concerned with the activation of a dynamic response to planetary conditions, which calls on humanity to take part in a process of individual, collective and planetary healing. The *Transformocene* tasks us with re-imagianing and renewing our relationship to nature and what it means to live in harmony as co-participants in life.

Transpersonal: Humanistic psychology's interest in human potential (including spirituality) resulted in the emergence of transpersonal psychology, which aimed to study experiences that are encountered *through* or *beyond* (trans) the individual ego. Classically, the transpersonal position embraces experiences of non-ordinary states of consciousness and does not consider them anomalous.

Transpersonal occupations: When people experience a reality *beyond* or *through* (trans) the personal ego, via altered or extreme states, it often results in a marked change in people's ways of doing and being. Transpersonal occupations are expressions of transformative states of consciousness in action.

Vector walk: Is a way of exploring and integrating different levels of experience (e.g. between consensus reality and the dreaming) as developed by Arnold Mindell. When we represent the various 'vectors' (directions) that make up our experiences, we are freed up to follow deeper associations that connect to our personal myth. For example, one direction could be represented as a 'consensus attitude' we are suffering from. However, another direction could connect to an interest in becoming a social activist. Working with these different directions helps us to find a superposition, where we connect to the pull of individuation. In the vector walk the natural world can be used to represent symbolic associations to our inner experiences.

References

Foreword by the Author

1. Reuters News. (2017). 'Girl, 9, sues Indian ministry over climate change action'. *The Guardian*, 8th April, p.22.
2. Safi, M. (2017). 'Farmers' suicides linked to climate change'. *The Guardian*, 1st August, p.13.
3. Milman, D. (2017). 'Study puts chance of staying below Paris climate target of 2C, at just 5%'. *The Guardian*, 1st August, p.6.
4. Milman, D. (2017). 'US federal workers are told: stop saying climate change'. *The Guardian*, 8th August, p.1-2.
5. Harvey, F. (2017). 'Trump has failed to scupper Paris climate change deal, says Gore'. *The Guardian*, 12th August, p.12.
6. Kurzweil, R. (1999). *The age of spiritual machines: When computers exceed human intelligence*. New York: Penguin.
7. Harari, Y.N. (2016). *Homo Deus: A brief history of tomorrow*. London: Vintage.
8. Storm, H. (2001). *My descent into death: And the message of love, which brought me back*. Forest Row, SU: Clairview Books.
9. Vrbata, A. (2014). 'Beyond the myth of "self-domination" (imaginal psychology in the pursuit of cultural shift)'. *Human Affairs*, 24, p.136-47.
10. Ronnberg, A. & Martin, K. (2010). *The book of symbols: Reflections on archetypal images*. Taschen: Cologne.
11. Brinkmann, S. (2017). 'Stop looking for yourself'. *The Observer Magazine*, 16th April, p.60.
12. Hillman, J. (1975). *Re-visioning psychology*. New York: Harper Colophon Books.
13. Collins, M. (2014). *The unselfish spirit: human evolution in a time of global crisis*. East Meon, Hampshire: Permanent Publications.
14. Stokes, P. (2002). *Philosophy: 100 essential thinkers*. London: Capella.
15. Campbell, J. (2001). *Thou art that: Transforming religious metaphor*. Novato, CA: New World Library.
16. Hollis, J. (2000). *The archetypal imagination*. College Station: Texas A&M University Press.

Introduction

1. Vaughan, A. 2016. 'Scientists herald a new epoch shaped by humanity's excess'. *The Guardian*, Friday 8th January, p.9.
2. Vince, G. (2014). *Adventures in the anthropocene: A journey to the heart of the planet we made*. London: Chatto & Windus.
3. Zalasiewicz, J. (2015). 'The earth stands on the brink of its sixth mass extinction'. *The Observer*, 21st June, p.30-1.
4. Capra, F. & Luisi, P.L. (2014). *The systems view of life: A unifying vision*. Cambridge: Cambridge University Press.
5. Rockström, J. (2015). 'The future of the planet is in the balance'. *The Observer*, 15th November, p.34-5.
6. Carrington, D. (2016). 'Welcome to the Anthropecene, the human-made Earth epoch'. *The Guardian*, 30th August, p.1, 3.
7. Carr, N. (2010). *The shallows: How the Internet is changing the way we think, read and remember*. London: Atlantic Books.
8. Vince, G. (2014). *Adventures in the anthropocene: A journey to the heart of the planet we made*. London: Chatto & Windus.
9. Ghosh, A. (2016). 'In the eye of the storm'. *The Guardian*, 29th October, p.16-7.
10. Harpur, P. (2002). *The philosophers' fire: A history of the imagination*. Glastonbury: The Squeeze Press.
11. Thompson, W.I. (1989). *The imaginary landscape: Myth and science*. New York: St Martin's Press.
12. Corbin, H. (1994). *The man of light in Iranian Sufism. Trans, Nancy Pearson*. New Lebanon: Omega Publications.
13. Marcuse, H. (1964/1991). *One-dimensional man*. London: Routledge.
14. Samuels, A. (1993). *The political psyche*. London: Routledge.
15. Jung, C.G. (1988). 'Jung on evil'. In *Facing evil: Confronting the dreadful power behind genocide, terrorism, and cruelty*, eds Woodruff, P. & Wilmer, H.A. p.257-65. Chicago: Open Court.
16. Capra, F. (2002). *The hidden connections: A science of sustainable living*. London: Harper Collins.
17. Jenkins, S. (2016). 'We're doing better than ever before. It's pessimism that clouds our vision'. *The Guardian*, 1st September, p.33.
18. Carrington, D. (2016). 'Tenth of UK wild species 'face extinction''. *The Guardian*, 14th September, p.14.
19. Toffler, A. (1970). *Future shock: A study of mass bewilderment in the face of accelerating change*. London: The Bodley Head.
20. Roszak, T. (1975). *Unfinished animal: The Aquarian frontier and the evolution of consciousness*. New York: Harper Colophon Books.
21. Mindell, A. (1993). *The shaman's body*. New York: Harper Collins.
22. Swimme, B. & Berry, T. (1992). *The universe story: From the primordial flaring forth to the ecozoic era*. Harper Collins: New York.
23. Thompson, W.I. (1995). The science of myth. In *Voices from the edge*, eds Brown, D.J. & McClen-Novick, R. p.271-99. Freedom, CA: The Crossing Press.
24. Eisenstein, C. (2013). *The more beautiful world our hearts know is possible*. Berkeley, CA: North Atlantic Books.
25. Collins, M. (2014). *The unselfish spirit: Human evolution in a time of global crisis*. East Meon, Hampshire: Permanent Publications.

26. Draper, B. (2016). *Soulfulness: Deepening the mindful life*. London: Hodder and Stoughton.
27. Thompson, W.I. (1976). *Evil and world order*. New York: Harper & Row.
28. Fox, M. (2016). *Sins of the spirit, blessings of the flesh: Transforming evil in soul and society*. Berkeley, CA: North Atlantic Books.
29. United Nations. (2015). *Transforming our world: The 2030 agenda for sustainable development*. Available at http://sustainable development.un.org/post2015/transforming our world. Accessed on 9th March, 2016.
30. Welsh Government. (2014). *Well-being of future generations: Impact assessment*. Available at http://gov.wales/docs//equality-impact-assessments/141210-eia-future-generations-bill-combined-impact-assessments-en.pdf. Accessed on 8th June, 2015.
31. Mindell, A. (1993). *The shaman's body*. New York: Harper Collins.
32. Mindell, A. (2013). *Dance of the ancient one: How the universe solves personal and world problems*. Portland, OR: Deep Democracy Institute.
33. Russell, P. (2005). 'Raising the IQ of the global brain'. In *Conversations on the edge of the apocalypse*, ed Brown, D.J. p.209-20. Basingstoke, Hampshire: Palgrave MacMillan.
34. Chopra, D. (2005). 'Quantum spirituality'. In *Conversations on the edge of the apocalypse*, ed Brown, D.J. p.221-6. Basingstoke, Hampshire: Palgrave MacMillan.
35. Whitmont, E.C. (1982). *Return of the goddess*. London: Arkana.
36. Housten, J. (1995). 'Forging the possible human'. In *Voices from the edge*, eds Brown, D.J. & McClen-Novick, R. p.231-51. Freedom, CA: The Crossing Press.
37. Ronnberg, A., and Martin, K. (2010). *The book of symbols: Reflections on archetypal images*. Cologne: Taschen.
38. Drury, N. (1991). *The visionary human: Mystical consciousness & paranormal perspectives*. Shaftesbury, Dorset: Element.
39. Garland, R. (1994). *Religion and the Greeks*. London: Bristol Classical Press.
40. Reiss, G. (2004). *Leap into living: Moving from fear into freedom*. Eugene, OR: Changing World Publications.
41. Rice-Oxley, M. (2017). 'Climate change live blog that sounded a global warning'. *The Guardian*, 28th January, p.52.
42. Whyte, D. (1998). *The heart aroused: Poetry and the preservation of the soul at work*. London: The Industrial Society.
43. Berman, M. (1981). *The reenchantment of the world*. Ithaca: Cornell University Press.
44. Kerr, M. & Key, D. (2012). The ecology of the unconscious. In *Vital signs: Psychological responses to ecological crisis*, eds Rust, M.J. & Totton, N. p.63-77. London: Karnac Books.

Three Propositions for Deeper Living

1. Harvey, F. (2013). 'Just 30 years to calamity if we carry on blowing the carbon budget, says IPCC'. *The Guardian*, 28th September, p.17.
2. McKie, R. (2016). 'Ten years ago, Nicholas Stern revealed the dangers of global warming to the economy. Now he says: "It's worse than I feared".' *The Observer*, 6th November, p.32.
3. Graham-Harrison, E. (2016). 'July confirmed as the hottest month ever'. *The Guardian*, 17th August, p.3.
4. Sophia, D.G. (2016). 'Sixth wildlife mass extinction to happen in 2020 experts say'. Available at www.natureworldnews.com/articles/20161027/30805/year-2020-era-wildlife-mass-extinction-.htm. Accessed on 24th November, 2016.
5. Vidal, J. (2016). 'Who will cull the beasts that are trashing the planet?' *The Guardian*, 19th December, p.25.
6. Gold, T. (2014). 'Materialism makes us sad'. *The Guardian*, 7th May, p.30.
7. Belton, T. (2014). *Happier people, healthier planet*. Bristol: SilverWood Books.
8. Emmott, S. (2013). 'It took 200,000 years for the population to reach one billion. Now our numbers increase by a billion every decade'. *The Observer*, 30th June, p.8-11.
9. Lucas, C. (2014). 'I didn't do this because I thought it was fun'. *The Guardian*, 15th April, p.27.
10. Van Vark, C. (2014). 'The Global Consumption Conundrum'. *The Guardian*, 17th October, p.39.
11. Berry, T. (1999). *The great work: Our way into the future*. New York: Random House.
12. Baring, A. (2012). *The dream of the cosmos: A quest for the soul*. Dorset: Archive Publishing.
13. Skolimowski, H. (1993). *A sacred place to dwell: Living with reverence upon the earth*. Rockport, MA: Element.
14. Lorimer, D., & Robinson, O. (2010). *A new renaissance: Transforming science, spirit and society*. Edinburgh: Floris Books.
15. Laszlo, E. (2008). *Quantum shift in the global brain*. Rochester, VER: Inner Traditions.
16. Laszlo, E. (2014). *The self-actualizing cosmos*. Rochester, VER: Inner Traditions.
17. Collins, M. (2014). *The unselfish spirit: Human evolution in a time of global crisis*. East Meon, Hampshire. Permanent Publications.
18. Von Franz, M.L. (1975/1998). *C.G. Jung: His myth in our time*. Toronto: Inner City Books.
19. Scarpelli, M. (2009). 'The earth, the song, the symbol'. *On soul and earth: The psychic value of place*, ed. E. Liotta, p.268-76. London: Routledge.
20. Clouston, T.J. (2014). 'Whose occupational balance is it anyway? The challenge of neoliberal capitalism and work-life imbalance. *British Journal of Occupational Therapy*, 77(10), p.507-15.
21. Neumann, E. (1954). *The origins and history of consciousness*. New York: Bollingen Foundation and Pantheon Books.
22. Trungpa, C. (1984). *Shambhala: The sacred path of the warrior*. Boston: Shambhala.
23. Leighton, T.D. (1998). *Bodhisattva archetypes: Classic Buddhist guides to awakening and their modern expression*. New York: Arkana.

24. Nyima Rinpoche, C. (1991). *The Bardo guidebook*. Hong Kong: Rangjong Yeshe Publications.
25. Mindell, A. (2013). *Dance of the ancient one: How the universe solves personal and world problems*. Portland, OR: Deep Democracy Institute.
26. Alvesson, M. (2013). *The triumph of emptiness: Consumption, higher education, and work organization*. Oxford: Oxford University Press.
27. Goodchild, V. (2012). *Songlines of the soul: Pathways to a new vision for a new century*. Lake Worth, FL: Nicolas-Hays.
28. Mindell, A. (1995). *Sitting in the fire: Large group transformation using conflict and diversity*. Portland, OR: Lao Tse Press.
29. Mindell, A. (2002). *The deep democracy of open forums*. Charlottesville, VA: Hampton Roads.
30. Mindell, A. (2007). *Earth-based psychology*. Portland, OR: Lao Tse Press.
31. Mindell, A. (2013). *Dance of the ancient one*. Portland, OR: Deep Democracy Exchange.
32. Mindell, A. (2017). *Conflict: Phases, forums and solutions*. North Charleston, SC: World Tao Press and A. Mindell.
33. Mindell, A. (1989). *Coma: Key to awakening*. Boston: Shambhala.
34. Gilbert, P. (2010). *The compassionate mind*. London: Constable & Robinson Ltd.
35. Halifax, J. (2000). Foreword. In *The power of compassion: Stories that open the heart, heal the soul, and change the world*, ed. P. Bloom, p.1-3. Charlottesville: Hampton Roads.
36. Thompson, W.I. (1989). *The imaginary landscape: Myth and science*. New York: St Martin's Press.
37. Moss, R. (2009). *The secret history of dreaming*. Novato, CA: New World Library.
38. Kingsnorth, P. (2016). The call of the wild. *The Guardian*, 23rd July, p.15-6.
39. Greenfield, S. (2003). *Tomorrow's people: How 21st-century technology is changing the way we think and feel*. London: Penguin.
40. Carrington, D. (2017). Beavers engineer rich habitats from degraded land. *The Guardian*, 19th July, p.13.
41. Skrbina, D. (2016). *The metaphysics of technology*. London: Routledge.
42. Roszak, T. (1968/1995). *The making of a counter culture: Reflections on the technocratic society and its youthful opposition*. Berkeley, CA: University of California Press.
43. Thompson, W.I. (1991). *Reimagination of the world: A critique of the new age, science, and popular culture* (co-authored with David Spangler). Santa Fe, NM: Bear & Company Publishing.
44. Thompson, W.I. (1976). *Evil and world order*. New York: Harper & Row.
45. Winston, R. (2005). *The story of God: A personal journey into the world of science and God*. London: Bantam Press.
46. Jones, K. (1993). *Beyond optimism: A Buddhist political ecology*. Oxford: John Carpenter Publishing.
47. Miles, B. (2003). *Hippie*. London: Bounty Books.
48. Rhodes-Dimmer, P. (1992). *The layman's guide to the New Age*. Teddington, Midd: Caduceus.
49. Metzner, R. (2010). *The expansion of consciousness*. Berkeley, CA: Regent Press for Green Earth Foundation.
50. Frank, T. (2017). How Steve Bannon captured America's spirit of revolt. *The Guardian*, 11th February, p.35.
51. Wachman, R. (2008). Who's to blame? Let's start the list with Thatcher and Reagan. *The Guardian*, 14th October. Available at www.theguardian.com/business/blog/2008/oct/14/creditcrunch-thatcher-reagan Accessed on, 15th February 2017.
52. Metcalf, S. (2017). The big idea that defines our era. *The Guardian*, 19th August, p.29-31.
53. Kaiser, D. (2011). *How the hippies saved physics*. New York: W.W. Norton & Company.
54. Capra, F. (1976/1991). *The Tao of physics: An exploration of the parallels between modern physics and eastern mysticism*. London: Flamingo.
55. Zukov, G. (1979). *The dancing Wu Li masters: An overview of the new physics*. New York: William Morrow & Company.
56. Capra, F., & Luisi, P.L. (2014). *The systems view of life: A unifying vision*. Cambridge: Cambridge University Press.
57. Roszak, T. (1972). *Where the wasteland ends: Politics and transcendence in postindustrial society*. New York: Doubleday & Company, Inc.
58. Roszak, T. (1975). *The unfinished animal: The Aquarian frontier and the evolution of consciousness*. New York: Harper Colophon Books.
59. Bloom, H. (1996). *Omens of Millennium*. London: Fourth Estate.
60. Sartori, P., & Walsh, K. (2017). *The transformative power of near-death experiences*. London: Watkins.
61. Roszak, T. (1978/2003). *Person/planet: The creative disintegration of industrial society*. Lincoln, NE: An Authors Guild Backinprint.com Edition.
62. Roszak, T. (1992/2001). *The voice of the earth: An exploration of ecopsychology*. Grand Rapids, MI: Phanes Press.
63. Sheldrake, R. (2012). *The science delusion: Freeing the spirit of enquiry*. London: Coronet.
64. Hubbard, B.M. (2012). *Emergence: The shift from ego to essence*. San Francisco: Hampton Roads Publishing.
65. William, A. (2016). *Medical medium: Life changing foods*. Carlsbad, CA: Hay House.
66. Conrad, P. (2017). 'Fanfare for Gods First Couple' book review of *The Rise and Fall of Adam and Eve*, The New Review (books). *The Observer*, 3rd September, p.33.

Introduction to Part One: The Imaginal Lineage

1. Austin, R. (2014). 'Sun and ice'. *A cold fire*. Stroud: Chrysalis Poetry.
2. O'Riordan, T. & Lenton, T. (2013). Preface. In *Addressing tipping points for a precarious future*, eds T. O'Riordan & T. Lenton, p.xv-xviii. Oxford: Oxford University Press. Published for The British Academy.

3. O'Riordan, T. Lenton, & Christie, I. (2013). Metaphors and systemic change. In *Addressing tipping points for a precarious future*, eds T. O'Riordan, & T. Lenton, p.3-20. Oxford: Oxford University Press. Published for The British Academy.

4. Foden, G. (2013). 'Skittles: The story of the tipping point metaphor and its relation to new realities'. In *Addressing tipping points for a precarious future*, eds T. O'Riordan & T. Lenton, p.49-72. Oxford: Oxford University Press. Published for The British Academy.

5. Hillman, J. (1975). Re-visioning psychology. New York: Harper Colophon Books.

6. Collins, M. (2014). *The unselfish spirit: Human evolution in a time of global crisis*. East Meon, Hampshire. Permanent Publications.

7. Hutchins, G. (2014). *The illusion of separation: Exploring the cause of our current crises*. Edinburgh: Floris Books.

8. Lenton, T. (2013). 'Tipping elements from a global perspective'. In *Addressing tipping points for a precarious future*, eds T. O'Riordan & T. Lenton, p.23-46. Oxford: Oxford University Press. Published for The British Academy.

9. Goodchild, V. (2012). *Songlines of the soul: Pathways to a new vision for a new century*. Lake Worth, FL: Nicolas-Hays.

10. Taylor, M. (2013). 'Commentary: Aligning contrasting perspectives of tipping points'. In *Addressing tipping points for a precarious future*, eds T. O'Riordan & T. Lenton, p.73-6. Oxford: Oxford University Press. Published for The British Academy.

11. Mindell, A. (2000). *Quantum mind: The edge between physics and psychology*. Portland, OR: Lao Tse Press.

12. Molyneaux, B.L. (1995). *The sacred earth*. London: Macmillan.

13. O'Riordan, T., & Lenton, T. (2013). 'Into a precarious future'. In *Addressing tipping points for a precarious future*, eds T. O'Riordan & T. Lenton, p.301-19. Oxford: Oxford University Press. Published for The British Academy.

14. Campbell, J. (2001). *Thou art that: Transforming religious metaphor*. Novato, CA: New World Library.

15. Hollis, J. (2000). *The archetypal imagination*. College Station: Texas A&M University Press.

16. Henderson, C. (2017). The wonder of you. Inner Life. *The Observer Magazine*, 29th October, p.68.

17. Comment. (2017). *The Observer*, 2nd July, p.32.

Chapter One

1. Thompson, W.I. (2013). *Beyond religion*. Great Barrington, MA: Lindisfarne Books.

2. Harari, Y.N. (2016). Come together. *The Guardian*, 10th September, p.16-7.

3. Harari, Y.N. (2011). *Sapiens: A brief history of humankind*. London: Vintage Books.

4. Jackson, R. (2012). A Gaian worldview. In *The song of the Earth: A synthesis of the scientific and spiritual worldviews*, eds M. Harland & W. Keepin, p.25-35. East Meon, Hampshire Permanent Publications.

5. Hughes, A.L. (2012). *The folly of scientism*. The New Atlantis, 37, p.32-50.

6. Pinker, S. (2013). 'Science is not your enemy: An impassioned plea to neglected novelists, embattled professors, and tenure-less historians'. Available at http://newrepublic.com/article/114127/science-not-enemy-humanities. Accessed on, 4th January, 2017.

7. Handwerk, B. (2015). 'Scientists replicated 100 psychology studies, and fewer than half got the same results'. Available at www.smithsonianmag.com/science-nature/scientists-replicated-100-psychology-studies-and-fewer-half-got-same-results-180956426/. Accessed on 4th January, 2017.

8. Wilber, K. (1985). *Quantum questions: Mystical writings of the world's great physicists*. Boston: Shambhala.

9. Marsh, H. (2017). 'Gene editing brings a world of extraordinary possibilities'. *The Guardian*, 3rd January, p.19.

10. Alexander, E. (2014). *The map of heaven: A neurosurgeon explores the mysteries of the afterlife and the truth about what lies beyond*. London: Piatkus.

11. Littlefair, S. (2016). Leading neuroscientists and Buddhists agree: "consciousness is everywhere". Available at, www.lionsroar.com/christof-koch-unites-buddhist-neuroscience-universal-nature-mind/. Accessed on 4th January, 2017.

12. Capra, F. & Luisi, P.L. (2014). *The systems view of life: A unifying vision*. Cambridge: Cambridge University Press.

13. Collins, M. (2014). *The unselfish spirit: Human evolution in a time of global crisis*. East Meon, Hampshire: Permanent Publications.

14. Jung, C.G. (1938/1966). *Psychology and religion*. New Haven: Yale University Press.

15. Token Rock, (2016). Ouroboros. Available at www.tokenrock.com/explain-ouroboros-70.html. Accessed on 18th March, 2016.

16. Gilchrist, C. (1984). *Alchemy: The great work*. London: Coronet.

17. Ramakrishnan, V. (2016). 'More than ever, science must be central to all our lives'. *The Observer*, Sunday 28th February, p.35.

18. Thompson, W.I. (1989). *The imaginary landscape: Myth and science*. New York: St Martin's Press.

19. Thompson, W.I. (1991). *Reimagination of the world: A critique of the new age, science, and popular culture* (co-authored with David Spangler). Santa Fe, NM: Bear & Company Publishing.

20. Thompson, W.I. (1976). *Evil and world order*. New York: Harper & Row.

21. Buhner, S.H. (2014). *Plant intelligence and the imaginal realm: Into the dreaming of the earth*. Rochester, VER: Bear & Company.

22. Roszak, T. (1972). *Where the wasteland ends: Politics and transcendence in postindustrial society*. New York: Doubleday & Company, Inc.

23. Thompson, W.I. (2013). *Beyond religion*. Great Barrington, MA: Lindisfarne Books.

24. Buhner, S.H. (2014). *Plant intelligence and the imaginal realm: Into the dreaming of the earth*.

25. Naydler, J. (1996). *Goethe on science: An anthology of Goethe's writings*. Edinburgh: Floris Books.

26. Shepherd, L. (1993). *Lifting the veil: The feminine face of science*. Boston: Shambhala.
27. Glass, D. & McCartney, M. (2016). 'Science, Ockham's razor and god'. *Philosophy Now*: 115, p.30-3.
28. Marcuse, H. (1964/1991). *One-dimensional man*. London: Routledge.
29. Stannard, R. (1982/2004). *Science and the renewal of belief*. Philadelphia: Templeton Foundation Press.
30. Walach, H. (2015). *Secular spirituality: The next step towards enlightenment*. London: Springer.
31. Zajonc, A. (1993). *Catching the light: The entwined history of light and mind*. New York: Oxford University Press.
32. Von Franz, M.L. (1998). *Dreams: A study of the dreams of Jung, Descartes, Socrates, and other historical figures*. Boston: Shambhala.
33. Wayan, C. (2016). Quod Vitae. Available at www.worlddreambank.org/q/quodvita.htm. Accessed on 16th February, 2016.
34. Ronnberg, A. & Martin, K. (2010). *The book of symbols: Reflections on archetypal images*. Cologne: Taschen.
35. Stevens, A. (1995). *Private myths: Dreams and dreaming*. London: Hamish Hamiltion.
36. Norris, R. (2016). 'Written in the stars: Aboriginal Australians could be the world's first astronomers'. *New Scientist*, 232(3104), p.153-5.
37. Dawkins, R. (2011). *The magic of reality: How we know what's really true*. London: Bantam Press.
38. Harpur, P. (2002). *The philosophers' fire: A history of the imagination*. Glastonbury: The Squeeze Press.
39. Zeller, M. (1975/1990). *The dream: The vision of the night*. Boston: Sigo Press.
40. Bailey, J. McLeish, K. & Spearman, D. (1981). *Gods and men: Myths and legends from the world's religions*. Oxford: Oxford University Press.
41. Roberts, A. & Roberts, J.M. (1975). *Dreamtime heritage: Australian aboriginal myths*. Adelaide: Rigby.
42. Laughlin, C.D. (2015). 'Dreams, societies and worldviews: A cross-cultural perspective'. In *Dreams and spirituality: A handbook for ministry, spiritual direction and counselling*, eds K. Adams, B.J. Koet & B. Koning, p.16-36. London: Canterbury Press.
43. Grant, S. (2015). We occupy the same land but tell very different stories. *The Guardian*, Monday 22nd February, p.6-9.
44. Roberts, A. & Mountford, C.P. (1971). *The first sunrise: Australian aboriginal myths*. Adelaide: Rigby.
45. Roberts, A. & Mountford, C.P. (1965). *The dreamtime: Australian aboriginal myths*. Adelaide: Rigby.
46. CBS News (2005). Ancient tribe survives tsunami. Available at www.cbsnews.com/new/ancient-tribe-survives-tsunami/ Accessed on 9th September, 2016.
47. Perry, J. (2014). *The edge of extinction: Travels with enduring people in vanishing lands*. Ithaca: Cornell University Press.
48. Harpur, P. (1994). *Daimonic reality: Understanding otherworld encounters*. London: Arkana.
49. Benson, H. (1991). 'Mind/body interaction including Tibetan studies'. In *Mind science: An East-West dialogue*, eds D. Goleman & R. Thurman, p.39-48. Boston: Wisdom Publications.
50. Sogyal, R. (1992). *The Tibetan book of living and dying*. London: Random House.
51. Norbu, C.N. (2012). *Rainbow body: The life and realization of a Tibetan yogin*, Togden Ugyen Tendzin, trans, A. Clemente. Berkeley, CA: North Atlantic Books.
52. Bernstein, J.S. (2005). *Living in the borderland: The evolution of consciousness and the challenge of healing trauma*. New York: Routledge.
53. Roszak, T. (1968/1995). *The making of a counter culture: Reflections on the technocratic society and its youthful opposition*. Berkeley, CA: University of California Press.
54. Kaku, M. (2011). *Physics of the future: The inventions that will transform lives*. London: Penguin Books.
55. Jenkins, S. (2016). 'Scientists aren't gods. They deserve the same scrutiny as everyone else'. *The Guardian*, 9th June, p.33.
56. Ramakrishnan, V. (2016). 'Science marches on via debate, not dogma'. *The Guardian* (letters), 20th June, p.24.
57. Thompson, W.I. (1996). *Coming into being: Artifacts and texts in the evolution of consciousness*. New York: St Martin's Griffin.
58. Butterly, P. (2017). 'A Hippocratic oath for young scientists'. *The Guardian* (letters), 6th May, p.36.
59. Hillman, J. (1996). *The soul's code: In search of character and calling*. London: Bantam Books.
60. Jung, C.G. (1988). Jung on evil. In *Facing evil: Confronting the dreadful power behind genocide, terrorism, and cruelty*, eds P. Woodruff & H.A. Wilmer, p.257-65. Chicago: Open Court.
61. Jaffé, A. (1983). *The myth of meaning in the work of CG Jung*. Zurich: Daimon.
62. Hardy, J. (1987/1996). *A psychology with a soul: Psychosynthesis in evolutionary context*. London: Woodgrange Press.
63. Jones, K. (1993). *Beyond optimism: A Buddhist political ecology*. Oxford: John Carpenter Publishing.

Chapter Two

1. Naess, A. (1995). 'Deepness of questions and the deep ecology movement'. In *Deep ecology for the 21st century: Readings on the philosophy and practice of the new environmentalism*, ed G. Sessions, p.205-12. Boston: Shambhala.
2. Collins, M. (2014). T*he unselfish spirit: Human evolution in a time of global crisis*. East Meon, Hampshire: Permanent Publications.
3. Roszak, T. (1992/2001). *The voice of the earth: A exploration of ecopsychology*. Grand Rapids, MI: Phanes Press.
4. Brooke, R. (1991). *Jung and phenomenology*. London: Routledge.
5. Jung, C.G. (1938/1966). *Psychology and religion*. New Haven: Yale University Press.

6. Washburn, M. (1994). *Transpersonal psychology in psychoanalytical perspective*. Albany, NY: State University of New York Press.

7. Washburn, M. (1995). *The ego and the dynamic ground: A transpersonal theory of human development*. Albany, NY: State University of New York Press.

8. Jung, C.G. ed Sabini, M. (2002/2016). *The earth has a soul: C.G. Jung's writings on nature, technology and modern life*. Berkeley, CA: North Atlantic Books.

9. Kingsley, P. (1999). *In the dark places of wisdom*. Shaftesbury, DOR: Element.

10. Fox, M. (2016). *Sins of the spirit, blessings of the flesh: Transforming evil in soul and society*. Berkeley, CA: North Atlantic Books.

11. Stokes, P. (2002). Philosophy: *100 essential thinkers*. London: Capella.

12. Thompson, W.I. (1996). *Coming into being: Artifacts and texts in the evolution of consciousness*. New York: St Martin's Griffin.

13. Thompson, W.I. (1976). *Evil and world order*. New York: Harper & Row.

14. Harari, Y.N. (2011). *Sapiens: A brief history of humankind*. London: Vintage Books.

15. Fox, M., & Sheldrake, R. (1996/2014). *The physics of angels: Exploring the realm where science and spirit meet*. Rhinebeck, NY: Monkfish Book Publishing.

16. All about heaven (2016). Parmenides. Available at www.allaboutheaven.org/sources/898/145/parmenides. Acessed on, 19th August, 2016.

17. Bussanich, J. (2016). The triumph of the archaic in the work of Peter Kingsley. Available at www.academia.edu/1668255/the_triumph_of_the_archaic_in_the_work_of_peter_kingsley. Accessed on 10th August, 2016.

18. Gowan, J.G. (1994). *Myths of dreaming: Interpreting aboriginal legends*. Bridport, Dorset: Prism Press.

19. Molyneaux, B.L. (1995). *The sacred earth*. London: Macmillan.

20. Mumford, J. (1997). *A chakra and Kundalini workbook: Psychospiritual techniques for health, rejuvenation, psychic powers and spiritual realization*. Woodbury, MINN: Llewellyn Publications.

21. Rickert, T. (2014). Parmenides, ontological enaction, and the prehistory of rhetoric. *Philosophy and Rhetoric*, 47(4), p.472-93.

22. Freke, T. & Gandy, P. (2001). *Jesus and the goddess: The secret teachings of the original Christians*. London: Thorsons.

23. Garfield, P. (1974/1995). *Creative dreaming*. New York: A Fireside Book.

24. Collins, M. (2013). 'Asklepian dreaming and the spirit of transpersonal healing: Linking the placebo response to therapeutic uses of self'. *Journal of Religion and Health*, 52, p.32-45.

25. Kaptchuk, T. & Kelley, J.M. (2013). The placebo effect and the power of imagination. Available at www.m.gulf-times.com/study/369485/the-placebo-effect-and-the-power-of-imagination. Accessed on 6th November, 2016.

26. Kaptchuk, T. & Croucher, M. (1986). *The healing arts: A journey through the faces of medicine*. London: British Broadcasting Corporation.

27. Whitmont, E. (1993). *The alchemy of healing: Psyche and soma*. Berkeley, CA: North Atlantic Books.

28. Fisher, S. (2016). 'The right kind of nothing'. *New Scientist*, 229(3064), p.32-4.

29. Dispenza, J. (2014). *You are the placebo: Making your mind matter*. Carlsbad, CA: Hay House.

30. Smith, S.M. (1995). *Getting into and out of mental ruts: A theory of fixation, incubation and insight*, eds R.J. Sternberg, J.E. Davidson, p.229-51. Cambridge, MA: MIT Press.

31. Baker, C. (2015). *Dark gold: The human shadow and the global crisis*. San Francisco: Next Revelations Press.

32. Jung, C.G. (1954). *Answer to Job*. London: Routledge & Kegan Paul.

33. Meade, M. (2010). *Fate and destiny: The two agreements of the soul*. Seattle: Green Fire Press.

34. Houston, J. (1995). 'Forging the possible human'. In V*oices from the edge*, eds D.J. Brow & R. McClen-Novick, p.231-51. Freedom, CA: The Crossing Press.

35. Shinoda Bolen, J. (2014). *Goddess in everywoman: Powerful archetypes in women's lives*. Harper: New York.

36. Goodchild, V. (2012). *Songlines of the soul: Pathways to a new vision for a new century*. Lake Worth, FL: Nicolas-Hays.

37. Moss, R. (2009). *The secret history of dreaming*. Novato, CA: New World Library.

38. Roszak, T. (1975). *The unfinished animal: The Aquarian frontier and the evolution of consciousness*. New York: Harper Colophon Books.

39. Harpur, P. (2002). *The philosophers' secret fire: A history of the imagination*. Glastonbury: The Squeeze Press.

40. Dourley, J.P. (2010). *On behalf of the mystical fool: Jung on the religious situation*. London: Routledge.

41. Dossey, L. (2012). *One mind: How our individual mind is part of a greater consciousness and why it matters*. London: Hay House.

42. Thompson, W.I. (1989). *The imaginary landscape: Myth and science*. New York: St Martin's Press.

43. Buhner, S.H. (2014). *Plant intelligence and the imaginal realm: Into the dreaming of the earth*. Rochester, VER: Bear & Company.

Chapter Three

1. Ashen, R.N. (1976). 'Foreword: World perspectives'. In Thompson, W.I. *Evil and world order*. New York: Harper & Row.

2. Thompson, W.I. (1989). *The imaginary landscape: Myth and science*. New York: St Martin's Press.

3. Thompson, W.I. (2013). *Beyond religion*. Great Barrington, MA: Lindisfarne Books.

4. Harrell, M. (2015). *Imaginal figures in everyday life: Stories from the world between matter and mind*. Ashville, NC: Chiron Publications.

5. Mindell, A. (2007). *Earth-based psychology: Path awareness from the teachings of Don Juan, Richard Feynman, and Lao Tse*. Portland, OR: Lao Tse Press.

6. Le Van, A. (1996). 'The gorgon Medusa'. Available at www. Perseus.mpiwg-berlin.mpg.de/classes/finALp.html. Accessed on 4th April 2016.
7. Whitmont, E.C. (1982). *Return of the goddess*. London: Arkana.
8. Nozedar, A. (2010). *The illustrated signs and symbols sourcebook*. London: Harper Collins.
9. George, D. (2016). 'The serpent-haired queen Medusa: Sovereign female wisdom'. Available at www.shedrums.com/Medusa.htm. Accessed on 4th April, 2016.
10. Baring, A. & Cashford, J. (1991). *The myth of the goddess: Evolution of an image*. London: Arkana
11. Ronnberg, A. & Martin, K. (2010). *The book of symbols: Reflections on archetypal images*. Taschen: Cologne.
12. Corbin, H. (1969/1981). *Alone with the alone: Creative imagination in the Sufism of Ibn'Arabi*. Princeton, NJ: Princeton University Press/ Bollingen Series.
13. Neumann, E. (1963). *The great mother: An analysis of the archetype*. Princeton, NJ: Bollingen – Princeton University Press.
14. Kelly, H.A. (2006). *Satan: A biography*. Cambridge: Cambridge University Press.
15. Winston, R. (2005). *The story of god: A personal journey into the world of science and religion*. London: Bantam Press.
16. Jakes, L. (2011). 'Mythic creatures – the snake'. Available at www.lizjakes.wordpress.com/category/snakes-in-greek-mythology/. Accessed on 18th March, 2016.
17. Pagels, E. (1988). *Adam, eve and the serpent*. New York: Vintage Books.
18. Campbell, J. (2001). *Thou art that: Transforming religious metaphor*. Novato, CA: New World Library.
19. Stannard, R. (1982/2004). *Science and the renewal of belief*. Philadelphia: Templeton Foundation Press.
20. Baring, A. (2013). *The dream of the cosmos: A quest for the soul*. Dorset: Archive Publishing.
21. Luke, H.M. (1981). *Woman, earth and spirit: The feminine in symbol and myth*. New York: Crossroad Publishing.
22. Narby, J. (1998). *The cosmic serpent: DNA and the origins of knowledge*. London: Weidenfeld & Nicolson.
23. Jung, C.G. (1983). *Memories, dreams, reflections*. London: Flamingo.
24. Molyneaux, B.L. (1995). *The sacred earth*. London: Macmillan Reference Books.
25. Bancroft, A. (1987). *Origins of the sacred: The spiritual journey in western tradition*. London: Arkana.
26. Bond, A. (2011). *The Walsingham story through 950 years*. Walsingham, Norfolk: P.T. Sterry.
27. Broadhurst, P. & Miller, H. (1989). *The sun and the serpent*. Launceston, Cornwall: Mythos.
28. Jones, K. & Griffiths, D, (1996). *The Goddess in Glastonbury*. Glastonbury: Ariadne Publications.
29. Artress, L. (1995). *Walking a sacred path: Rediscovering the labyrinth as a spiritual tool*. New York: Riverhead Books.
30. Sunderland, T.J. (2004). *Walking the labyrinth*. Norwich: Tchenka.
31. Perera, S.B. (1981). *Descent to the Goddess: A way of initiation for women*. Toronto: Ineer City Books.
32. Lovelock, J. (1991). *Gaia: The practical science of planetary medicine*. London: Gaia Books.
33. Buhner, S.H. (2014). *Plant intelligence and the imaginal realm: Into the dreaming of the earth*. Rochester, VER: Bear & Company.
34. Gimbutas, M. (1995). 'Learning the language of the goddess'. In *Voices from the edge*, eds D.J. Brown & R. McClen-Novick, p.7-24. Freedom, CA: The Crossing Press.
35. Senensky, S.S. (2003). *Healing and empowering the feminine: A labyrinth journey*. Wilmette, ILL: Chiron Publications.
36. Baker, C. (1996). *Reclaiming the dark feminine: The price of desire*. Tempe, AZ: New Falcon Publications.
37. Jung, E. (1985). *Animus and anima: Two essays*. Dallas: Spring Publications.
38. Lamb Lash, J. (2006). *Not in his image: Gnostic vision, sacred ecology, and the future of belief*. White River Junction, VER: Chelsea Green Publishing.
39. Schaup, S. (1997). *Sophia: Aspects of the divine feminine, past and present*. York Beach, Ma: Nicolas-Hays.
40. Online etymological dictionary (2016). www.etymonline.com Accessed on 27th June, 2016.
41. Bernstein, J.S. (2005). *Living in the borderland: The evolution of consciousness and the challenge of healing trauma*. London: Routledge.
42. Collins, M. (2014). *The unselfish spirit: Human evolution in a time of global crisis*. East Meon, Hampshire: Permanent Publications.

Chapter Four

1. Hillman, J., & Shamdasani, S. (2013). *Lament of the dead: Psychology after Jung's Red Book*. New York: W.W. Norton & Company.
2. Collins, M. (2014). *The unselfish spirit: Human evolution in a time of global crisis*. East Meon, Hampshire Permanent Publications.
3. Naydler, J. (1996). *Goethe on science: An anthology of Goethe's scientific writings*. Edinburgh: Floris Books.
4. Bernstein, J.S. (2005). *Living in the borderland: The evolution of consciousness and the challenge of healing trauma*. London: Routledge.
5. Grof, S. (2000). *Psychology of the future: Lessons from modern consciousness research*. Albany, NY: State University of New York Press.
6. Boseley, S. (2016). 'Scientists pinning hope on psychedelic help for depression'. *The Guardian*, 3rd December, p.12.
7. Collins, M. (2004). 'Psychiatric shaman'. In *Alternative to war: Creative aftermath of worldwork 2004*, eds S. Halprin & U. Hohler, p.51. Eugene, OR: Changing World Publications.
8. Hillman, J. & Ventura, M. (1992). *We've had a hundred years of psychotherapy and the world's getting worse*. New York: Harper Collins.

9. Ronnberg, A. & Martin, K. (2010). *The book of symbols: Reflections on archetypal images.* Cologne: Taschen.

10. Mindell, A. (1988). *City shadows: Psychological interventions in psychiatry.* London: Arkana.

11. Klein, N. (2014). *This changes everything: Capitalism vs. the climate.* London: Allen Lane

12. O'Riordan, T. (2014). 'Preface: Preparing humanity for a damaged planet'. Collins, M. In *The unselfish spirit: Human evolution in a time of global crisis.* p.xiii-xvi. East Meon, Hampshire: Permanent Publications.

13. Callicott, J.B. (2013). *Thinking like a planet: The land ethic and the earth ethic.* Oxford: Oxford University Press.

14. Swimme, B. & Berry, T. (1992). *The universe story: From the primordial flaring forth to the ecozoic era.* New York: Harper One.

15. Jones, K. (1993). *Beyond optimism: A Buddhist political ecology.* Oxford: John Carpenter Publications.

16. Wikipedia (2016). 'Kogi People'. Available at www.en.wikipedia.org/wiki/kogi_people. Accessed on 12th February, 2016.

17. The Tairona Heritage Trust. (2008). 'Kogi religion and cosmology'. Available at www. tairona.myzen.co.uk/index.php/culture/kogi_religion_and_cosmology. Accessed on 12th February, 2016.

18. Reddy, J. (2013). 'What Colombia's Kogi people can teach us about the environment'. *The Guardian.* Available at www.theguardian.com/sustainable-business/colombia-kogi-environment-destruction. Accessed on 12th February, 2016.

19. Zajonc, A. (1993). *Catching the light: The entwined history of light and mind.* New York: Oxford University Press.

20. Eisenstein, C. (2013). *The more beautiful world our hearts know is possible.* Berkeley, CA: North Atlantic Books.

21. Corbin, H. (1969/1981). *Alone with the alone: Creative imagination in the Sufism of Ibn'Arabi.* Princeton, NJ: Princeton University Press/ Bollingen Series.

22. Roszak, T. (1975). *The unfinished animal: The Aquarian frontier and the evolution of consciousness.* New York: Harper & Row.

23. Thompson, W.I. (1996). *Coming into being: Artifacts and texts in the evolution of consciousness.* New York: St Martin's Griffin.

24. Thompson, W.I. (1989).*The imaginary landscape: Myth and science.* New York: St Martin's Press.

25. Thompson, W.I. (1995). The science of Myth. In *Voices from the edge,* eds D.J. Brown & R. McClen-Novick, p.270-99. Freedom, CA: The Crossing Press.

26. Wikipedia. (2016). 'Eureka'. Available at http://en.m.wikipedia.org-wiki-eureka Accessed on 12th February, 2016.

27. Diamond, S.A. (1996). *Anger, madness and the daimonic: The psychological genesis of violence, evil and creativity.* Albany, NY: State University of New York Press.

28. McNiff, S. (1995). *Earth angels: Engaging the sacred in everyday things.* Boston: Shambhala.

29. Shweder, R. (1995). 'Santa on the cross'. In *The truth about truth: De-confusing and re-constructing the postmodern world,* ed W.T. Anderson, p.72-8. New York: Jeremy P. Tarcher/ Penguin – A New Consciousness Reader.

30. Shamdasani, S. (2003). *Jung and the making of modern psychology: The dream of a science.* Cambridge: Cambridge University Press.

31. Von Franz, M.L. (1998). C.G. Jung: *His myth in our time.* Toronto: Inner City Books.

32. Harpur, P. (1994). *Daimonic reality: Understanding otherworld encounters.* London: Arkana.

33. Larsen, S. (1996). *The mythic imagination: The quest for meaning through personal mythology.* Rochester, VER: Inner Traditions International.

34. Hillman, J. (1983). *Inter views.* Woodstock, CON: Spring Publications.

35. Garfield, P. (1974/1995). *Creative dreaming.* New York: A Fireside Book.

36. Famous Scientists. (2016). 'Seven great examples of scientific discoveries made in dreams'. Available at www.famousscientists.org/7-great-examples-of-scientific-discoveries-made-in-dreams. Accessed on 30th October, 2016.

37. Moss, R. (2009). *The secret history of dreaming.* Novato, CA: New World Library.

38. Dossey, L. (2012). *One mind: How our individual mind is part of a greater consciousness and why it matters.* London: Hay House.

39. Peake, A. (2012). *The daemon: A guide to your extraordinary secret self.* London: Arcturus.

40. Foster, S.J. (2011). *Risky business: A Jungian view of environmental disasters and the nature archetype.* Toronto: Inner City Books.

41. Goodchild, V. (2012). *Songlines of the soul: Pathways to a new vision for a new century.* Lake Worth, FL: Nicolas-Hays.

42. Main, R. (2007). *Revelations of chance: Synchronicity as spiritual experience.* Albany, NY: State University of New York.

43. Roszak, T. (1972). *Where the wasteland ends: Politics and transcendence in postindustrial society.* New York: Doubleday & Company, Inc.

44. Black, J. (2013). *The sacred history: How angels, mystics and higher intelligence made our world.* London: Quercus.

45. Harrell, M. (2015). *Imaginal figures in everyday life: Stories from the world between matter and mind.* Ashville, NC: Chiron Publications.

46. Laughlin, C.D. (2015). Dreams, societies and worldviews: A cross-cultural perspective. In *Dreams and spirituality: A handbook for ministry, spiritual direction and counselling,* eds K. Adams, B.J. Koet & B. Koning, p.16-36. London: Canterbury Press.

47. Swimme, B., & Berry, T. (1992). *The universe story: From the primordial flaring forth to the ecozoic era.* New York: Harper One.

48. 'Erysichthon'. Available at www.01greekmythology.blogspot.com. Accessed on 8th February 2018.

49. Spangler, D. (1991). *Reimagination of the world: A critique of the new age, science, and popular culture* (co-authored with William Irwin Thompson). Santa Fe, NM: Bear & Company Publishing.

50. Mindell, A. (1993). *The shaman's body: A new shamanism for transforming health, relationships and the community*. New York: Harper San Francisco.
51. Begg, E. (1984). *Myth and today's consciousness*. London: Coventure.
52. Ford, D. (1998). *The dark side of the light chasers: Reclaiming your power, creativity, brilliance, and dreams*. New York: Riverhead Books.

Introduction to Part Two: The Redemptive Quest

1. Austin, R. (2014). The prisoner. In *A cold fire*. Stroud: Chrysalis Poetry.
2. Laszlo, E & Kingsley, L.D. (2013). *Dawn of the Akashic Age: New consciousness, quantum resonance and the future of the world*. Rochester, VER: Inner Traditions.
3. Smith, D. (2017). 'Warnings as Trump scraps Obama's climate change policies'. *The Guardian*, 29th March, p.2.
4. Milman, O. (2017). 'Fossil fuels order likely to unleash coastal fury'. *The Guardian*, 29th April, p.24.
5. Arroyo, V. (2017). 'US is the biggest loser on the planet thanks to Trump's calamitous act'. *The Observer*, 4th June, p.34.
6. Tacey, D. (2009). *Edge of the sacred: Jung, psyche, Earth*. Einsiedeln, SW: Daimon Verlag.
7. Collins, M. (2014). *The unselfish spirit: Human evolution in a time of global crisis*. East Meon, Hampshire: Permanent Publications.
8. Eliade, M. (1954). *The myth of the eternal return*. New York: Bollingen Foundation, published by Pantheon Books, NY. Translated by W.R. Trask.
9. Nicoll, M. (1952). *Living time*. London: Vincent Stuart.
10. Goodchild, V. (2012). *Songlines of the soul: Pathways to a new vision for a new century*. Lake Worth, FL: Nicolas-Hays.
11. Mindell, A. (2000). *Quantum mind: The edge between physics and psychology*. Portland, OR: Lao Tse Press.
12. Nicoll, M. (1957). *Psychological commentaries on the teaching of Gurdjieff and Ouspensky, volume 2*. London: Vincent Stuart.
13. Metzner, R. (1886/1998). *The unfolding self: Varieties of transformative experience*. Novato, CA: Origin Press.
14. Von Franz, M.L. (1995). *Shadow and evil in fairy tales*. Boston: Shambhala.

Chapter Five

1. Rockström, J. (2015). 'The future of the planet is in the balance'. *The Observer*, 15th November, p.34-5
2. Greenfield, S. (2003). *Tomorrow's people: How 21st century technology is changing the way we think and feel*. London: Penguin.
3. Roszak, T. (1972). *Where the wasteland ends: Politics and transcendence in postindustrial society*. New York: Doubleday & Company, Inc.
4. Shepherd, L. (1993). *Lifting the veil: The feminine face of science*. Boston: Shambhala.
5. Thompson, W.I. (1976). *Evil and world order*. New York: Harper & Row.

6. Buhner, S.H. (2014). *Plant intelligence and the imaginal realm: Into the dreaming of the earth*. Rochester, VER: Bear & Company.
7. McKenna, J. (2016). 'Pope Francis says destroying the environment is a sin'. *The Guardian*, 1st September. Available at www.theguardian.com/world/2016/sep/01/pope-francis-calls-on-christians-to-embrace-gree-agenda?0p19G=c. Accessed on 15th September, 2016.
8. Nicoll, M. (1954). *The mark*. London: Vincent Stuart.
9. Begg, E. (1984). *Myth and today's consciousness*. London: Coventure.
10. Mercatante, A.S. (1978). *Good and evil: Mythology and folklore*. New York: Harper Row.
11. Harpur, P. (2002). *The philosophers' secret fire: A history of the imagination*. Glastonbury, Somerset: The Squeeze Press.
12. Mavromataki, M. (1997). *Greek mythology and religion*. Athens: Haitalis.
13. Gill, N.S. (2015). .What was Pandora's box?. Available at www.ancienthistory.about.com/grecoromanmyths/a/050410Pandora_and_her_boxor_pithos_htm. Accessed on 27th January, 2016.
14. Solnit, R. (2016). 'Hope is a gift you do not have to surrender'. *The Guardian*, Review; Saturday 16th July, p.2-4.
15. Stirling, B. (2005). 'Future culture and subcultures'. In *Conversations on the edge of the apocalypse*, ed D.J. Brown, p.155-66. Basingstoke, Hampshire: Palgrave MacMillan.
16. Roszak, T. (1975). *The unfinished animal: The Aquarian frontier and the evolution of consciousness*. New York: Harper Colophon Books.
17. Roszak, T. (1978/2003). *Person/planet: The creative disintegration of industrial society*. Lincoln, NE: An Authors Guild Backinprint.com Edition.
18. Baker, C. (2015). *Dark gold: The human shadow and the global crisis*. San Francisco: Next Revelations Press.
19. Collins, M. (2014). *The unselfish spirit: Human evolution in a time of global crisis*. East Meon, Hampshire: Permanent Publications.
20. Luke, H. (2001). The only freedom. In *Gathering sparks*, eds Appelbaum, D. & Kulin, J. p.18-26. New York: Parabola Books.
21. Thompson, W.I. (1995). 'The science of Myth'. In *Voices from the edge*, eds Brown D.J. & McClen-Novick, R. p.270-99. Freedom, CA: The Crossing Press.
22. Patterson, C. (2016). 'Does anyone even give a monkey's?' *The Guardian*, Saturday 6th February, p.35.
23. Carotenuto, A. (1994). *The call of the daimon: Love and truth in the writings of Franz Kafka. The trial and the castle*. Wilmette, ILL: Chiron Publications.
24. Devlin, H. (2017). Science falling victim to 'crisis of narcissism'. *The Guardian*, 21st January, p.19.
25. Buranyi, S. (2017). 'The science fraud squad'. *The Guardian*, 1st February, p.25-6.
26. Vidal, J. (2016). 'Who will cull the beasts that are trashing the planet?' *The Guardian*, 19th December, p.25.

27. Inman, P. (2016). 'A deal for freer trade or corporate greed? Here's the truth about TTIP'. *The Observer*, Sunday 3rd January, p.36-7.

28. Monbiot, G. (2016). 'TTIP may be dead, but a worse trade deal is coming'. *The Guardian*, 7th September, p.29.

29. Guggenbühl-Craig, A. (1991). Quacks, charlatans and false prophets. In *Meeting the shadow: The hidden power of the dark side of human nature*, eds Zweig, C. & Abrams, J. p.110-6. New York: Jeremy P. Tarcher/Perigee. A New Consciousness Reader.

30. El-Hai, J. (2013). *The Nazi and the psychiatrist: Hermann Göring, Dr Douglas M. Kelley, and a fatal meeting of minds at the end of WW11*. New York: Public Affairs.

31. Ford, D. (1998). *The dark side of the light chasers: Reclaiming your power, creativity, brilliance, and dreams*. New York: Riverhead Books.

32. Von Franz, M.L. (1998). *C.G. Jung: His myth in our time*. Toronto: Inner City Books.

33. Weick, K.E. (1988). 'Small sins and large evils'. In *Facing evil: Confronting the dreadful power behind genocide, terrorism, and cruelty*, eds Woodruff, P. & Wilmer, H.A. p.83-92. Chicago: Open Court.

34. Sannella, L. (1989). 'Kundalini: classical and clinical'. In *Spiritual emergency: When personal transformation becomes a crisis*, eds Grof, S. & Grof, C. p.99-108. Los Angeles, CA: Jeremy P. Tarcher.

35. Breaux, C. (1989). *Journey into consciousness: The chakras, tantra and Jungian psychology*. York Beach, MAI: Nicolas-Hays.

36. Mindell, A. (1993). *The shaman's body: A new shamanism for transforming health, relationships and the community*. New York: Harper San Francisco.

37. Harrell, M. (2015). *Imaginal figures in everyday life: Stories from the world between matter and mind*. Asheville, NC: Chiron Publications/ Inner Quest Books.

38. Kenrick, D.T. (2011). 'Have you had a homicidal fantasy today?' *Psychology Today*. Available at www.psychologytoday.com/blo// sex-murder-and-the-meaning-of-life/201105/ have-you-had-homicidal-fantasy-today. Accessed on 3rd April, 2016.

39. Eichman, W.C. (1991). 'Meeting the dark side in spiritual practice'. In *Meeting the shadow: The hidden power of the dark side of human nature*, eds Zweig, C. & Abrams, J. p.134-6. New York: Jeremy P. Tarcher/Perigee. A New Consciousness Reader.

40. Jung, C.G. (2009). *The red book: Liber Novus* (editor, Shamadasni, S.). New York: W.W. Norton & Company.

41. Hillman, J. (1991). 'The cure of the shadow'. In *Meeting the shadow: The hidden power of the dark side of human nature*, eds Zweig, C. & Abrams, J. p.242-3. New York: Jeremy P. Tarcher/Perigee. A New Consciousness Reader.

42. Buergenthal, T. (2009). *A lucky child: A memoir of surviving Auschwitz as a young boy*. London: Profile Books.

43. Rees, L. (2005). *Auschwitz: The Nazis and the 'final solution'*. London: BBC Books.

44. Cadwalladr, C. (2016). 'Extreme right 'has hijacked Google's search engine ranking''. *The Observer*, 4th December, p.5.

45. Von Franz, M.L. (1995). *Shadow and evil in fairy tales*. Boston: Shambhala.

46. Audergon, A. (2005). *The war hotel: Psychological dynamics in violent conflict*. London: Whurr Publishers.

Chapter Six

1. Jung, C.G. (1983). *Memories, dreams, reflections*. London: Fontana.

2. Campbell, J. (2004). *Pathways to bliss: Mythology and personal transformation*. Novato, CA: New World Library.

3. Eliade, M. (1960). *Myths, dreams and mysteries*. London: Harvill Press.

4. Alexander, E. (2012). *Proof of heaven: A neuro-surgeon's journey into the afterlife*. London: Piatkus.

5. Ronnberg, A. & Martin, K. (2010). *The book of symbols: Reflections on archetypal images*. Cologne: Taschen.

6. Romig, R. (2012). 'What do we mean by "evil"? *The New Yorker*. Available at www. newyorker.com/books/page-turner/what-do-we-mean-by-evil. Accessed on 3rd April, 2016.

7. Thompson, W.I. (1989). *The imaginary landscape: Myth and science*. New York: St Martin's Press.

8. Thompson, W.I. (1976). *Evil and world order*. New York: Harper & Row.

9. Jung, C.G. (2009). *Red book: Liber Novus*, ed. S. Shamdasani. New York: W.W. Norton Company.

10. Jung, C.G. (1988). 'Jung on evil'. In *Facing evil: Confronting the dreadful power behind genocide, terrorism, and cruelty*, eds Woodruff, P. & Wilmer, H.A. p.257-64. Chicago: Open Court.

11. Levy, P. (2013). *Dispelling wetiko: Breaking the curse of evil*. Berkeley, CA: North Atalantic Books.

12. Odajnyk, V.W. (1976). *Jung and politics: The political and social ideas of C.G. Jung*. New York: New York University Press.

13. Jung, C.G. (1991). The problem of evil today. In *Meeting the shadow: The hidden power of the dark side of human nature*, eds Zweig, C. & Abrams, J. p.170-2. New York: Jeremy P. Tarcher/Perigee. A New Consciousness Reader.

14. Fox, M. (2016). *Sins of the spirit, blessings of the flesh: Transforming evil in soul and society*. Berkeley, CA: North Atlantic Books.

15. Russell, J.B. (1988). 'The evil one'. In *Facing evil: Confronting the dreadful power behind genocide, terrorism, and cruelty*, ed Woodruff, P. & Wilmer, H.A. p.47-61. Chicago: Open Court.

16. Capra, F. & Luisi, P.L. (2014). *The systems view of life: A unifying vision*. Cambridge: Cambridge University Press.

17. Eisenstein, C. (2013). *The more beautiful world our hearts know is possible*. Berkeley, CA: North Atlantic Books.

18. Chakrabortty, A. (2017). 'One blunt heckler has shown just how much economists are failing us'. *The Guardian*, 10th January, p.31.

19. Townsend, M. (2017). 'Ginger's life on the street: a battle with people's disgust, illness...and the cold'. *The Guardian*, p.34.

20. Elliott, L. (2017). 'Eight men richer than half of humanity says Oxfam, as global elite gather in Davos'. *The Guardian*, 16th January, p.3.

21. Macaskill, W. (2015). *Doing good better*. London: Guardian Books and Faber & Faber.

22. Chu, B. (2017). 'Donald Trump's Wall Street deregulation slammed as 'the last thing we need' by ECB head Mario Draghi'. *The Independent*. Available at www.google.co.uk/amp/www.independent.co.uk/news/business/news/donald-trump-wall-street-deregulation-european-central-bank-president-mario-draghi-a7565411.html%3Famp Accessed on 21st March, 2017.

23. Vaughan, L. & Finch, G. (2017). 'How bankers fixed the world's most important number'. *The Guardian*, 18th January, p.23-5.

24. Eisenstein, C. (2011). *Sacred economics: Money, gift and society in the age of transition*. Berkeley, CA: Evolver Editions.

25. Monbiot, G. (2017). 'At last – an economic model that won't destroy the planet'. *The Guardian*, 12th April, p.35.

26. Williams, Z. (2016). 'Me!' *The Guardian*, Thursday 3rd March, p.6-9.

27. Jacobs, B. (2016). 'Trump labels Clinton "The Devil" and suggests election will be rigged'. *The Guardian*, 2nd August. Available at www.theguardian.com/us-news/2016/aug/02/donald-trump-calls-hilary-clinton-the-devil-and-suggests-election-will-be-rigged. Accessed on 10th August, 2016.

28. Jung, C.G. (1983). *Memories, dreams, reflections*. London: Flamingo.

29. Williams, Z. (2017). 'German-born political theorist JHannah Arendt coined the phrase 'the banality of evil' while writing about the Nazias in the 60s'. *The Guardian*, 2nd February, p.6-9.

30. Stevens, A. (1995). *Private myths: Dreams and dreaming*. London: Hamish Hamilton.

31. Bolen, J.S. (1992). *Ring of power: A Jungian understanding of Wagner's Ring cycle*. New York: Harper Collins.

32. Hillman, J. (1996). *The soul's code: In search of character and calling*. London: Bantam Books.

33. Cooke, R. (2016). 'Hitler's Germany was a place of complete chaos. Meth kept people in the system without their having to think about it'. *The Observer*: New Review, 25th September, p.17-8.

34. Jung, C.G. 'In Stein', M. ed (1995). *Jung on evil*. London: Routledge.

35. Asthana, A. (2016). 'Casey raises alarm over a lack of social cohesion'. *The Guardian*, 5th December, p.9.

36. Monbiot, G. (2016). 'Trump's climate denial is just one of the forces that point towards war'. *The Guardian*, 23rd November, p.37.

37. Snyder, T. (2015). 'Hitler's world may not be so far away'. *The Guardian*, Wednesday 16th September, p.33-5.

38. El-Hai, J. (2013). *The Nazi and the psychiatrist: Hermann Göring, Dr Douglas M. Kelley, and a fatal meeting of minds at the end of WWII*. New York: Public Affairs.

39. Hitler, A. (2015). *Mein Kampf*. Ahmedabad: Jaico Publishing House.

40. Dee, N. (1991). *Understanding dreams: How to benefit from the power of your dreams*. London: Thorsons.

41. Winston, R. (2005). *The story of god: A personal journey into the world of science and religion*. London: Bantam Press.

42. Newsweek. (2016). *Hitler: Special Edition*. New York: Newsweek.

43. More 4, (2016). *Hitler's hidden drug habit*. More 4, 2nd October.

44. Hilberg, R. (1988). 'The holocaust'. In *Facing evil: Confronting the dreadful power behind genocide, terrorism, and cruelty*, eds Woodruff, P. & Wilmer, H.A. p.99-110. Chicago: Open Court.

45. Weick, K.E. (1988). Small sins and large evils. In *Facing evil: Confronting the dreadful power behind genocide, terrorism, and cruelty*, eds Woodruff, P. & Wilmer, H.A. p.83-92. Chicago: Open Court.

46. Baker, C. (2015). *Dark gold: The human shadow and the global crisis*. San Francisco: Next Revelations Press.

47. Zeller, M. (1975/1990). *The dream: The vision of the night*. Boston: Sigo Press.

48. Ford, D. (1998). *The dark side of the light chasers: Reclaiming your power, creativity, brilliance, and dreams*. New York: Riverhead Books.

49. Harrell, M. (2015). *Imaginal figures in everyday life: Stories from the world between matter and mind*. Asheville, NC: Chiron Publications/ Inner Quest Books.

50. Cooke, R. (2016). 'Hitler's Germany was a place of complete chaos. Meth kept people in the system without their having to think about it'. *The Observer*: New Review, 25th September, p.17-8.

51. Sanford, J. (1981). *Evil: The shadow side of reality*. New York: The Crossroad Publishing Company.

52. BBC. (2016). *Himmler: The decent one*. Storyville, BBC4, Sunday 6th March.

53. Sanford, J. (1987/1993). *Jung and the problem of evil: The strange trial of Mr. Hyde*. Boston: Sigo Press.

54. Larsen, S. (1996). *The mythic imagination: The quest for meaning through personal mythology*. Rochester, VER: Inner Traditions International.

55. Frey-Rohn, L. (1991) 'How to deal with evil'. In *Meeting the shadow: The hidden power of the dark side of human nature*, eds Zweig, C. & Abrams, J. p.264-8. New York: Jeremy P. Tarcher/Perigee. A New Consciousness Reader.

56. Corbin, H. (1994). *The man of light in Iranian Sufism*. New Lebanon: Omega Publications. Translated by N. Pearson.

57. Pagels, E. (1995). *The origin of Satan*. New York: Vintage Books.

58. Jung, C.G. (1954). *Answer to Job*. London: Routledge & Kegan Paul.

59. Roszak, T. (1975). *The unfinished animal: The Aquarian frontier and the evolution of consciousness*. New York: Harper Colophon Books.

60. Pagels, E. (1988). *Adam, Eve and the serpent*. New York: Vintage Books.

61. Angelou, M. (1988). 'That which lives after us'. In *Facing evil: Confronting the dreadful power behind genocide, terrorism, and cruelty*, eds Woodruff, P. & Wilmer, H.A. p.21-46. Chicago: Open Court.
62. Kalsched, D. (1996). *The inner world of trauma: Archetypal defences of the human spirit*. London: Routledge.
63. Sparrow, G.S. (1995). *I am with you always: True stories of encounters with Jesus*. London: MacMillan.
64. Roszak, T. (1972). *Where the wasteland ends*. New York: Doubleday and Company.
65. Roszak, T. (1978/2003). *Person/planet: The creative disintegration of industrial society*. Lincoln, NE: An Authors Guild Backinprint. com Edition.
66. Peck, M.S. (1988). 'Healing institutional evil'. In *Facing evil: Confronting the dreadful power behind genocide, terrorism, and cruelty*, eds Woodruff, P. & Wilmer, H.A. p.189-207. Chicago: Open Court.
67. Von Franz, M.L. (1995). *Shadow and evil in fairy tales*. Boston: Shambhala.

Chapter Seven

1. Collins, M. (2014). *The unselfish spirit: Human evolution in a time of global crisis*. East Meon, Hampshire: Permanent Publications.
2. Otto, R. (1958). *The idea of the holy*. London: Oxford University Press.
3. Dourley, J.P. (2010). *On behalf of the mystical fool: Jung on the religious situation*. London: Routledge.
4. Shamdasani, S. (2003). *Jung and the making of modern psychology: The dream of a science*. Cambridge: Cambridge University Press.
5. Hillman, J. & Shamdasani, S. (2013). *Lament of the dead: Psychology after Jung's Red Book*. New York: W.W. Norton & Company.
6. Odajnyk, V.W. (1976). *Jung and politics: The political and social ideas of C.G. Jung*. New York: New York University Press.
7. Zeller, M. (1975/1990). *The dream: The vision of the night*. Boston: Sigo Press.
8. Roszak, T. (1972). *Where the wasteland ends: Politics and transcendence in postindustrial society*. New York: Doubleday & Company, Inc.
9. Harpur, P. (2002). *The philosophers' secret fire: A history of the imagination*. Glastonbury: The Squeeze Press.
10. Harpur, P. (1994). *Daimonic reality: Understanding otherworld encounters*. London: Penguin/Arkana.
11. Jung, C.G. (2009). *The Red Book*: Liber Novus, ed. S. Shamdasani. New York: W.W. Norton & Company.
12. Marstrand-Strong, H. (2012). 'Ancient prophecies and the vision quest as a path to oneness'. In *The song of the earth: A synthesis of the scientific and spiritual worldviews*, eds Harland, M. & Keepin, W. p.102-7. East Meon, Hampshire: Permanent Publications.
13. Hesse, H. (1919). Quoted in L. Dossey. (2013). *One mind: How our individual mind is part of a greater consciousness and why it matters*. Carlsbad, CA: Hay House.
14. Owen, M. (2002). *Jung and the Native American moon cycles: Rhythms of influence*. Berwick, ME: Nicolas-Hays, Inc.
15. Jung, C.G. (1983). *Memories, dreams, reflections*. London: Fontana.
16. Deloria, V. (2009). *C.G. Jung and the Sioux traditions: Dreams, visions, nature, and the primitive*, eds Deloria, P.J. & Bernstein, J.S. New Orleans, LOU: Spring Journal Books.
17. Suzuki, D. & Knudtson, P. (1992). *Wisdom of the elders: Sacred native stories of nature*. New York: Bantam Books.
18. Laughlin, C.D. (2015). 'Dreams, societies and worldviews: A cross cultural perspective'. In *Dreams and spirituality: A handbook for ministry, spiritual direction and counselling*, eds Adams, K. Koet, B.J. & Koning, B. p.16-36. London: Canterbury Press.
19. Mindell, A. (1982). *Dreambody: The body's role in revealing the self*. London: Arkana.
20. Thompson, W.I. (1976). *Evil and world order*. New York: Harper & Row.
21. Huang, C.A. (1988). 'Tai Ji'. In *Facing evil: Confronting the dreadful power behind genocide, terrorism, and cruelty*, eds Woodruff, P. & Wilmer, H.A. p.176-81. Chicago: Open Court.
22. Swimme, B. & Berry, T. (1992). *The universe story. From the primordial flaring forth to the ecozoic era*. New York: Harper One.
23. Neumann, E. (1968). 'Mystical man'. In *The mystic vision: Papers from the Eranos yearbooks*, ed Campbell, J. p.375-415. New York: Bollingen Foundation.
24. Woolger, R. (1987). *Other lives, other selves: A Jungian psychotherapist discusses past lives*. London: Thorsons.
25. Jawar, M. (2014). Children who seemingly remember past lives. *Psychology Today*. Available at, www.psychologytoday.com/blog/feeling-too-much-/201412/children-who-seemingly-remember-past-lives. Accessed on, 5th December, 2016.
26. Laszlo, E. (2012). *The Akasha paradigm: Revolution in science, evolution in consciousness*. Tillson, NY: Waterfront Press & Worthy Shorts.
27. Castello, M.S. (2012). 'How trauma is carried across generations: Holding the secret history of our ancestors'. *Psychology Today*. Available at www.psychologytoday.com/blog/the-me-in-we/201205/how-trauma-is-carried-across-generations. Accessed on 7th May, 2017.
28. Mindell, A. (1993). *The shaman's body: A new shamanism for transforming health, relationships and the community*. New York: Harper San Francisco.
29. Ronnberg, A. & Martin, K. (2010). *The book of symbols: Reflections on archetypal images*. Cologne: Taschen.
30. Fox, M. (2016). *Sins of the spirit, blessings of the flesh: Transforming evil in soul and society*. Berkeley, CA: North Atlantic Books.

Chapter Eight

1. Thompson, W.I. (1976). *Evil and world order*. New York: Harper & Row.
2. Thompson, W.I. (1989). *The imaginary landscape: Myth and science*. New York: St Martin's Press.
3. Peake, A. (2008). *The Daemon: A guide to your extraordinary secret self*. London: Arcturus.
4. Harpur, P. (2002). *The philosophers' secret fire: A history of the imagination*. Glastonbury: The Squeeze Press.
5. Otto, R. (1958). *The idea of the holy*. London: Oxford University Press.
6. Garland, R. (1994). *Religion and the Greeks*. London: Bristol Classical Press.
7. Diamond, S.A. (1996). *Anger, madness and the daimonic: The psychological genesis of violence, evil, and creativity*. Albany, NY: State University of New York Press.
8. Harpur, P. (1994). *Daimonic reality: Understanding otherworld encounters*. London: Penguin/Arkana.
9. Roszak, T. (1975). *Unfinished animal: The Aquarian frontier and the evolution of consciousness*. New York: Harper Colophon Books.
10. El-Hai, J. (2013). *The Nazi and the psychiatrist: Hermann Göring, Dr Douglas M. Kelley, and a fatal meeting of minds at the end of WW11*. New York: Public Affairs.
11. Mindell, A. (1993). *The shaman's body: A new shamanism for transforming health, relationships and the community*. New York: Harper San Francisco.
12. McKirahan, R.D. (1994). *Philosophy before Socrates*. Indianapolis: Hackett Publishing Company.
13. Carotenuto, A. (1989). *The call of the daimon: Love and truth in the writings of Franz Kafka. The trial and the castle*. Wilmette, ILL: Chiron Publications.
14. Sanford, J.A. (1995). *Fate, love and ecstasy: Wisdom from the lesser-known goddesses of the Greeks*. Wilmette, ILL: Chiron Publications.
15. May, R. (1969). *Love and will*. New York: W.W. Norton & Company.
16. Callicott, J.B. (2013). *Thinking like a planet: The land ethic and the earth ethic*. Oxford: Oxford University Press.
17. Webb, J.F. (1993). *The Beatitudes: A summary of Jesus' inner teaching*. London: CTS Publications.
18. Prabhavananda, S. (1992). *The Sermon on the Mount according to Vedanta*. Hollywood, CA: Vedanta Press.
19. Dennis, S.L. (2001). *Embrace of the daimon: Sensuality and the imagination of forbidden imagery in depth psychology*. York Beach, MAI: Nicolas-Hays.
20. Diamond, S.A. (1991). 'Redeeming our devils and demons'. In *Meeting the shadow: The hidden power of the dark side of human nature*, eds Zweig, C. & Abrams, J. p.180-5. New York: Jeremy P. Tarcher/Perigee. A New Consciousness Reader.
21. Tacey, D. (editor). (2012). *The Jung reader*. London: Routledge.
22. Hillman, J. (1996). *The soul's code: In search of character and calling*. London: Bantam Books.
23. Von Franz, M.L. (1998). *C.G. Jung: His myth in our time*. Toronto: Inner City Books.
24. Jung, C.G. (1983). *Memories, dreams, reflections*. London: Fontana.
25. La Chapelle, D. (2001). *Navigating the tides of change: Stories from science, the sacred, and a wise planet*. Gabriola Island, VC: New Society Publishers.
26. Hillman, J. & Shamdasani, S. (2013). *Lament of the dead: Psychology after Jung's Red Book*. New York: W.W. Norton & Company.
27. Black, J. (2013). *The sacred history: How angels, mystics and higher intelligence made our world*. London: Quercus.
28. Johnson, R.A. (1993). *The fisher king and the handless maiden: Understanding the wounded feeling function in masculine and feminine psychology*. New York: Harper One.
29. Matthews, J. (1997). *Healing the wounded king: Soul work and the quest for the grail*. Shaftesbury, Dorset: Element.
30. Jung, C.G. (2009). *The Red Book: Liber Novus*, ed Shamdasani, S. New York: W.W. Norton & Company.
31. Harpur, P. (2002). *The philosophers' secret fire: A history of the imagination*. Glastonbury: The Squeeze Press.
32. What Is. (2016). *Hierarchy*. Available at Whatis. techtarget.com. Accessed on 24th October 2016.
33. Yeats, W.B. (1925/2008). *A vision, volume XIII: The collected works of W.B. Yeats*, eds Paul, C.E. & Harper, M.H. New York: Scribner.
34. Bradshaw, G.A. (2012). 'Restoring our daemons'. In *Vital signs: Psychological responses to ecological crisis*, eds Rust, M.J. & Totton, N. p.89-103. London: Karnac Books.
35. Hinds, J. (2016). 'Eudemonic philosophy and human(istic) – nature relationships in ecotherapy'. In *Ecotherapy: Theory, research and practice*, eds Jordan, M. & Hinds, J. p.45-57. London: Palgrave.

Introduction to Part Three: The Emancipatory Edge

1. Austin, R. (2014). Philosopher. In *A cold fire*. Stroud: Chrysalis Poetry.
2. Rust, M.J., & Totton, N. (2012). Introduction. In *Vital signs: Psychological responses to ecological crisis*, eds Rust, M.J. & Totton, N. p.xv-xxii. London: Karnac Books.
3. O'Riordan, T. (2013). 'Sustaining markets, establishing well-being, and promoting social virtue for transformational tipping points'. In *Addressing tipping points for a precarious future*, eds O'Riordan, T. & Lenton, T. p.173-87. Oxford: Oxford University Press. Published for The British Academy.
4. Laszlo, E. (2007). *Science and the akashic field: An integral theory of everything*. Rochester, VER: Inner Traditions.

5. Freeman, L. (2013). 'Contemplative consciousness'. In *Addressing tipping points for a precarious future*, eds O'Riordan, T. & Lenton, T. p.151-64. Oxford: Oxford University Press. Published for The British Academy.

6. Taylor, B. (2010). *Dark green religion: Nature spirituality and the planetary future*. Berkeley, CA: University of California Press.

7. Metzner, R. (1999). *Green psychology: Transforming our relationship to the earth*. Rochester, VER: Inner Traditions.

8. Goodchild, V. (2012). *Songlines of the soul: Pathways to a new vision for a new century*. Lake Worth, FL: Nicolas-Hays.

9. Grof, S. (2006). *When the impossible happens: Adventures in non-ordinary realities*. Boulder, CO: Sounds True.

10. Tompkins, P. & Beddos, T. (2016). *Proof of angels*. London: Simon and Schuster.

11. Sartori, P. & Walsh, K. (2017). *The transformative power of near-death experiences*. London: Watkins

12. Mindell, A. (1988). *City Shadows: Psychological interventions in psychiatry*. London: Arkana.

13. Lorimer, D. (1990). *Whole in one: The near-death experience and the ethic of interconnectedness*. London: Arkana.

14. Jung, C.G. (1983). *Memories, dreams, reflections*. London: Flamingo.

15. Fabricus, J. (1976/1994). *Alchemy: The medieval alchemists and their royal art*. London: Diamond Books.

16. Whitehouse, M. (2008). *Total Kabbalah*. San Francisco: Chronicle Books.

17. Berry, T. (1999). *The great work: Our way into the future*. New York: Bell Tower.

18. Kingsley, L.D. (2014). *The phoenix generation: A new era of connection, compassion and consciousness*. London: Watkins Publishing.

19. Gibbs, S. (2017). 'Experts issue warning on killer robots: Once this Pandora's box is opened, it will be hard to close'. *The Guardian*, 21st August, p.7.

Chapter Nine

1. Levine, S. (1993). *A year to live: How to live this life as if it were your last*. London: Thorsons.

2. Thompson, W.I. (1995). 'The science of Myth'. In *Voices from the edge*, eds Brown, D.J. & McClen-Novick, R. p.270-99. Freedom, CA: The Crossing Press.

3. Nuwer, R. (2015). *What it's really like to die*. Available at www.bbc.com/future/story/20150303-what -its-really-like-to-die. Accessed on 4th April, 2016.

4. Sartori, P. (2014). *The wisdom of near death experiences: How understanding NDEs can help us live more fully*. London: Watkins Publishing.

5. Jovanovic, P. (1995). *An inquiry into the existence of guardian angels*. New York: M. Evans and Company.

6. Dossey, L. (2012). *One mind: How our individual mind is part of a greater consciousness and why it matters*. Carlsbad, CA: Hay House.

7. Collins, M. (2016). *The unselfish spirit: Human evolution in a time of global crisis*. East Meon, Hampshire: Permanent Publications.

8. Long, J.A. (2013). 'Life review, changed beliefs, universal order and purpose, and the near-death experience, part 4 soulmates'. Available at www.nderf.org/NDERF/Research/purpose_lifereview.htm. Accessed on 26th April, 2016.

9. Thompson, W.I. (2013). *Beyond religion*. Great Barrington, MA: Lindisfarne Books.

10. Wikipedia. (2017). *The myth of Er*. Available at, http://en.m.wikipedia.org/wiki/Myth_of_Er. Accessed on 12th January, 2017.

11. Ronnberg, A. & Martin, K. (2010). *The book of symbols: Reflections on archetypal images*. Cologne: Taschen.

12. Buhner, S.H. (2014). *Plant intelligence and the imaginal realm: Into the dreaming of the earth*. Rochester, VER: Bear & Company.

13. Meade, M. (2010). *Fate and destiny: The two agreements of the soul*. Seattle: Greenfire Press.

14. Alexander, E. (2014). *The map of heaven: A neurosurgeon explores the mysteries of the afterlife and the truth about what lies beyond*. London: Piatkus.

15. El-Hai, J. (2013). *The Nazi and the psychiatrist: Hermann Göring, Dr Douglas M. Kelley, and a fatal meeting of minds at the end of WWII*. New York: Public Affairs.

16. Moss, R. (2009). *The secret history of dreaming*. Novato, CA: New World Library.

17. La Chapelle, D. (2001). *Navigating the tides of change: Stories from science, the sacred, and a wise planet*. Gabriola Island, VC: New Society Publishers.

18. Krishnamurti, J. (2005). *Facing a world in crisis: What life teaches us in challenging times*. Boston: Shambhala.

19. Hillman, J. (1996). *The soul's code: In search of character and calling*. London: Bantam Books.

20. Skrbina, D. (2016). *The metaphysics of technology*. London: Routledge.

21. Thompson, W.I. (1989). *The imaginary landscape: Myth and science*. New York: St Martin's Press.

22. Adams, T. (2016). 'Is there too much stress?' *The Observer*, Sunday 14th February, p.8-11.

23. Jung, C.G. M. Sabini, ed (2002/2016). *C.G. Jung on nature, technology and modern life*. Berkeley, CA: North Atlantic Books.

24. Arthur, C. (2015). 'Homo sapiens will be split into a handful of gods and the rest of us'. *The Observer*, Sunday 8th November, p.42-3.

25. Boyle, M. (2016). 'Why I've decided to live without technology'. *The Guardian*, 19th December, p.27.

26. Bloom, H. (1996). *Omens of Millennium*. London: Fourth Estate.

27. Harris, J. (2017). 'They call it fun, but the digital giants are turning workers into robots'. *The Guardian*, 21st January, p.39.

28. Cadwalladr, C. (2017). 'Robert Mercer, a computer scientist and hedge-fund mogul, uses big data and artificial intelligence to wage information wars that disable mainstream media. And he's winning'. *The Observer*. The New Review, 26th February, p.8-11.

29. Carr, N. (2010). *The shallows: How the Internet is changing the way we think, read and remember*. London: Atlantic Books.

30. Benady, D. (2016). 'Are we ready for the rise of the robots?' *The Guardian*, Wednesday 30th March, p.25.

31. Allen, K. (2016). 'The machines are rising – but we still need the human touch'. *The Observer*, Sunday 13th March, p.42.

32. Turkle, S. (2011). *Alone together: Why we expect more from technology and less from each other*. New York: Basic Books.

33. Greenfield, S. (2003). *Tomorrow's people: How 21st century technology is changing the way we think and feel*. London: Penguin Books.

34. Noughton, J. (2016). 'Forget ideology: The new threats to liberal democracy are coming from technology and bioscience'. *The Observer*, 28th August, p.30-1.

35. Hern, A. (2016). 'The computer that learns by thinking'. *The Guardian*, Tuesday 15th March, p.9.

36. Solon, O. (2017). 'Cards are stacked against humanity after artificial intelligence wins poker contest'. *The Guardian*, 1st Febuary, p.3.

37. Millar, J. (2016). 'The momentous advance in artificial intelligence demands a new set of ethics'. *The Observer*, Sunday 13th March, p.33.

38. Sample, I. (2017). 'Set up watchdog for artificial intelligence, say tech experts'. *The Guardian*, 28th January, p.9.

39. Sample, I. (2017). 'When bots go bad: How Wikipedia's helpers ended up locked in conflict'. *The Guardian*, 24th February, p.3.

40. Chatfield, T. (2016). 'How much should we fear the rise of artificial intelligence?' *The Guardian*, Friday 18th March, p.35.

41. Firth-Butterfield, K. (2017). 'First came noughts and crosses, then chess. Now artificial intelligence has managed to beat pros at the poker table'. *The Observer*. In Focus, 5th February, p.28-9.

42. Tucker, I. (2016). 'Humanity's biggest fear is becoming irrelevant'. *The Observer*, 27th November, p.22-3.

43. Borody, W.A. (2013). 'The Japanese roboticist Masahiro Mori's Buddhist inspired concept of "The Uncanny Valley"'. (*Bukimi no Tani Genshō*). *Journal of Evolution and Technology*, 2(1), 31-44.

44. Global Mail. (2013). Japan's love affair with robots. Available at http://newsfeed.time. com/2013/02/21/watch-japans-love-affair-with-robots-explained/. Accessed on 8th December, 2016.

45. BBC. (2016). *The immortalist*. BBC2, Horizon. Wednesday 16th March.

46. Japan Times. (2014). 'Japan's suicide rate exceeds world average: WHO report'. Available at www.japantimes.co.jp/news/2014/09/04/national/japans-suicide -rate-exceeds-world-average-who-report/#.WDshG-IYWJV. Accessed on 27th November, 2016.

47. Haworth, A. (2013). 'Why have young people in Japan stopped having sex?' *The Guardian*. Available at www.the guardian.com/world/2013/oct/20/young-people-japan-stopped-having-sex?0p19G=c. Accessed on 27th November, 2016.

48. Davis, N. (2016). 'Big steps in bionics offer the chance to walk again – and be superhuman'. *The Guardian*, 26th December, p.13.

49. O' Connell, M. (2017). "Goodbye body, hello posthuman machine'. *The Observer*, Science and Tech, 26th March, p.19-21.

50. Wong, J.C. (2016). 'I am a robot. I'm also a lawyer, a nurse, a waiter and a teacher'. *The Observer*, Sunday 20th March, p.35.

51. Kursweil, R. (2005). 'Designing higher intelligence'. In *Conversations on the edge of the apocalypse*, ed Brown, D.J. p.105-20. Basingstoke: Palgrave MacMillan.

52. Donnelly, P. (2017). 'Why rage against the machines when we could be friends?' *The Observer*, 30th April, p.44.

53. Fox, M. (2016). *Sins of the spirit, blessings of the flesh: Transforming evil in soul and society*. Berkley, CA: North Atlantic Books.

54. Jung, C.G. (2009). *The Red Book: Liber Novus*, ed. S. Shamdasani. New York: W.W. Norton & Company.

55. Macfarlane, R. (2016). 'What have we done?' *The Guardian*, Saturday 2nd April, p.2-3.

56. Bartlett, J. (2017). *Secrets of Silicon Valley, part one*. BBC 2, Sunday 6th August.

57. Bartlett, J. (2017). *Secrets of Silicon Valley, part two*. BBC 2, Sunday 13th August.

58. Giono, J. (1953/1996). *The man who planted trees*. London: Haverhill Press.

Chapter Ten

1. Spangler, D. & Thompson, W.I. (1991). *Reimagination of the world: A critique of the new age, science, and popular culture*. Santa Fe, NM: Bear & Company Publishing.

2. Hillman, J. & Shamdasani, S. (2013). *Lament of the dead: Psychology after Jung's Red Book*. New York: W.W. Norton & Company.

3. Godden, R. (1996). *A pocket book of spiritual poems*. London: Hodder & Stoughton.

4. Fuller, R.B. (1970). *I seem to be a verb*. New York: Bantam Books.

5. Fuller, R.B. (1963). *No more second hand God*. Carbondale: Southern Illinois Press.

6. Collins, M. (2014). *The unselfish spirit: Human evolution in a time of global crisis*. East Meon, Hampshire: Permanent Publications.

7. Mindell, A. (2013). *Dance of the ancient one: How the universe solves personal and world problems*. Portland, OR: Deep Democracy Institute.

8. Jung, C.G. (2009). *The red book: Liber Novus*. (Shamdasani, S. ed). New York: W.W. Norton & Company.

9. Jung, C.G. (1983). *Memories, dreams, reflections*. London: Flamingo.

10. Dass, R. (1970). *Doing your own being*. London: Neville Spearman.

11. Jung C.G. (1940). *The integration of the personality.* London: Kegan Paul, Trench, Trubner & Co. Ltd.
12. Van Der Post, L. (1976). *Jung and the story of our time.* London: The Hogarth Press.
13. Collins, M. (2007). 'Engaging self-actualisation through occupational intelligence'. *Journal of Occupational Science*, 14(2), p.92-9.
14. Collins, M. (2011). 'The Akashic field and archetypal occupations: Transforming human potential through doing and being'. *World Futures*, 67(7), 453-79.
15. Hoffmann, Y. (1975). *The sound of the one hand: 281 Zen koans with answers.* London: Sheldon Press.
16. Churton, T. (2005). *The golden builders: Alchemists, rosicrucians, and the first freemasons.* Boston, MA: Weiser Books.
17. Singer, J. (1973). *Boundaries of the soul: The practice of Jung's psychology.* London: Victor Gollancz.
18. Jung, C.G. (1927). Cited in Scarpelli, M. 'The earth, the song, the symbol'. In *On soul and earth*, ed Liotta, E. p.268-76. London: Routledge.
19. Roszak, T. (1975). *Unfinished animal: The Aquarian frontier and the evolution of consciousness.* New York: Harper Colophon Books.
20. Hillman, J. (1983). *Inter Views.* Woodstock, Conn: Spring Publications.
21. Von Franz, M.L. (1998). *C.G. Jung: His myth in our time.* Toronto: Inner City Books.
22. Harpur, P. (2002). *The philosophers' secret fire: A history of the imagination.* Glastonbury: The Squeeze Press.
23. Harpur, P. (1994). *Daimonic reality: Understanding otherworld encounters.* London: Penguin/Arkana.
24. Roszak, T. (1978/2003). *Person/planet: The creative disintegration of industrial society.* Lincoln, NE: iUniverse.
25. McNiff, S. (1995). *Earth angels: Engaging the sacred in everyday things.* Boston: Shambhala.
26. Zeller, M. (1975/1990). *The dream: The vision of the night.* Boston: Sigo Press.
27. Dossey. L. (2012). *One mind: How our individual mind is part of a greater consciousness and why it matters.* Carlsbad, CA: Hay House.
28. La Chapelle, D. (2001). *Navigating the tides of change: Stories from science, the sacred, and a wise planet.* Gabriola Island, BC: New Society Publishers.
29. Mitchell, E. (2008). *The way of the explorer: An Apollo astronaut's journey through the material and mystical worlds.* Franklin Lakes, NJ: New Page Books.
30. Kingsnorth, P. (2016). 'The call of the wild'. *The Guardian*, 23rd July, p.15-6.
31. Moss, R. (2009). *The secret history of dreaming.* Novato, CA: New World Library.
32. Jung, C.G. In Sabini, M. ed (2002/2016). *C.G. Jung on nature, technology and modern life.* Berkeley, CA: North Atlantic Books.
33. Garfield, P. (1974/1995). *Creative dreaming.* New York: A Fireside Book.
34. Buhner, S.H. (2014). *Plant intelligence and the imaginal realm: Into the dreaming of the earth.* Rochester, VER: Bear & Company.
35. Meade, M. (2010). *Fate and destiny: The two agreements of the soul.* Seattle: Greenfire Press.
36. Farmer-Knowles, H. (2010). *The healing plants bible: The definitive guide to herbs, trees and flowers.* London: Octopus Publishing.
37. Ywahoo, D. (2012). 'Voices of our ancestors'. In *The song of the earth: A synthesis of the scientific and spiritual worldviews*, eds Harland, M. & Keepin, W. p.118-9. East Meon, Hampshire: Permanent Publications.
38. Goodchild, V. (2012). *Songlines of the soul: Pathways to a new vision for a new century.* Lake Worth, FL: Nicolas-Hays.
39. Abram, D. (2010). *Becoming animal: A earthly cosmology.* New York: Vintage Books.
40. Tompkins, P. & Bird, C. (1973). *The secret life of plants: A fascinating account of the physical, emotional, and spiritual relations between plants and man.* New York: Harper.
41. Harland, M. & Keepin, W. (2012). 'Introduction'. In *The song of the earth: A synthesis of the scientific and spiritual worldviews*, eds Harland, M. & Keepin, W. p.xi-xiv. East Meon, Hampshire: Permanent Publications.
42. Roszak, T. (1972). *Where the wasteland ends: Politics and transcendence in postindustrial society.* New York: Doubleday & Company, Inc.
43. Jung, C.G. (1988). 'Jung on evil'. In *Facing evil: Confronting the dreadful power behind genocide, terrorism, and cruelty*, eds Woodruff, P. & Wilmer, H.A. p.257-73. Chicago: Open Court.

Chapter Eleven

1. Collins, M. (2014). *The unselfish spirit: Human evolution in a time of global crisis.* East Meon, Hampshire: Permanent Publications.
2. Skolimowski, H. (1993). *A sacred place to dwell: Living with reverence upon the earth.* Rockport, MA: Element.
3. Paulson, G.L. (2003). *Kundalini and the chakras.* St Paul, MINN: Lewellyn Publications.
4. O'Riordan, T. (2014). 'Preparing humanity for a damaged planet'. Preface, in Collins, M. *The unselfish spirit: Human evolution in a time of global crisis.* East Meon: Permanent Publications.
5. Black, RE., Cesar, GV., Walker, SP., Zulfiqar, AB., Parul, C., de Onis, M., Majid, E, Grantham-McGregor, S., Katz, J., Martorell, R., Uauy, R., The Maternal and Child Nutrition Study Group. (2013). 'Maternal and child undernutrition and overweight in low-income and middle-income countries'. *Lancet*, Volume 382, No. 9890, p.427-451. Available at www.thelancet.com/journals/lancet/article/PIIS0140-6736%2813%2960937-X/abstract. Accessed on 20th August, 2015.
6. Judith, A. (1996/2004). *Eastern body, western mind: Psychology and the chakra system as a path to the self.* Berkeley, CA: Celestial Arts.

7. Jung, C.G. (1996). *The psychology of Kundalini yoga: Notes of the seminar given in 1932 by C.G. Jung*, edited by S. Shamdasani. Princeton, NJ: Princeton University Press. Bollingen Series XCIX.

8. Breaux, C. (1989). *Journey into consciousness: The chakras, tantra and Jungian psychology*. York Beach, MAI: Nicolas-Hays.

9. Chitrabhanu, G.S. (1979). *The psychology of enlightenment: Meditations on the seven energy centers*. Berkeley, CA: Asian Humanities Press, edited by L. Miller.

10. Fox, M. (2016). *Sins of the spirit, blessings of the flesh: Transforming evil in soul and society*. Berkeley, CA: North Atlantic Books.

11. Khalsa, D.S. & O'Keefe, D. (2016). *Kundalini yoga*. London: Gaia.

12. Mindell, A. (2004). *The quantum mind and healing. How to listen and respond to your body's symptoms*. Charlottesville, VA: Hampton Roads.

13. Jung, C.G. In Sabini, M. ed (2002/2016). *C.G. Jung on nature, technology and modern life*. Berkeley, CA: North Atlantic Books.

14. Dalai Lama, HH. (1996). *The good heart: His Holiness the Dalai Lama explores the heart of Christianity – and of humanity*. London: Rider.

15. Hanh, T.N. (1998). *The heart of the Buddha's teaching: Transforming suffering into peace, joy and liberation*. London: Rider.

16. Logothetis, A.S. (2001). *The heart: An orthodox and spiritual guide*. Nafpaktos, GR: Brotherhood of the Transfiguration of our Saviour Jesus Christ.

17. Llewellyn, V.L. (2012). *Prayer of the heart in Christian and Sufi mysticism*. Point Reyes, CA: Golden Sufi Center.

18. Corbin, H. (1969/1981). *Alone with the alone: Creative imagination in the Sufism of Ibn 'Arabī*. Princeton, NJ: Princeton University Press. Bollingen Series XCI.

19. Thompson, W.I. (1995). 'The science of Myth'. In *Voices from the edge*, eds Brown, D.J. & McClen-Novick, R. p.270-99. Freedom, CA: The Crossing Press.

20. Peake, A. (2008). *The Daemon: A guide to your extraordinary secret self*. London: Arcturus.

21. Corbin, H. (1978/1994). *The man of light in Iranian Sufism*. Translated by N. Pearson. New Lebanon, NY: Omega Publications.

22. Harpur, P. (1994). *Daimonic reality: Understanding otherworld encounters*. London: Penguin/Arkana.

23. Katra, J. & Targ, R. (2011). *The heart of the mind: Using our mind to transform our consciousness*. Guildford: White Crow Books.

24. Myers, P.Z. (2010). A change in who we are. In *This will change everything: Ideas that will shape the future*, ed Brockman, J. p.8-9. New York: Harper Perennial.

25. Geiger, J. (2013). *The angel effect: We are never alone*. New York: Weinstein Books.

26. Mitchell, E. (2008). *The way of the explorer: An Apollo astronaut's journey through the material and mystical worlds*. Franklin Lakes, NJ: New Page Books.

27. Alexander, E. (2012). *Proof of heaven: A neurosurgeon's journey into the afterlife*. London: Piatkus.

28. Rinpoche, B. (1993). *Death and the art of dying in Tibetan Buddhism*. San Francisco: Clear Point Press.

29. Harari, Y.N. (2011). *Sapiens: A brief history of humankind*. London: Vintage Books.

30. Thompson, W.I. (1976). *Evil and world order*. New York: Harper & Row.

31. Spangler, D. & Thompson, W.I. (1991). *Reimagination of the world: A critique of the new age, science, and popular culture*. Santa Fe, NM: Bear & Company Publishing.

32. McNiff, S. (1995). *Earth angels: Engaging the sacred in everyday things*. Boston: Shambhala.

33. Byrne, L. (2008). *Angels in my hair*. London: Century.

34. Jovanovic, P. (1995). *An inquiry into the existence of guardian angels*. New York: M. Evans and Company.

35. Black, J. (2013). *The sacred history: How angels, mystics and higher intelligence made our world*. London: Quercus.

36. Moss, R. (2009). *The secret history of dreaming*. Novato, CA: New World Library.

37. Cruz, J.C. (1997). *Mysteries, marvels, miracles in the lives of the saints*. Charlotte, N. CA: Tan Books.

38. Hillman, J. (1996). *The soul's code: In search of character and calling*. London: Bantam Books.

39. Sanford, J.A. (1995). *Fate, love and ecstasy: Wisdom from the lesser-known goddesses of the Greeks*. Wilmette, ILL: Chiron Publications.

40. Zajonc, A. (1993). *Catching the light: The entwined history of light and mind*. New York: Oxford University Press.

41. Dennis, S.L. (2001). *Embrace of the daimon: Sensuality and the imagination of forbidden imagery in depth psychology*. York Beach, MAI: Nicolas-Hays.

42. Bronowski, J. (1973). *Ascent of man*. London: BBC Books.

43. Ronnberg, A., & Martin, K. (2010). *The book of symbols: Reflections on archetypal images*. Cologne: Taschen.

44. Fox, M., Sheldrake, R. (1996/2014). *The physics of angels: Exploring the realm where science and spirit meet*. Rhinebeck, NY: Monkfish Book Publishing.

45. Brice, M. (2013). 'Senator Mark Kirk reportedly saw angels after suffering from stroke'. Available at http://medical daily.com/ senator-mark-kirk-reportedly-saw-angels-after-suffering-stroke-244149. Accessed on 24th November 2016.

46. Hamilton, M.L. (2013). '"I would still be drowned in tears": Spiritualism in Abraham Lincoln's White House'. Master of Arts Thesis. San Diego State University. Available at www. sdsu-dspace.calstate.edu. Accessed on 24th October, 2017.

47. Dossey, L. (2009). *The power of premonitions: How knowing the future can shape our lives*. New York: Dutton.

48. Byrne, L. (2015). *Love from heaven*. London: Coronet.
49. Ford, D. (1998). *The dark side of the light chasers: Reclaiming your power, creativity, brilliance and dreams*. New York: Riverhead Books.

Chapter Twelve

1. Collins, M. (2014). *The unselfish spirit: Human evolution in a time of global crisis*. East Meon, Hampshire: Permanent Publications.
2. Taylor, B. (2010). *Dark green religion: Nature spirituality and the planetary culture*. Berkeley: University of California Press.
3. Mindell, A. (2010). *Process Mind: A user's guide to connecting with the mind of God*. Wheaton, Ill: Quest Books.
4. Skepteco, (2012). 'Does the spiritual have a place in permaculture?' Available at https://skepteco.wordpress.com/2012/01/09/does-the-spiritual-have-a-Place-in-permaculture/. Accessed on 21st September, 2016.
5. Manuel Navarrete, D., Kay, J.J. & Dolderman, D. (2004). 'Ecological integrity discourses: Linking ecology with cultural transformations'. *Human Ecology Review*, 11(3), p.215-29.
6. Fox, W. (1990). 'Transpersonal ecology: "Psychologizing" ecophilosophy'. *The Journal of Transpersonal Psychology*, 22(1), p.59-96.
7. Tarnas, R. (2006). *Cosmos and psyche: Intimations of a new world view*. New York: Viking.
8. Dass, R. (1970). *Doing your own being*. London: Neville Spearman.
9. Capra, F. & Luisi, P.L. (2014). *The systems view of life: A unifying vision*. Cambridge: Cambridge University Press.
10. Gibson, C. & Bang, J.M. (2015). *Permaculture: A spiritual perspective*. Forres: Findhorn Press.
11. Macnamara, L. (2012). *People and permaculture: Caring and designing for ourselves, each other and the planet*. East Meon: Permanent Publications.
12. Dunwell, M. (2016). 'Bill Mollison. Obituary'. *The Guardian*, 19th October, p.35.
13. Eliade, M. (1979). *From primitives to Zen: A thematic sourcebook of the history of religions*. London: Collins.
14. Cleary, T. (1992). *Wen-Tzu, understanding the mysteries: Further teachings of Lao Tzu*. Boston: Shambhala.
15. Campbell, J. (2004). *Pathways to bliss: Mythology and personal transformation*. Novato, CA: New World Library.
16. Hinduism Today. (1990). 'Computing the mathematical face of God: S. Ramanujan'. Posted by Maharaj, J. Available at www.hindunet.org/alt_hindu/1995_Mar_2/msg00033.html. Accessed on 4th April, 2016.
17. Maryboy, N.C. (2009). 'Cosmic serpent: A global archetype'. Available at www.cosmicserpent.org/about-us/the-cosmic-serpent. Accessed on 18th March, 2016.
18. Kaden, H. (2008). *Some memories of my life*. Turvey: Turvey Monastery.
19. Mindell, A. (2007). *Earth-based psychology: Path awareness from the teachings of Don Juan, Richard Feynman, and Lao Tse*. Portland, OR: Lao Tse Press.
20. Alexander, E. (2014). *The map of heaven: A neurosurgeon explores the mysteries of the afterlife and the truth about what lies beyond*. London: Piatkus.

Afterword

1. Begg, E. (1984). *Myth and today's consciousness*. London: Coventure.
2. Masters, J.J. (1999). *Finding Freedom: Writings from death row*. Junction City, CA: Padma Publishing.
3. Kripananda, S. (1984). 'Kundalini: The energy of transformation'. In *Ancient wisdom and modern science*, ed Grof, S. p.79-93. Albany, NY: State University of New York Press.
4. Jones, K. (1993). *Beyond optimism: A Buddhist political ecology*. Oxford: John Carpenter Publishing.
5. Ronnberg, A. & Martin, K. (2010). *The book of symbols: Reflections on archetypal images*. Cologne: Taschen.
6. Black, J. (2014). 'The warriors of the Rainbow prophecy'. Available at www.ancient-origins.net/myths-legends/warriors-rainbow-prophecy-001577?nopaging=1. Accessed on 27th January, 2017.
7. Wikipedia. (2017). Legend of the Rainbow Warriors. Available at https://en.m.wikipedia.org/wiki/Legend_of_the_Rainbow_Warriors. Accessed on 27th January, 2017.
8. Trungpa, C. (1984). *Shambhala: The sacred path of the warrior*. Boston: Shambhala.
9. Mindell, A. (1993). *The shaman's body: A new shamanism for transforming health, relationships and the community*. New York: Harper San Francisco.
10. Mindell, A. (2017). *Conflict: Phases, forums and solutions*. North Charleston, SC: World Tao Press and A. Mindell.
11. Habday, A.J. (1981). 'Seeking a moist heart: Native American ways of helping the spirit'. In *Historical roots, ecumenical routes*, ed Fox, M. p.317-29. Santa Fe, NM: Bear and Company.

Useful Connections

As well as the extensive reading list in the reference section, these websites may be helpful.

https://spiritualcrisisnetwork.uk
A very helpful UK-based website that provides important information about spiritual crisis.

www.iapop.com
A very useful list of international practitioners of process-oriented psychology as formulated by Arnold Mindell and colleagues (process work). The process work paradigm is an excellent approach that uses creative ways of promoting awareness and integrating the wisdom found in altered and extreme states of consciousness, as well as body symptoms and relationship conflicts.

www.epiczoetic.co.uk
The author's website, offering holistic coaching for individuals, groups and organisations seeking to engage their transformative potential.

www.emergingproud.com
An international social activist campaign that supports people's non-ordinary spiritual experiences, which aims to build bridges with mainstream psychiatry.

www.eurotas.org
A website representing a wide range of European transpersonal practitioners.

Index

Enjoyed this book?
You might like these...

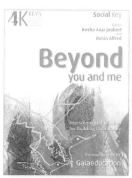 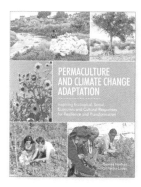 

Subscribe to a better world

Each issue of *Permaculture Magazine International* is hand crafted, sharing practical, innovative solutions, money saving ideas and global perspectives from a grassroots movement in over 170 countries

Print subscribers receive FREE digital access to our complete 25 years of back issues plus bonus content

To subscribe call 01730 823 311 or visit:

www.permaculture.co.uk

See our North American specific edition at: **https://permaculturemag.org**